# CIRCLE OF FIRE

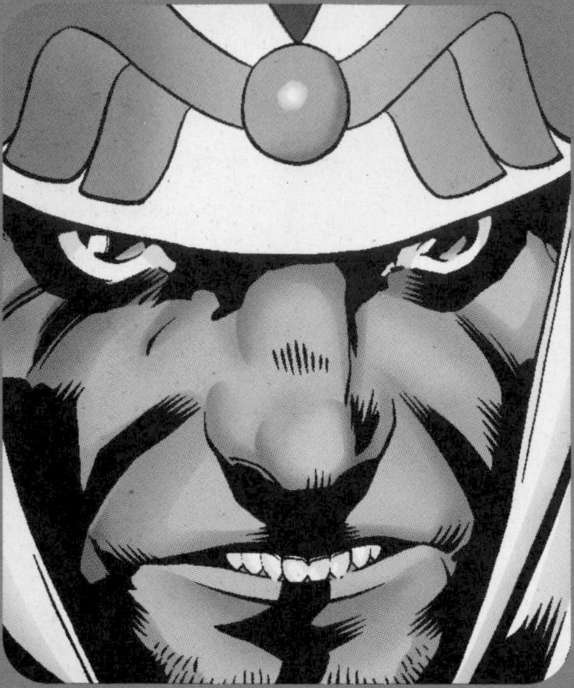

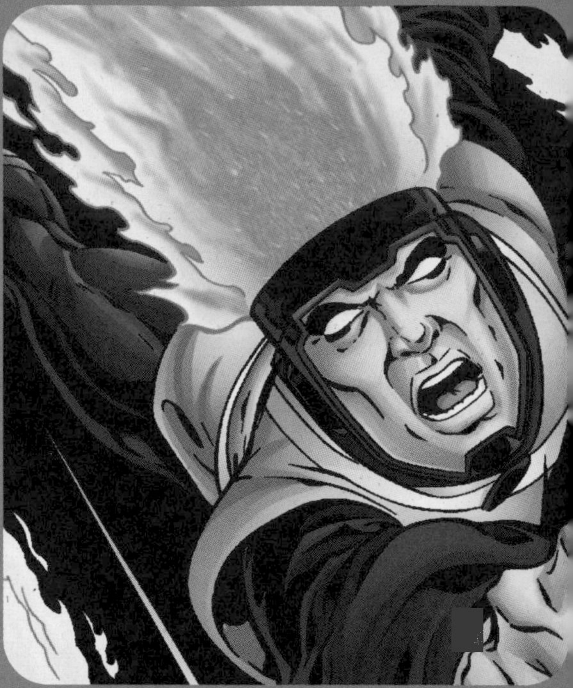

# CIRCLE OF FIRE

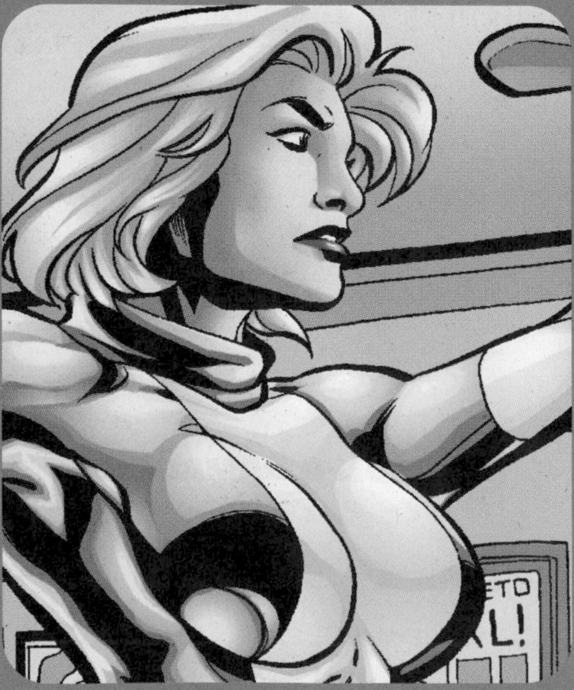

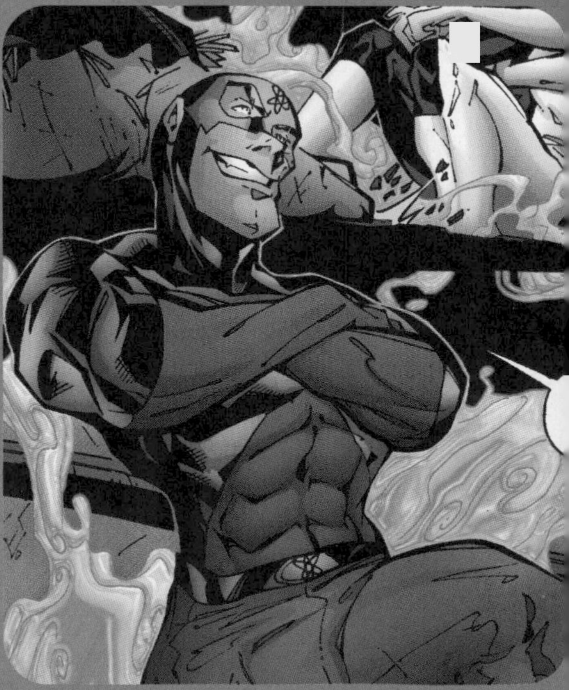

**BRIAN K. VAUGHAN**
**SCOTT BEATTY**
**JAY FAERBER**
**JUDD WINICK**
Writers

**NORM BREYFOGLE**
**TREVOR McCARTHY**
**PETE WOODS**
**CARY NORD**
**RON RANDALL**
**RANDY GREEN**
**ROBERT TERANISHI**
Pencillers

**JOHN LOWE**
**RAY KRYSSING**
**STEVE BIRD**
**JOHN NYBERG**
**KEITH AIKEN**
**TYSON McADOO**
**ANDREW PEPOY**
**JOHN STANISCI**
**MARK LIPKA**
**DAN DAVIS**
**WAYNE FAUCHER**
**CLAUDE ST. AUBIN**
Inkers

**TOM McCRAW**
**GLENN WHITMORE**
**MOOSE BAUMANN**
**SHANNON BLANCHARD**
Colorists

**SEAN KONOT**
Letterer

**CARY NORD**
**RODOLFO DAMAGGIO**
**DARRYL BANKS**
**MARK LIPKA**
**KEVIN NOWLAN**
Original Covers

**GREEN LANTERN: CIRCLE OF FIRE**

Published by DC Comics. Cover and compilation copyright © 2002 DC Comics. All Rights Reserved.

Originally published in single magazine form as GREEN LANTERN: CIRCLE OF FIRE 1 & 2, GREEN LANTERN/ATOM 1, GREEN LANTERN/POWER GIRL 1, GREEN LANTERN/ADAM STRANGE 1, GREEN LANTERN/FIRESTORM 1, GREEN LANTERN/GREEN LANTERN 1. Copyright © 2000 DC Comics.
All Rights Reserved. All characters, their distinctive likenesses and related indicia featured in this publication are trademarks of DC Comics.
The stories, characters, and incidents featured in this publication are entirely fictional.
DC Comics does not read or accept unsolicited submissions of ideas, stories or artwork.

DC Comics, 1700 Broadway, New York, NY 10019
A division of Warner Bros. - An AOL Time Warner Company
Printed in Canada. First Printing.
ISBN: 1-56389-806-3
Cover illustration by Darryl Banks and Kevin Nowlan.
Cover color by Chris Sotomayor.

CIRCLE OF FIRE

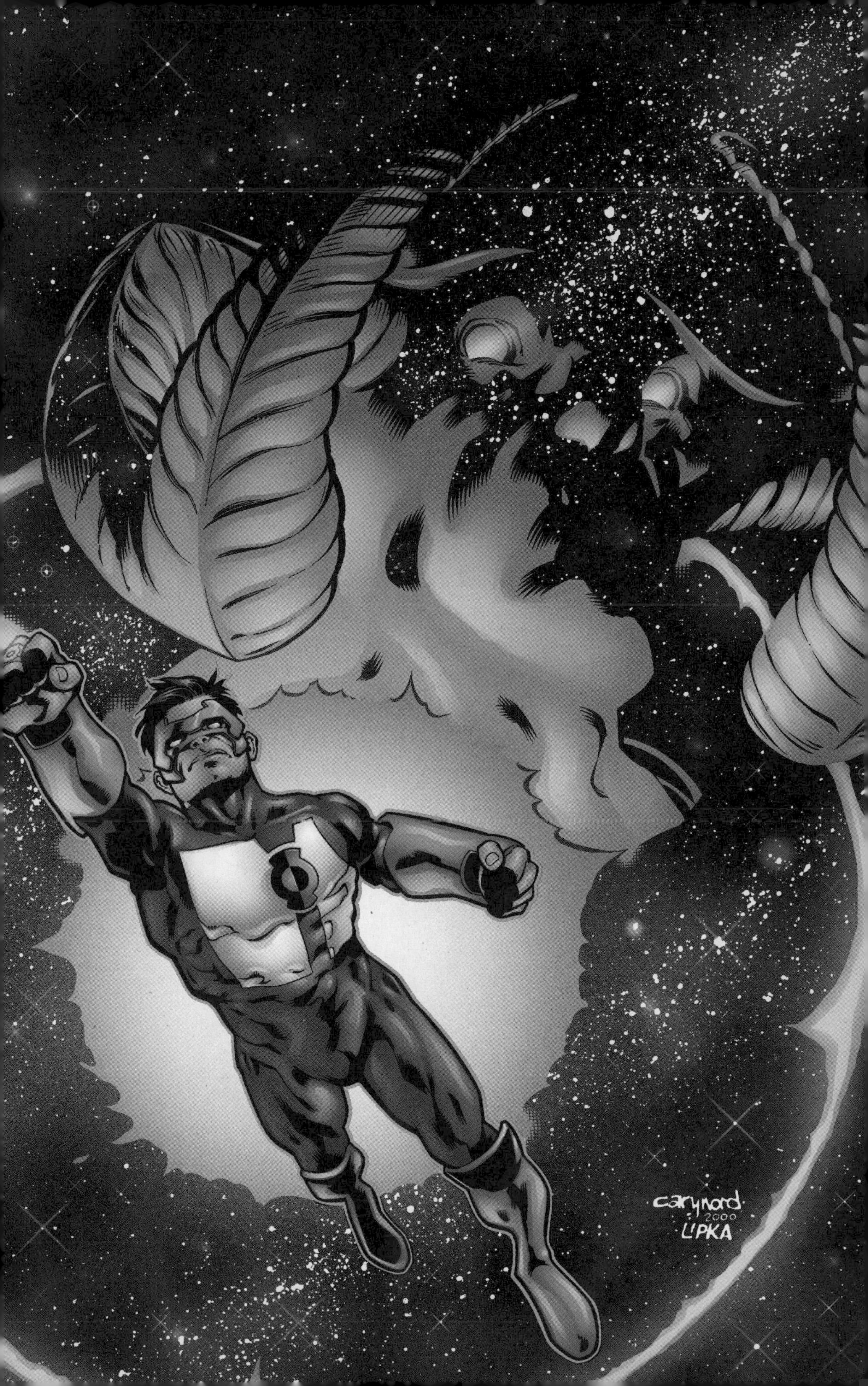
carynord
2000
LIPKA

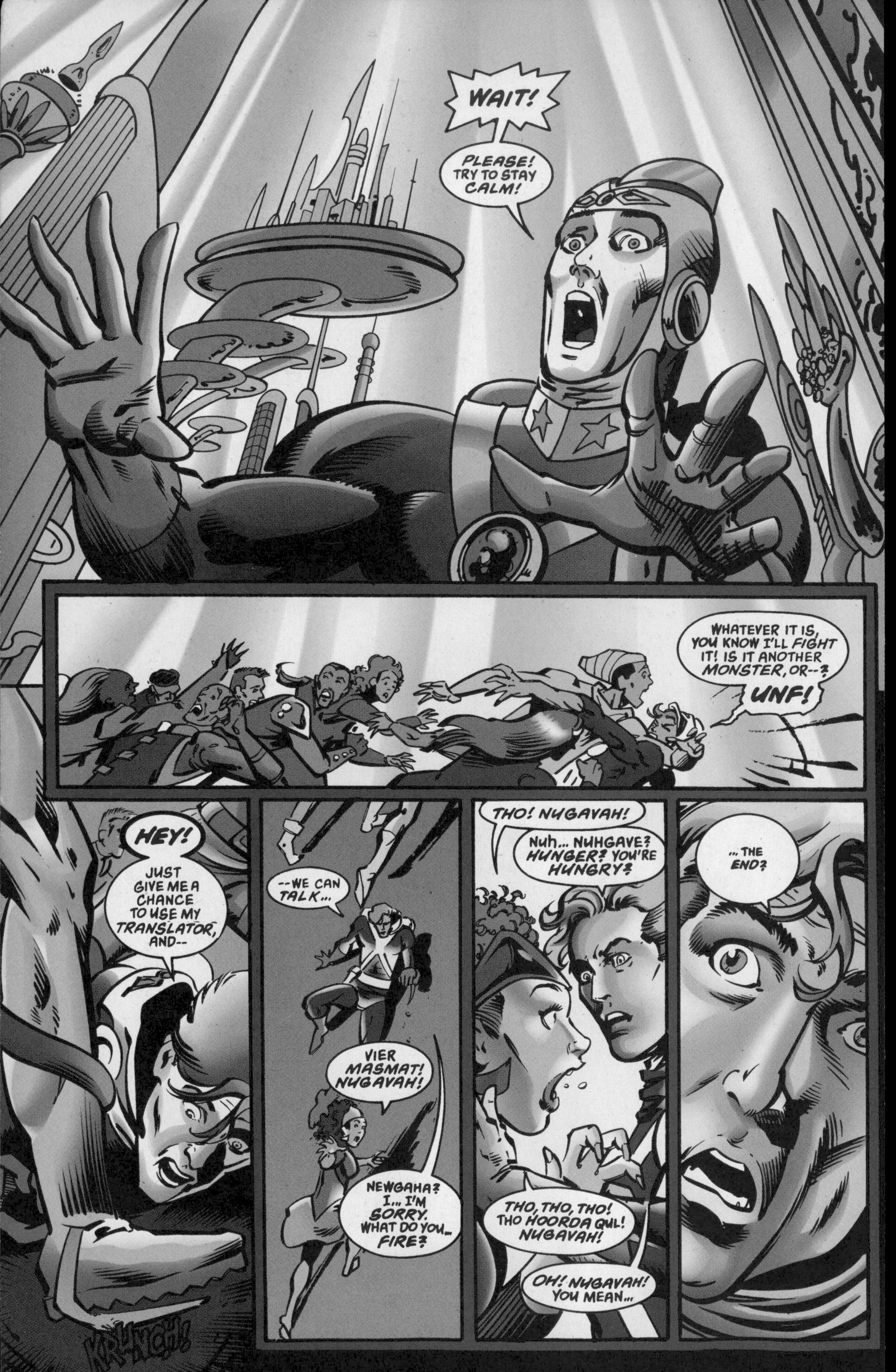

WAIT!
PLEASE! TRY TO STAY CALM!
WHATEVER IT IS, YOU KNOW I'LL FIGHT IT! IS IT ANOTHER MONSTER, OR--?
UNF!
HEY!
JUST GIVE ME A CHANCE TO USE MY TRANSLATOR, AND--
--WE CAN TALK...
VIER MASMAT! NUGAVAH!
NEWGAHA? I... I'M SORRY. WHAT DO YOU... FIRE?
THO! NUGAVAH!
Nuh... NUHGAVE? HUNGER? YOU'RE HUNGRY?
THO, THO, THO! THO HOORDA QUL! NUGAVAH!
OH! NUGAVAH! YOU MEAN...
... THE END?

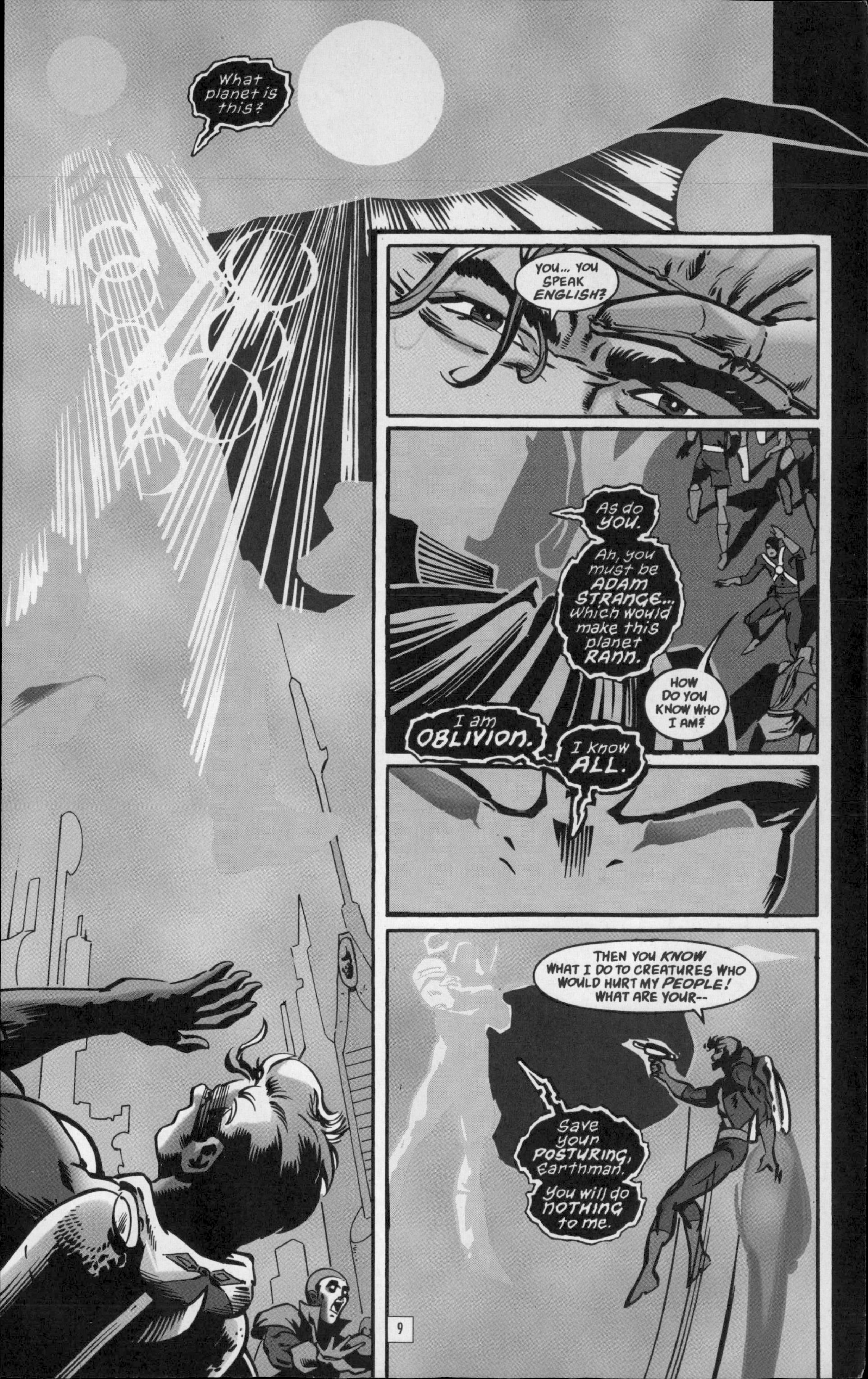
What planet is this?
YOU... YOU SPEAK ENGLISH?
As do YOU.
Ah, you must be ADAM STRANGE... Which would make this planet RANN.
HOW DO YOU KNOW WHO I AM?
I am OBLIVION.
I know ALL.
THEN YOU KNOW WHAT I DO TO CREATURES WHO WOULD HURT MY PEOPLE! WHAT ARE YOUR--
Save your POSTURING, Earthman.
You will do NOTHING to me.

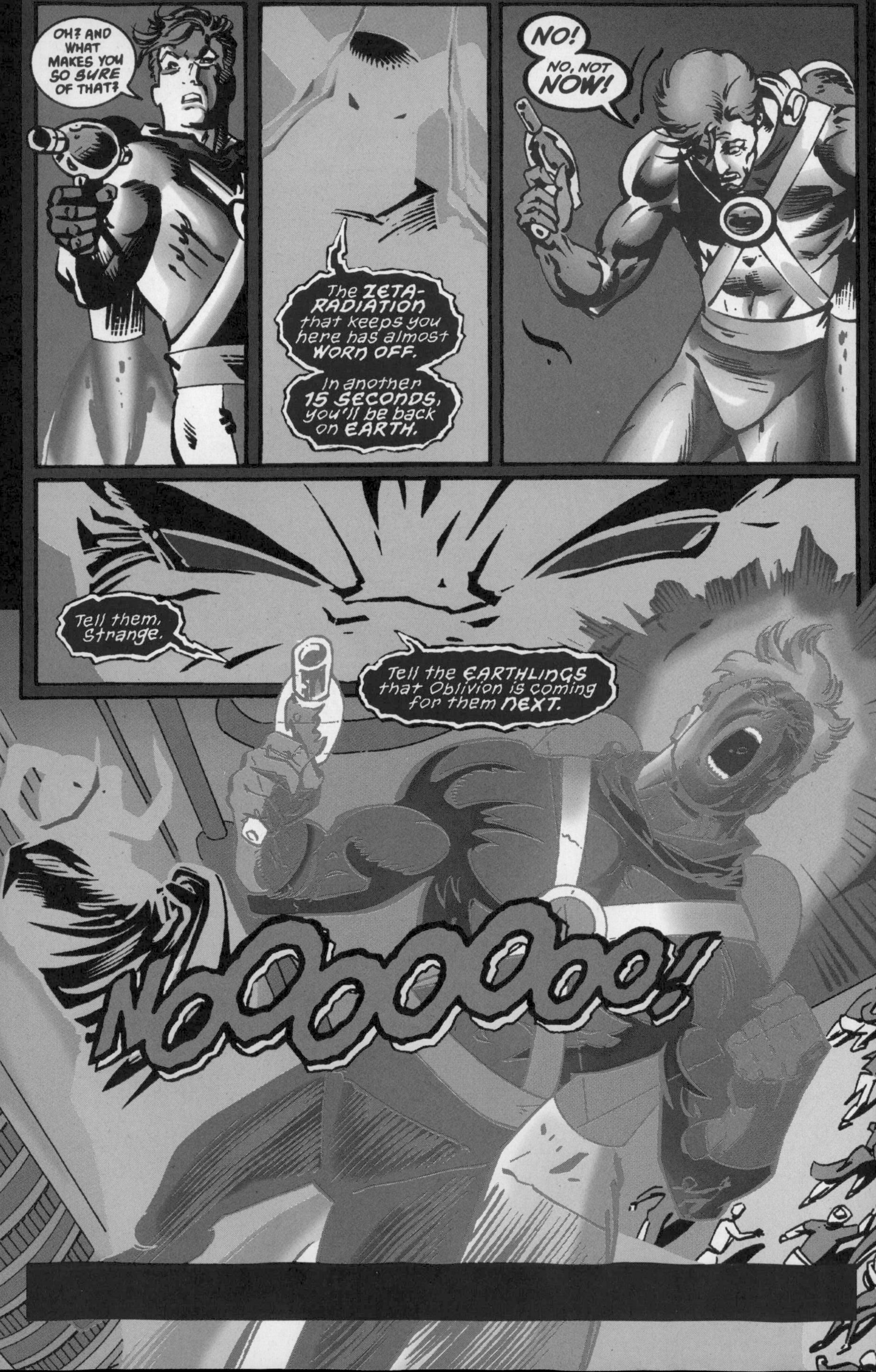
OH? AND WHAT MAKES YOU SO SURE OF THAT?
The ZETA-RADIATION that keeps you here has almost WORN OFF.
In another 15 SECONDS, you'll be back on EARTH.
NO!
NO, NOT NOW!
Tell them, Strange.
Tell the EARTHLINGS that Oblivion is coming for them NEXT.
NOOOOOOO!

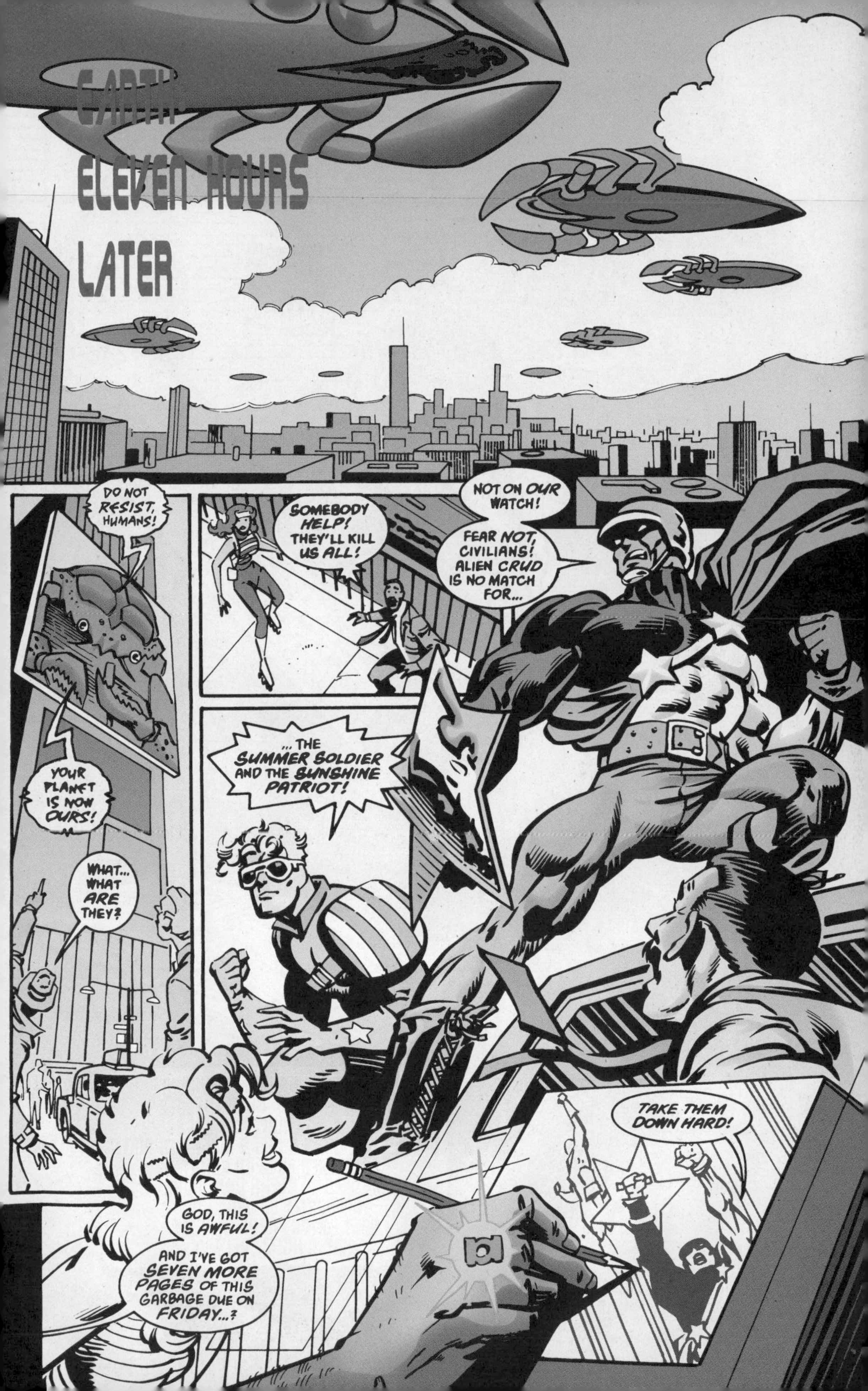
EARTH
ELEVEN HOURS
LATER
DO NOT RESIST, HUMANS!
YOUR PLANET IS NOW OURS!
WHAT... WHAT ARE THEY?
SOMEBODY HELP! THEY'LL KILL US ALL!
NOT ON OUR WATCH!
FEAR NOT, CIVILIANS! ALIEN CRUD IS NO MATCH FOR...
...THE SUMMER SOLDIER AND THE SUNSHINE PATRIOT!
TAKE THEM DOWN HARD!
GOD, THIS IS AWFUL!
AND I'VE GOT SEVEN MORE PAGES OF THIS GARBAGE DUE ON FRIDAY...?

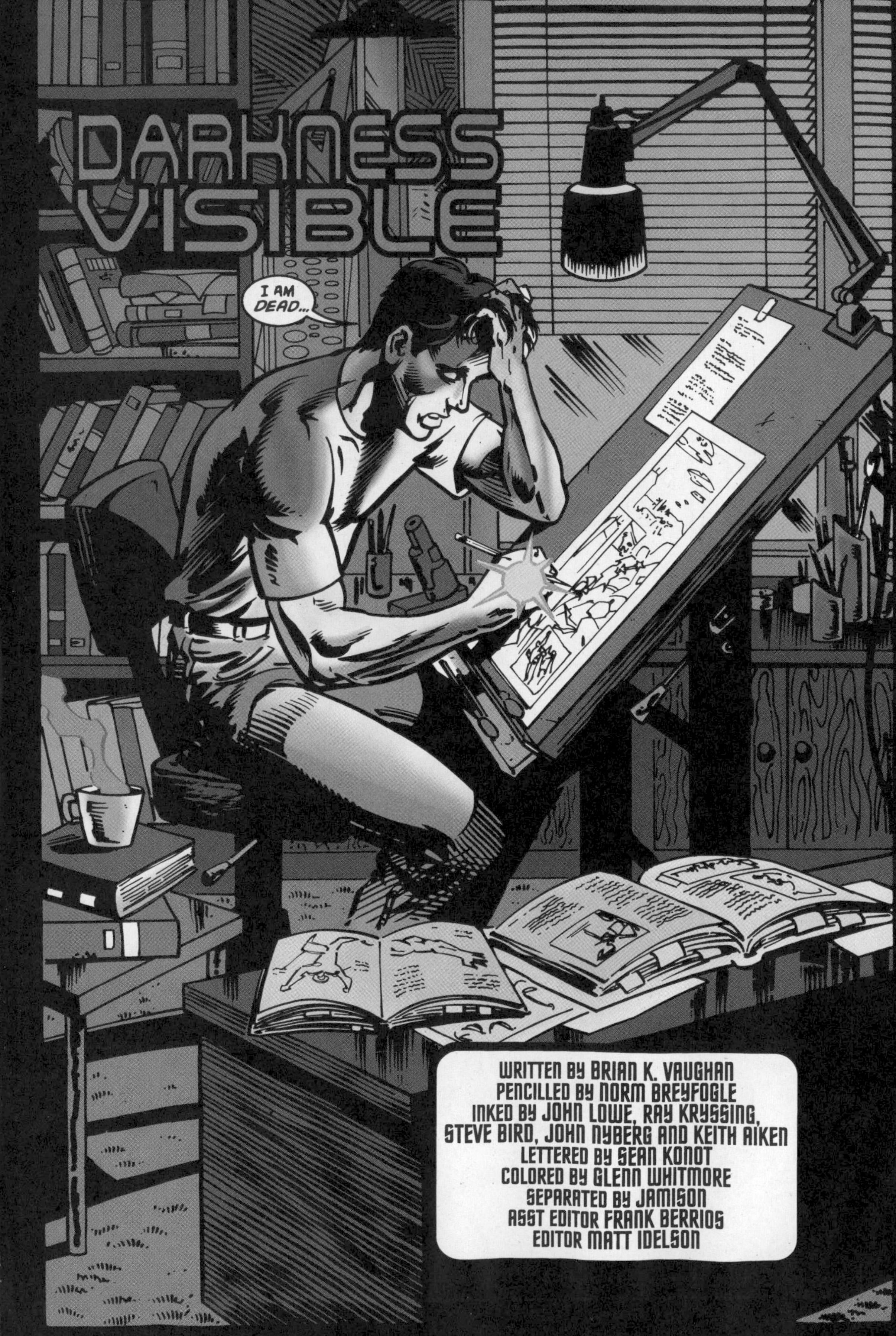
DARKNESS VISIBLE
I AM DEAD...
WRITTEN BY BRIAN K. VAUGHAN
PENCILLED BY NORM BREYFOGLE
INKED BY JOHN LOWE, RAY KRYSSING, STEVE BIRD, JOHN NYBERG AND KEITH AIKEN
LETTERED BY SEAN KONOT
COLORED BY GLENN WHITMORE
SEPARATED BY JAMISON
ASST EDITOR FRANK BERRIOS
EDITOR MATT IDELSON

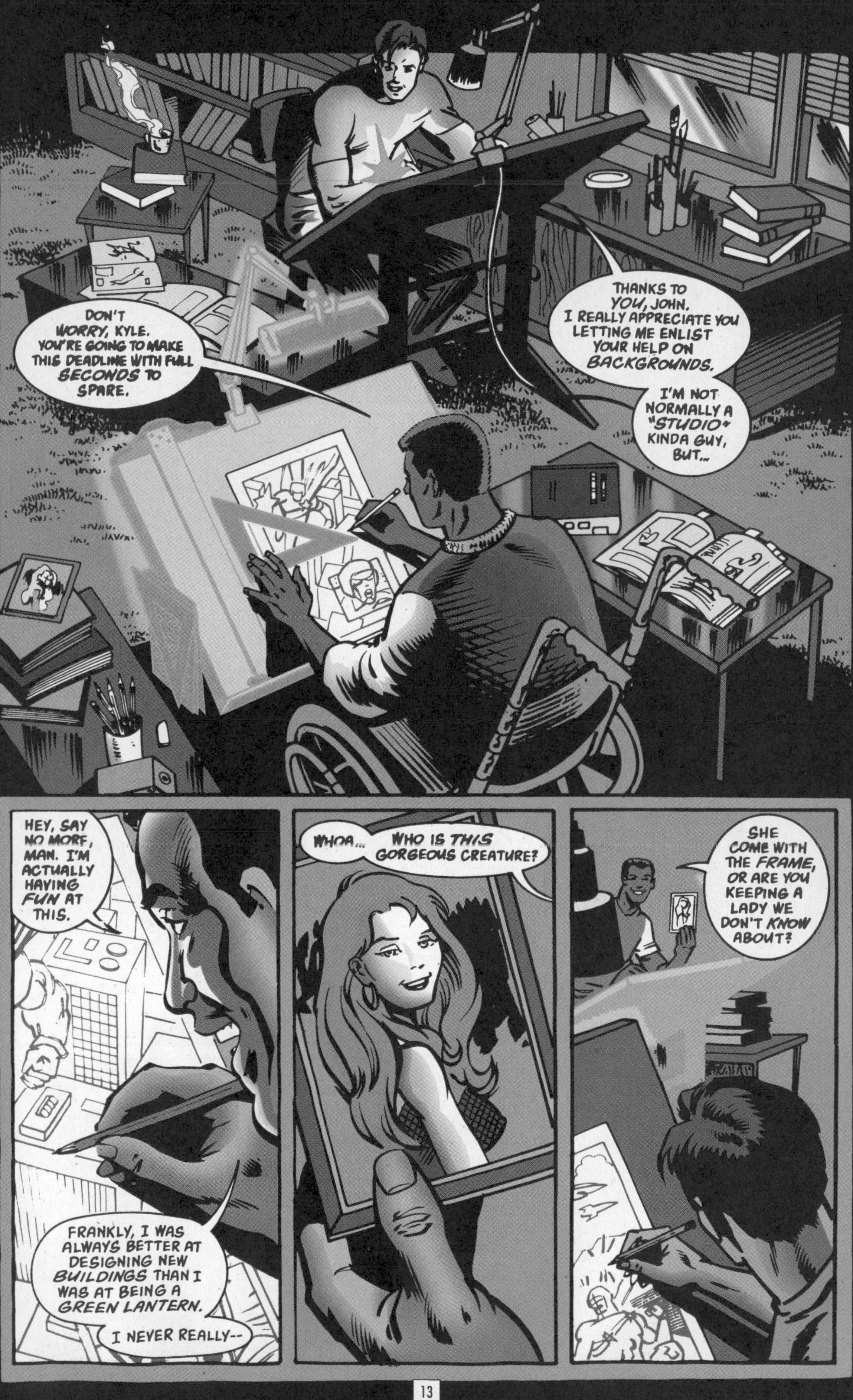
DON'T WORRY, KYLE. YOU'RE GOING TO MAKE THIS DEADLINE WITH FULL SECONDS TO SPARE.
THANKS TO YOU, JOHN. I REALLY APPRECIATE YOU LETTING ME ENLIST YOUR HELP ON BACKGROUNDS.
I'M NOT NORMALLY A "STUDIO" KINDA GUY, BUT...
HEY, SAY NO MORE, MAN. I'M ACTUALLY HAVING FUN AT THIS.
FRANKLY, I WAS ALWAYS BETTER AT DESIGNING NEW BUILDINGS THAN I WAS AT BEING A GREEN LANTERN.
I NEVER REALLY--
WHOA... WHO IS THIS GORGEOUS CREATURE?
SHE COME WITH THE FRAME, OR ARE YOU KEEPING A LADY WE DON'T KNOW ABOUT?

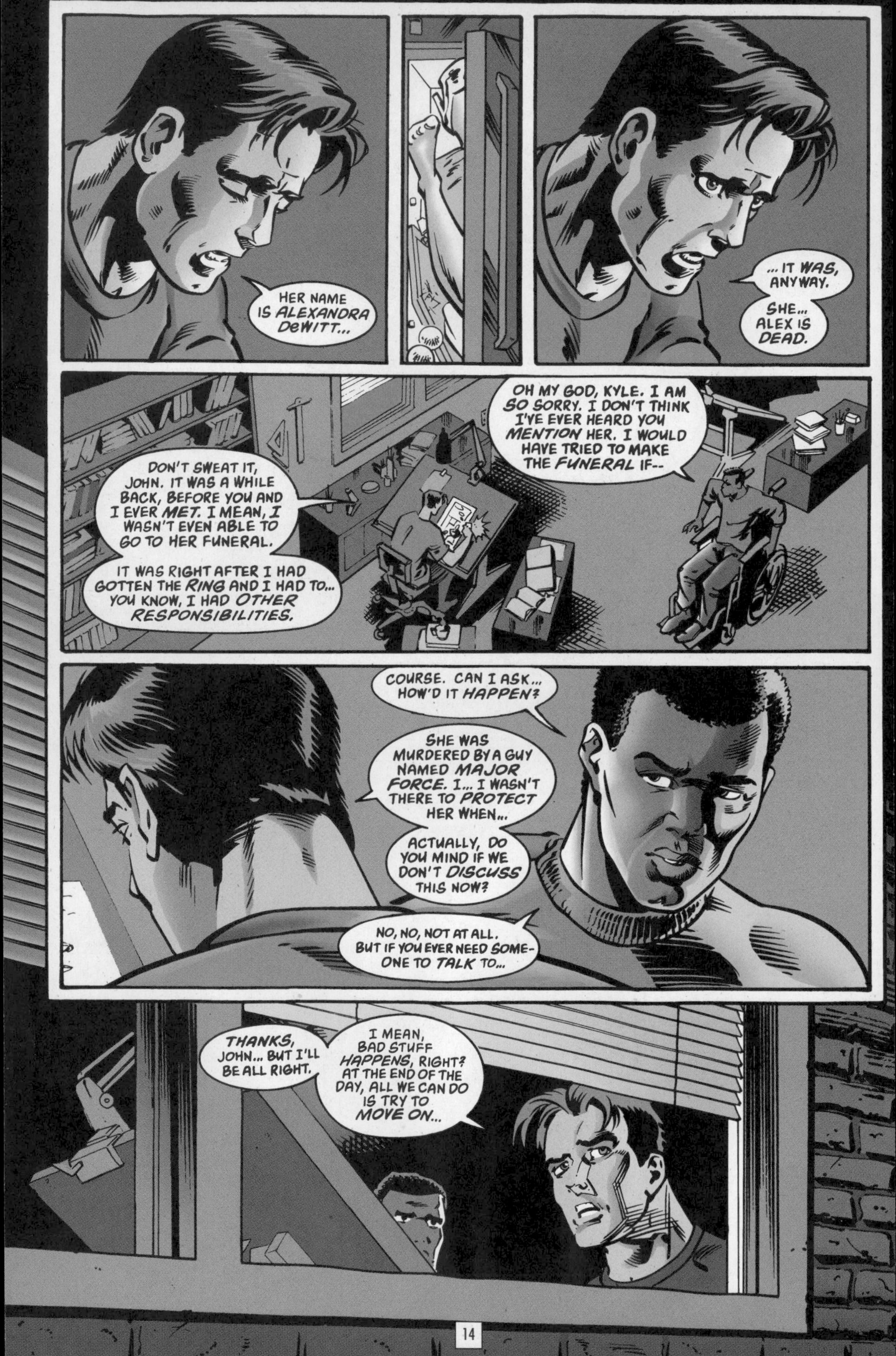
HER NAME IS ALEXANDRA DeWITT...
...IT WAS, ANYWAY.
SHE... ALEX IS DEAD.
DON'T SWEAT IT, JOHN. IT WAS A WHILE BACK, BEFORE YOU AND I EVER MET. I MEAN, I WASN'T EVEN ABLE TO GO TO HER FUNERAL.
IT WAS RIGHT AFTER I HAD GOTTEN THE RING AND I HAD TO... YOU KNOW, I HAD OTHER RESPONSIBILITIES.
OH MY GOD, KYLE. I AM SO SORRY. I DON'T THINK I'VE EVER HEARD YOU MENTION HER. I WOULD HAVE TRIED TO MAKE THE FUNERAL IF--
COURSE. CAN I ASK... HOW'D IT HAPPEN?
SHE WAS MURDERED BY A GUY NAMED MAJOR FORCE. I... I WASN'T THERE TO PROTECT HER WHEN...
ACTUALLY, DO YOU MIND IF WE DON'T DISCUSS THIS NOW?
NO, NO, NOT AT ALL. BUT IF YOU EVER NEED SOME-ONE TO TALK TO...
THANKS, JOHN... BUT I'LL BE ALL RIGHT.
I MEAN, BAD STUFF HAPPENS, RIGHT? AT THE END OF THE DAY, ALL WE CAN DO IS TRY TO MOVE ON...

WELCOME TO IVY UNIVERSITY FOUNDED 1749

**ALL RIGHT, MR. RAYMOND, WHAT IS THE *SIXTH* MOST ABUNDANT ELEMENT IN OUR PLANET'S CRUST?**

Uh... *SODIUM?*

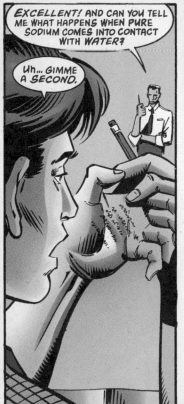

**EXCELLENT! AND CAN YOU TELL ME WHAT HAPPENS WHEN PURE SODIUM COMES INTO CONTACT WITH *WATER?***

Uh... GIMME A *SECOND.*

**RONALD, YOU'RE NOT GOING TO BE ABLE TO CHECK YOUR *CRIB SHEET* WHEN *DARKSEID* IS FEEDING YOU YOUR OWN *HEART.***

**HEY, TAKE IT *EASY,* PROFESSOR PALMER! I'VE ALREADY MEMORIZED MORE CHEMISTRY FACTOIDS THAN ANY OTHER DUMB JOCK IN THE *HISTORY* OF DUMB JOCKS!**

**THINGS WERE JUST A LOT EASIER WHEN PROFESSOR *STEIN* WAS STILL AROUND...**

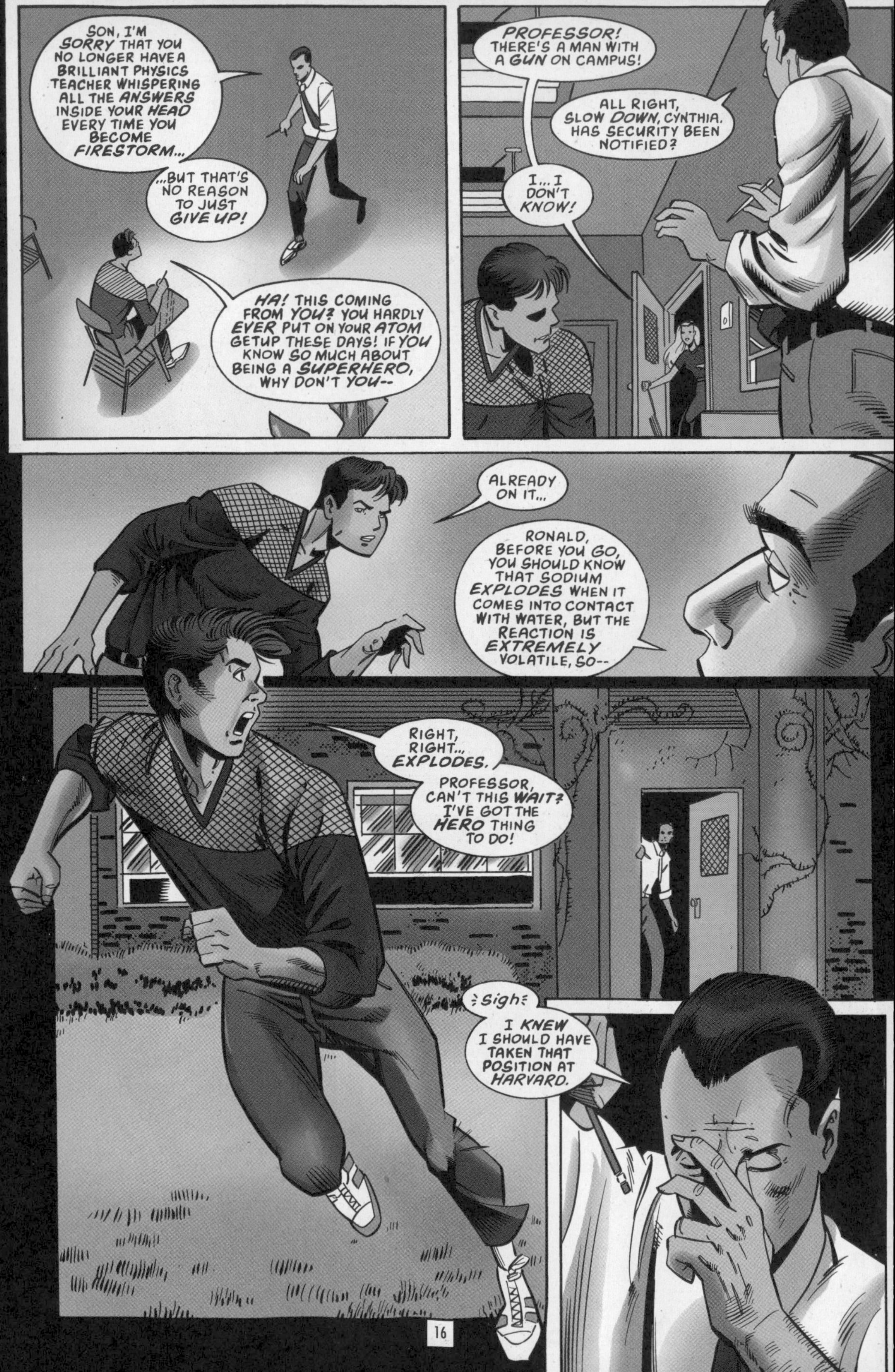
SON, I'M SORRY THAT YOU NO LONGER HAVE A BRILLIANT PHYSICS TEACHER WHISPERING ALL THE ANSWERS INSIDE YOUR HEAD EVERY TIME YOU BECOME FIRESTORM...
...BUT THAT'S NO REASON TO JUST GIVE UP!
HA! THIS COMING FROM YOU? YOU HARDLY EVER PUT ON YOUR ATOM GETUP THESE DAYS! IF YOU KNOW SO MUCH ABOUT BEING A SUPERHERO, WHY DON'T YOU--
PROFESSOR! THERE'S A MAN WITH A GUN ON CAMPUS!
ALL RIGHT, SLOW DOWN, CYNTHIA. HAS SECURITY BEEN NOTIFIED?
I... I DON'T KNOW!
ALREADY ON IT...
RONALD, BEFORE YOU GO, YOU SHOULD KNOW THAT SODIUM EXPLODES WHEN IT COMES INTO CONTACT WITH WATER, BUT THE REACTION IS EXTREMELY VOLATILE, SO--
RIGHT, RIGHT... EXPLODES.
PROFESSOR, CAN'T THIS WAIT? I'VE GOT THE HERO THING TO DO!
Sigh
I KNEW I SHOULD HAVE TAKEN THAT POSITION AT HARVARD.

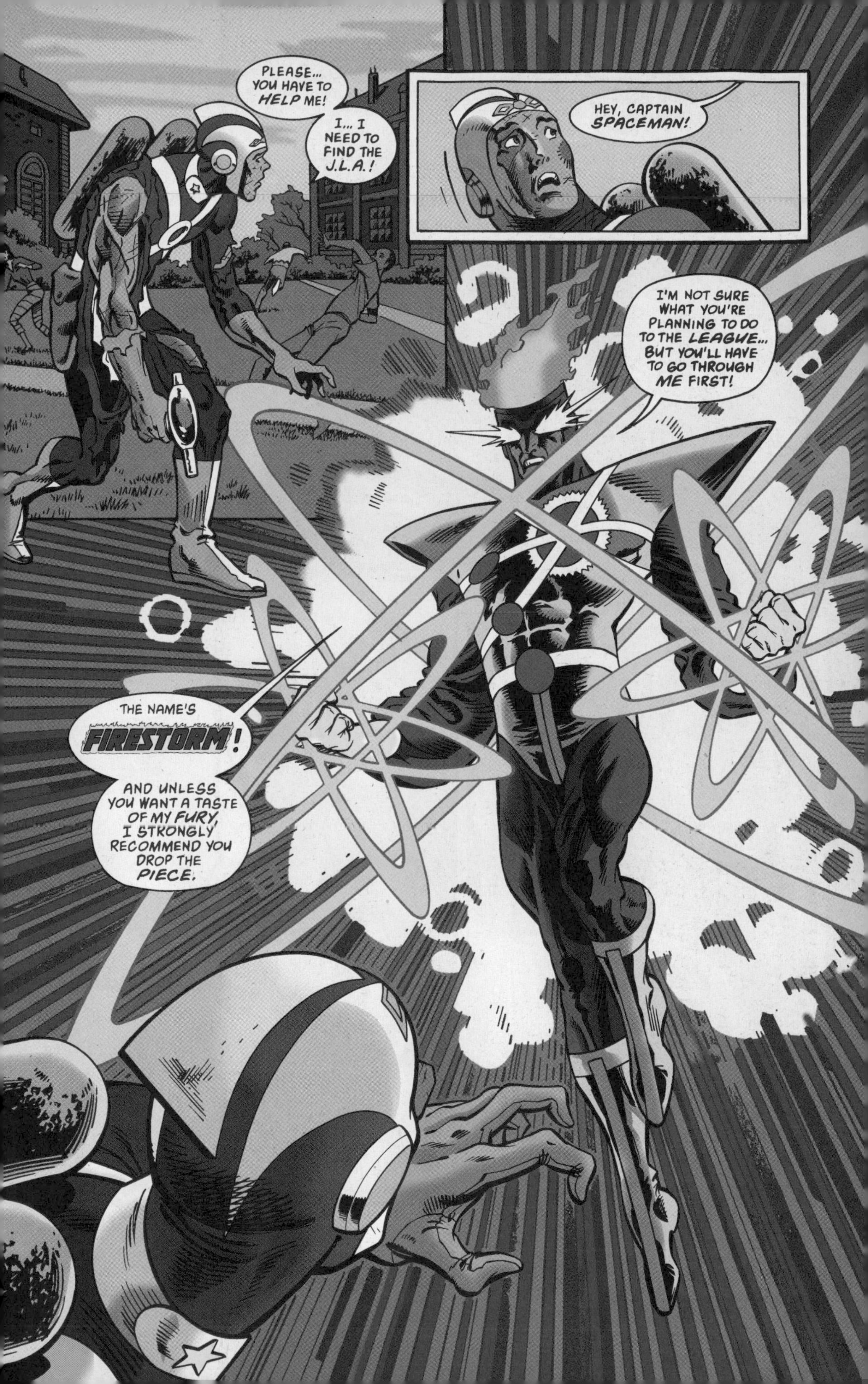
PLEASE... YOU HAVE TO HELP ME!
I... I NEED TO FIND THE J.L.A.!
HEY, CAPTAIN SPACEMAN!
I'M NOT SURE WHAT YOU'RE PLANNING TO DO TO THE LEAGUE... BUT YOU'LL HAVE TO GO THROUGH ME FIRST!
THE NAME'S FIRESTORM!
AND UNLESS YOU WANT A TASTE OF MY FURY, I STRONGLY RECOMMEND YOU DROP THE PIECE.

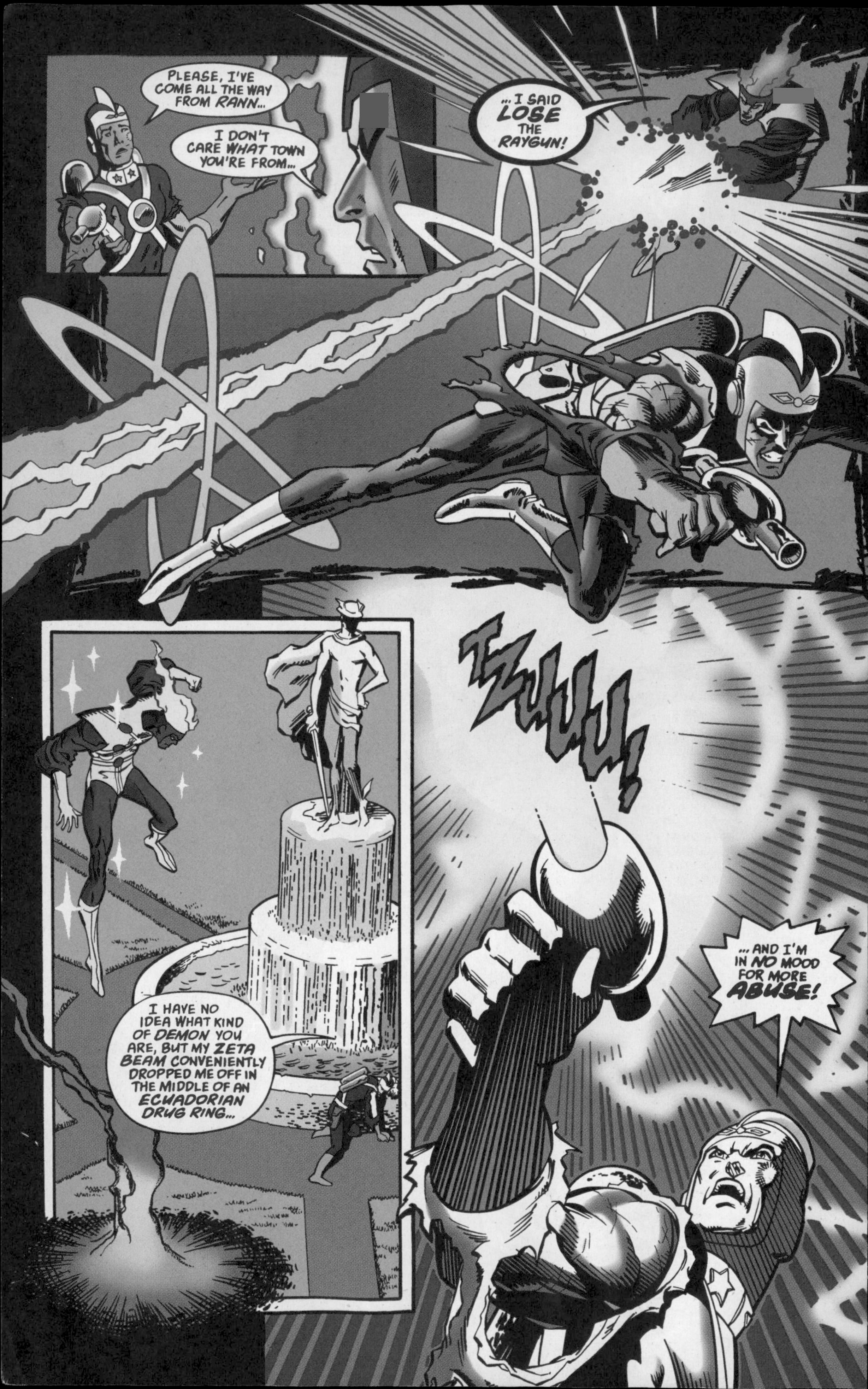
PLEASE, I'VE COME ALL THE WAY FROM RANN...
I DON'T CARE WHAT TOWN YOU'RE FROM...
...I SAID LOSE THE RAYGUN!
TZUUU!
I HAVE NO IDEA WHAT KIND OF DEMON YOU ARE, BUT MY ZETA BEAM CONVENIENTLY DROPPED ME OFF IN THE MIDDLE OF AN ECUADORIAN DRUG RING...
...AND I'M IN NO MOOD FOR MORE ABUSE!

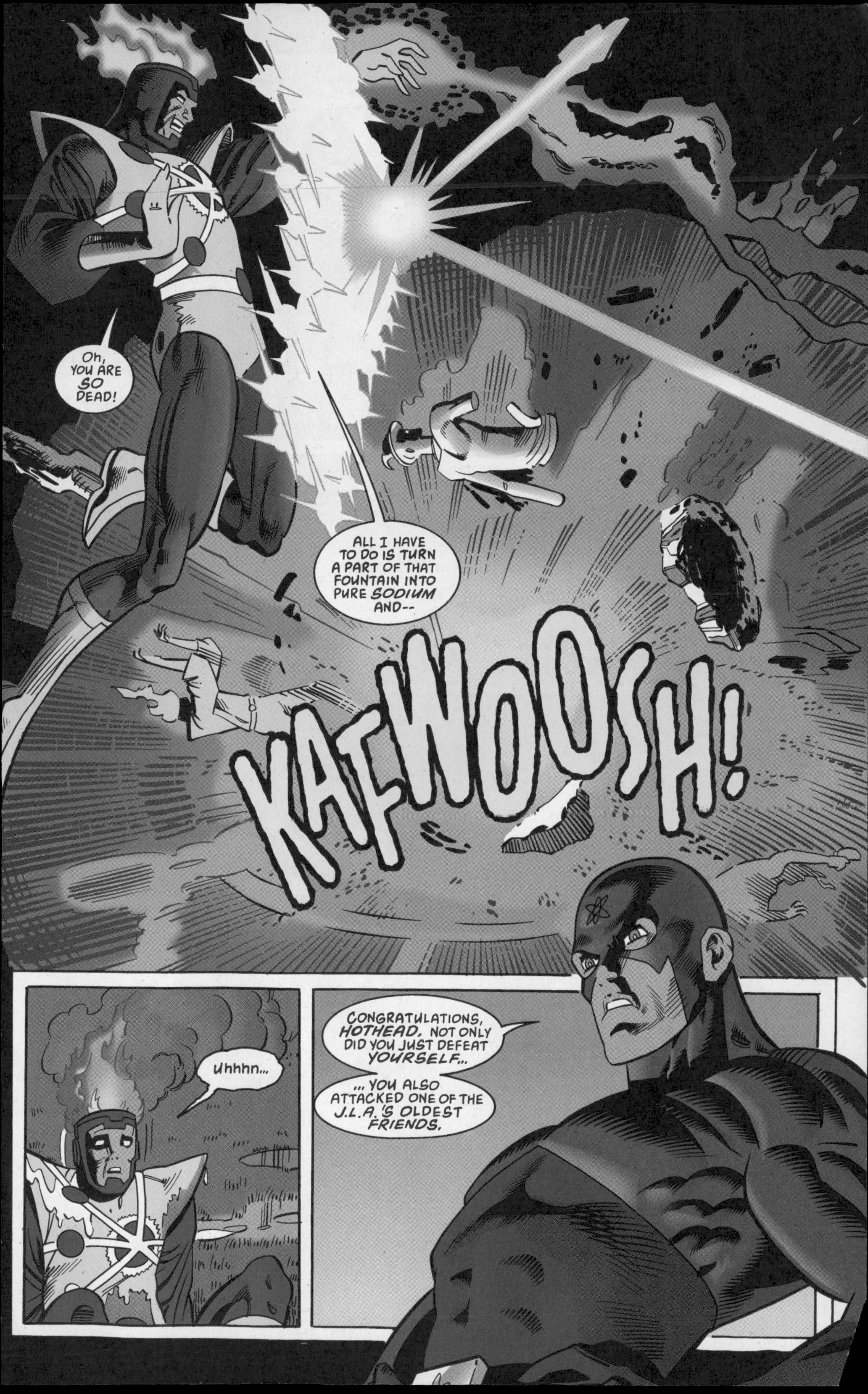
Oh, YOU ARE SO DEAD!
ALL I HAVE TO DO IS TURN A PART OF THAT FOUNTAIN INTO PURE SODIUM AND--
KAFWOOSH!
Uhhhn...
CONGRATULATIONS, HOTHEAD. NOT ONLY DID YOU JUST DEFEAT YOURSELF...
... YOU ALSO ATTACKED ONE OF THE J.L.A.'S OLDEST FRIENDS.

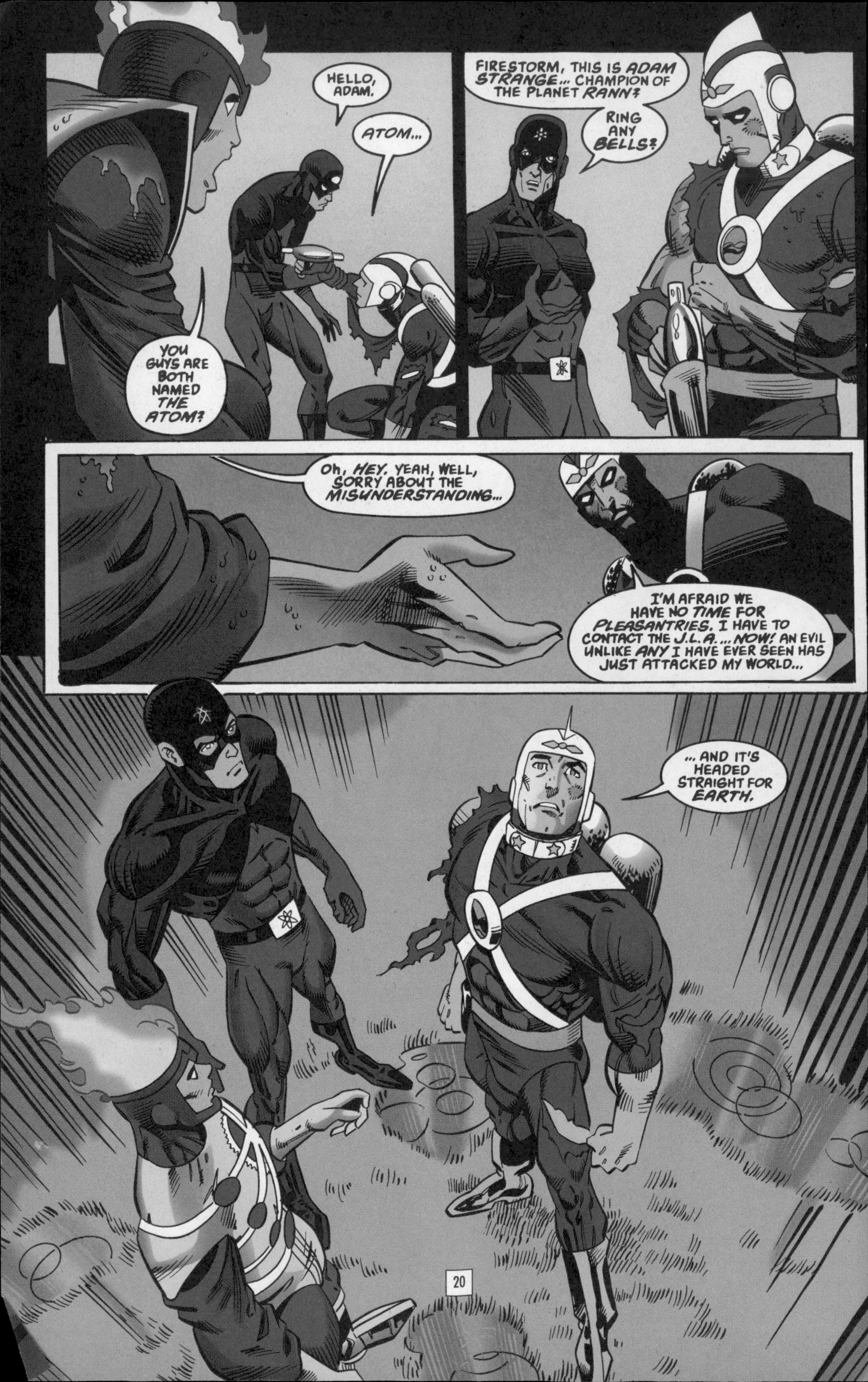
HELLO, ADAM.
ATOM...
YOU GUYS ARE BOTH NAMED THE ATOM?
FIRESTORM, THIS IS ADAM STRANGE... CHAMPION OF THE PLANET RANN?
RING ANY BELLS?
Oh, HEY. YEAH, WELL, SORRY ABOUT THE MISUNDERSTANDING...
I'M AFRAID WE HAVE NO TIME FOR PLEASANTRIES. I HAVE TO CONTACT THE J.L.A. ... NOW! AN EVIL UNLIKE ANY I HAVE EVER SEEN HAS JUST ATTACKED MY WORLD...
... AND IT'S HEADED STRAIGHT FOR EARTH.

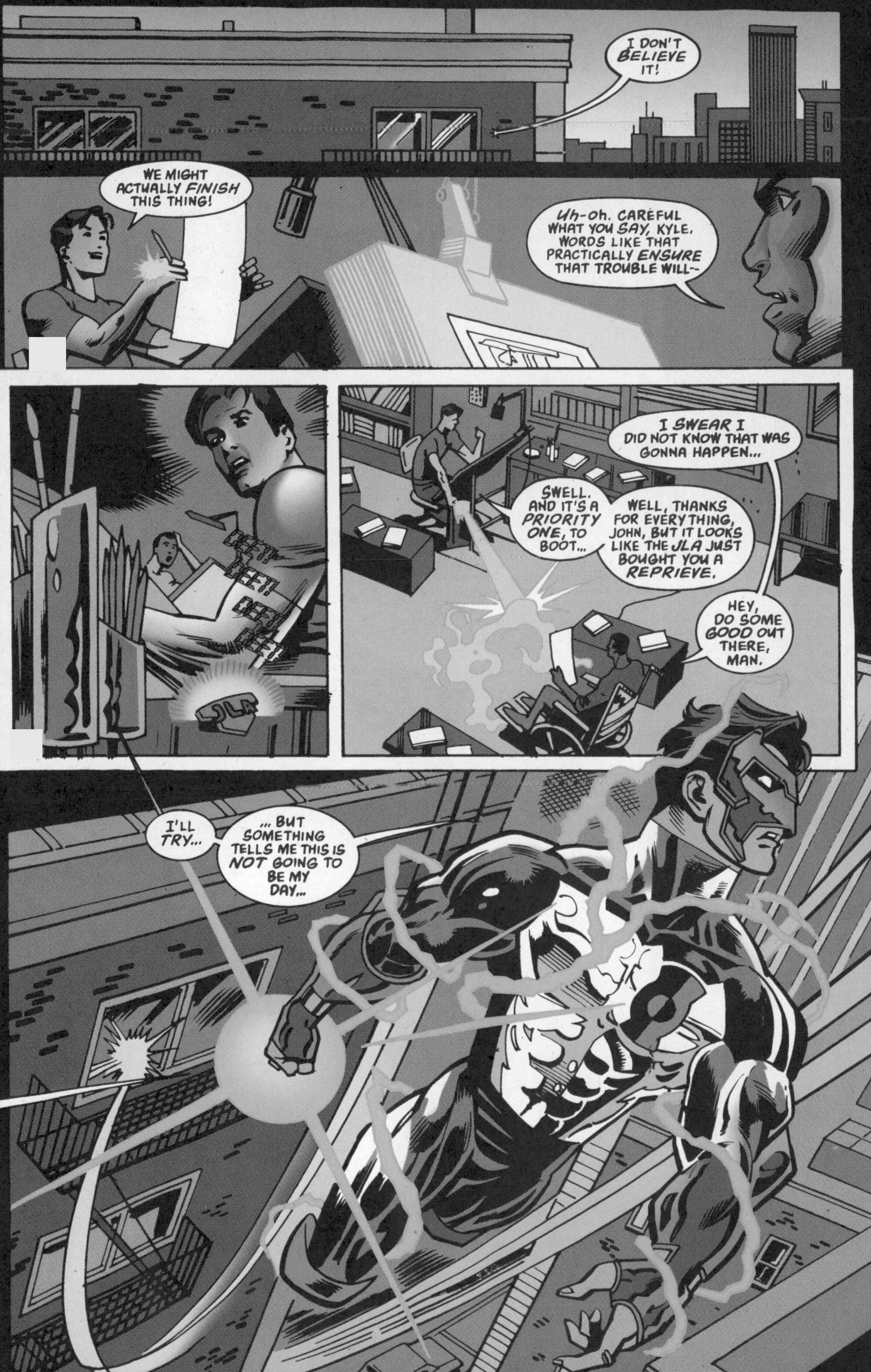
I DON'T BELIEVE IT!
WE MIGHT ACTUALLY FINISH THIS THING!
Uh-oh. CAREFUL WHAT YOU SAY, KYLE. WORDS LIKE THAT PRACTICALLY ENSURE THAT TROUBLE WILL--
DEET! DEET! DEET! DEET!
I SWEAR I DID NOT KNOW THAT WAS GONNA HAPPEN...
SWELL. AND IT'S A PRIORITY ONE, TO BOOT...
WELL, THANKS FOR EVERYTHING, JOHN, BUT IT LOOKS LIKE THE JLA JUST BOUGHT YOU A REPRIEVE.
HEY, DO SOME GOOD OUT THERE, MAN.
I'LL TRY...
...BUT SOMETHING TELLS ME THIS IS NOT GOING TO BE MY DAY...

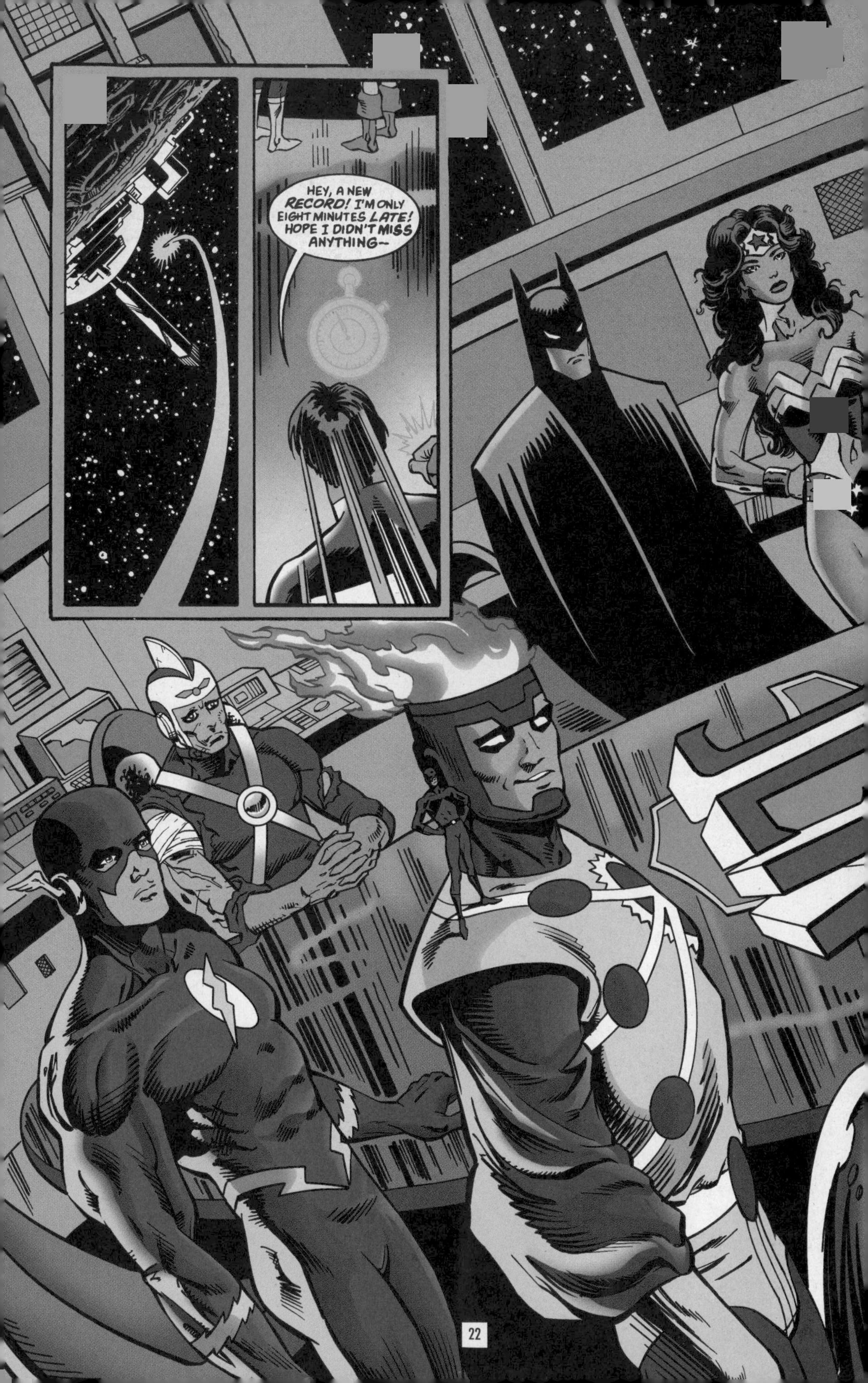
HEY, A NEW RECORD! I'M ONLY EIGHT MINUTES LATE! HOPE I DIDN'T MISS ANYTHING--

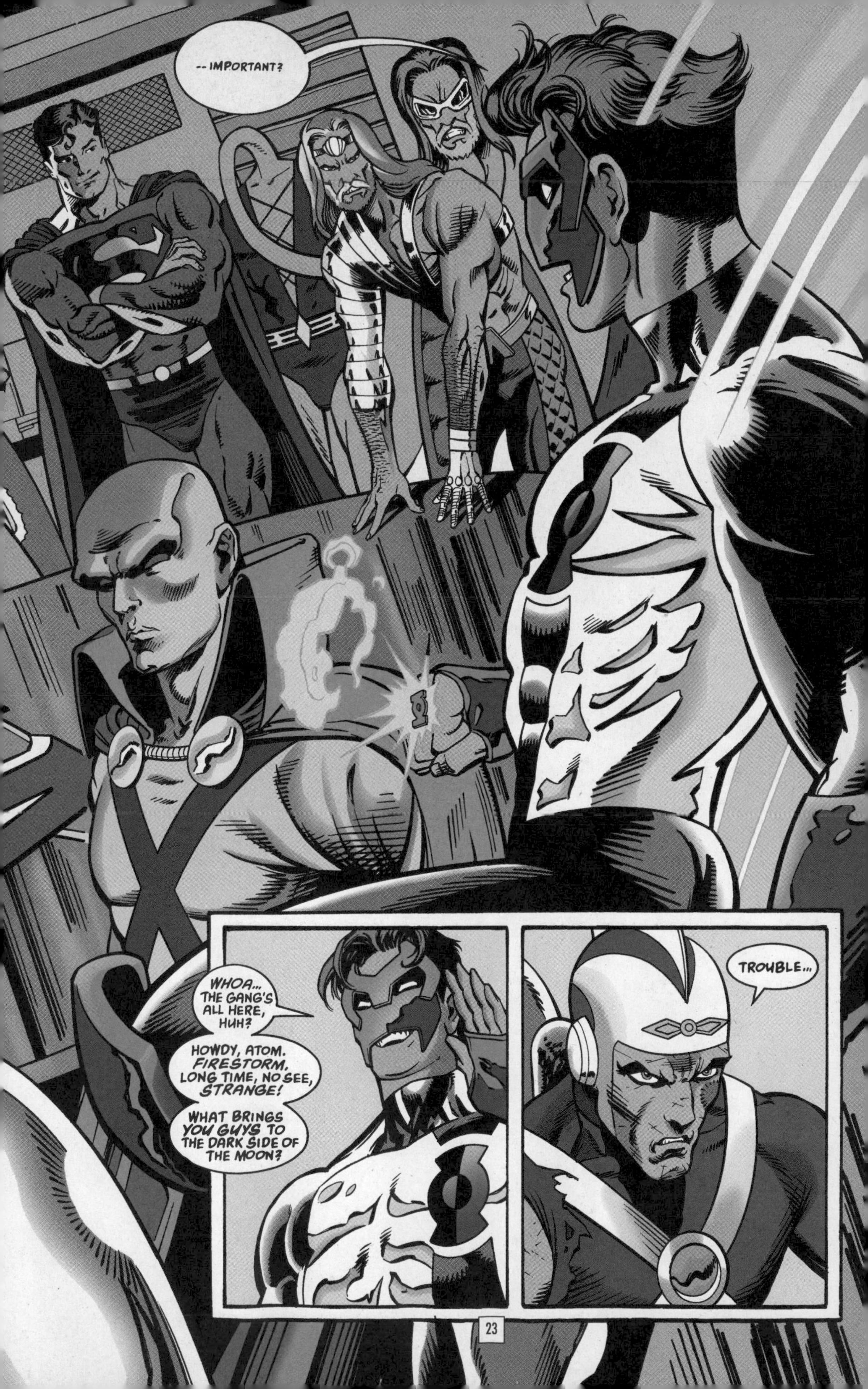
-- IMPORTANT?
WHOA... THE GANG'S ALL HERE, HUH?
HOWDY, ATOM. FIRESTORM. LONG TIME, NO SEE, STRANGE!
WHAT BRINGS YOU GUYS TO THE DARK SIDE OF THE MOON?
TROUBLE...

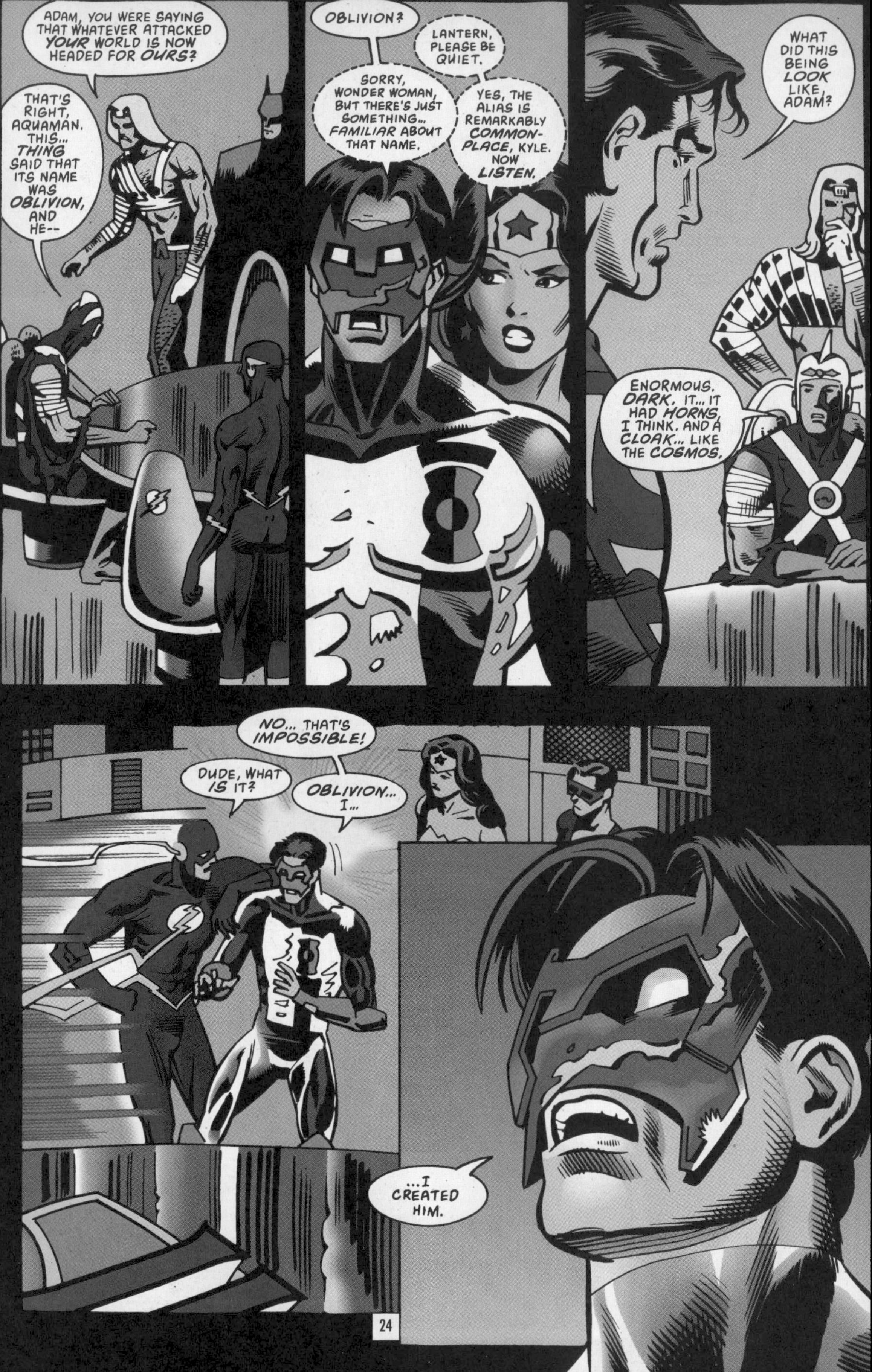
ADAM, YOU WERE SAYING THAT WHATEVER ATTACKED YOUR WORLD IS NOW HEADED FOR OURS?
THAT'S RIGHT, AQUAMAN. THIS... THING SAID THAT ITS NAME WAS OBLIVION, AND HE--
OBLIVION?
SORRY, WONDER WOMAN, BUT THERE'S JUST SOMETHING... FAMILIAR ABOUT THAT NAME.
LANTERN, PLEASE BE QUIET.
YES, THE ALIAS IS REMARKABLY COMMON-PLACE, KYLE. NOW LISTEN.
WHAT DID THIS BEING LOOK LIKE, ADAM?
ENORMOUS. DARK. IT... IT HAD HORNS, I THINK. AND A CLOAK... LIKE THE COSMOS.
NO... THAT'S IMPOSSIBLE!
DUDE, WHAT IS IT?
OBLIVION... I...
...I CREATED HIM.

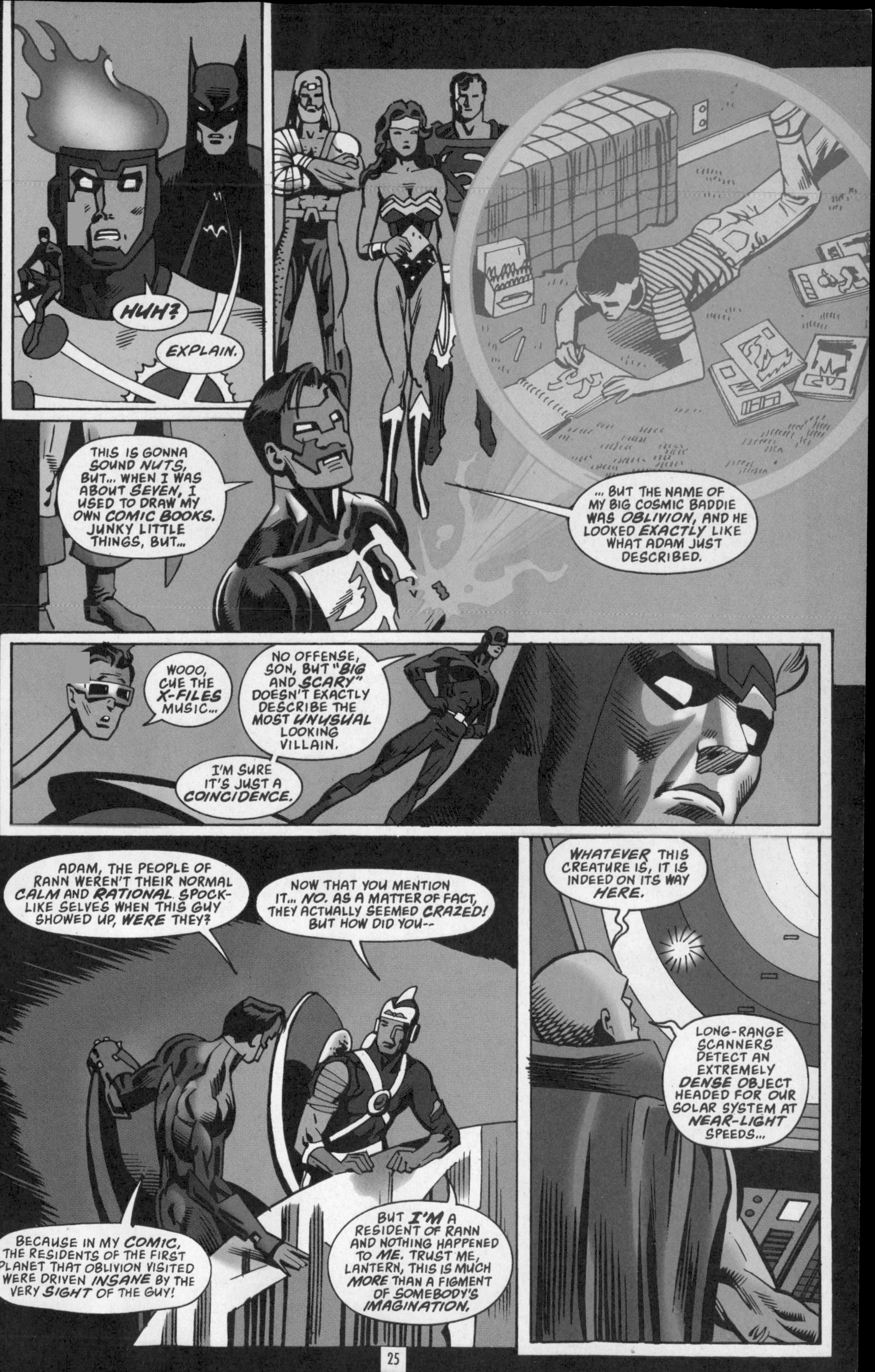

HUH?
EXPLAIN.
THIS IS GONNA SOUND NUTS, BUT... WHEN I WAS ABOUT SEVEN, I USED TO DRAW MY OWN COMIC BOOKS. JUNKY LITTLE THINGS, BUT...
... BUT THE NAME OF MY BIG COSMIC BADDIE WAS OBLIVION, AND HE LOOKED EXACTLY LIKE WHAT ADAM JUST DESCRIBED.
WOOO, CUE THE X-FILES MUSIC...
NO OFFENSE, SON, BUT "BIG AND SCARY" DOESN'T EXACTLY DESCRIBE THE MOST UNUSUAL LOOKING VILLAIN.
I'M SURE IT'S JUST A COINCIDENCE.
ADAM, THE PEOPLE OF RANN WEREN'T THEIR NORMAL CALM AND RATIONAL SPOCK-LIKE SELVES WHEN THIS GUY SHOWED UP, WERE THEY?
NOW THAT YOU MENTION IT... NO. AS A MATTER OF FACT, THEY ACTUALLY SEEMED CRAZED! BUT HOW DID YOU--
BECAUSE IN MY COMIC, THE RESIDENTS OF THE FIRST PLANET THAT OBLIVION VISITED WERE DRIVEN INSANE BY THE VERY SIGHT OF THE GUY!
BUT I'M A RESIDENT OF RANN AND NOTHING HAPPENED TO ME. TRUST ME, LANTERN, THIS IS MUCH MORE THAN A FIGMENT OF SOMEBODY'S IMAGINATION.
WHATEVER THIS CREATURE IS, IT IS INDEED ON ITS WAY HERE.
LONG-RANGE SCANNERS DETECT AN EXTREMELY DENSE OBJECT HEADED FOR OUR SOLAR SYSTEM AT NEAR-LIGHT SPEEDS...

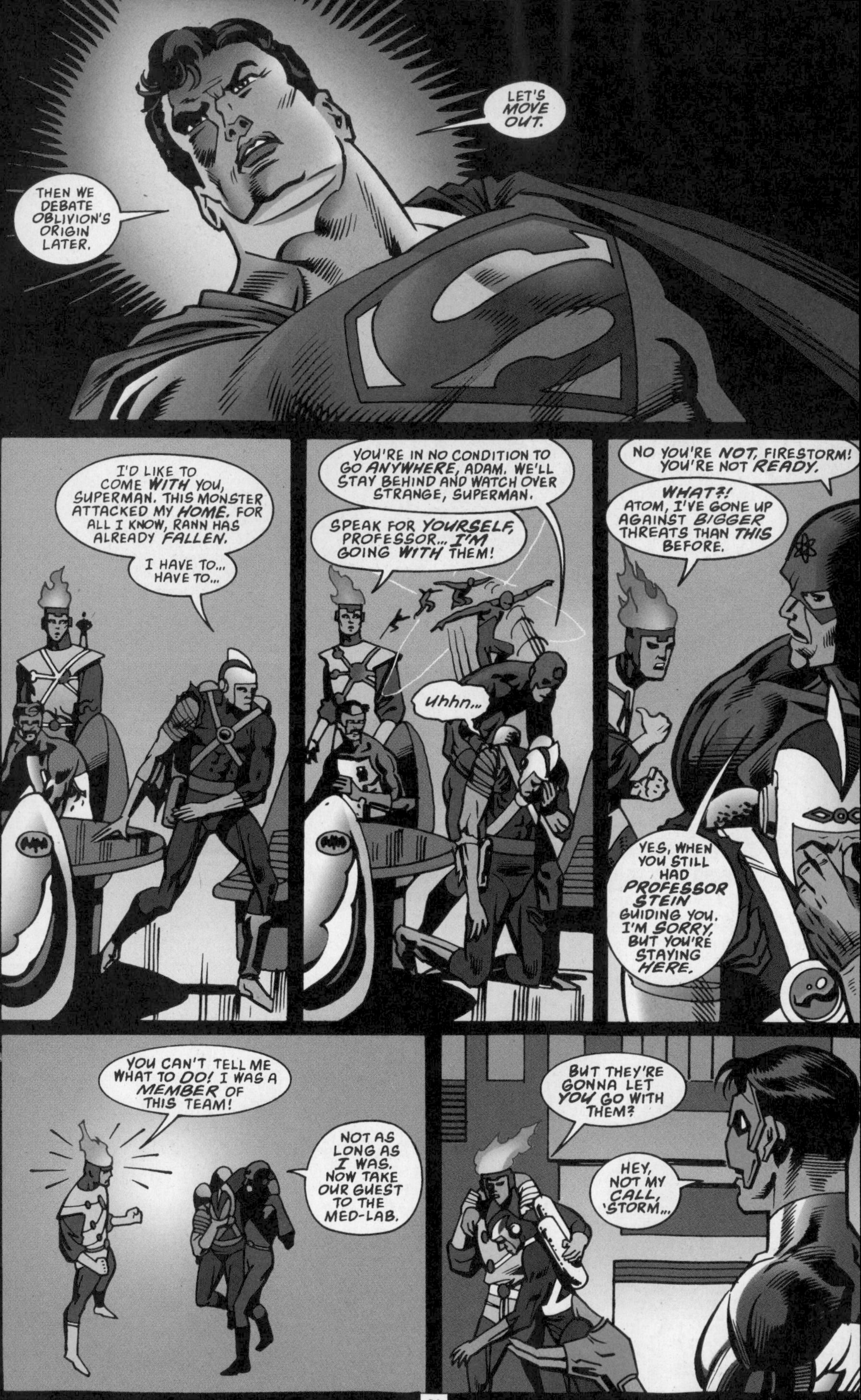
LET'S MOVE OUT.
THEN WE DEBATE OBLIVION'S ORIGIN LATER.
I'D LIKE TO COME WITH YOU, SUPERMAN. THIS MONSTER ATTACKED MY HOME. FOR ALL I KNOW, RANN HAS ALREADY FALLEN.
I HAVE TO... HAVE TO...
YOU'RE IN NO CONDITION TO GO ANYWHERE, ADAM. WE'LL STAY BEHIND AND WATCH OVER STRANGE, SUPERMAN.
SPEAK FOR YOURSELF, PROFESSOR... I'M GOING WITH THEM!
uhhn...
NO YOU'RE NOT, FIRESTORM! YOU'RE NOT READY.
WHAT?! ATOM, I'VE GONE UP AGAINST BIGGER THREATS THAN THIS BEFORE.
YES, WHEN YOU STILL HAD PROFESSOR STEIN GUIDING YOU. I'M SORRY, BUT YOU'RE STAYING HERE.
YOU CAN'T TELL ME WHAT TO DO! I WAS A MEMBER OF THIS TEAM!
NOT AS LONG AS I WAS. NOW TAKE OUR GUEST TO THE MED-LAB.
BUT THEY'RE GONNA LET YOU GO WITH THEM?
HEY, NOT MY CALL, 'STORM...

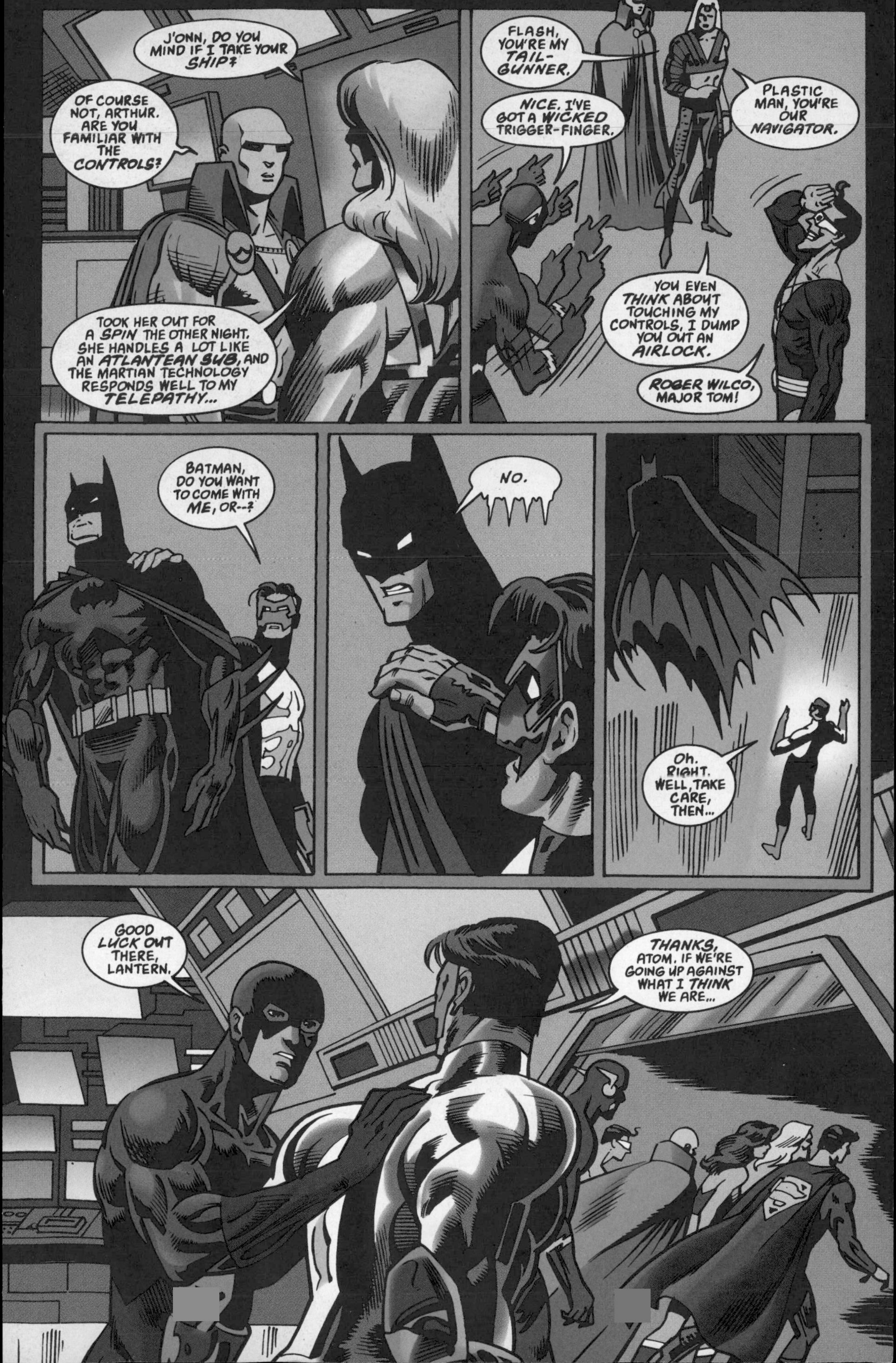
J'ONN, DO YOU MIND IF I TAKE YOUR SHIP?
OF COURSE NOT, ARTHUR. ARE YOU FAMILIAR WITH THE CONTROLS?
TOOK HER OUT FOR A SPIN THE OTHER NIGHT. SHE HANDLES A LOT LIKE AN ATLANTEAN SUB, AND THE MARTIAN TECHNOLOGY RESPONDS WELL TO MY TELEPATHY...
FLASH, YOU'RE MY TAIL-GUNNER.
NICE. I'VE GOT A WICKED TRIGGER-FINGER.
PLASTIC MAN, YOU'RE OUR NAVIGATOR.
YOU EVEN THINK ABOUT TOUCHING MY CONTROLS, I DUMP YOU OUT AN AIRLOCK.
ROGER WILCO, MAJOR TOM!
BATMAN, DO YOU WANT TO COME WITH ME, OR--?
NO.
Oh. RIGHT. WELL, TAKE CARE, THEN...
GOOD LUCK OUT THERE, LANTERN.
THANKS, ATOM. IF WE'RE GOING UP AGAINST WHAT I THINK WE ARE...

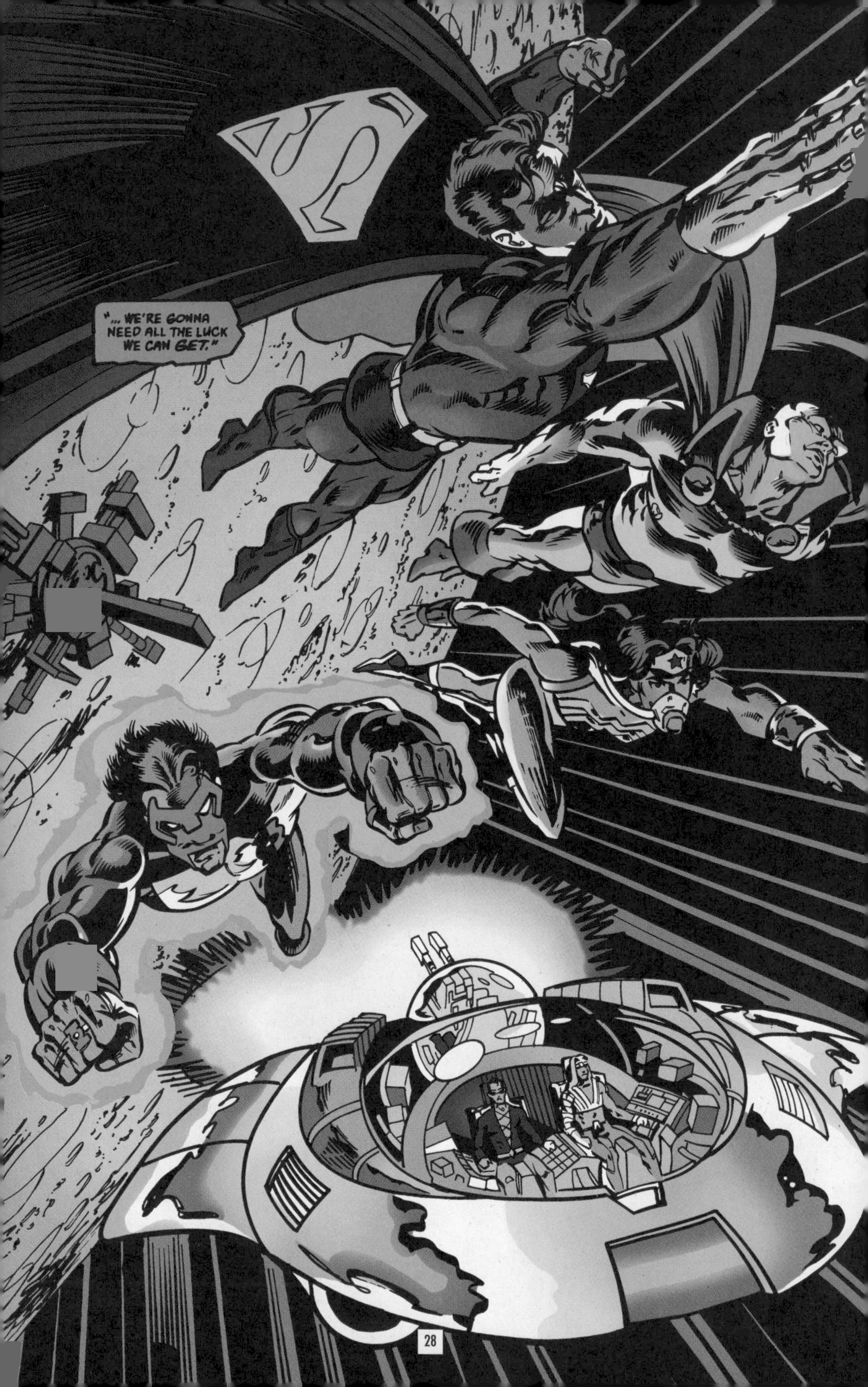
"... WE'RE GONNA NEED ALL THE LUCK WE CAN GET."

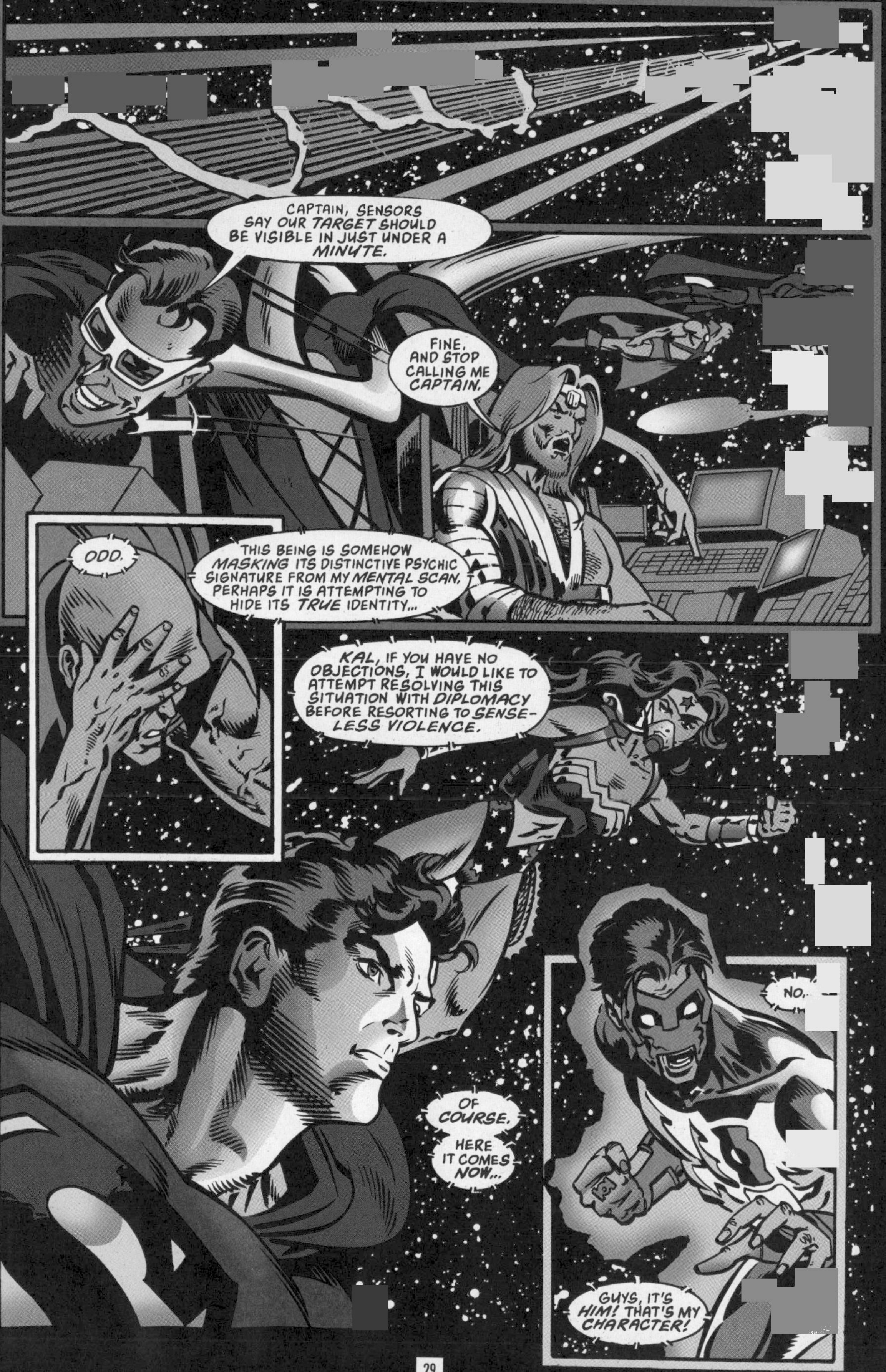

CAPTAIN, SENSORS SAY OUR TARGET SHOULD BE VISIBLE IN JUST UNDER A MINUTE.
FINE, AND STOP CALLING ME CAPTAIN.
ODD.
THIS BEING IS SOMEHOW MASKING ITS DISTINCTIVE PSYCHIC SIGNATURE FROM MY MENTAL SCAN. PERHAPS IT IS ATTEMPTING TO HIDE ITS TRUE IDENTITY...
KAL, IF YOU HAVE NO OBJECTIONS, I WOULD LIKE TO ATTEMPT RESOLVING THIS SITUATION WITH DIPLOMACY BEFORE RESORTING TO SENSELESS VIOLENCE.
OF COURSE.
HERE IT COMES NOW...
NO.
GUYS, IT'S HIM! THAT'S MY CHARACTER!

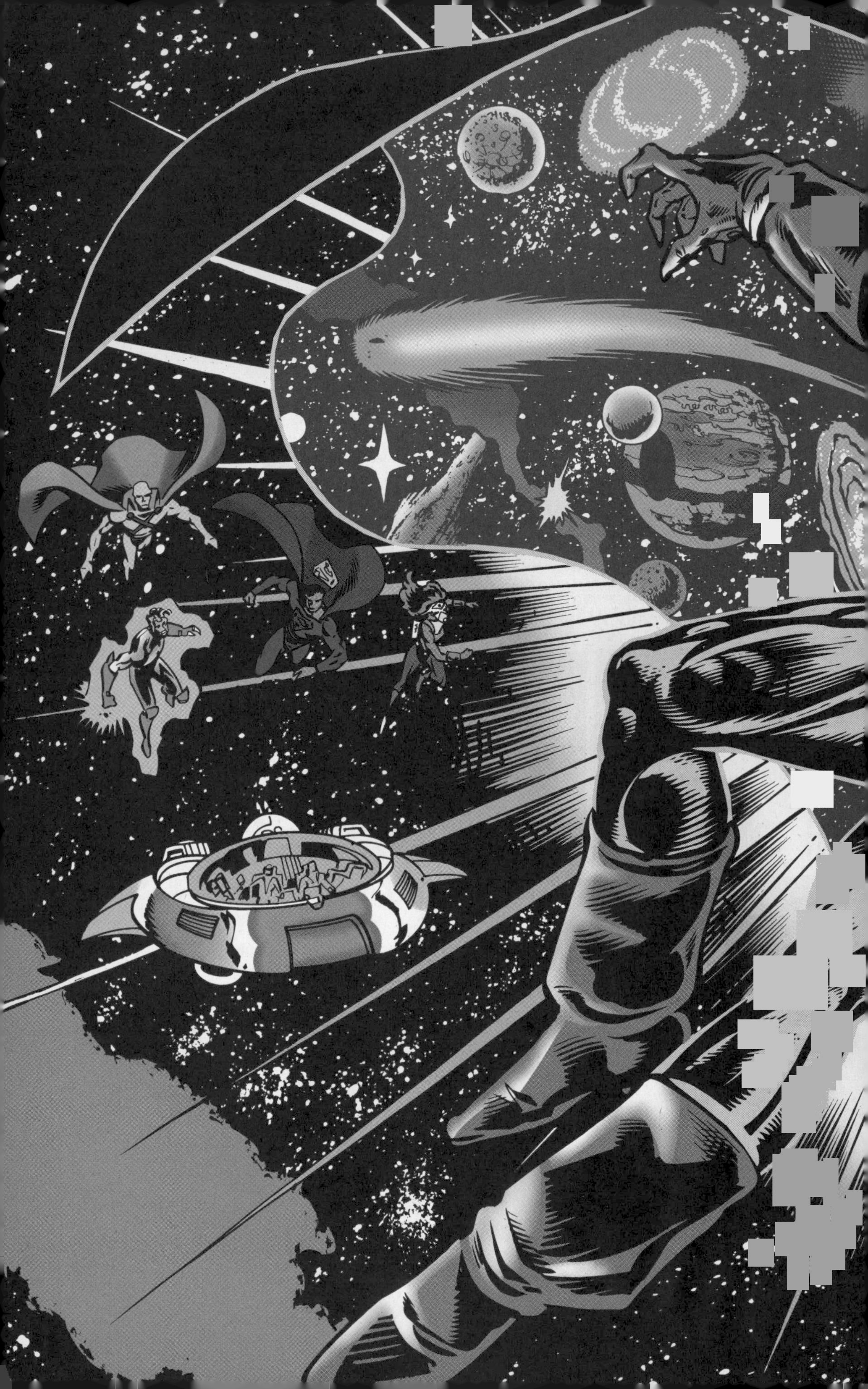

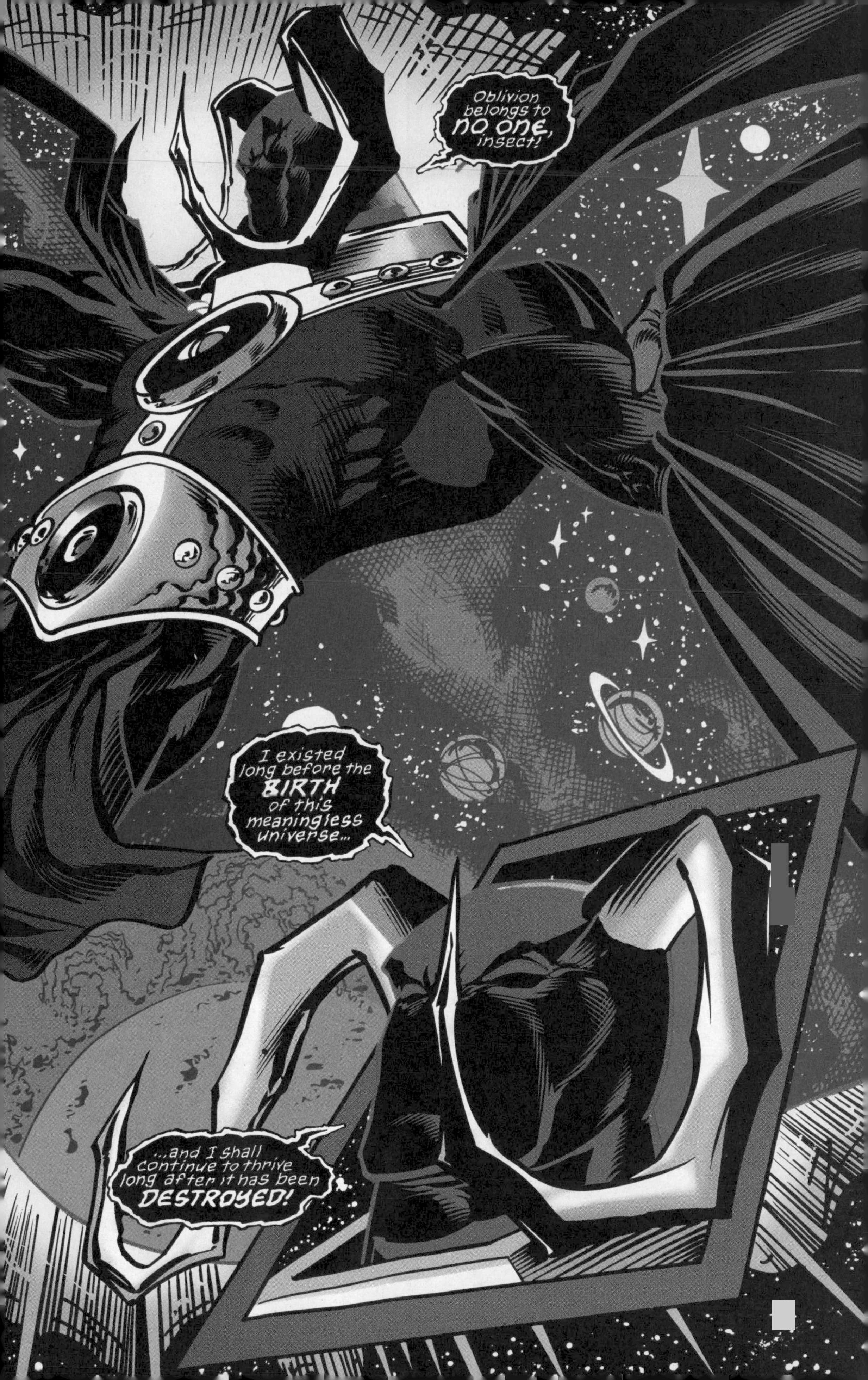

Oblivion belongs to NO ONE, insect!
I existed long before the BIRTH of this meaningless universe...
...and I shall continue to thrive long after it has been DESTROYED!

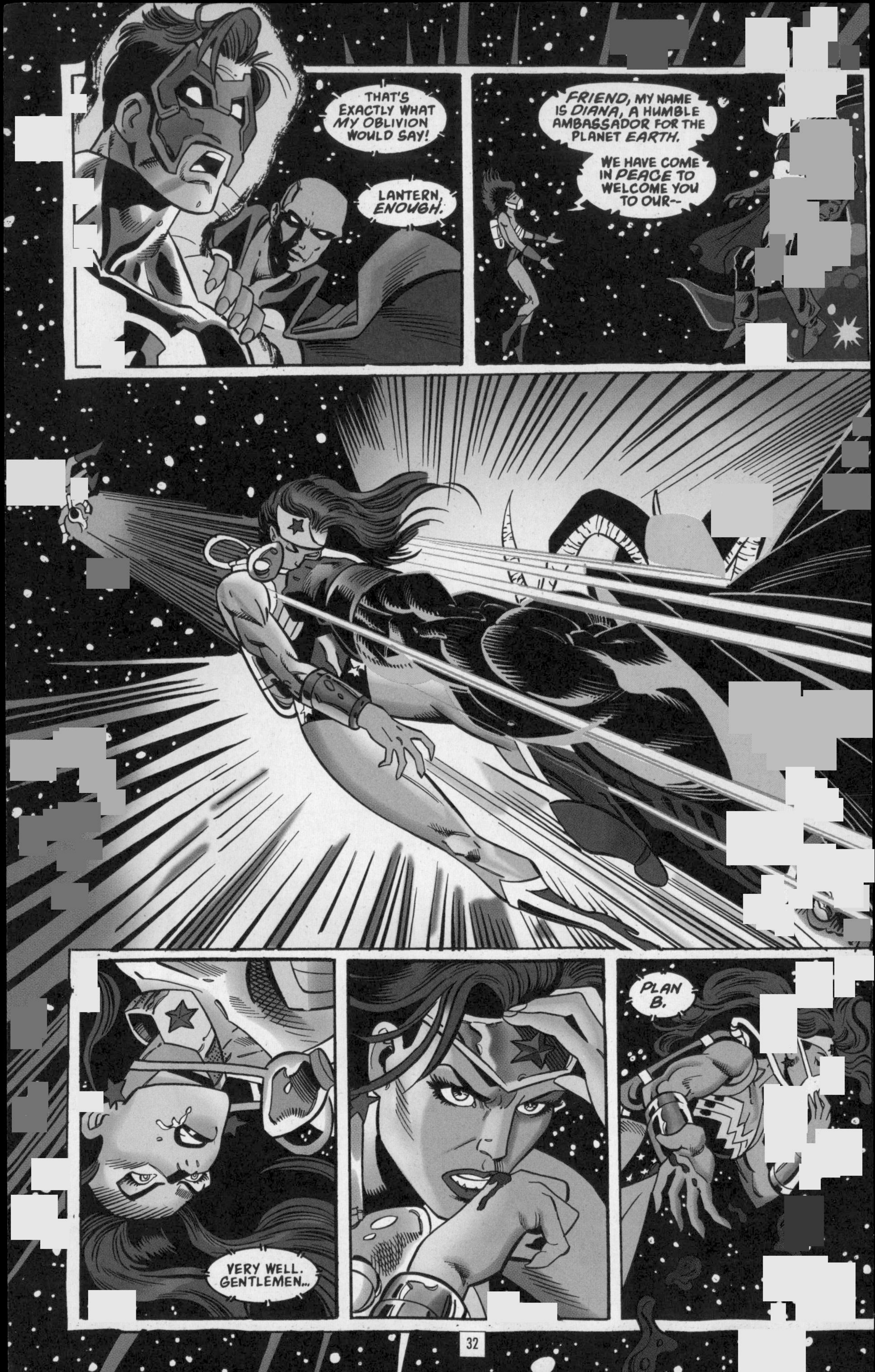
THAT'S EXACTLY WHAT MY OBLIVION WOULD SAY!
LANTERN, ENOUGH.
FRIEND, MY NAME IS DIANA, A HUMBLE AMBASSADOR FOR THE PLANET EARTH.
WE HAVE COME IN PEACE TO WELCOME YOU TO OUR--
VERY WELL. GENTLEMEN...
PLAN B.

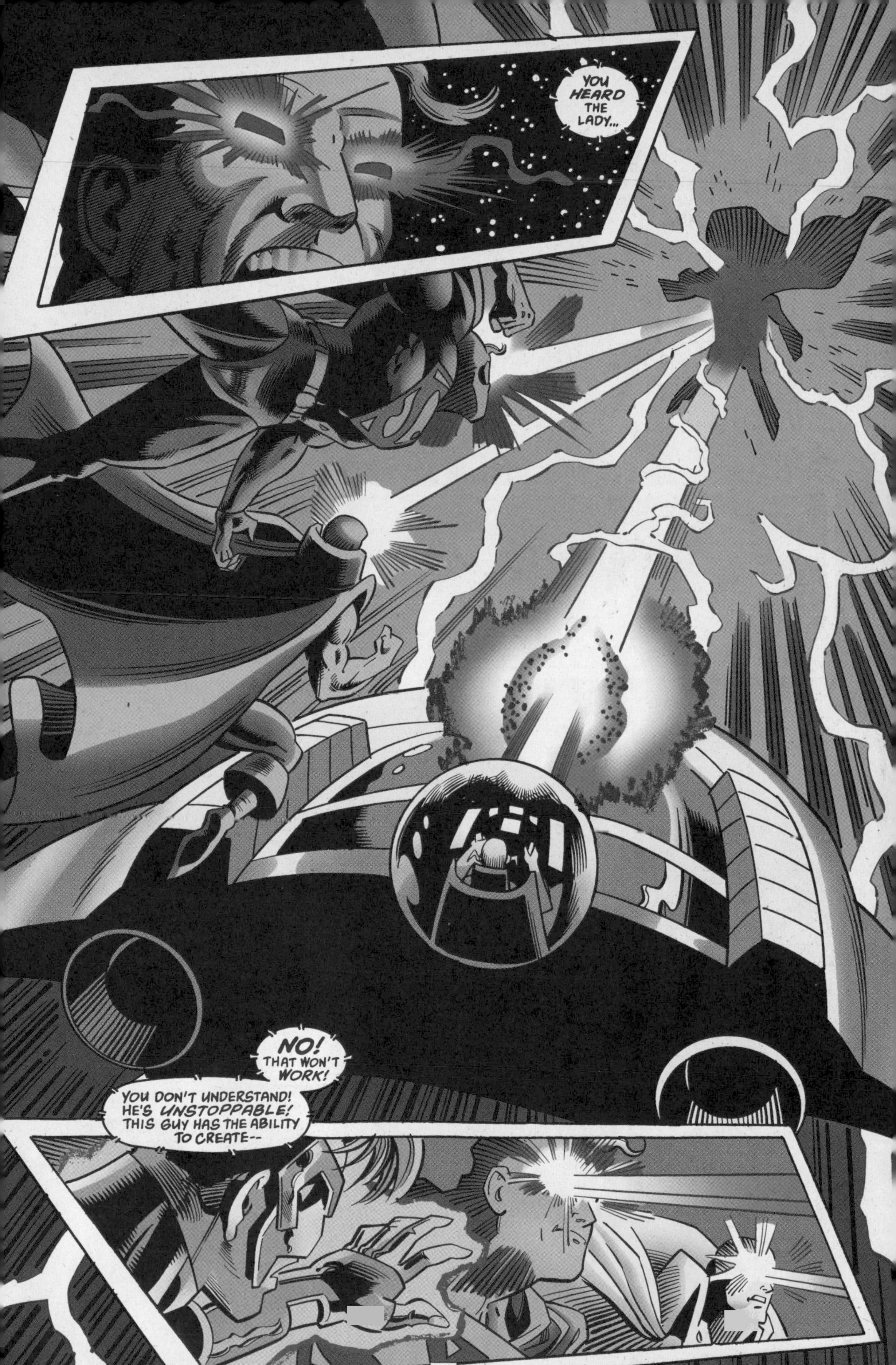
YOU HEARD THE LADY...
NO! THAT WON'T WORK!
YOU DON'T UNDERSTAND! HE'S UNSTOPPABLE! THIS GUY HAS THE ABILITY TO CREATE--

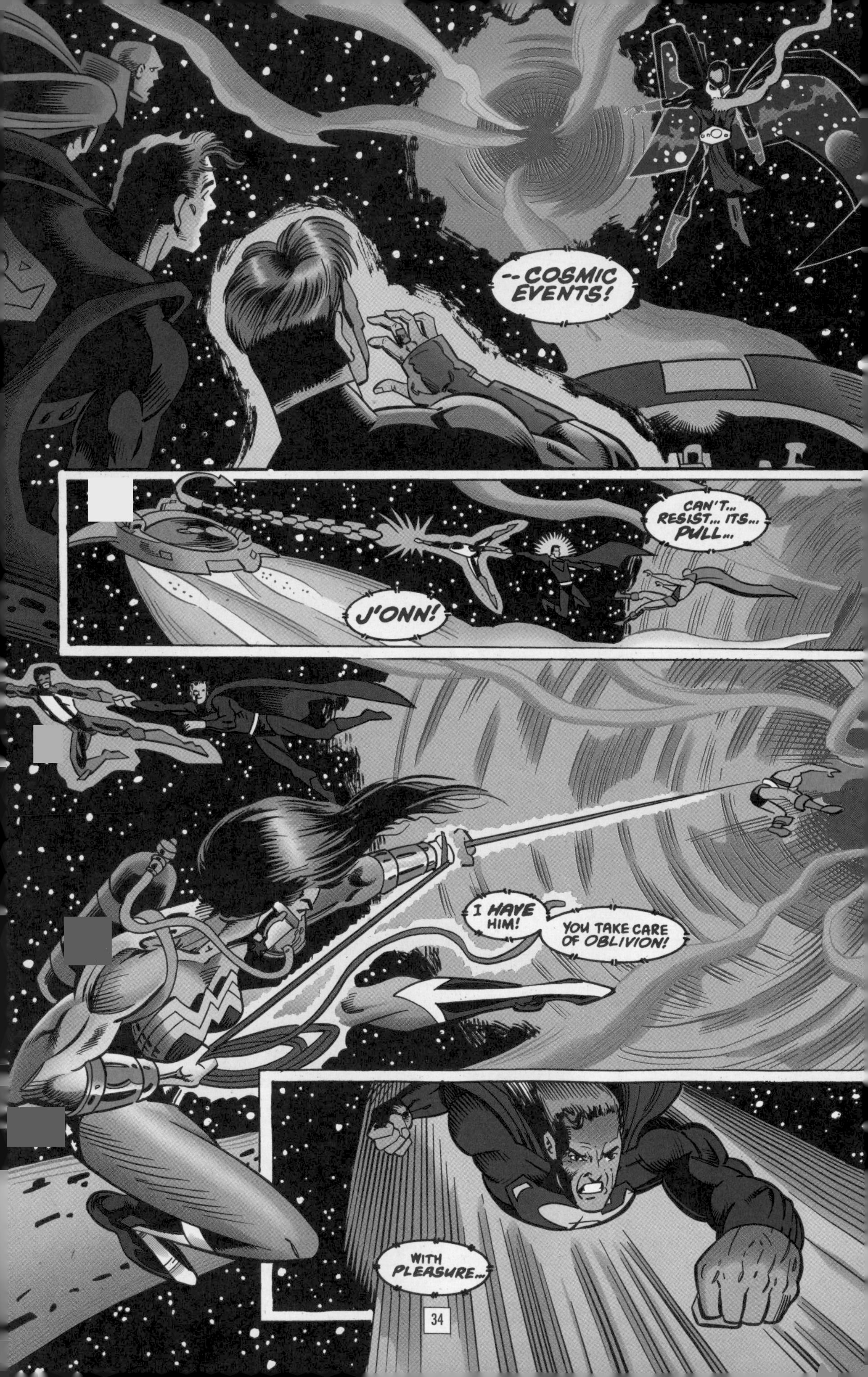
--COSMIC EVENTS!
CAN'T... RESIST... ITS... PULL...
J'ONN!
I HAVE HIM!
YOU TAKE CARE OF OBLIVION!
WITH PLEASURE...

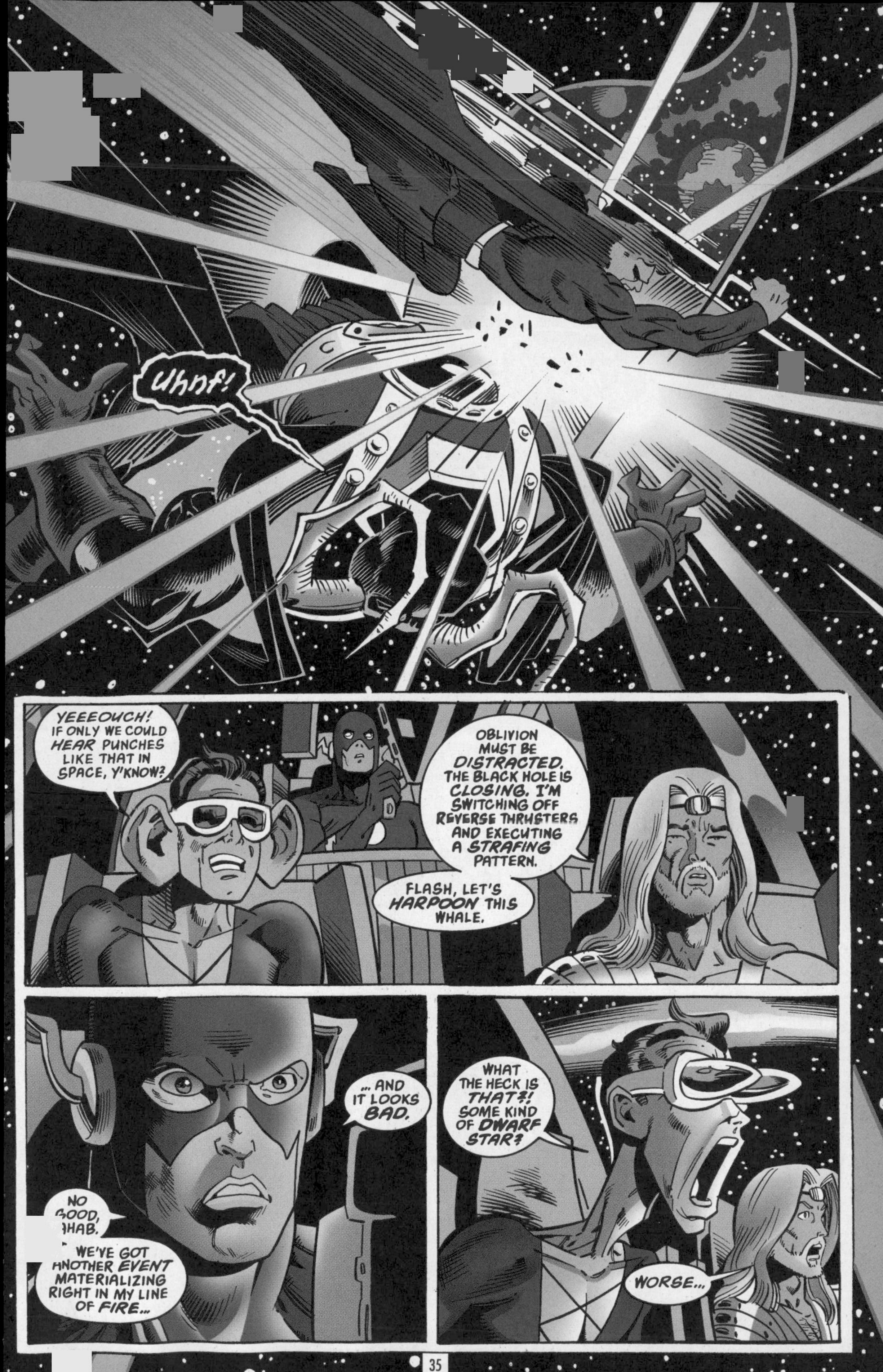

UHNF!
YEEEOUCH! IF ONLY WE COULD HEAR PUNCHES LIKE THAT IN SPACE, Y'KNOW?
OBLIVION MUST BE DISTRACTED. THE BLACK HOLE IS CLOSING. I'M SWITCHING OFF REVERSE THRUSTERS AND EXECUTING A STRAFING PATTERN.
FLASH, LET'S HARPOON THIS WHALE.
NO GOOD, HAB.
WE'VE GOT NOTHER EVENT MATERIALIZING RIGHT IN MY LINE OF FIRE...
...AND IT LOOKS BAD.
WHAT THE HECK IS THAT?! SOME KIND OF DWARF STAR?
WORSE...

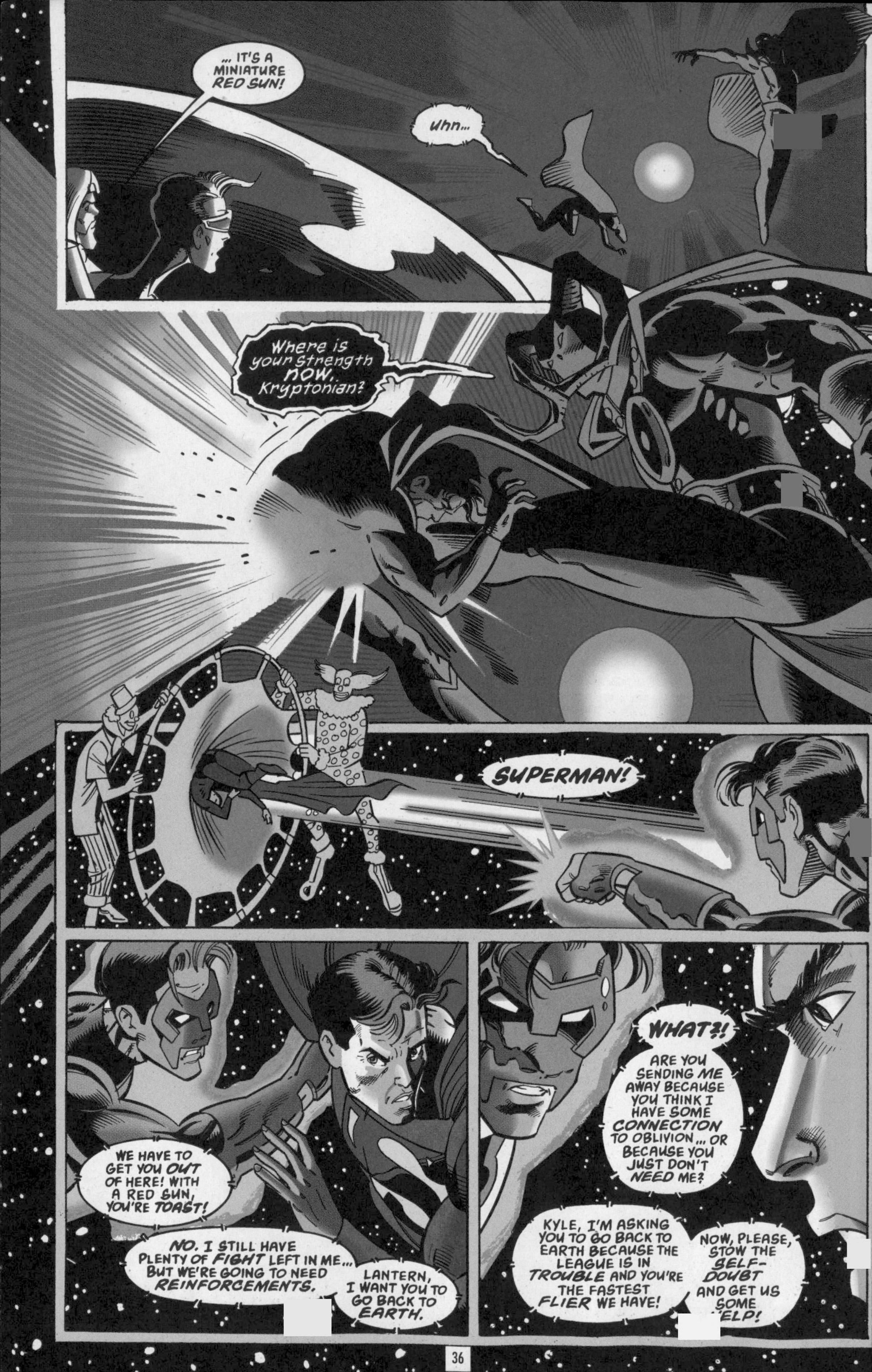
... IT'S A MINIATURE RED SUN!
Uhn...
Where is your strength now, Kryptonian?
SUPERMAN!
WE HAVE TO GET YOU OUT OF HERE! WITH A RED SUN, YOU'RE TOAST!
NO. I STILL HAVE PLENTY OF FIGHT LEFT IN ME... BUT WE'RE GOING TO NEED REINFORCEMENTS.
LANTERN, I WANT YOU TO GO BACK TO EARTH.
WHAT?!
ARE YOU SENDING ME AWAY BECAUSE YOU THINK I HAVE SOME CONNECTION TO OBLIVION... OR BECAUSE YOU JUST DON'T NEED ME?
KYLE, I'M ASKING YOU TO GO BACK TO EARTH BECAUSE THE LEAGUE IS IN TROUBLE AND YOU'RE THE FASTEST FLIER WE HAVE!
NOW, PLEASE, STOW THE SELF-DOUBT AND GET US SOME ELP!

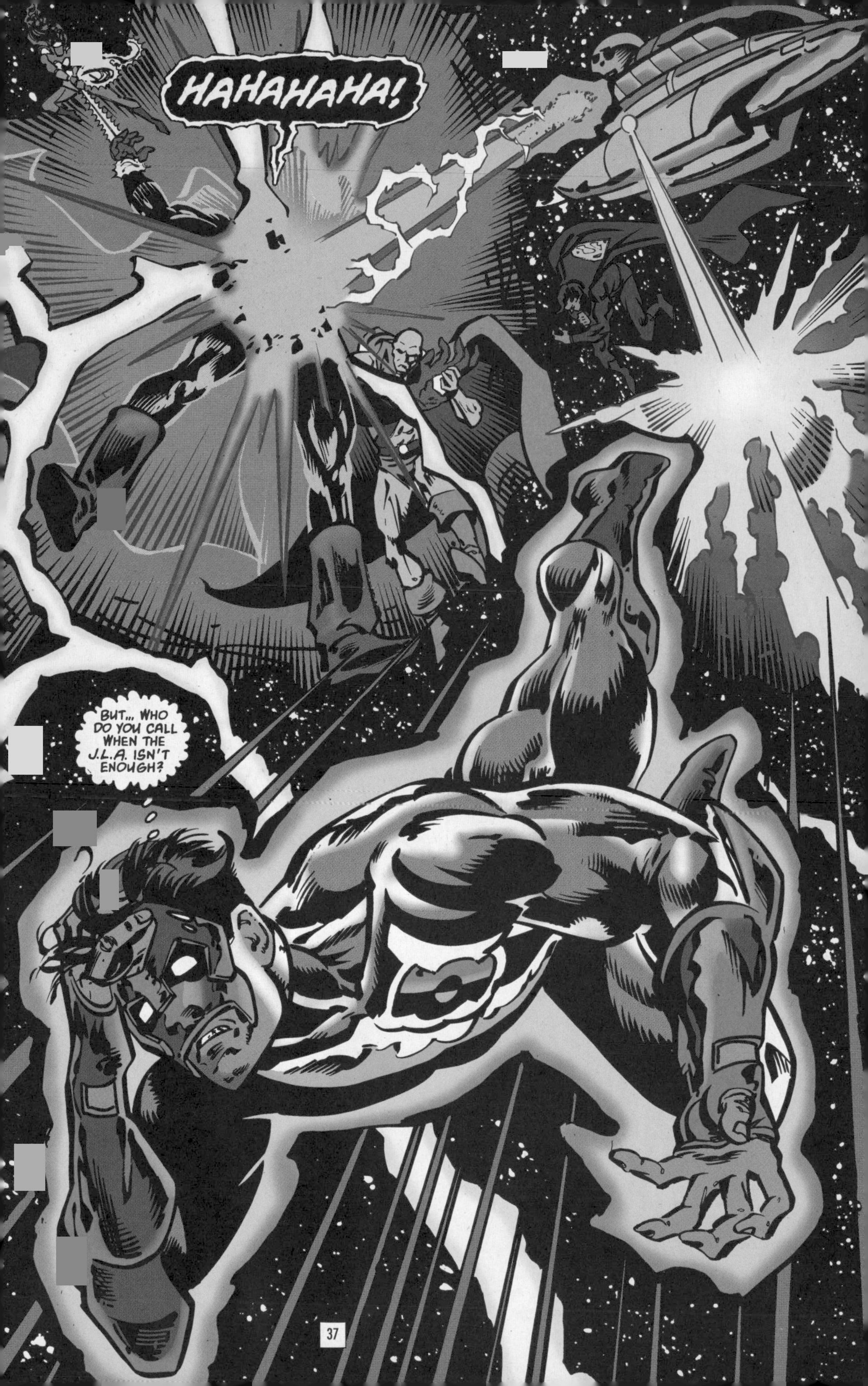
HAHAHAHA!
BUT... WHO DO YOU CALL WHEN THE J.L.A. ISN'T ENOUGH?

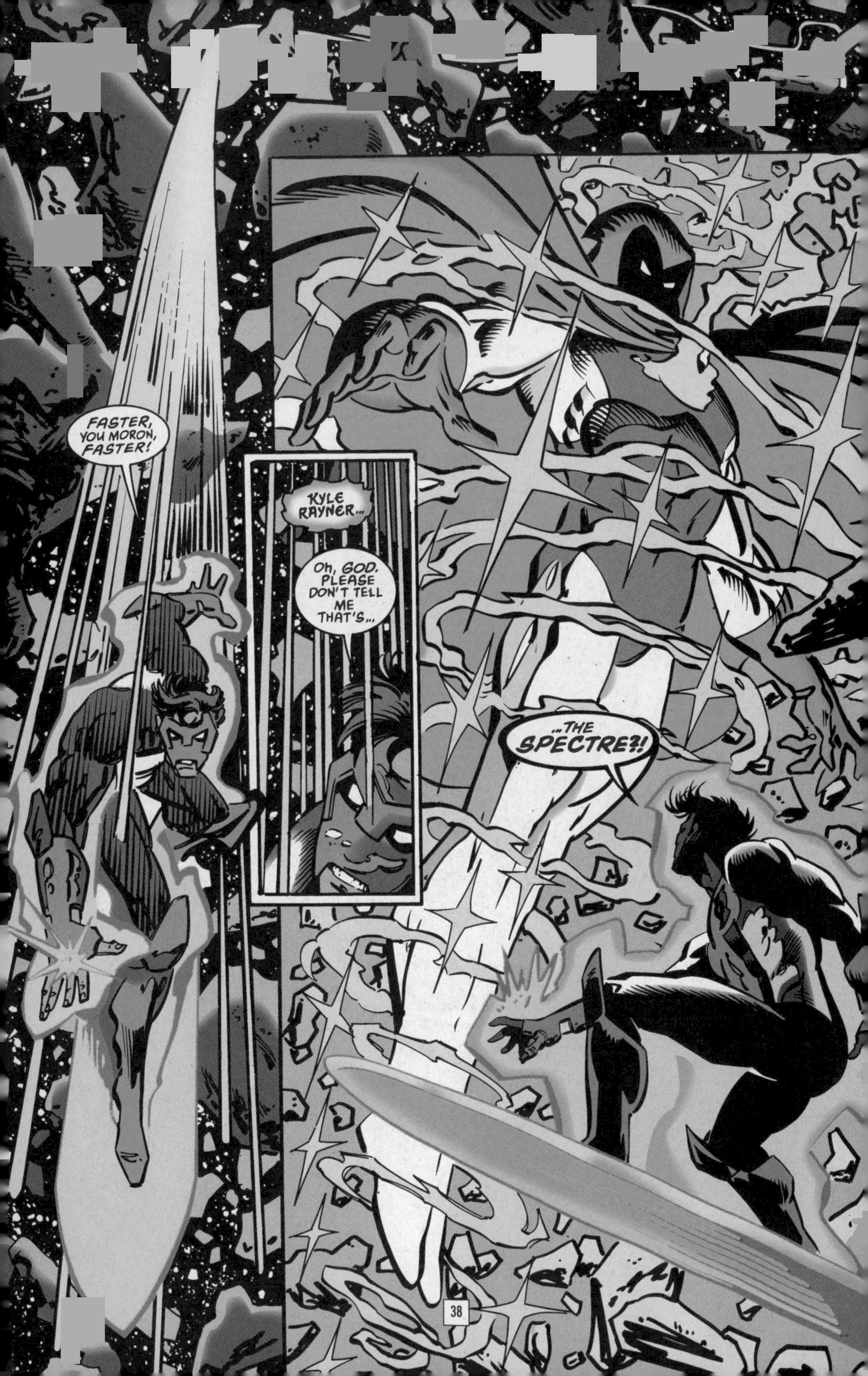
FASTER, YOU MORON, FASTER!
KYLE RAYNER...
Oh, GOD. PLEASE DON'T TELL ME THAT'S...
...THE SPECTRE?!

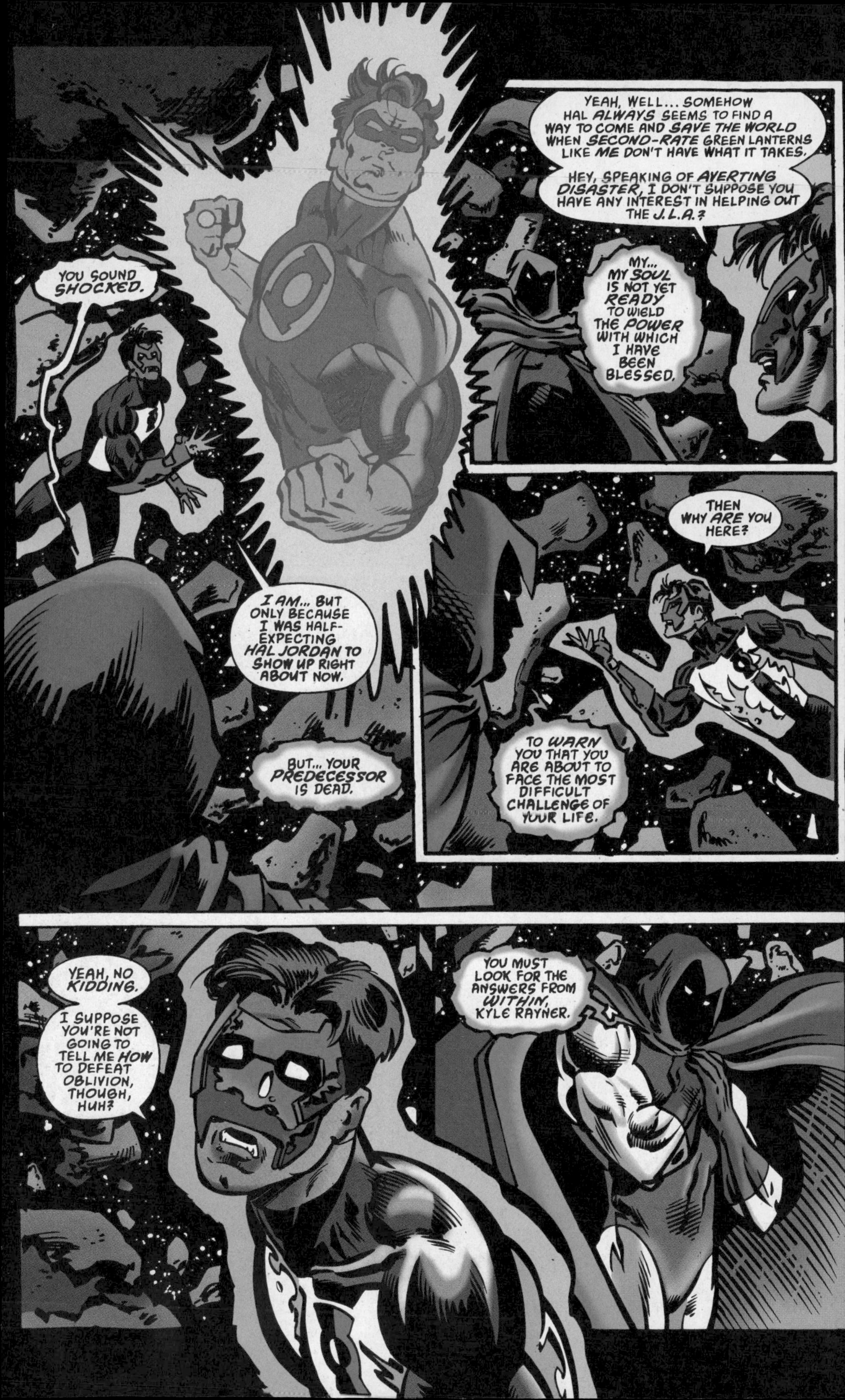
YOU SOUND SHOCKED.
I AM... BUT ONLY BECAUSE I WAS HALF-EXPECTING HAL JORDAN TO SHOW UP RIGHT ABOUT NOW.
BUT... YOUR PREDECESSOR IS DEAD.
YEAH, WELL... SOMEHOW HAL ALWAYS SEEMS TO FIND A WAY TO COME AND SAVE THE WORLD WHEN SECOND-RATE GREEN LANTERNS LIKE ME DON'T HAVE WHAT IT TAKES.
HEY, SPEAKING OF AVERTING DISASTER, I DON'T SUPPOSE YOU HAVE ANY INTEREST IN HELPING OUT THE J.L.A.?
MY... MY SOUL IS NOT YET READY TO WIELD THE POWER WITH WHICH I HAVE BEEN BLESSED.
THEN WHY ARE YOU HERE?
TO WARN YOU THAT YOU ARE ABOUT TO FACE THE MOST DIFFICULT CHALLENGE OF YOUR LIFE.
YEAH, NO KIDDING.
I SUPPOSE YOU'RE NOT GOING TO TELL ME HOW TO DEFEAT OBLIVION, THOUGH, HUH?
YOU MUST LOOK FOR THE ANSWERS FROM WITHIN, KYLE RAYNER.

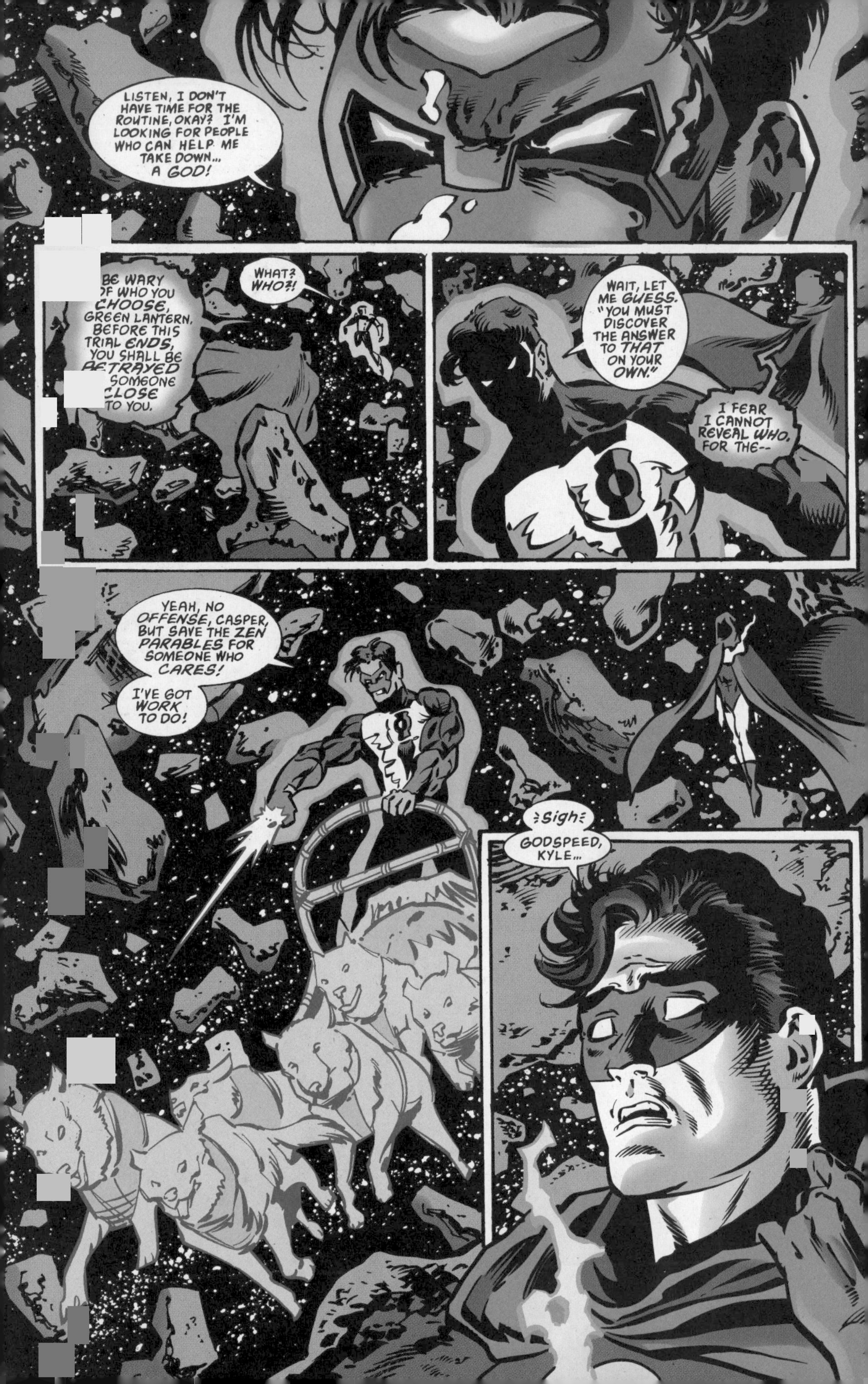
LISTEN, I DON'T HAVE TIME FOR THE ROUTINE, OKAY? I'M LOOKING FOR PEOPLE WHO CAN HELP ME TAKE DOWN... A GOD!
BE WARY OF WHO YOU CHOOSE, GREEN LANTERN. BEFORE THIS TRIAL ENDS, YOU SHALL BE BETRAYED BY SOMEONE CLOSE TO YOU.
WHAT? WHO?!
WAIT, LET ME GUESS. "YOU MUST DISCOVER THE ANSWER TO THAT ON YOUR OWN."
I FEAR I CANNOT REVEAL WHO, FOR THE--
YEAH, NO OFFENSE, CASPER, BUT SAVE THE ZEN PARABLES FOR SOMEONE WHO CARES!
I'VE GOT WORK TO DO!
Sigh
GODSPEED, KYLE...

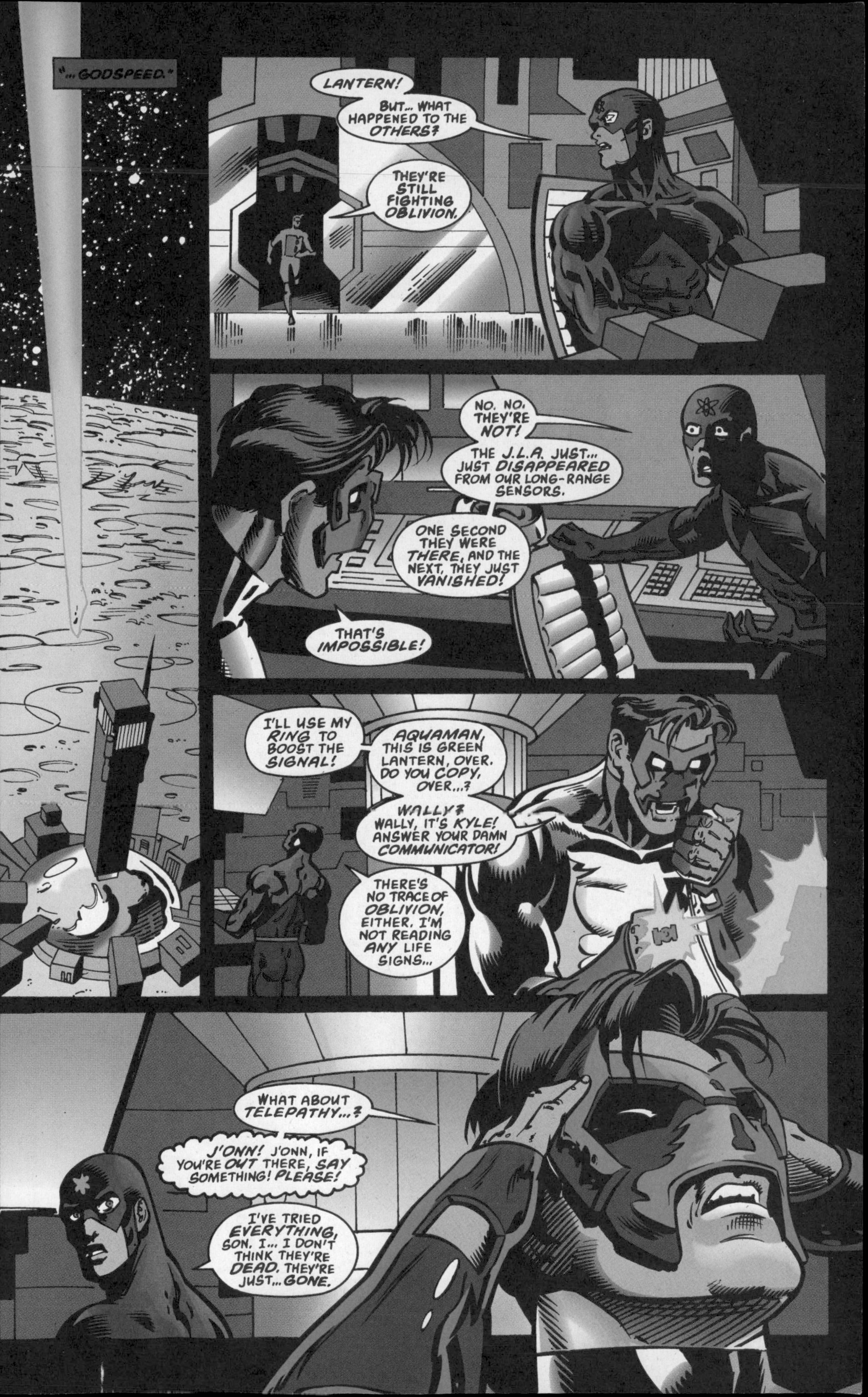
"...GODSPEED."
LANTERN!
BUT... WHAT HAPPENED TO THE OTHERS?
THEY'RE STILL FIGHTING OBLIVION.
NO. NO. THEY'RE NOT!
THE J.L.A. JUST... JUST DISAPPEARED FROM OUR LONG-RANGE SENSORS.
ONE SECOND THEY WERE THERE, AND THE NEXT, THEY JUST VANISHED!
THAT'S IMPOSSIBLE!
I'LL USE MY RING TO BOOST THE SIGNAL!
AQUAMAN, THIS IS GREEN LANTERN, OVER. DO YOU COPY, OVER...?
WALLY? WALLY, IT'S KYLE! ANSWER YOUR DAMN COMMUNICATOR!
THERE'S NO TRACE OF OBLIVION, EITHER. I'M NOT READING ANY LIFE SIGNS...
WHAT ABOUT TELEPATHY...?
J'ONN! J'ONN, IF YOU'RE OUT THERE, SAY SOMETHING! PLEASE!
I'VE TRIED EVERYTHING, SON. I... I DON'T THINK THEY'RE DEAD. THEY'RE JUST... GONE.

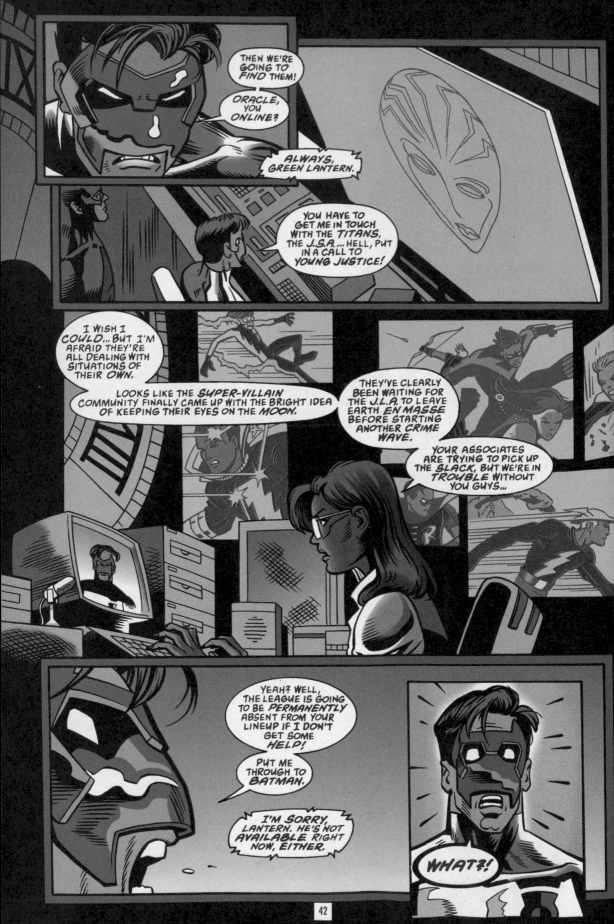

THEN WE'RE GOING TO *FIND* THEM!

ORACLE, YOU *ONLINE*?

ALWAYS, *GREEN LANTERN*.

YOU HAVE TO GET ME IN TOUCH WITH THE *TITANS*, THE *J.S.A.*... HELL, PUT IN A CALL TO *YOUNG JUSTICE*!

I WISH I *COULD*... BUT I'M AFRAID THEY'RE ALL DEALING WITH SITUATIONS OF THEIR *OWN*.

LOOKS LIKE THE *SUPER-VILLAIN* COMMUNITY FINALLY CAME UP WITH THE BRIGHT IDEA OF KEEPING THEIR EYES ON THE *MOON*.

THEY'VE CLEARLY BEEN WAITING FOR THE *J.L.A.* TO LEAVE EARTH *EN MASSE* BEFORE STARTING ANOTHER *CRIME WAVE*.

YOUR ASSOCIATES ARE TRYING TO PICK UP THE *SLACK*, BUT WE'RE IN *TROUBLE* WITHOUT YOU GUYS...

YEAH? WELL, THE LEAGUE IS GOING TO BE *PERMANENTLY* ABSENT FROM YOUR LINEUP IF I DON'T GET SOME *HELP*!

PUT ME THROUGH TO *BATMAN*.

I'M SORRY, LANTERN. HE'S NOT *AVAILABLE* RIGHT NOW, EITHER.

WHAT?!

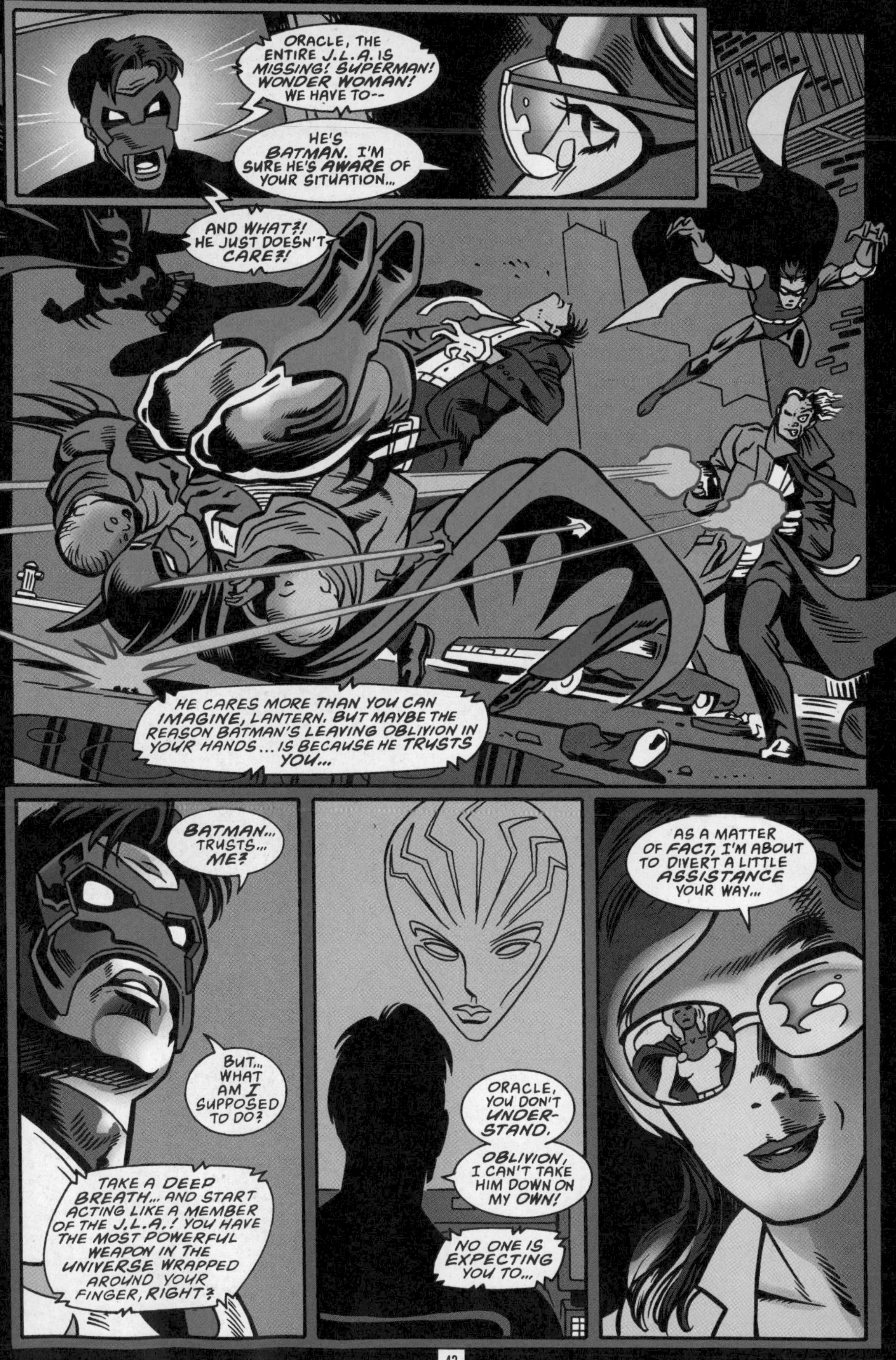
ORACLE, THE ENTIRE J.L.A. IS MISSING! SUPERMAN! WONDER WOMAN! WE HAVE TO--
HE'S BATMAN. I'M SURE HE'S AWARE OF YOUR SITUATION...
AND WHAT?! HE JUST DOESN'T CARE?!
HE CARES MORE THAN YOU CAN IMAGINE, LANTERN. BUT MAYBE THE REASON BATMAN'S LEAVING OBLIVION IN YOUR HANDS... IS BECAUSE HE TRUSTS YOU...
BATMAN... TRUSTS... ME?
BUT... WHAT AM I SUPPOSED TO DO?
TAKE A DEEP BREATH... AND START ACTING LIKE A MEMBER OF THE J.L.A.! YOU HAVE THE MOST POWERFUL WEAPON IN THE UNIVERSE WRAPPED AROUND YOUR FINGER, RIGHT?
ORACLE, YOU DON'T UNDER-STAND.
OBLIVION, I CAN'T TAKE HIM DOWN ON MY OWN!
NO ONE IS EXPECTING YOU TO...
AS A MATTER OF FACT, I'M ABOUT TO DIVERT A LITTLE ASSISTANCE YOUR WAY...

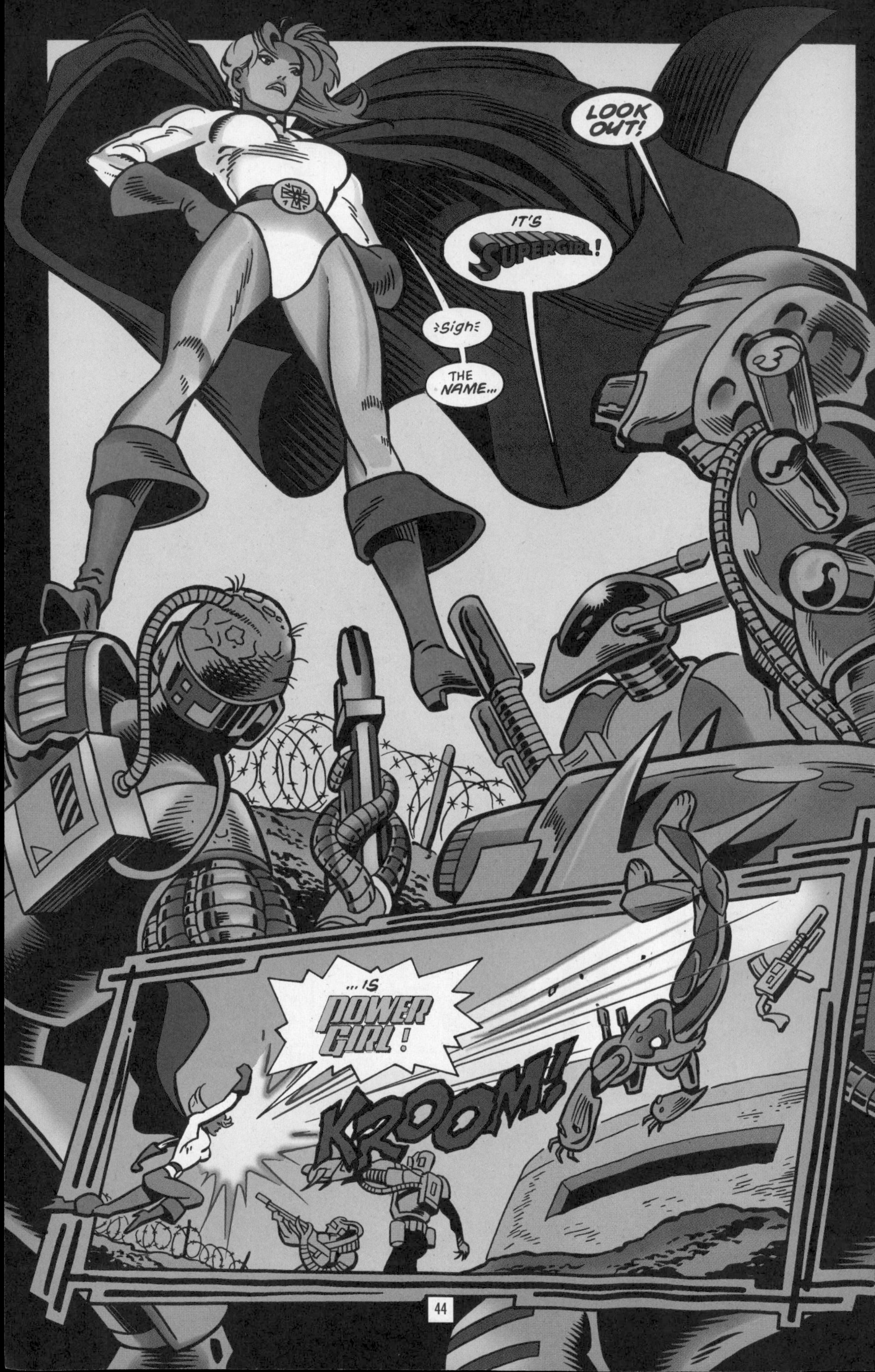
LOOK OUT!
IT'S SUPERGIRL!
Sigh
THE NAME...
...IS POWER GIRL!
KROOM!

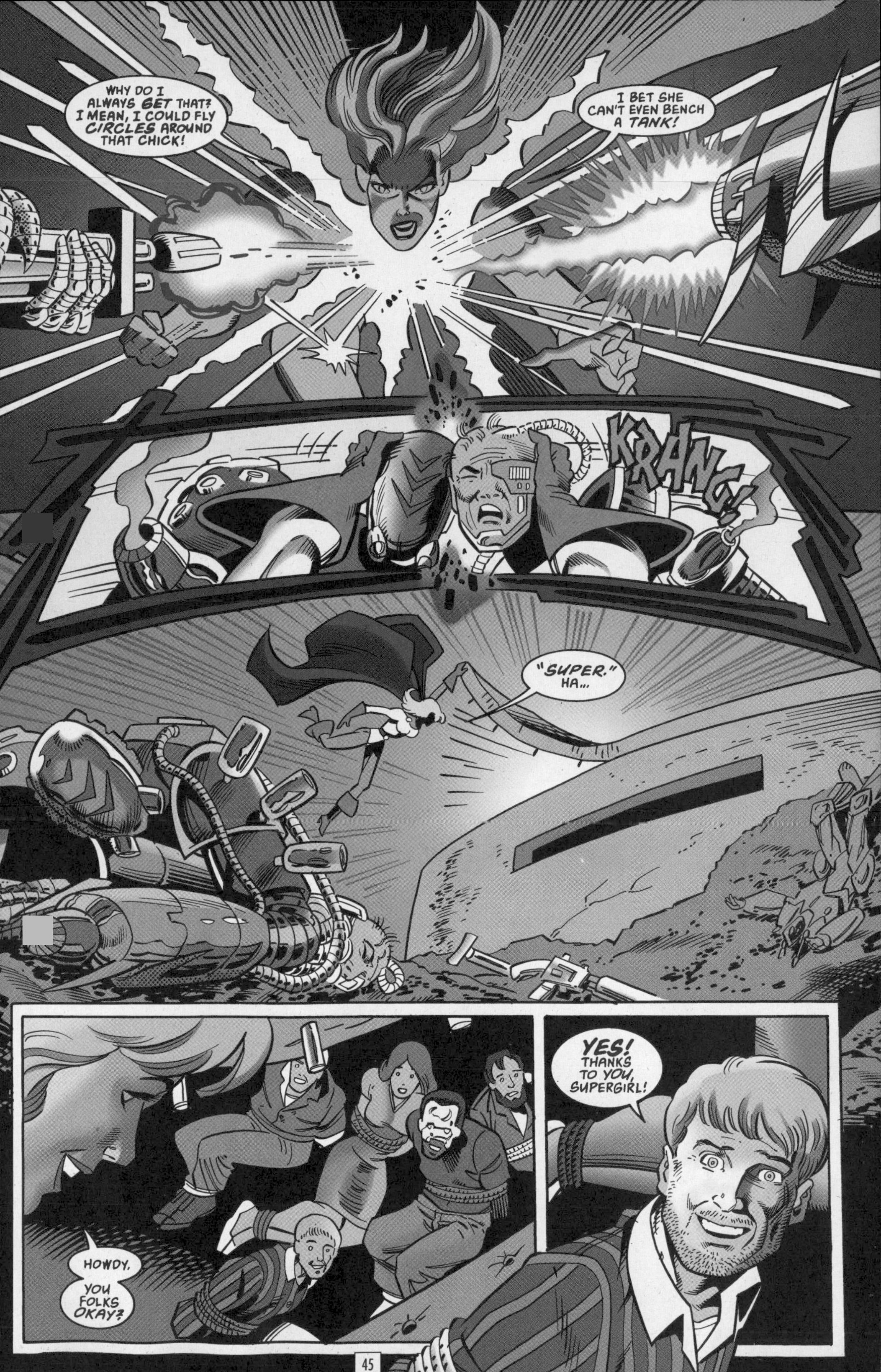
WHY DO I ALWAYS GET THAT? I MEAN, I COULD FLY CIRCLES AROUND THAT CHICK!
I BET SHE CAN'T EVEN BENCH A TANK!
KRANG!
"SUPER." HA...
HOWDY. YOU FOLKS OKAY?
YES! THANKS TO YOU, SUPERGIRL!

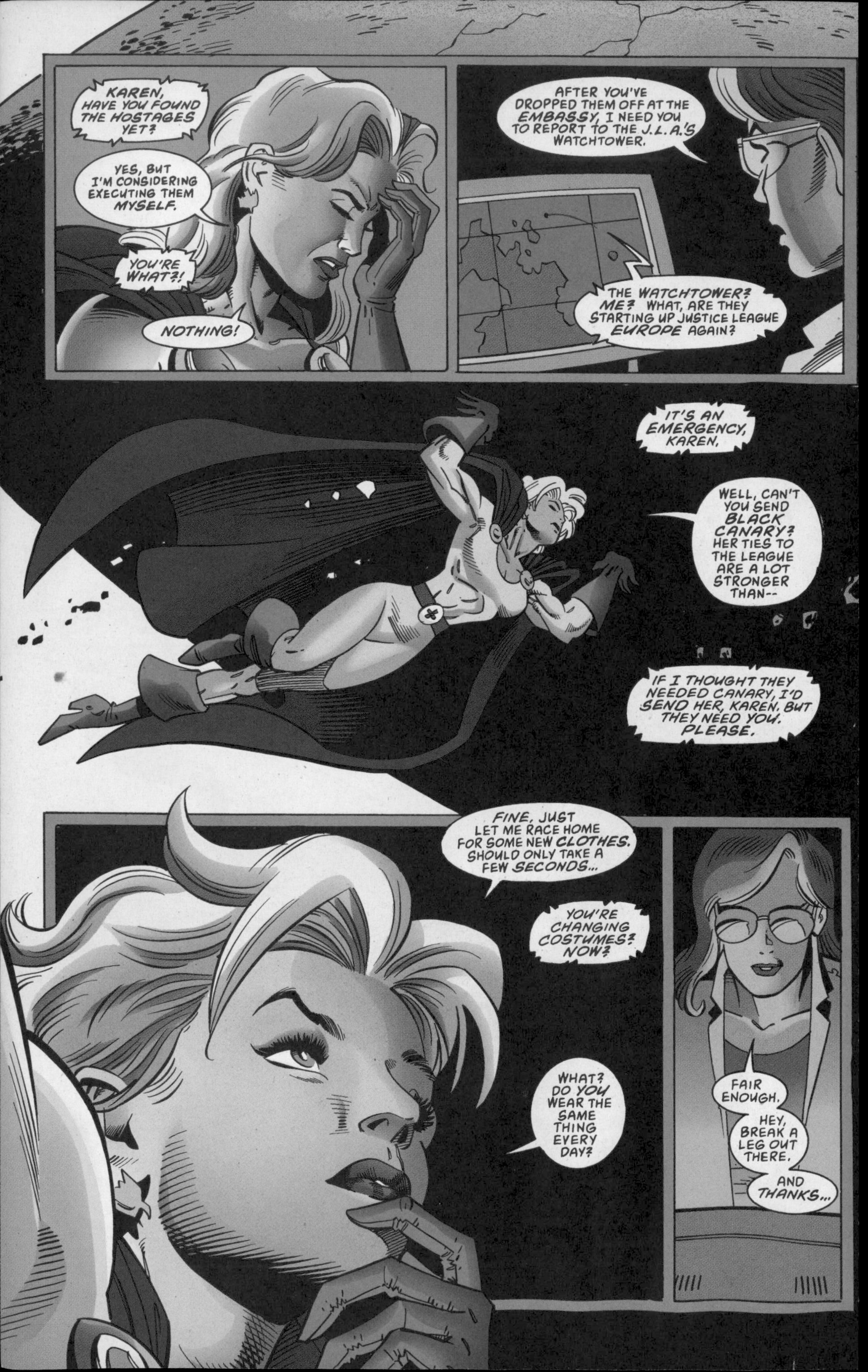
KAREN, HAVE YOU FOUND THE HOSTAGES YET?
YES, BUT I'M CONSIDERING EXECUTING THEM MYSELF.
YOU'RE WHAT?!
NOTHING!
AFTER YOU'VE DROPPED THEM OFF AT THE EMBASSY, I NEED YOU TO REPORT TO THE J.L.A.'S WATCHTOWER.
THE WATCHTOWER? ME? WHAT, ARE THEY STARTING UP JUSTICE LEAGUE EUROPE AGAIN?
IT'S AN EMERGENCY, KAREN.
WELL, CAN'T YOU SEND BLACK CANARY? HER TIES TO THE LEAGUE ARE A LOT STRONGER THAN--
IF I THOUGHT THEY NEEDED CANARY, I'D SEND HER, KAREN. BUT THEY NEED YOU. PLEASE.
FINE. JUST LET ME RACE HOME FOR SOME NEW CLOTHES. SHOULD ONLY TAKE A FEW SECONDS...
YOU'RE CHANGING COSTUMES? NOW?
WHAT? DO YOU WEAR THE SAME THING EVERY DAY?
FAIR ENOUGH.
HEY, BREAK A LEG OUT THERE.
AND THANKS...

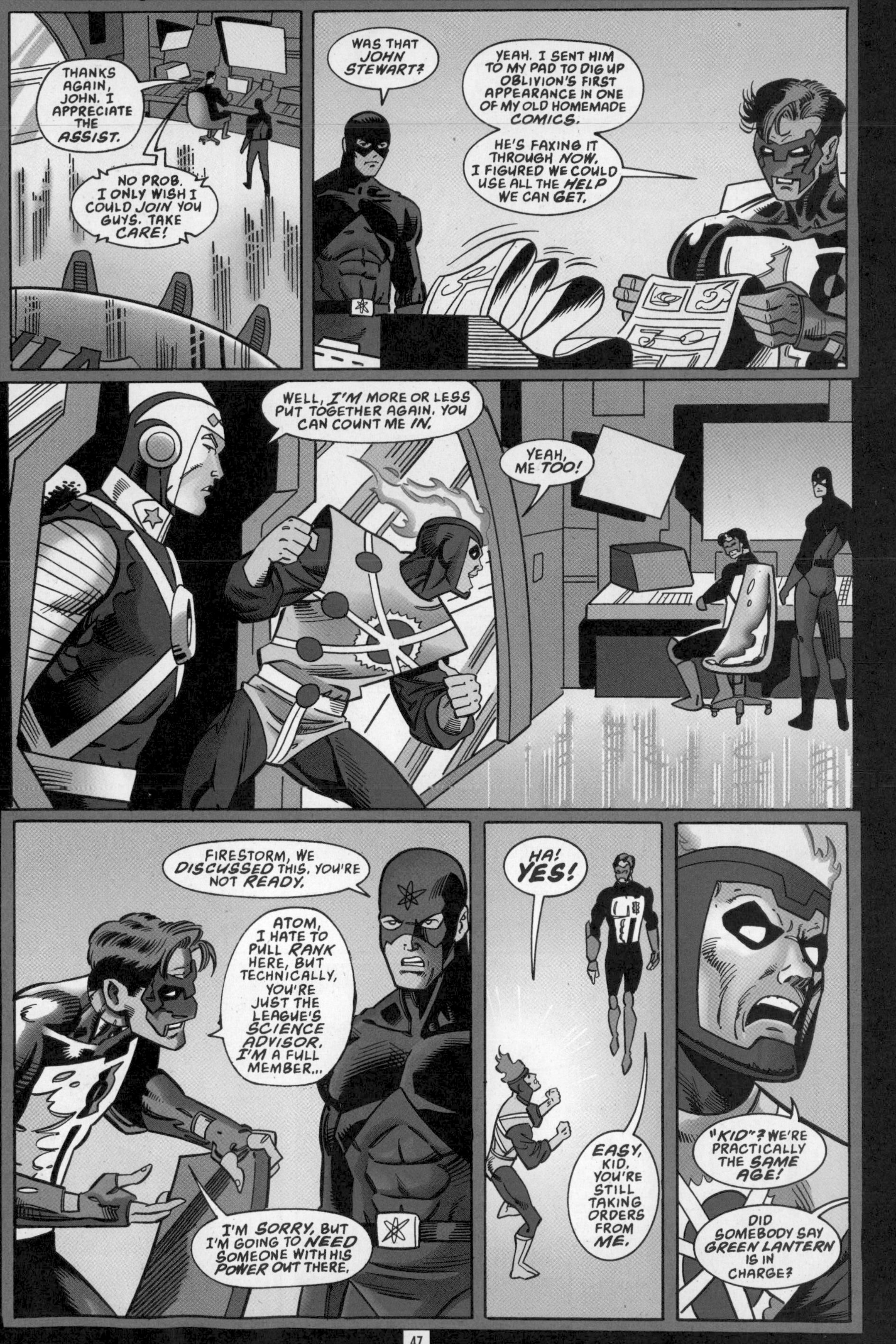
THANKS AGAIN, JOHN. I APPRECIATE THE ASSIST.
NO PROB. I ONLY WISH I COULD JOIN YOU GUYS. TAKE CARE!
WAS THAT JOHN STEWART?
YEAH. I SENT HIM TO MY PAD TO DIG UP OBLIVION'S FIRST APPEARANCE IN ONE OF MY OLD HOMEMADE COMICS.
HE'S FAXING IT THROUGH NOW. I FIGURED WE COULD USE ALL THE HELP WE CAN GET.
WELL, I'M MORE OR LESS PUT TOGETHER AGAIN. YOU CAN COUNT ME IN.
YEAH, ME TOO!
FIRESTORM, WE DISCUSSED THIS. YOU'RE NOT READY.
ATOM, I HATE TO PULL RANK HERE, BUT TECHNICALLY, YOU'RE JUST THE LEAGUE'S SCIENCE ADVISOR. I'M A FULL MEMBER...
I'M SORRY, BUT I'M GOING TO NEED SOMEONE WITH HIS POWER OUT THERE.
HA! YES!
EASY, KID. YOU'RE STILL TAKING ORDERS FROM ME.
"KID"? WE'RE PRACTICALLY THE SAME AGE!
DID SOMEBODY SAY GREEN LANTERN IS IN CHARGE?

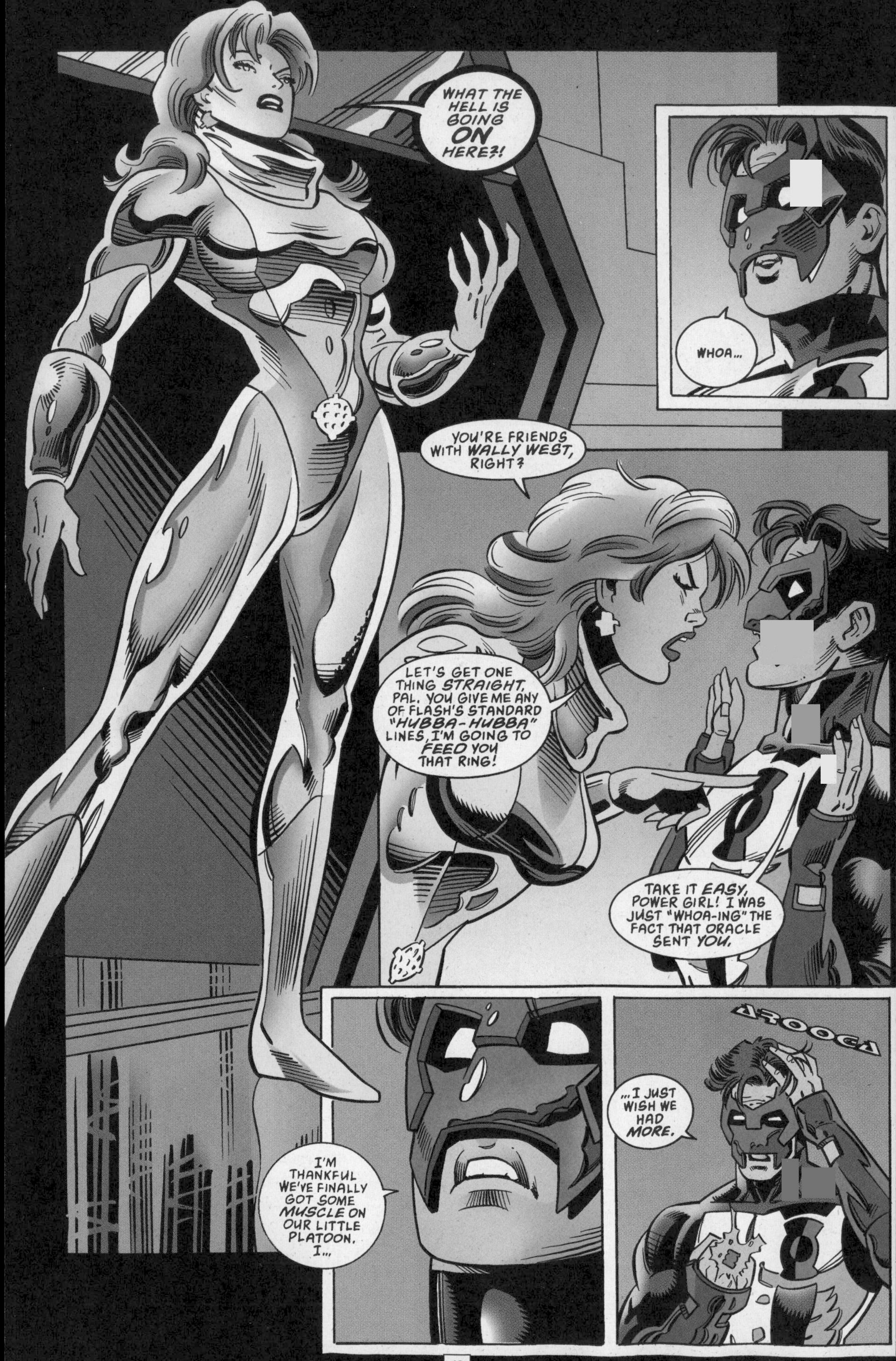
WHAT THE HELL IS GOING ON HERE?!
WHOA...
YOU'RE FRIENDS WITH WALLY WEST, RIGHT?
LET'S GET ONE THING STRAIGHT, PAL. YOU GIVE ME ANY OF FLASH'S STANDARD "HUBBA-HUBBA" LINES, I'M GOING TO FEED YOU THAT RING!
TAKE IT EASY, POWER GIRL! I WAS JUST "WHOA-ING" THE FACT THAT ORACLE SENT YOU.
I'M THANKFUL WE'VE FINALLY GOT SOME MUSCLE ON OUR LITTLE PLATOON. I...
...I JUST WISH WE HAD MORE.

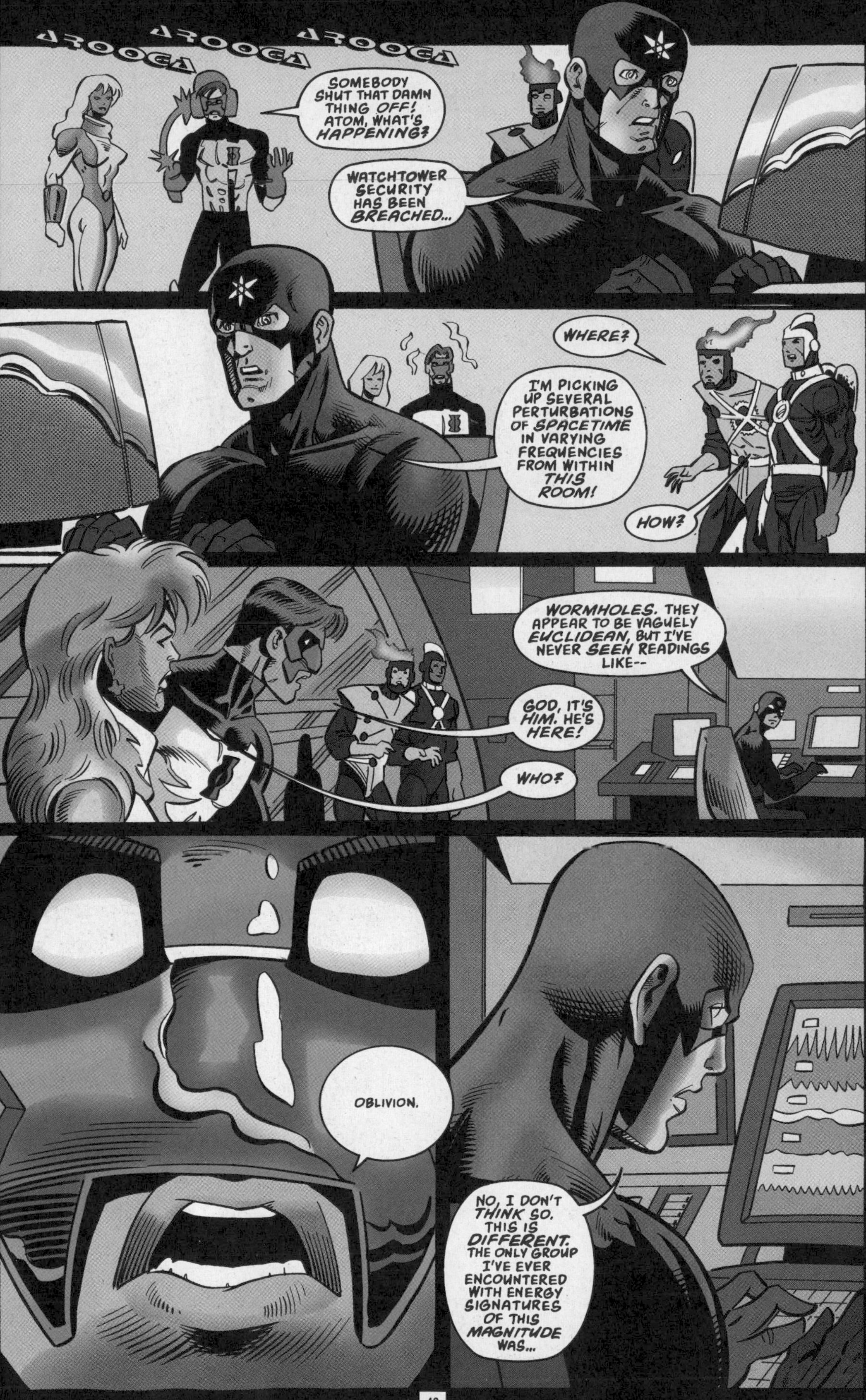
AROOGA AROOGA AROOGA
SOMEBODY SHUT THAT DAMN THING OFF! ATOM, WHAT'S HAPPENING?
WATCHTOWER SECURITY HAS BEEN BREACHED...
WHERE?
I'M PICKING UP SEVERAL PERTURBATIONS OF SPACETIME IN VARYING FREQUENCIES FROM WITHIN THIS ROOM!
HOW?
WORMHOLES. THEY APPEAR TO BE VAGUELY EUCLIDEAN, BUT I'VE NEVER SEEN READINGS LIKE--
GOD, IT'S HIM. HE'S HERE!
WHO?
OBLIVION.
NO, I DON'T THINK SO. THIS IS DIFFERENT. THE ONLY GROUP I'VE EVER ENCOUNTERED WITH ENERGY SIGNATURES OF THIS MAGNITUDE WAS...

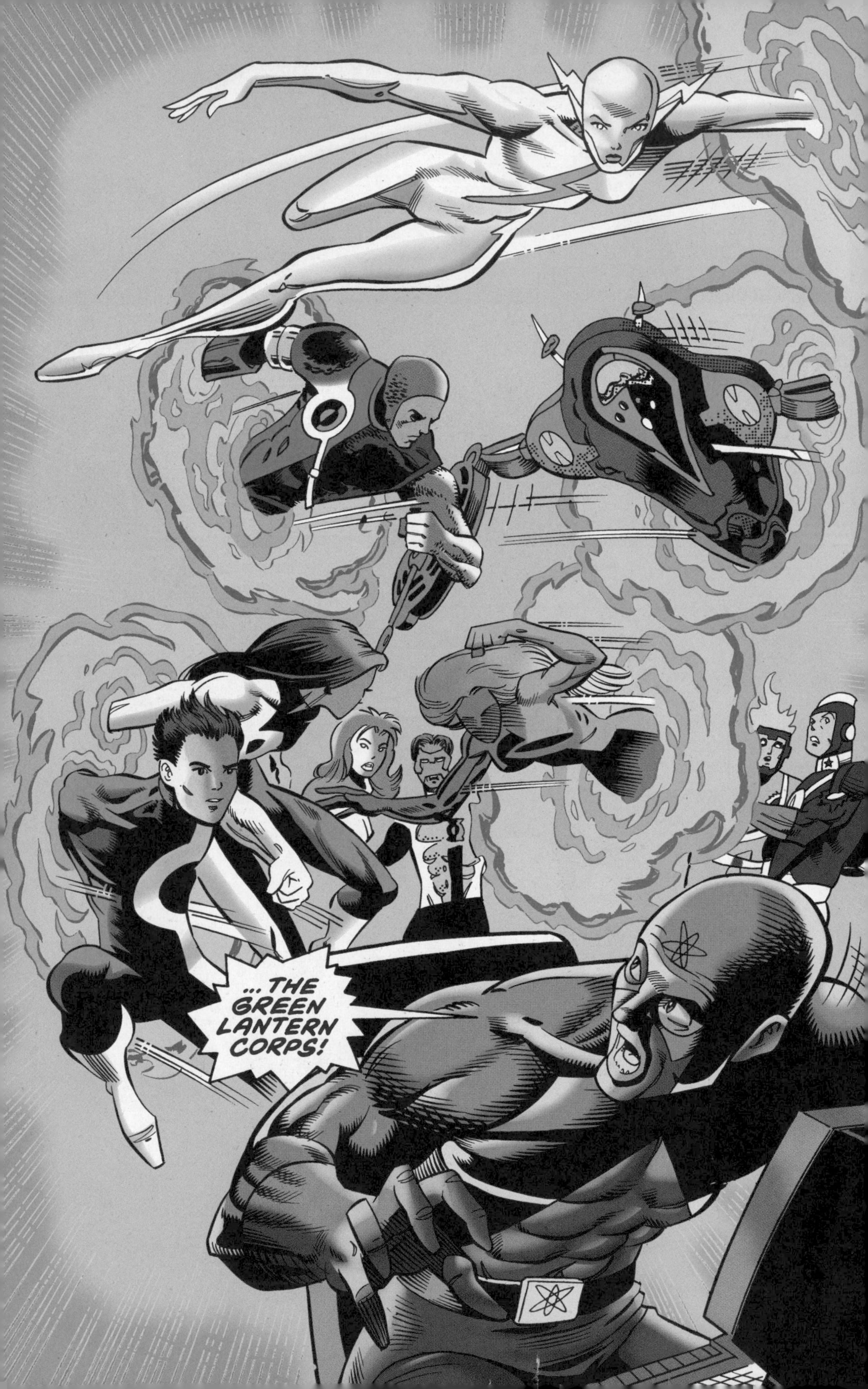
...THE GREEN LANTERN CORPS!

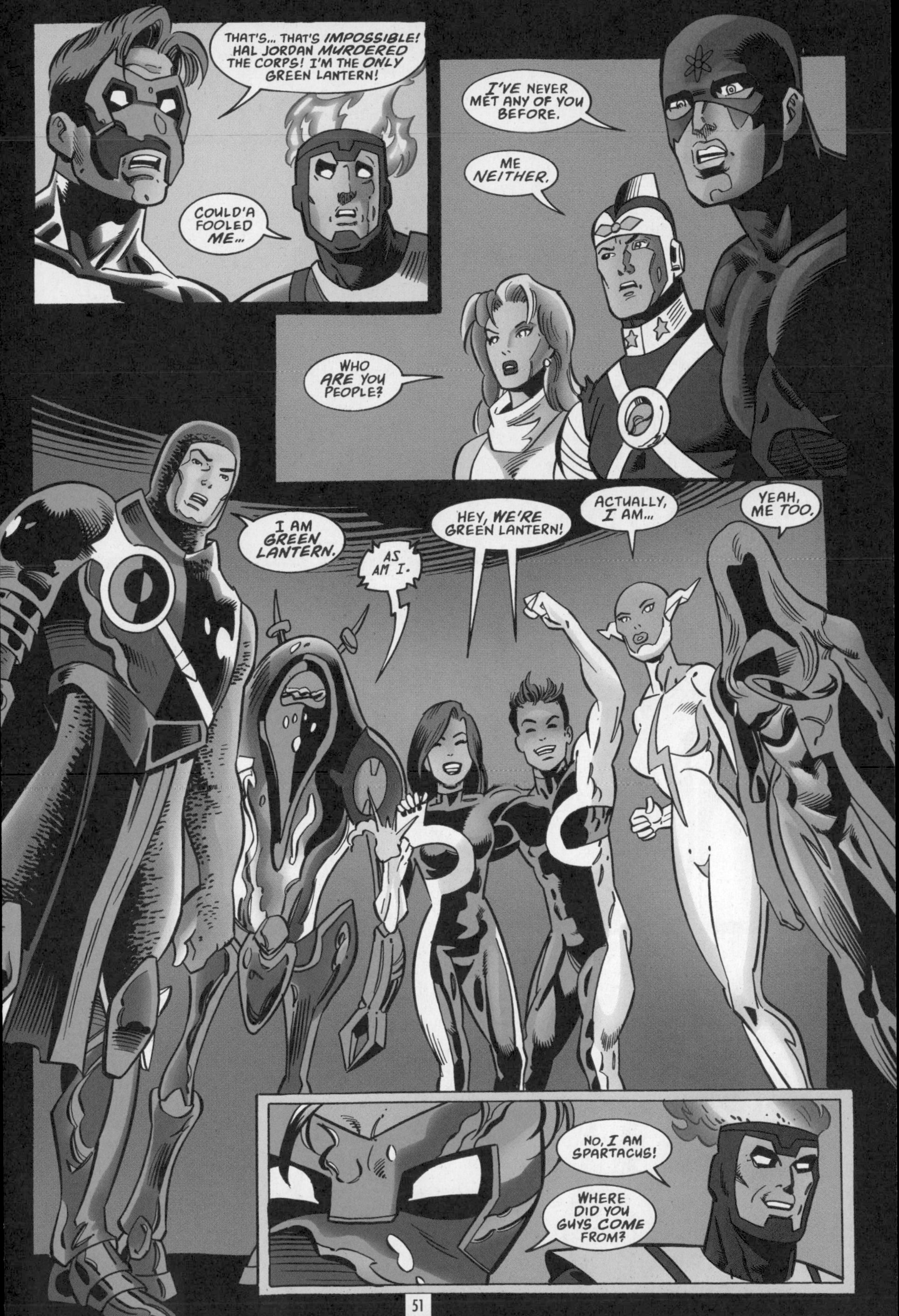
THAT'S... THAT'S IMPOSSIBLE! HAL JORDAN MURDERED THE CORPS! I'M THE ONLY GREEN LANTERN!
COULD'A FOOLED ME...
I'VE NEVER MET ANY OF YOU BEFORE.
ME NEITHER.
WHO ARE YOU PEOPLE?
I AM GREEN LANTERN.
AS AM I.
HEY, WE'RE GREEN LANTERN!
ACTUALLY, I AM...
YEAH, ME TOO.
NO, I AM SPARTACUS!
WHERE DID YOU GUYS COME FROM?

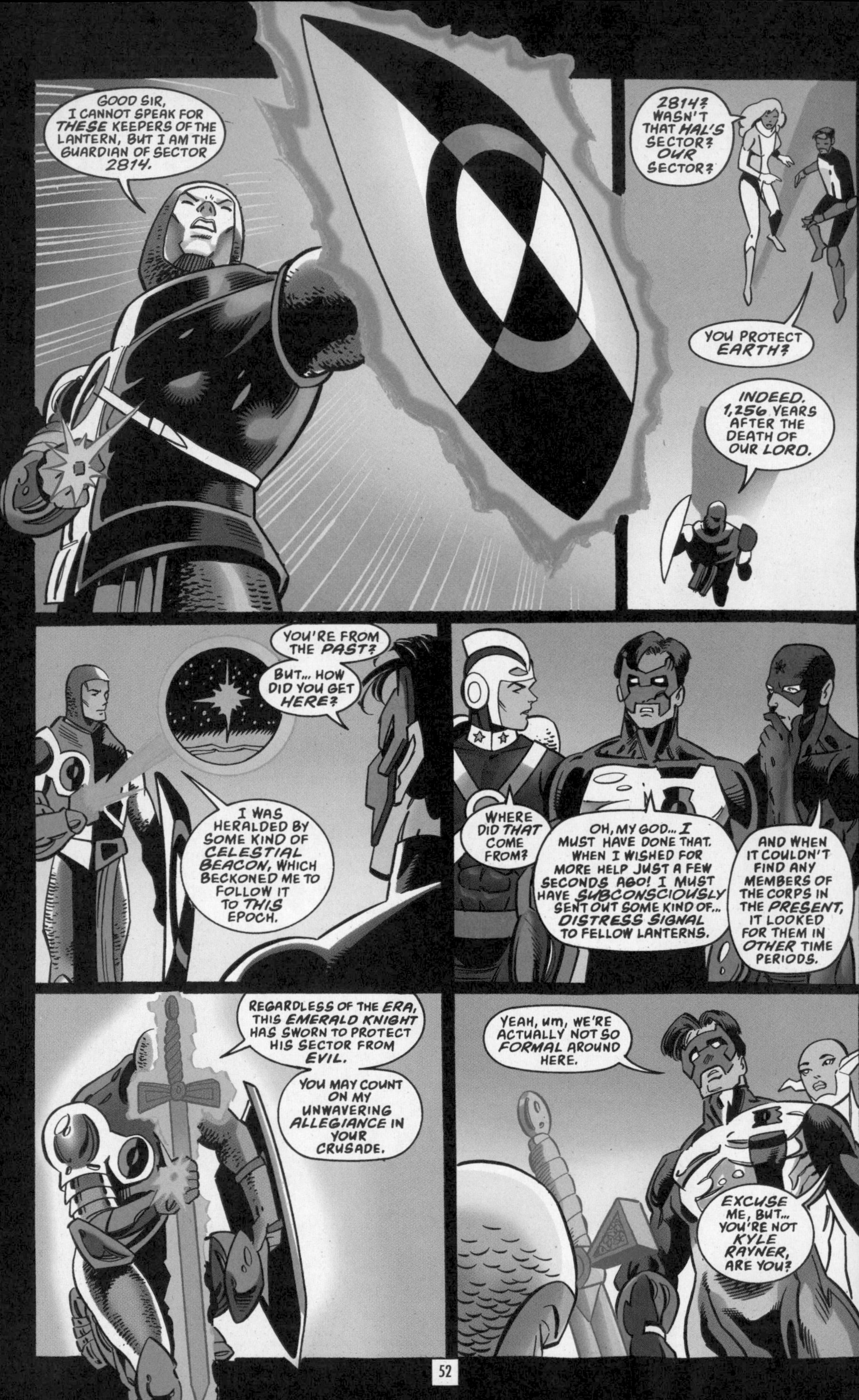
GOOD SIR, I CANNOT SPEAK FOR THESE KEEPERS OF THE LANTERN, BUT I AM THE GUARDIAN OF SECTOR 2814.
2814? WASN'T THAT HAL'S SECTOR? OUR SECTOR?
YOU PROTECT EARTH?
INDEED. 1,256 YEARS AFTER THE DEATH OF OUR LORD.
YOU'RE FROM THE PAST?
BUT... HOW DID YOU GET HERE?
I WAS HERALDED BY SOME KIND OF CELESTIAL BEACON, WHICH BECKONED ME TO FOLLOW IT TO THIS EPOCH.
WHERE DID THAT COME FROM?
OH, MY GOD... I MUST HAVE DONE THAT. WHEN I WISHED FOR MORE HELP JUST A FEW SECONDS AGO! I MUST HAVE SUBCONSCIOUSLY SENT OUT SOME KIND OF... DISTRESS SIGNAL TO FELLOW LANTERNS.
AND WHEN IT COULDN'T FIND ANY MEMBERS OF THE CORPS IN THE PRESENT, IT LOOKED FOR THEM IN OTHER TIME PERIODS.
REGARDLESS OF THE ERA, THIS EMERALD KNIGHT HAS SWORN TO PROTECT HIS SECTOR FROM EVIL.
YOU MAY COUNT ON MY UNWAVERING ALLEGIANCE IN YOUR CRUSADE.
YEAH, UM, WE'RE ACTUALLY NOT SO FORMAL AROUND HERE.
EXCUSE ME, BUT... YOU'RE NOT KYLE RAYNER, ARE YOU?

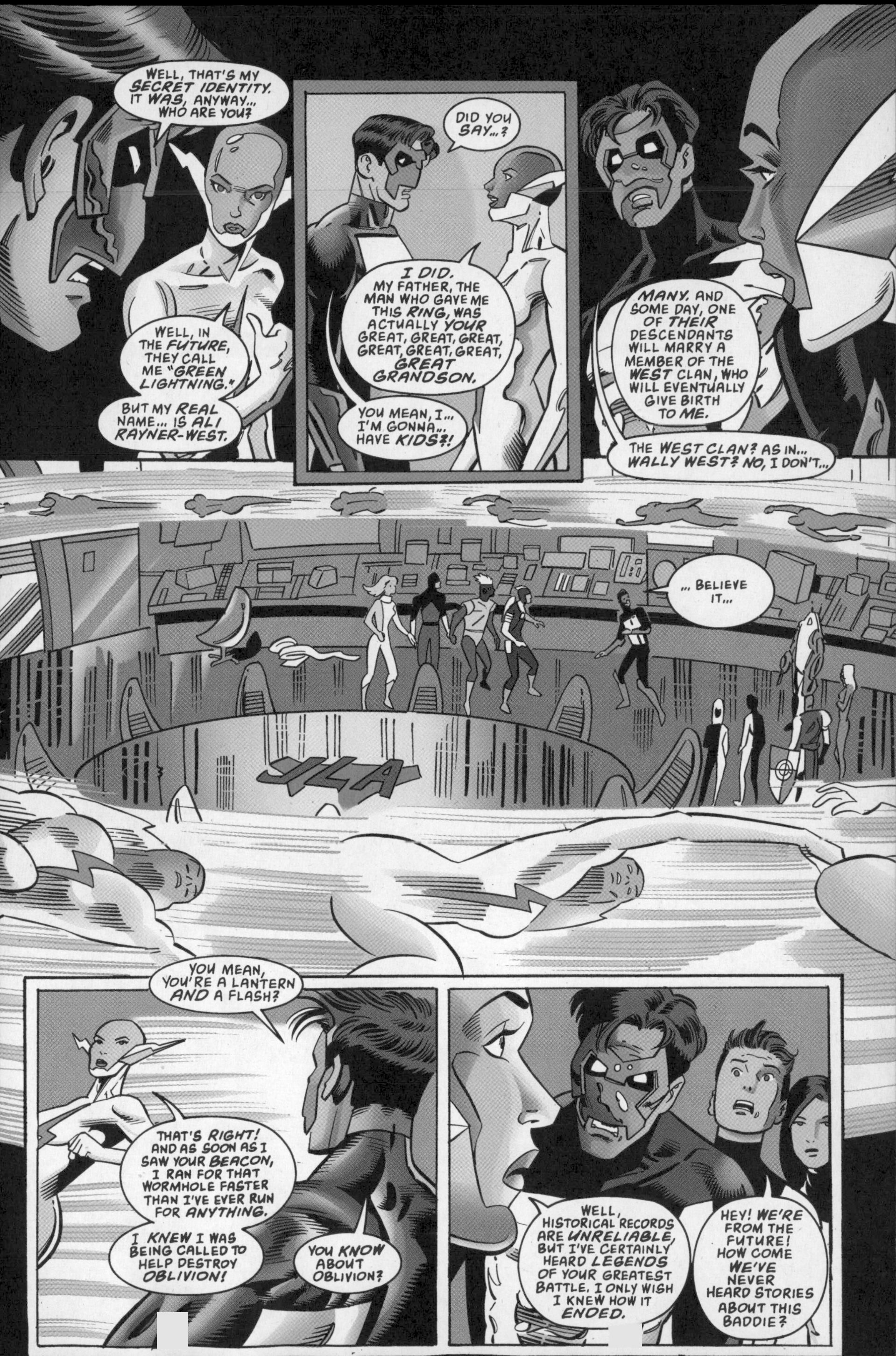

WELL, THAT'S MY SECRET IDENTITY. IT WAS, ANYWAY... WHO ARE YOU?
WELL, IN THE FUTURE, THEY CALL ME "GREEN LIGHTNING."
BUT MY REAL NAME... IS ALI RAYNER-WEST.
DID YOU SAY...?
I DID. MY FATHER, THE MAN WHO GAVE ME THIS RING, WAS ACTUALLY YOUR GREAT, GREAT, GREAT, GREAT, GREAT, GREAT, GREAT GRANDSON.
YOU MEAN, I... I'M GONNA... HAVE KIDS?!
MANY. AND SOME DAY, ONE OF THEIR DESCENDANTS WILL MARRY A MEMBER OF THE WEST CLAN, WHO WILL EVENTUALLY GIVE BIRTH TO ME.
THE WEST CLAN? AS IN... WALLY WEST? NO, I DON'T...
... BELIEVE IT...
JLA
YOU MEAN, YOU'RE A LANTERN AND A FLASH?
THAT'S RIGHT! AND AS SOON AS I SAW YOUR BEACON, I RAN FOR THAT WORMHOLE FASTER THAN I'VE EVER RUN FOR ANYTHING.
I KNEW I WAS BEING CALLED TO HELP DESTROY OBLIVION!
YOU KNOW ABOUT OBLIVION?
WELL, HISTORICAL RECORDS ARE UNRELIABLE, BUT I'VE CERTAINLY HEARD LEGENDS OF YOUR GREATEST BATTLE. I ONLY WISH I KNEW HOW IT ENDED.
HEY! WE'RE FROM THE FUTURE! HOW COME WE'VE NEVER HEARD STORIES ABOUT THIS BADDIE?

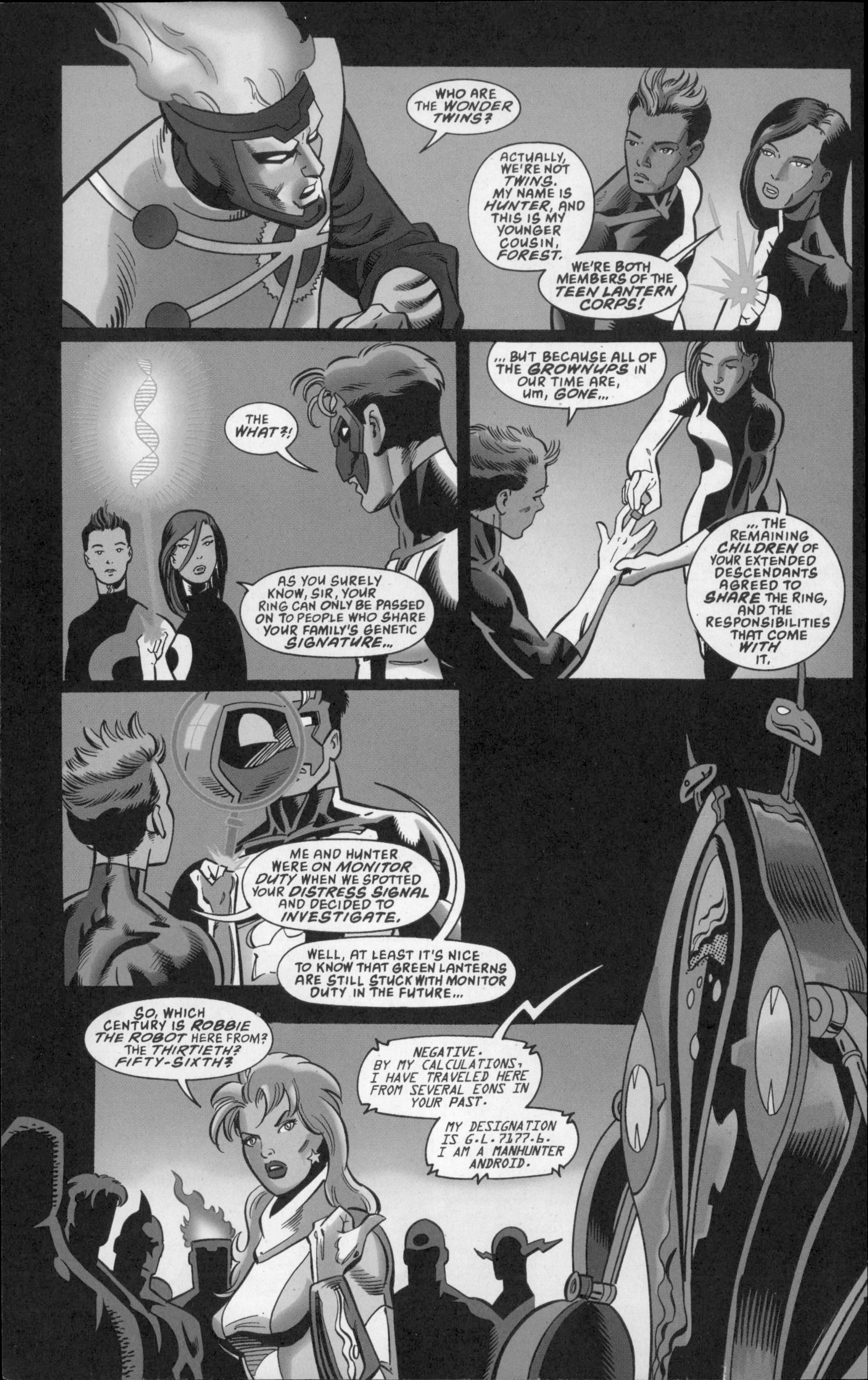
WHO ARE THE WONDER TWINS?
ACTUALLY, WE'RE NOT TWINS. MY NAME IS HUNTER, AND THIS IS MY YOUNGER COUSIN, FOREST.
WE'RE BOTH MEMBERS OF THE TEEN LANTERN CORPS!
THE WHAT?!
AS YOU SURELY KNOW, SIR, YOUR RING CAN ONLY BE PASSED ON TO PEOPLE WHO SHARE YOUR FAMILY'S GENETIC SIGNATURE...
...BUT BECAUSE ALL OF THE GROWNUPS IN OUR TIME ARE, UM, GONE...
...THE REMAINING CHILDREN OF YOUR EXTENDED DESCENDANTS AGREED TO SHARE THE RING, AND THE RESPONSIBILITIES THAT COME WITH IT.
ME AND HUNTER WERE ON MONITOR DUTY WHEN WE SPOTTED YOUR DISTRESS SIGNAL AND DECIDED TO INVESTIGATE.
WELL, AT LEAST IT'S NICE TO KNOW THAT GREEN LANTERNS ARE STILL STUCK WITH MONITOR DUTY IN THE FUTURE...
SO, WHICH CENTURY IS ROBBIE THE ROBOT HERE FROM? THE THIRTIETH? FIFTY-SIXTH?
NEGATIVE. BY MY CALCULATIONS, I HAVE TRAVELED HERE FROM SEVERAL EONS IN YOUR PAST.
MY DESIGNATION IS G.L. 7177.6. I AM A MANHUNTER ANDROID.

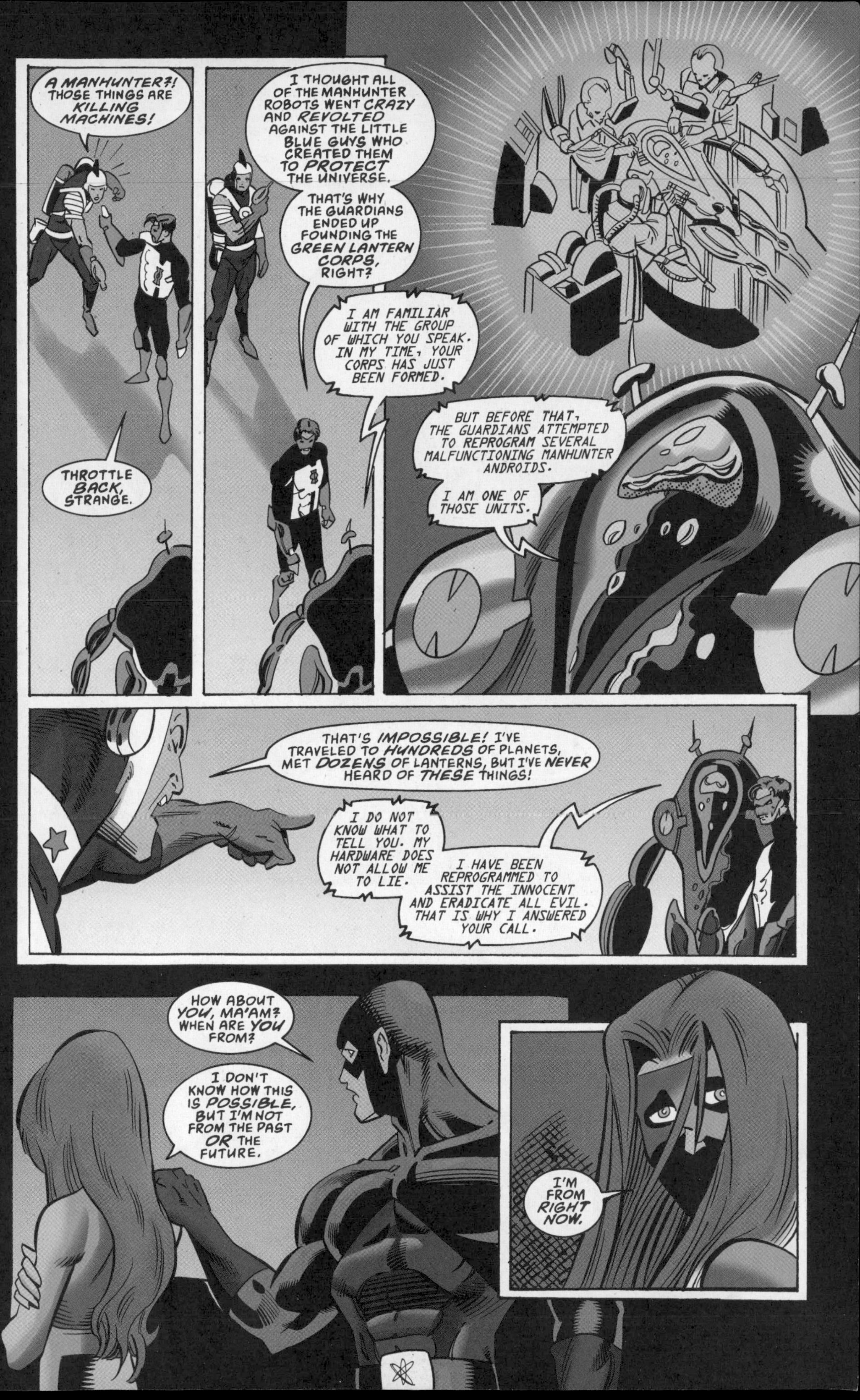
A MANHUNTER?! THOSE THINGS ARE KILLING MACHINES!
THROTTLE BACK, STRANGE.
I THOUGHT ALL OF THE MANHUNTER ROBOTS WENT CRAZY AND REVOLTED AGAINST THE LITTLE BLUE GUYS WHO CREATED THEM TO PROTECT THE UNIVERSE.
THAT'S WHY THE GUARDIANS ENDED UP FOUNDING THE GREEN LANTERN CORPS, RIGHT?
I AM FAMILIAR WITH THE GROUP OF WHICH YOU SPEAK. IN MY TIME, YOUR CORPS HAS JUST BEEN FORMED.
BUT BEFORE THAT, THE GUARDIANS ATTEMPTED TO REPROGRAM SEVERAL MALFUNCTIONING MANHUNTER ANDROIDS.
I AM ONE OF THOSE UNITS.
THAT'S IMPOSSIBLE! I'VE TRAVELED TO HUNDREDS OF PLANETS, MET DOZENS OF LANTERNS, BUT I'VE NEVER HEARD OF THESE THINGS!
I DO NOT KNOW WHAT TO TELL YOU. MY HARDWARE DOES NOT ALLOW ME TO LIE.
I HAVE BEEN REPROGRAMMED TO ASSIST THE INNOCENT AND ERADICATE ALL EVIL. THAT IS WHY I ANSWERED YOUR CALL.
HOW ABOUT YOU, MA'AM? WHEN ARE YOU FROM?
I DON'T KNOW HOW THIS IS POSSIBLE, BUT I'M NOT FROM THE PAST OR THE FUTURE.
I'M FROM RIGHT NOW.

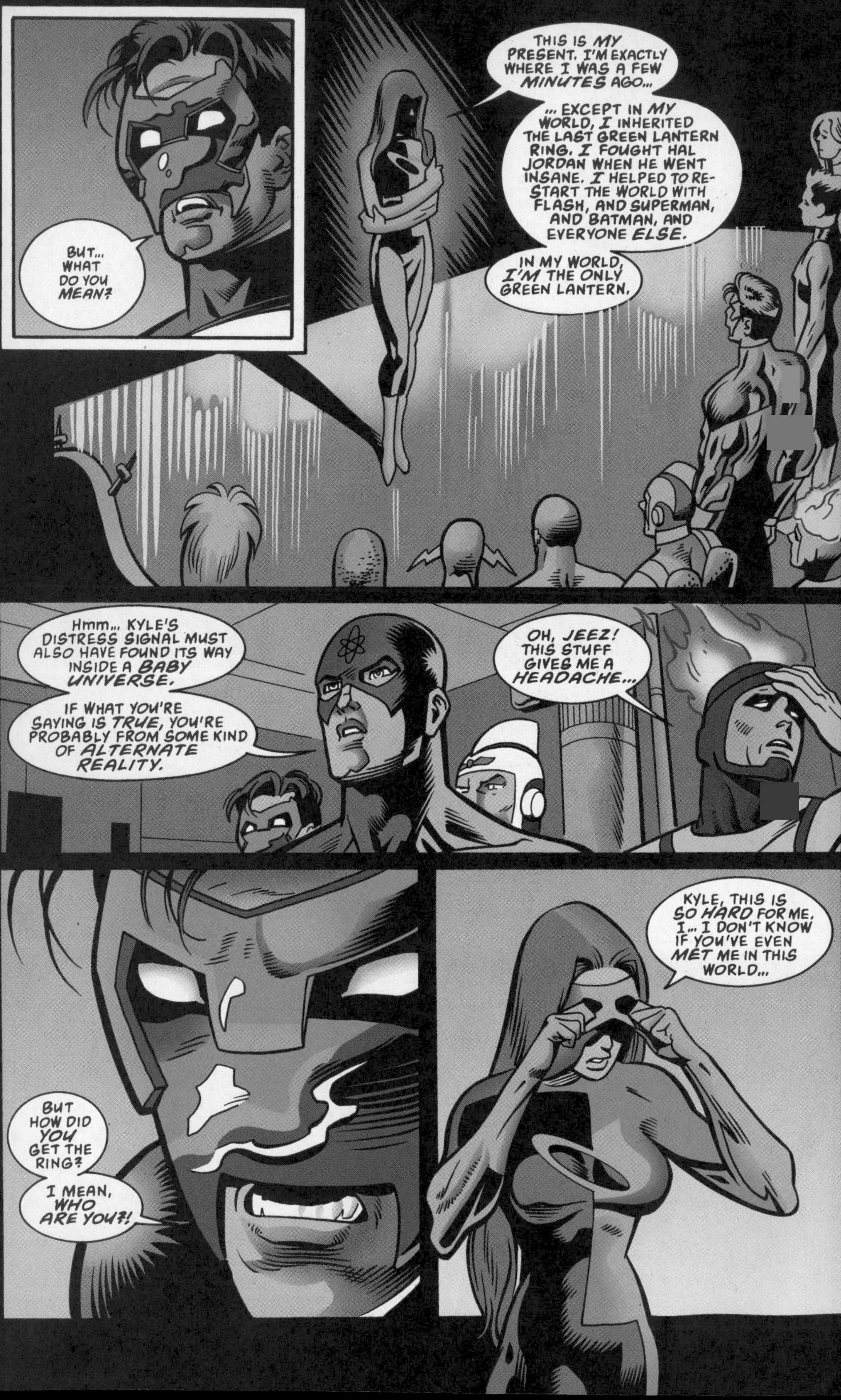
BUT... WHAT DO YOU MEAN?
THIS IS MY PRESENT. I'M EXACTLY WHERE I WAS A FEW MINUTES AGO...
... EXCEPT IN MY WORLD, I INHERITED THE LAST GREEN LANTERN RING. I FOUGHT HAL JORDAN WHEN HE WENT INSANE. I HELPED TO RE-START THE WORLD WITH FLASH, AND SUPERMAN, AND BATMAN, AND EVERYONE ELSE.
IN MY WORLD, I'M THE ONLY GREEN LANTERN.
Hmm... KYLE'S DISTRESS SIGNAL MUST ALSO HAVE FOUND ITS WAY INSIDE A BABY UNIVERSE.
IF WHAT YOU'RE SAYING IS TRUE, YOU'RE PROBABLY FROM SOME KIND OF ALTERNATE REALITY.
OH, JEEZ! THIS STUFF GIVES ME A HEADACHE...
BUT HOW DID YOU GET THE RING?
I MEAN, WHO ARE YOU?!
KYLE, THIS IS SO HARD FOR ME. I... I DON'T KNOW IF YOU'VE EVEN MET ME IN THIS WORLD...

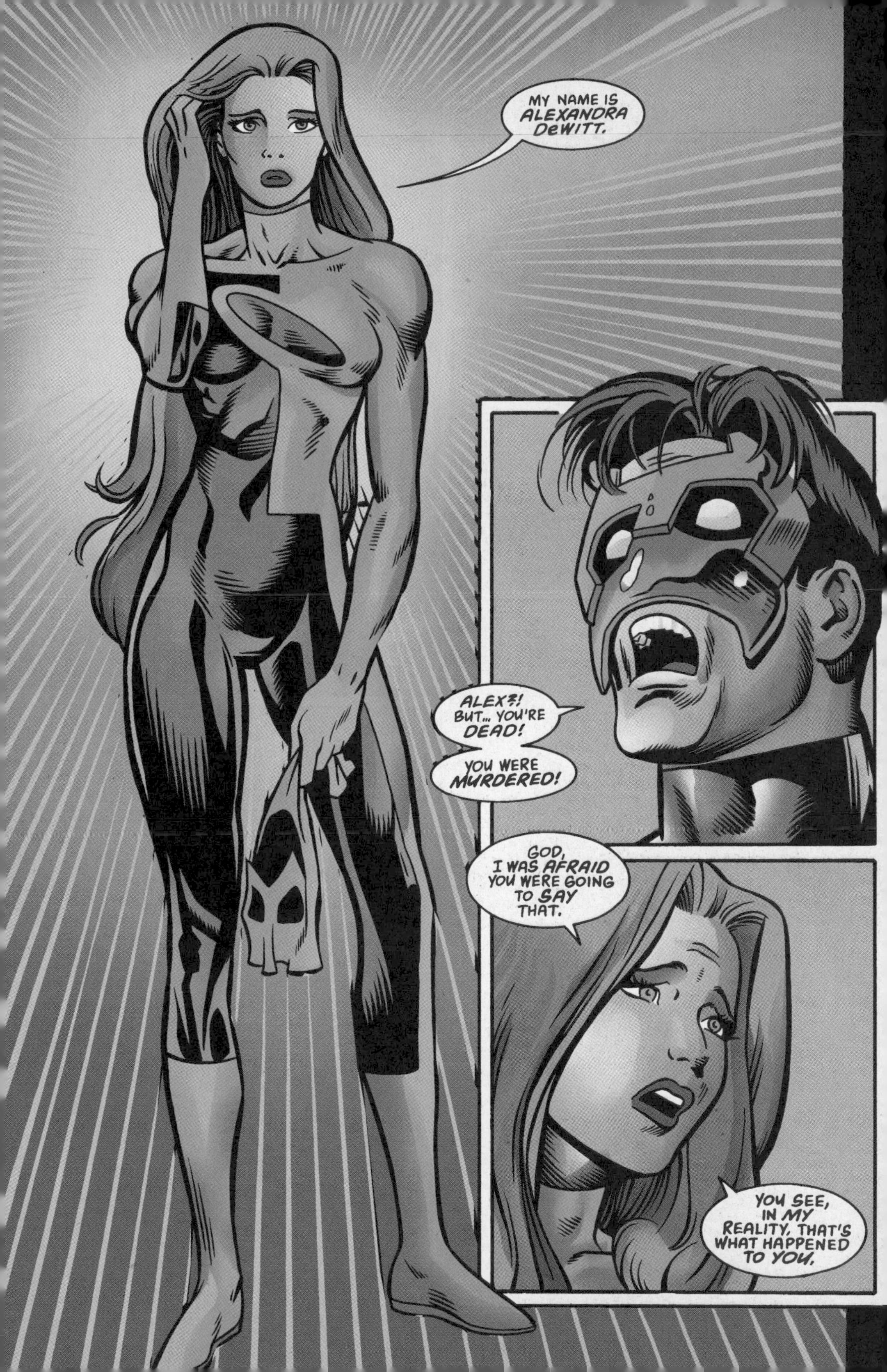
MY NAME IS ALEXANDRA DeWITT.
ALEX?! BUT... YOU'RE DEAD!
YOU WERE MURDERED!
GOD, I WAS AFRAID YOU WERE GOING TO SAY THAT.
YOU SEE, IN MY REALITY, THAT'S WHAT HAPPENED TO YOU.

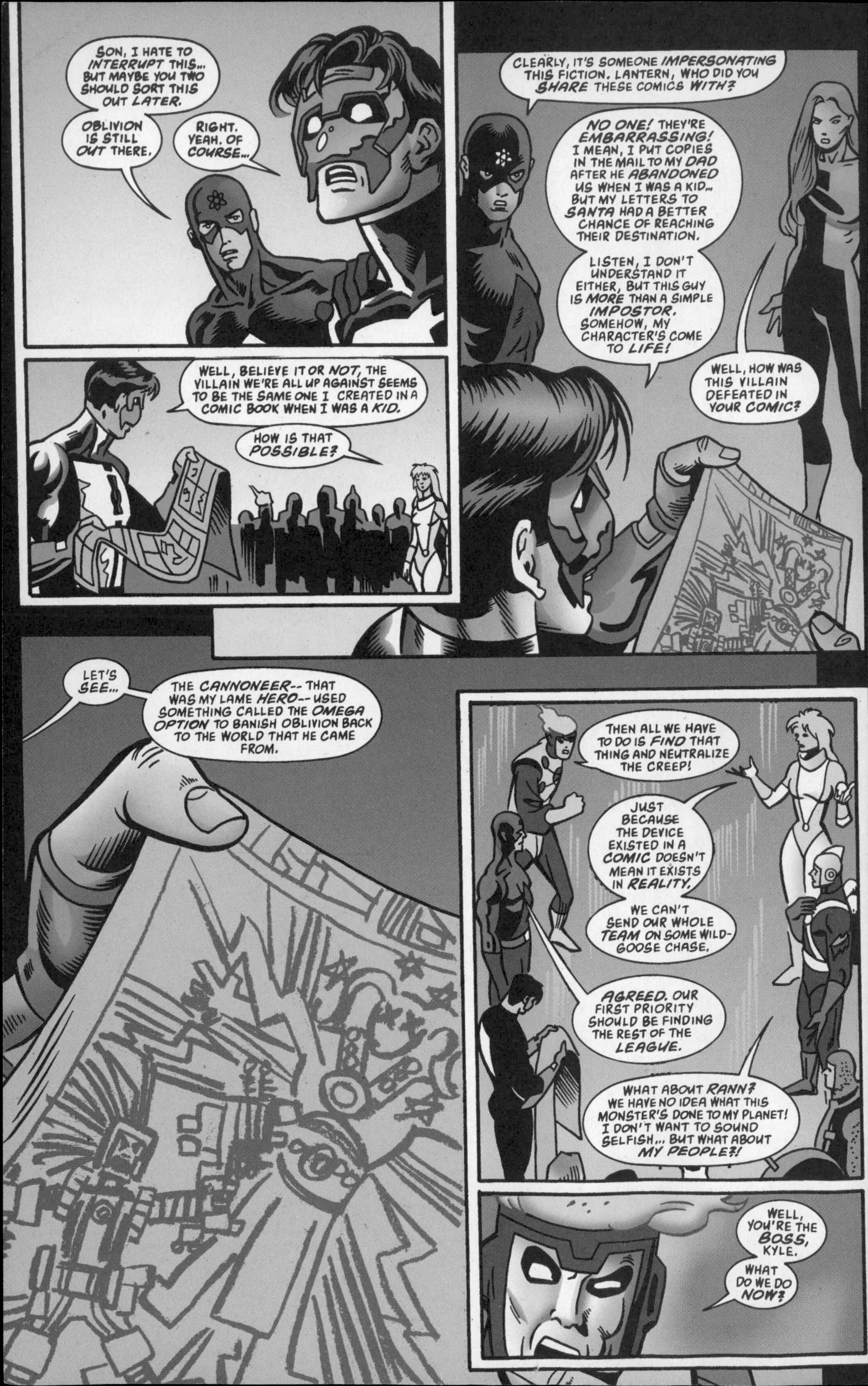
SON, I HATE TO INTERRUPT THIS... BUT MAYBE YOU TWO SHOULD SORT THIS OUT LATER.
OBLIVION IS STILL OUT THERE.
RIGHT. YEAH. OF COURSE...
CLEARLY, IT'S SOMEONE IMPERSONATING THIS FICTION. LANTERN, WHO DID YOU SHARE THESE COMICS WITH?
NO ONE! THEY'RE EMBARRASSING! I MEAN, I PUT COPIES IN THE MAIL TO MY DAD AFTER HE ABANDONED US WHEN I WAS A KID... BUT MY LETTERS TO SANTA HAD A BETTER CHANCE OF REACHING THEIR DESTINATION.
LISTEN, I DON'T UNDERSTAND IT EITHER, BUT THIS GUY IS MORE THAN A SIMPLE IMPOSTOR. SOMEHOW, MY CHARACTER'S COME TO LIFE!
WELL, BELIEVE IT OR NOT, THE VILLAIN WE'RE ALL UP AGAINST SEEMS TO BE THE SAME ONE I CREATED IN A COMIC BOOK WHEN I WAS A KID.
HOW IS THAT POSSIBLE?
WELL, HOW WAS THIS VILLAIN DEFEATED IN YOUR COMIC?
LET'S SEE...
THE CANNONEER-- THAT WAS MY LAME HERO-- USED SOMETHING CALLED THE OMEGA OPTION TO BANISH OBLIVION BACK TO THE WORLD THAT HE CAME FROM.
THEN ALL WE HAVE TO DO IS FIND THAT THING AND NEUTRALIZE THE CREEP!
JUST BECAUSE THE DEVICE EXISTED IN A COMIC DOESN'T MEAN IT EXISTS IN REALITY.
WE CAN'T SEND OUR WHOLE TEAM ON SOME WILD-GOOSE CHASE.
AGREED. OUR FIRST PRIORITY SHOULD BE FINDING THE REST OF THE LEAGUE.
WHAT ABOUT RANN? WE HAVE NO IDEA WHAT THIS MONSTER'S DONE TO MY PLANET! I DON'T WANT TO SOUND SELFISH... BUT WHAT ABOUT MY PEOPLE?!
WELL, YOU'RE THE BOSS, KYLE.
WHAT DO WE DO NOW?

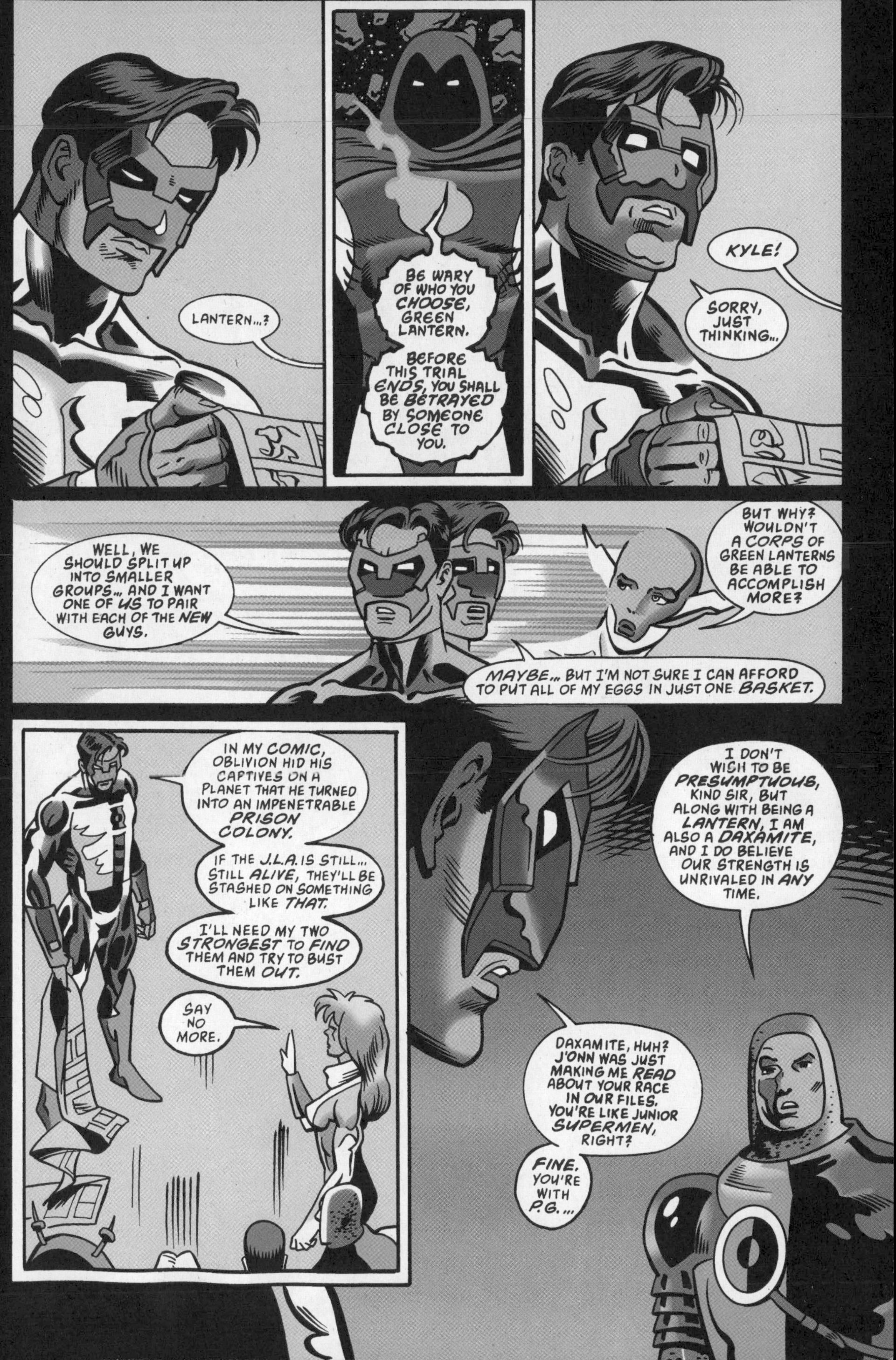
LANTERN...?
BE WARY OF WHO YOU CHOOSE, GREEN LANTERN.
BEFORE THIS TRIAL ENDS, YOU SHALL BE BETRAYED BY SOMEONE CLOSE TO YOU.
KYLE!
SORRY, JUST THINKING...
WELL, WE SHOULD SPLIT UP INTO SMALLER GROUPS... AND I WANT ONE OF US TO PAIR WITH EACH OF THE NEW GUYS.
BUT WHY? WOULDN'T A CORPS OF GREEN LANTERNS BE ABLE TO ACCOMPLISH MORE?
MAYBE... BUT I'M NOT SURE I CAN AFFORD TO PUT ALL OF MY EGGS IN JUST ONE BASKET.
IN MY COMIC, OBLIVION HID HIS CAPTIVES ON A PLANET THAT HE TURNED INTO AN IMPENETRABLE PRISON COLONY.
IF THE J.L.A. IS STILL... STILL ALIVE, THEY'LL BE STASHED ON SOMETHING LIKE THAT.
I'LL NEED MY TWO STRONGEST TO FIND THEM AND TRY TO BUST THEM OUT.
SAY NO MORE.
I DON'T WISH TO BE PRESUMPTUOUS, KIND SIR, BUT ALONG WITH BEING A LANTERN, I AM ALSO A DAXAMITE, AND I DO BELIEVE OUR STRENGTH IS UNRIVALED IN ANY TIME.
DAXAMITE, HUH? J'ONN WAS JUST MAKING ME READ ABOUT YOUR RACE IN OUR FILES. YOU'RE LIKE JUNIOR SUPERMEN, RIGHT?
FINE. YOU'RE WITH P.G. ...

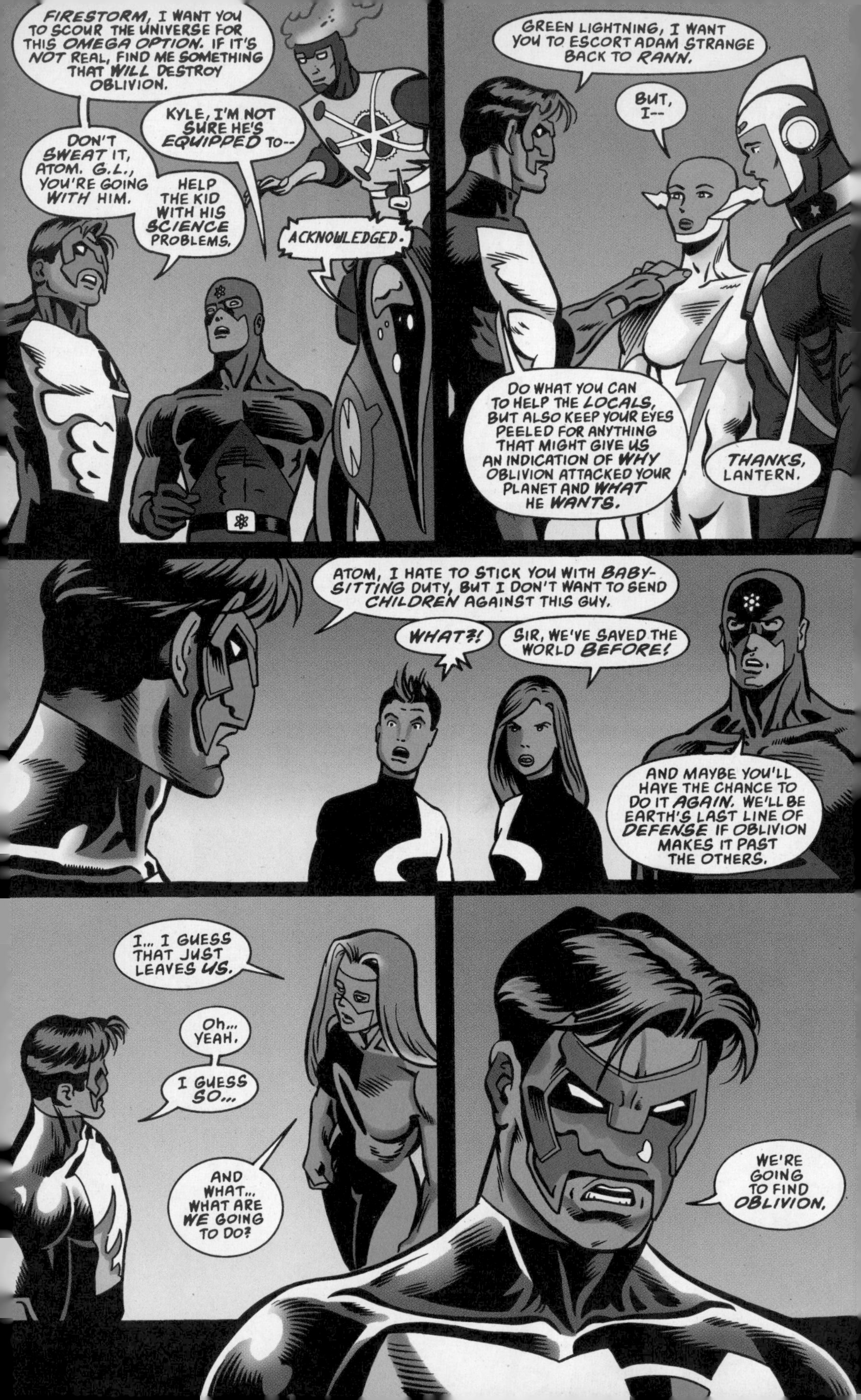
FIRESTORM, I WANT YOU TO SCOUR THE UNIVERSE FOR THIS OMEGA OPTION. IF IT'S NOT REAL, FIND ME SOMETHING THAT WILL DESTROY OBLIVION.
KYLE, I'M NOT SURE HE'S EQUIPPED TO--
DON'T SWEAT IT, ATOM. G.L., YOU'RE GOING WITH HIM.
HELP THE KID WITH HIS SCIENCE PROBLEMS.
ACKNOWLEDGED.
GREEN LIGHTNING, I WANT YOU TO ESCORT ADAM STRANGE BACK TO RANN.
BUT, I--
DO WHAT YOU CAN TO HELP THE LOCALS, BUT ALSO KEEP YOUR EYES PEELED FOR ANYTHING THAT MIGHT GIVE US AN INDICATION OF WHY OBLIVION ATTACKED YOUR PLANET AND WHAT HE WANTS.
THANKS, LANTERN.
ATOM, I HATE TO STICK YOU WITH BABY-SITTING DUTY, BUT I DON'T WANT TO SEND CHILDREN AGAINST THIS GUY.
WHAT?!
SIR, WE'VE SAVED THE WORLD BEFORE!
AND MAYBE YOU'LL HAVE THE CHANCE TO DO IT AGAIN. WE'LL BE EARTH'S LAST LINE OF DEFENSE IF OBLIVION MAKES IT PAST THE OTHERS.
I... I GUESS THAT JUST LEAVES US.
Oh... YEAH.
I GUESS SO...
AND WHAT... WHAT ARE WE GOING TO DO?
WE'RE GOING TO FIND OBLIVION.

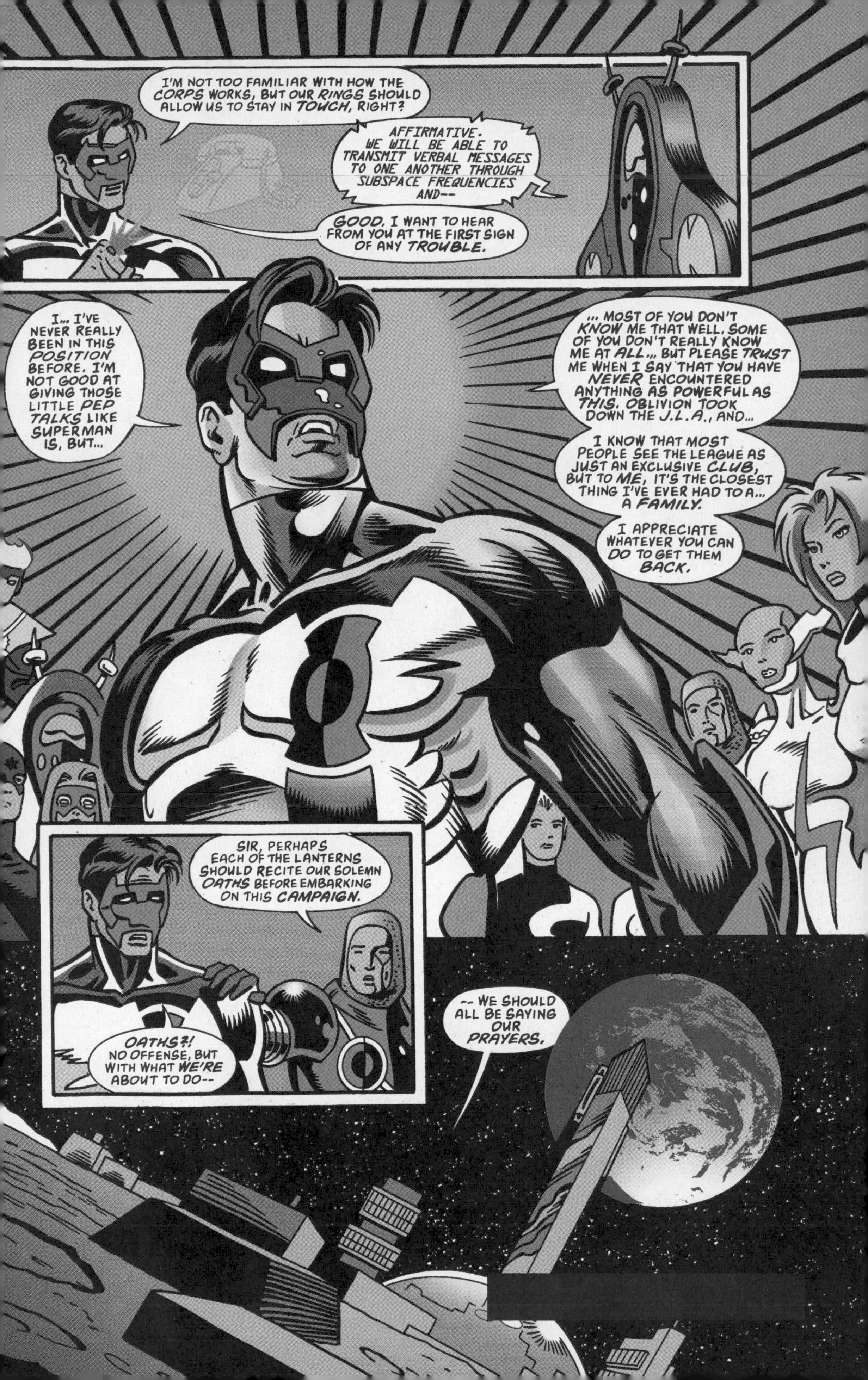
I'M NOT TOO FAMILIAR WITH HOW THE CORPS WORKS, BUT OUR RINGS SHOULD ALLOW US TO STAY IN TOUCH, RIGHT?
AFFIRMATIVE. WE WILL BE ABLE TO TRANSMIT VERBAL MESSAGES TO ONE ANOTHER THROUGH SUBSPACE FREQUENCIES AND--
GOOD. I WANT TO HEAR FROM YOU AT THE FIRST SIGN OF ANY TROUBLE.
I... I'VE NEVER REALLY BEEN IN THIS POSITION BEFORE. I'M NOT GOOD AT GIVING THOSE LITTLE PEP TALKS LIKE SUPERMAN IS, BUT...
... MOST OF YOU DON'T KNOW ME THAT WELL. SOME OF YOU DON'T REALLY KNOW ME AT ALL... BUT PLEASE TRUST ME WHEN I SAY THAT YOU HAVE NEVER ENCOUNTERED ANYTHING AS POWERFUL AS THIS. OBLIVION TOOK DOWN THE J.L.A., AND...
I KNOW THAT MOST PEOPLE SEE THE LEAGUE AS JUST AN EXCLUSIVE CLUB, BUT TO ME, IT'S THE CLOSEST THING I'VE EVER HAD TO A... A FAMILY.
I APPRECIATE WHATEVER YOU CAN DO TO GET THEM BACK.
SIR, PERHAPS EACH OF THE LANTERNS SHOULD RECITE OUR SOLEMN OATHS BEFORE EMBARKING ON THIS CAMPAIGN.
OATHS?! NO OFFENSE, BUT WITH WHAT WE'RE ABOUT TO DO--
-- WE SHOULD ALL BE SAYING OUR PRAYERS.
[redacted]

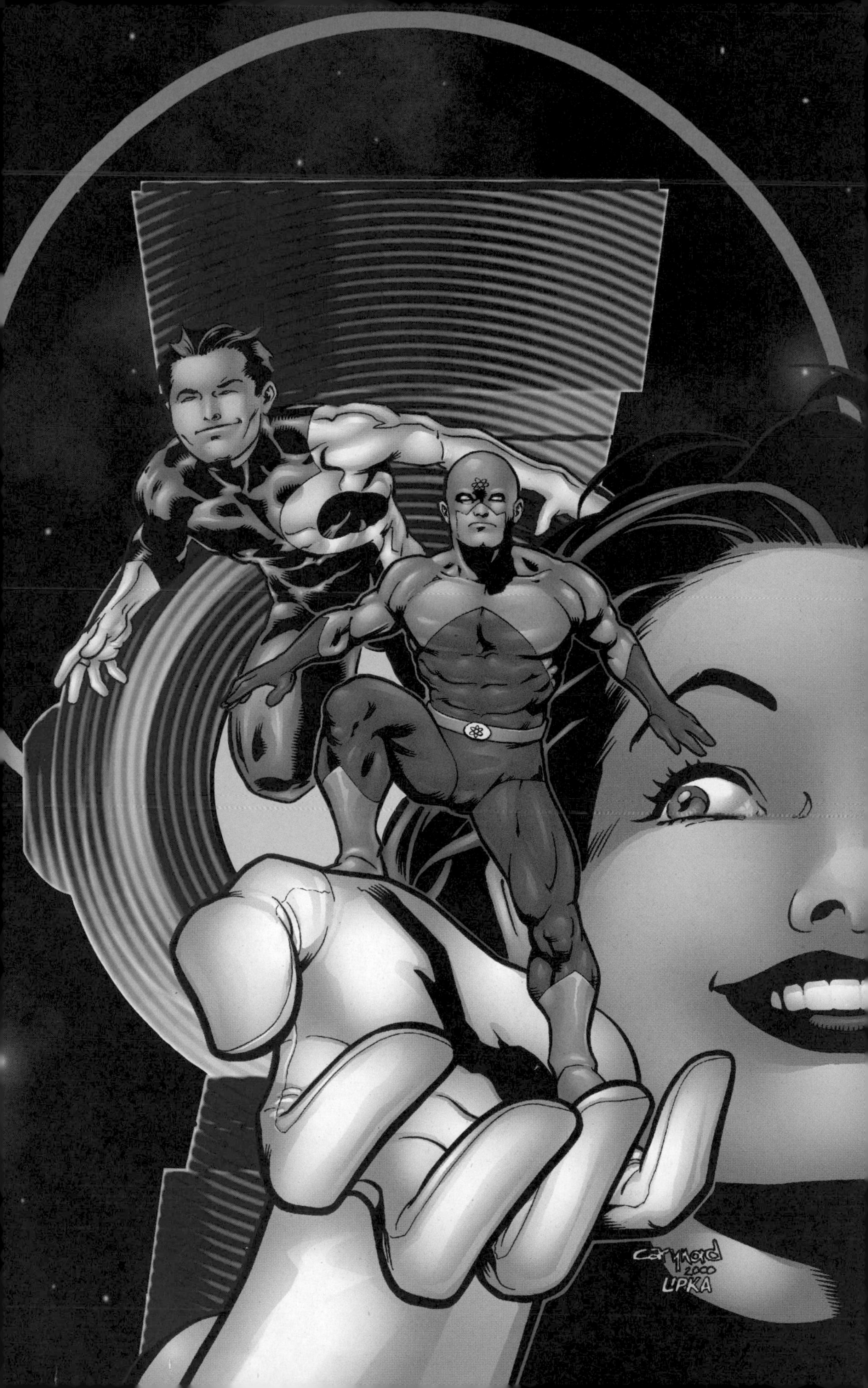
carynord
2000
LIPKA

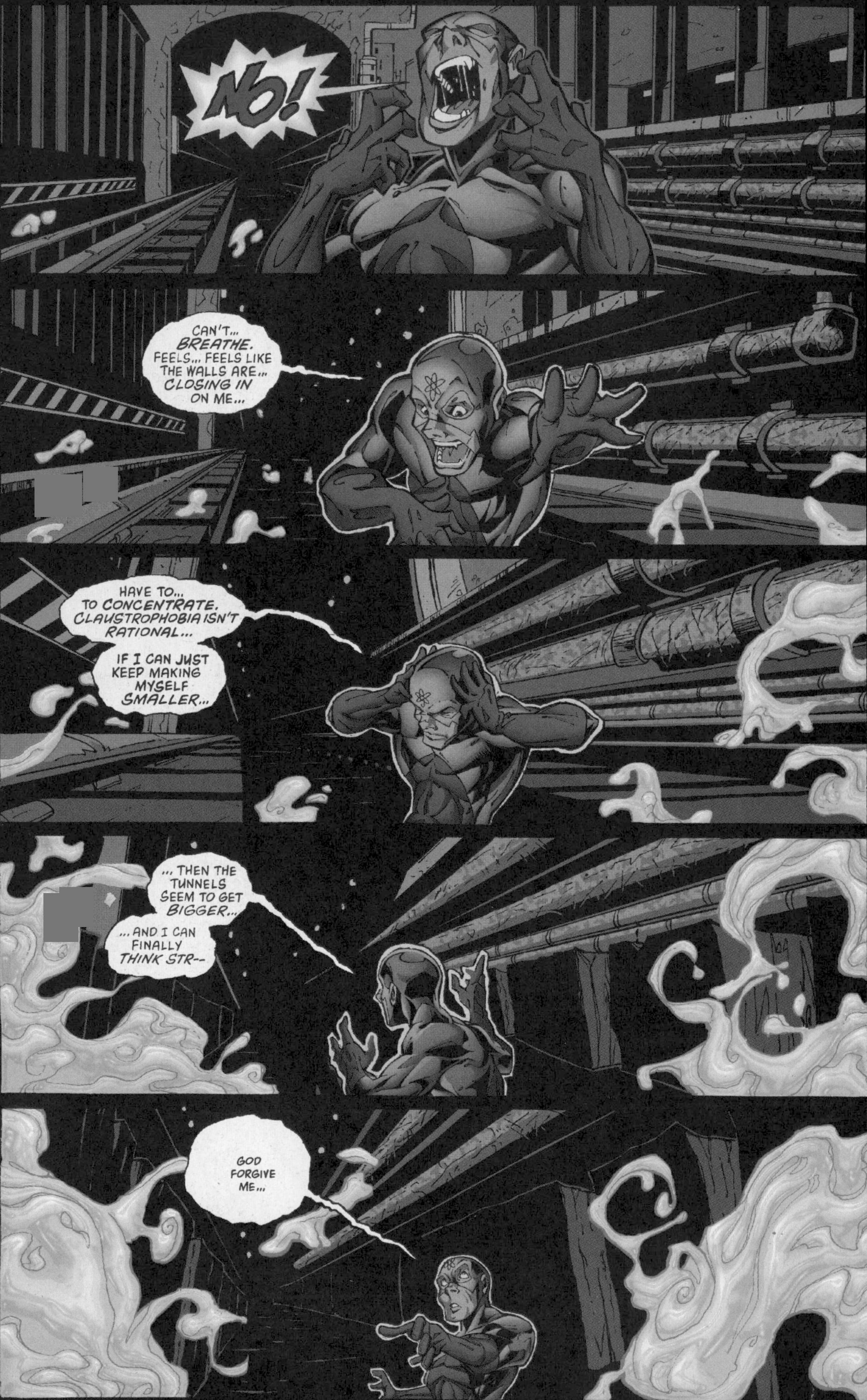
NO!
CAN'T... BREATHE. FEELS... FEELS LIKE THE WALLS ARE... CLOSING IN ON ME...
HAVE TO... TO CONCENTRATE. CLAUSTROPHOBIA ISN'T RATIONAL...
IF I CAN JUST KEEP MAKING MYSELF SMALLER...
... THEN THE TUNNELS SEEM TO GET BIGGER...
... AND I CAN FINALLY THINK STR--
GOD FORGIVE ME...

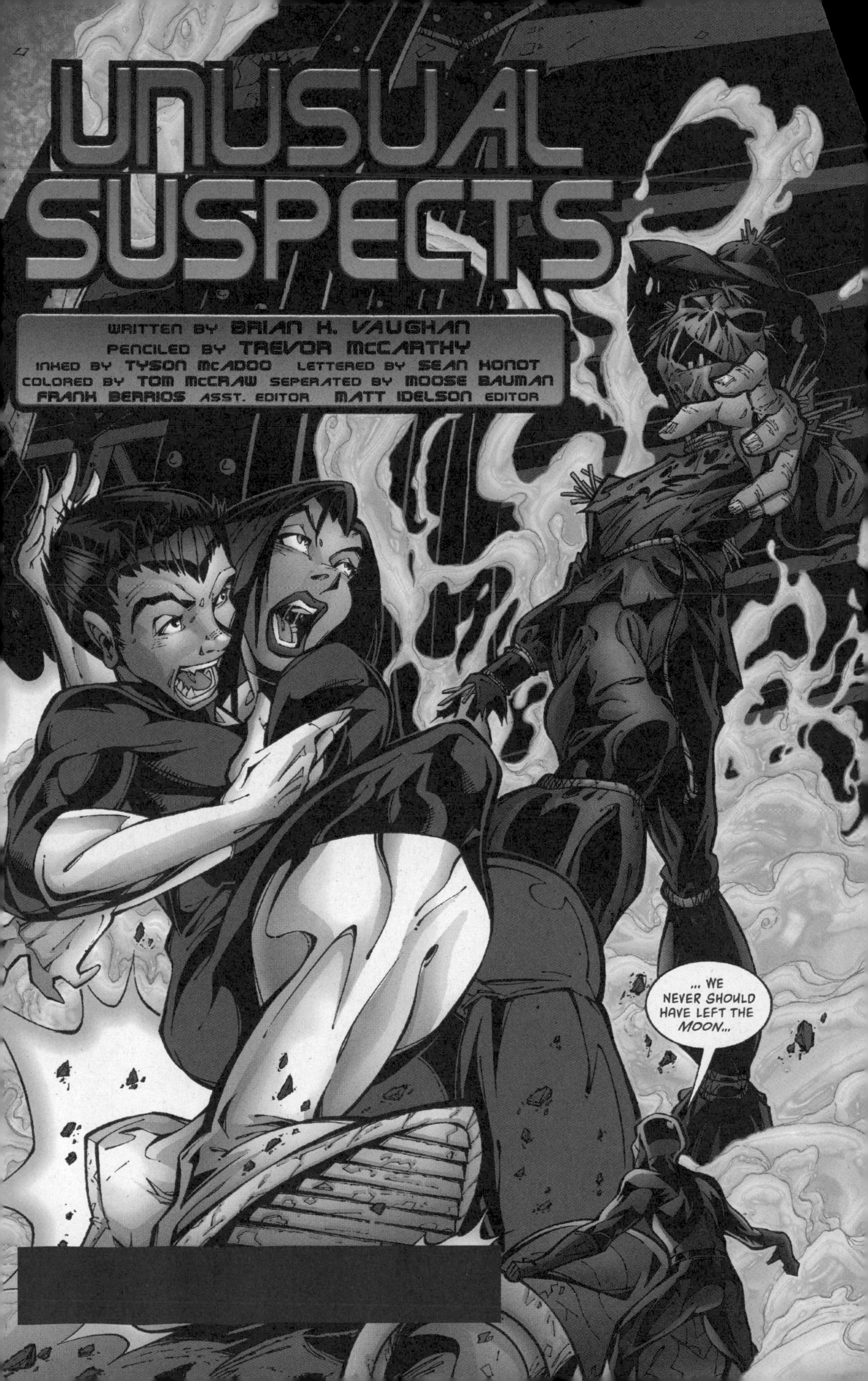
UNUSUAL SUSPECTS
WRITTEN BY BRIAN K. VAUGHAN
PENCILED BY TREVOR McCARTHY
INKED BY TYSON McADOO LETTERED BY SEAN KONOT
COLORED BY TOM McCRAW SEPERATED BY MOOSE BAUMAN
FRANK BERRIOS ASST. EDITOR MATT IDELSON EDITOR
... WE NEVER SHOULD HAVE LEFT THE MOON...

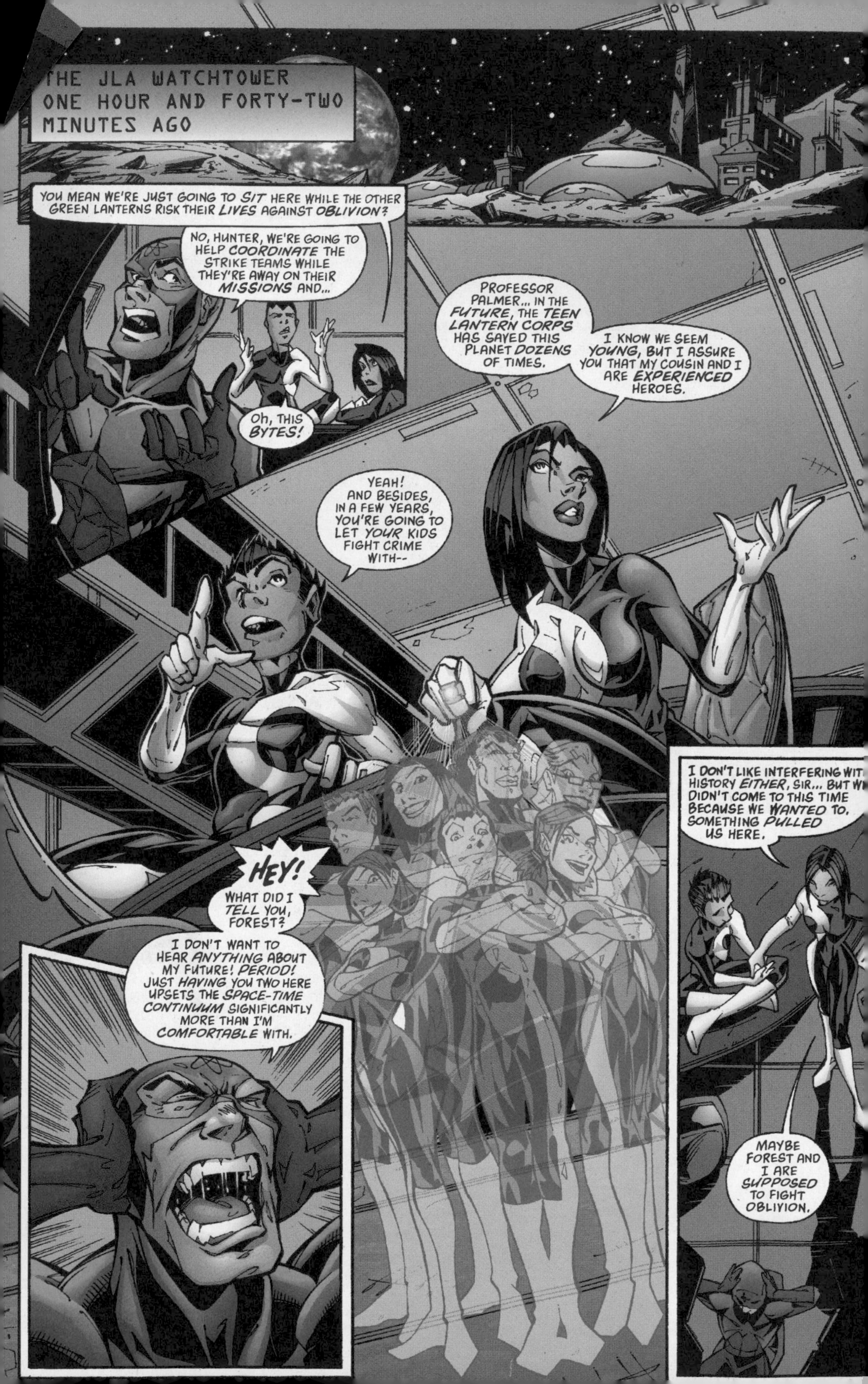
THE JLA WATCHTOWER ONE HOUR AND FORTY-TWO MINUTES AGO
YOU MEAN WE'RE JUST GOING TO SIT HERE WHILE THE OTHER GREEN LANTERNS RISK THEIR LIVES AGAINST OBLIVION?
NO, HUNTER, WE'RE GOING TO HELP COORDINATE THE STRIKE TEAMS WHILE THEY'RE AWAY ON THEIR MISSIONS AND...
Oh, THIS BYTES!
PROFESSOR PALMER... IN THE FUTURE, THE TEEN LANTERN CORPS HAS SAVED THIS PLANET DOZENS OF TIMES.
I KNOW WE SEEM YOUNG, BUT I ASSURE YOU THAT MY COUSIN AND I ARE EXPERIENCED HEROES.
YEAH! AND BESIDES, IN A FEW YEARS, YOU'RE GOING TO LET YOUR KIDS FIGHT CRIME WITH--
HEY!
WHAT DID I TELL YOU, FOREST?
I DON'T WANT TO HEAR ANYTHING ABOUT MY FUTURE! PERIOD! JUST HAVING YOU TWO HERE UPSETS THE SPACE-TIME CONTINUUM SIGNIFICANTLY MORE THAN I'M COMFORTABLE WITH.
I DON'T LIKE INTERFERING WIT HISTORY EITHER, SIR... BUT W DIDN'T COME TO THIS TIME BECAUSE WE WANTED TO. SOMETHING PULLED US HERE.
MAYBE FOREST AND I ARE SUPPOSED TO FIGHT OBLIVION.

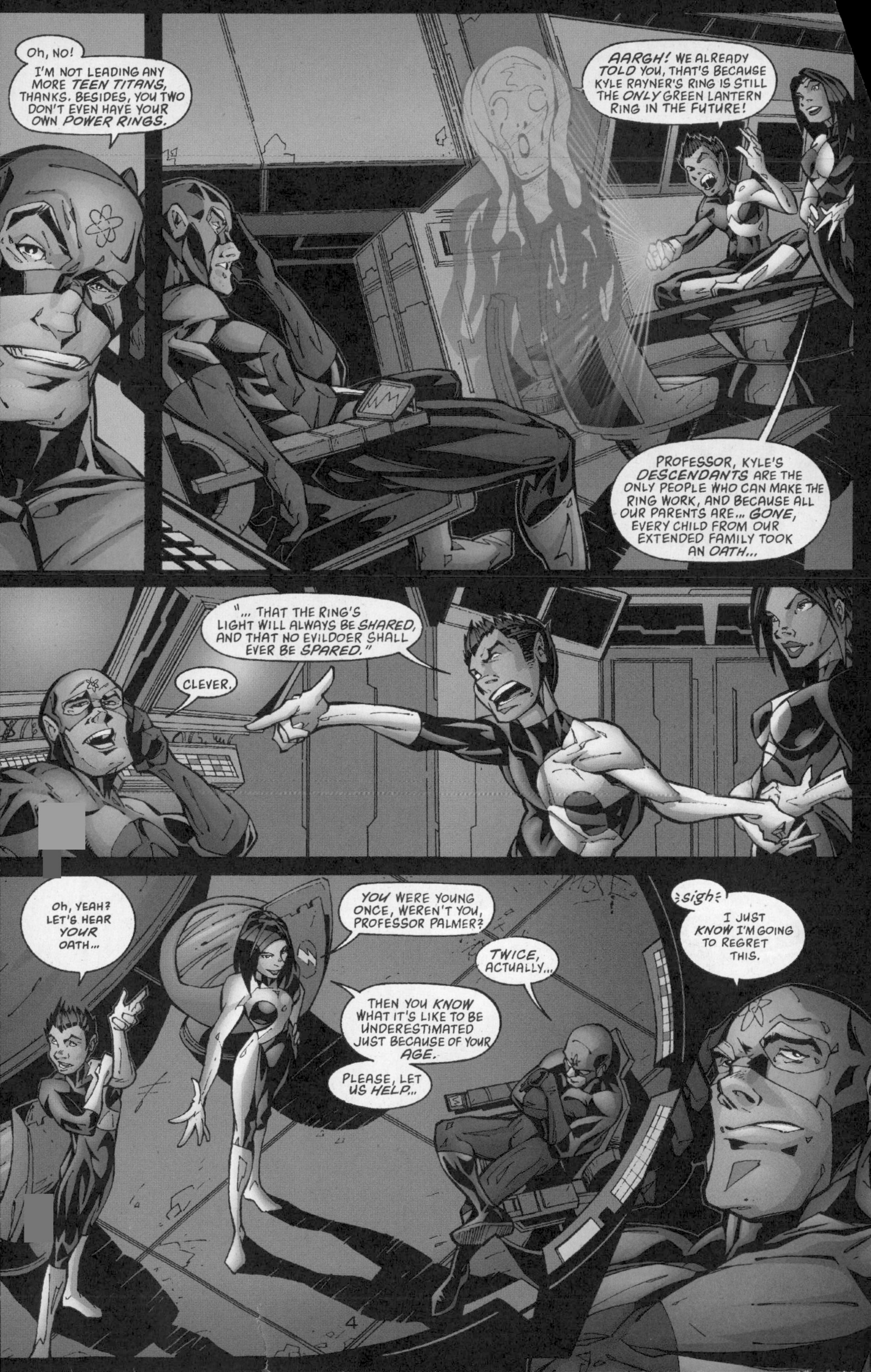

Oh, NO! I'M NOT LEADING ANY MORE TEEN TITANS, THANKS. BESIDES, YOU TWO DON'T EVEN HAVE YOUR OWN POWER RINGS.
AARGH! WE ALREADY TOLD YOU, THAT'S BECAUSE KYLE RAYNER'S RING IS STILL THE ONLY GREEN LANTERN RING IN THE FUTURE!
PROFESSOR, KYLE'S DESCENDANTS ARE THE ONLY PEOPLE WHO CAN MAKE THE RING WORK, AND BECAUSE ALL OUR PARENTS ARE... GONE, EVERY CHILD FROM OUR EXTENDED FAMILY TOOK AN OATH...
"... THAT THE RING'S LIGHT WILL ALWAYS BE SHARED, AND THAT NO EVILDOER SHALL EVER BE SPARED."
CLEVER.
Oh, YEAH? LET'S HEAR YOUR OATH...
YOU WERE YOUNG ONCE, WEREN'T YOU, PROFESSOR PALMER?
TWICE, ACTUALLY...
THEN YOU KNOW WHAT IT'S LIKE TO BE UNDERESTIMATED JUST BECAUSE OF YOUR AGE.
PLEASE, LET US HELP...
sigh
I JUST KNOW I'M GOING TO REGRET THIS.

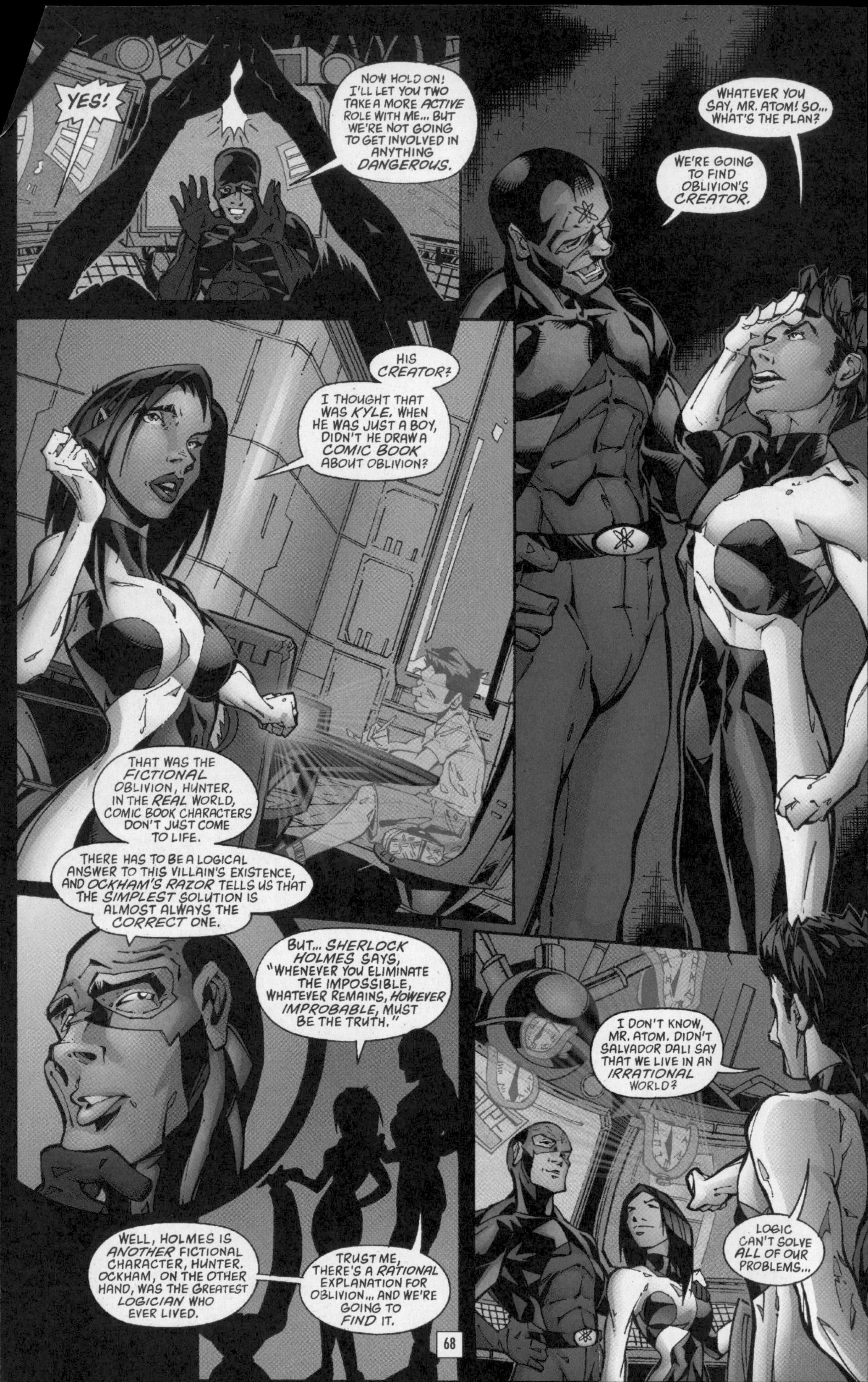
YES!
NOW HOLD ON! I'LL LET YOU TWO TAKE A MORE ACTIVE ROLE WITH ME... BUT WE'RE NOT GOING TO GET INVOLVED IN ANYTHING DANGEROUS.
WHATEVER YOU SAY, MR. ATOM! SO... WHAT'S THE PLAN?
WE'RE GOING TO FIND OBLIVION'S CREATOR.
HIS CREATOR?
I THOUGHT THAT WAS KYLE. WHEN HE WAS JUST A BOY, DIDN'T HE DRAW A COMIC BOOK ABOUT OBLIVION?
THAT WAS THE FICTIONAL OBLIVION, HUNTER. IN THE REAL WORLD, COMIC BOOK CHARACTERS DON'T JUST COME TO LIFE.
THERE HAS TO BE A LOGICAL ANSWER TO THIS VILLAIN'S EXISTENCE, AND OCKHAM'S RAZOR TELLS US THAT THE SIMPLEST SOLUTION IS ALMOST ALWAYS THE CORRECT ONE.
BUT... SHERLOCK HOLMES SAYS, "WHENEVER YOU ELIMINATE THE IMPOSSIBLE, WHATEVER REMAINS, HOWEVER IMPROBABLE, MUST BE THE TRUTH."
WELL, HOLMES IS ANOTHER FICTIONAL CHARACTER, HUNTER. OCKHAM, ON THE OTHER HAND, WAS THE GREATEST LOGICIAN WHO EVER LIVED.
TRUST ME, THERE'S A RATIONAL EXPLANATION FOR OBLIVION... AND WE'RE GOING TO FIND IT.
I DON'T KNOW, MR. ATOM. DIDN'T SALVADOR DALI SAY THAT WE LIVE IN AN IRRATIONAL WORLD?
LOGIC CAN'T SOLVE ALL OF OUR PROBLEMS...

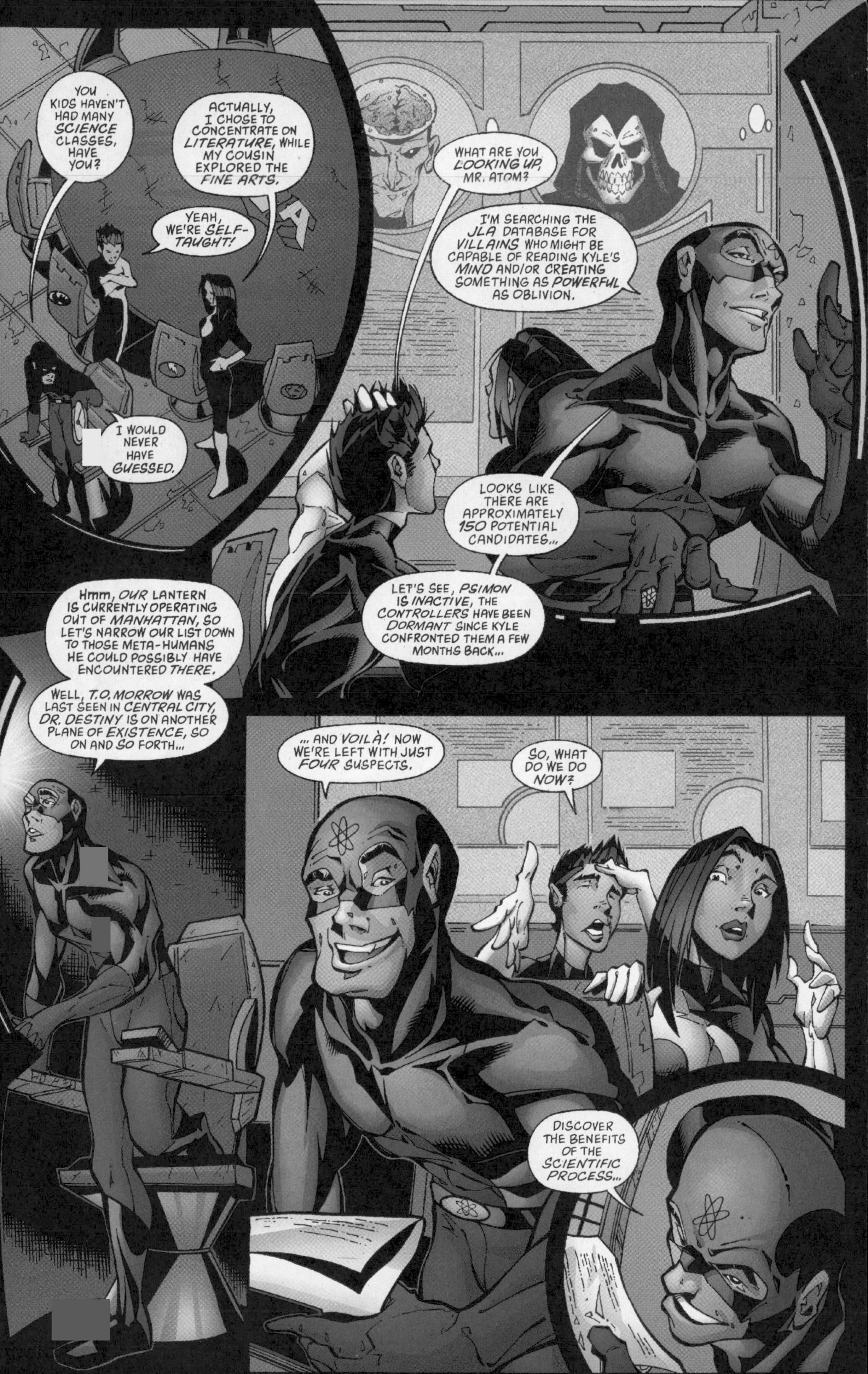
YOU KIDS HAVEN'T HAD MANY SCIENCE CLASSES, HAVE YOU?
ACTUALLY, I CHOSE TO CONCENTRATE ON LITERATURE, WHILE MY COUSIN EXPLORED THE FINE ARTS.
YEAH, WE'RE SELF-TAUGHT!
I WOULD NEVER HAVE GUESSED.
WHAT ARE YOU LOOKING UP, MR. ATOM?
I'M SEARCHING THE JLA DATABASE FOR VILLAINS WHO MIGHT BE CAPABLE OF READING KYLE'S MIND AND/OR CREATING SOMETHING AS POWERFUL AS OBLIVION.
LOOKS LIKE THERE ARE APPROXIMATELY 150 POTENTIAL CANDIDATES...
LET'S SEE, PSIMON IS INACTIVE, THE CONTROLLERS HAVE BEEN DORMANT SINCE KYLE CONFRONTED THEM A FEW MONTHS BACK...
Hmm, OUR LANTERN IS CURRENTLY OPERATING OUT OF MANHATTAN, SO LET'S NARROW OUR LIST DOWN TO THOSE META-HUMANS HE COULD POSSIBLY HAVE ENCOUNTERED THERE.
WELL, T.O. MORROW WAS LAST SEEN IN CENTRAL CITY, DR. DESTINY IS ON ANOTHER PLANE OF EXISTENCE, SO ON AND SO FORTH...
...AND VOILÀ! NOW WE'RE LEFT WITH JUST FOUR SUSPECTS.
SO, WHAT DO WE DO NOW?
DISCOVER THE BENEFITS OF THE SCIENTIFIC PROCESS...

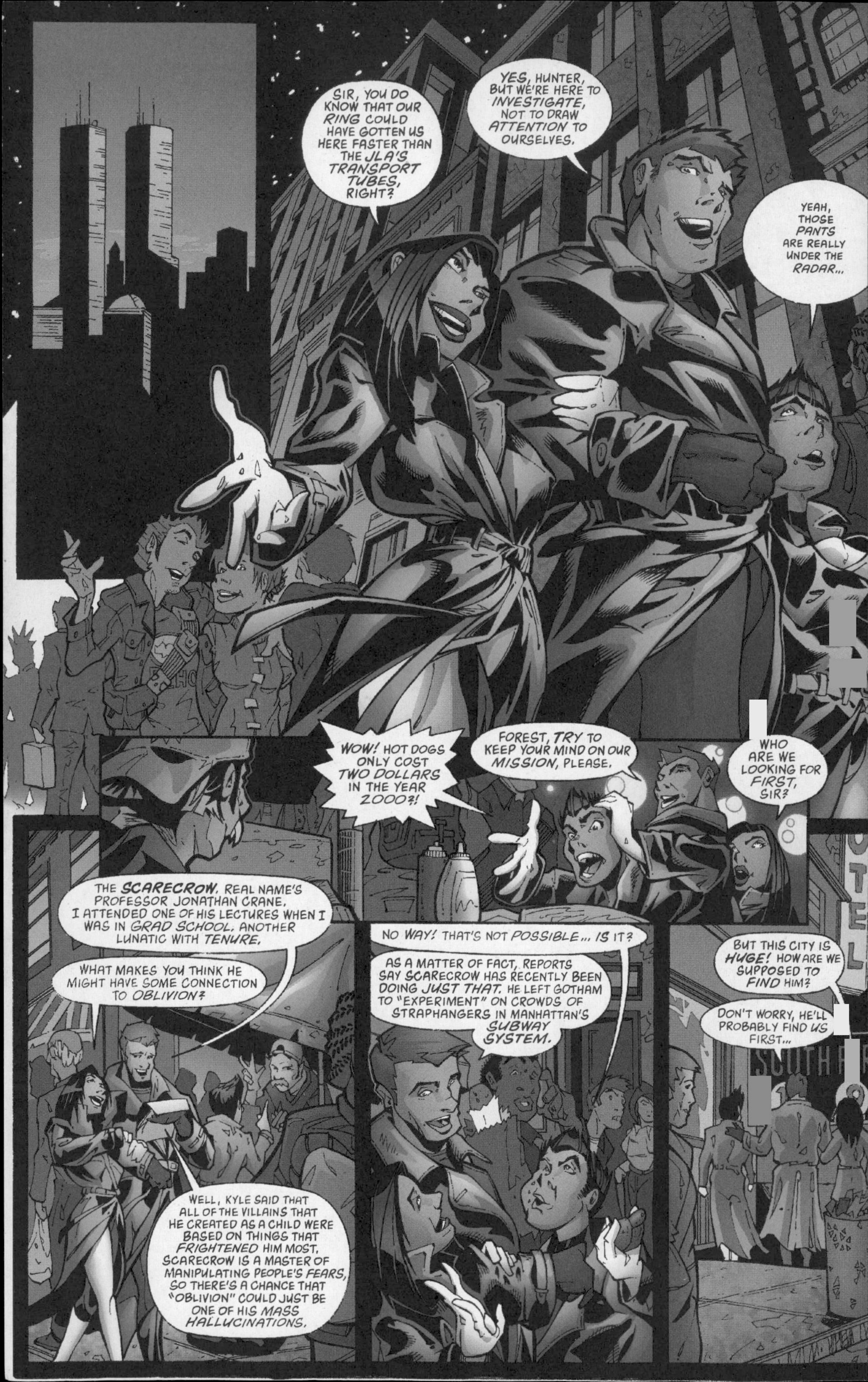

SIR, YOU DO KNOW THAT OUR RING COULD HAVE GOTTEN US HERE FASTER THAN THE JLA'S TRANSPORT TUBES, RIGHT?
YES, HUNTER, BUT WE'RE HERE TO INVESTIGATE, NOT TO DRAW ATTENTION TO OURSELVES.
YEAH, THOSE PANTS ARE REALLY UNDER THE RADAR...
WOW! HOT DOGS ONLY COST TWO DOLLARS IN THE YEAR 2000?!
FOREST, TRY TO KEEP YOUR MIND ON OUR MISSION, PLEASE.
WHO ARE WE LOOKING FOR FIRST, SIR?
THE SCARECROW. REAL NAME'S PROFESSOR JONATHAN CRANE. I ATTENDED ONE OF HIS LECTURES WHEN I WAS IN GRAD SCHOOL. ANOTHER LUNATIC WITH TENURE.
WHAT MAKES YOU THINK HE MIGHT HAVE SOME CONNECTION TO OBLIVION?
WELL, KYLE SAID THAT ALL OF THE VILLAINS THAT HE CREATED AS A CHILD WERE BASED ON THINGS THAT FRIGHTENED HIM MOST. SCARECROW IS A MASTER OF MANIPULATING PEOPLE'S FEARS, SO THERE'S A CHANCE THAT "OBLIVION" COULD JUST BE ONE OF HIS MASS HALLUCINATIONS.
NO WAY! THAT'S NOT POSSIBLE... IS IT?
AS A MATTER OF FACT, REPORTS SAY SCARECROW HAS RECENTLY BEEN DOING JUST THAT. HE LEFT GOTHAM TO "EXPERIMENT" ON CROWDS OF STRAPHANGERS IN MANHATTAN'S SUBWAY SYSTEM.
BUT THIS CITY IS HUGE! HOW ARE WE SUPPOSED TO FIND HIM?
DON'T WORRY, HE'LL PROBABLY FIND US FIRST...

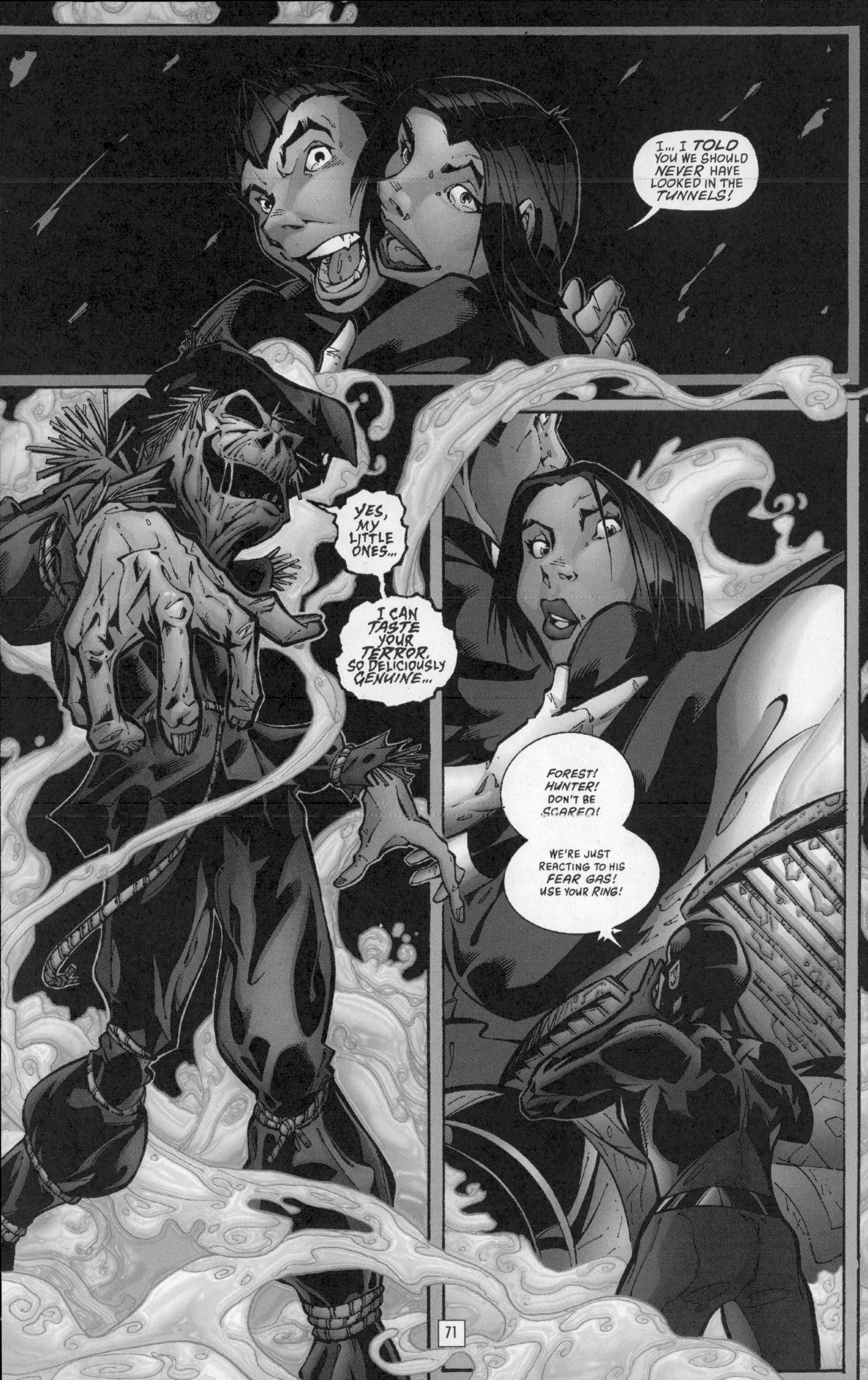
I... I TOLD YOU WE SHOULD NEVER HAVE LOOKED IN THE TUNNELS!
YES, MY LITTLE ONES...
I CAN TASTE YOUR TERROR, SO DELICIOUSLY GENUINE...
FOREST! HUNTER! DON'T BE SCARED!
WE'RE JUST REACTING TO HIS FEAR GAS! USE YOUR RING!

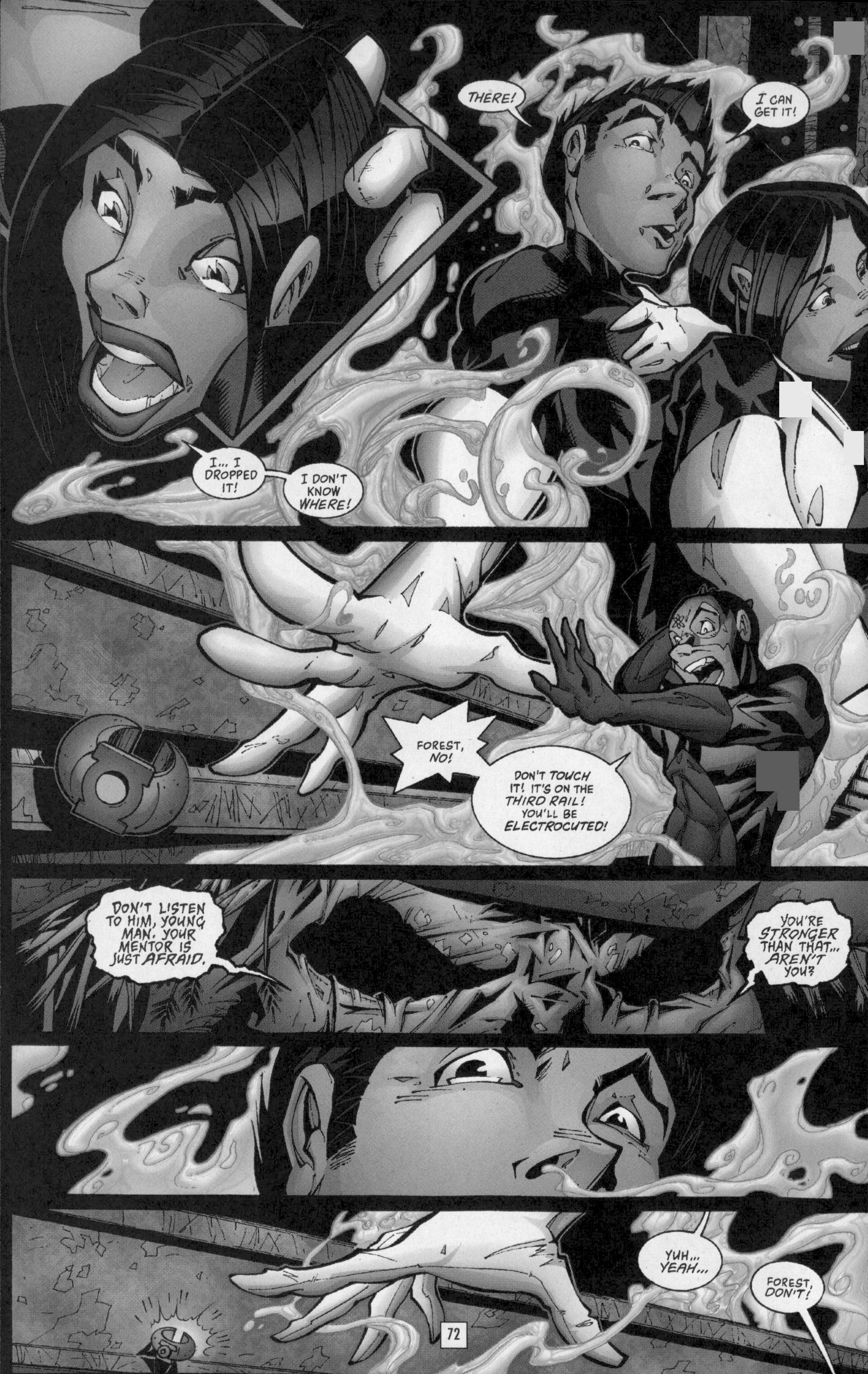
THERE!
I CAN GET IT!
I... I DROPPED IT!
I DON'T KNOW WHERE!
FOREST, NO!
DON'T TOUCH IT! IT'S ON THE THIRD RAIL! YOU'LL BE ELECTROCUTED!
DON'T LISTEN TO HIM, YOUNG MAN. YOUR MENTOR IS JUST AFRAID.
YOU'RE STRONGER THAN THAT... AREN'T YOU?
YUH... YEAH...
FOREST, DON'T!

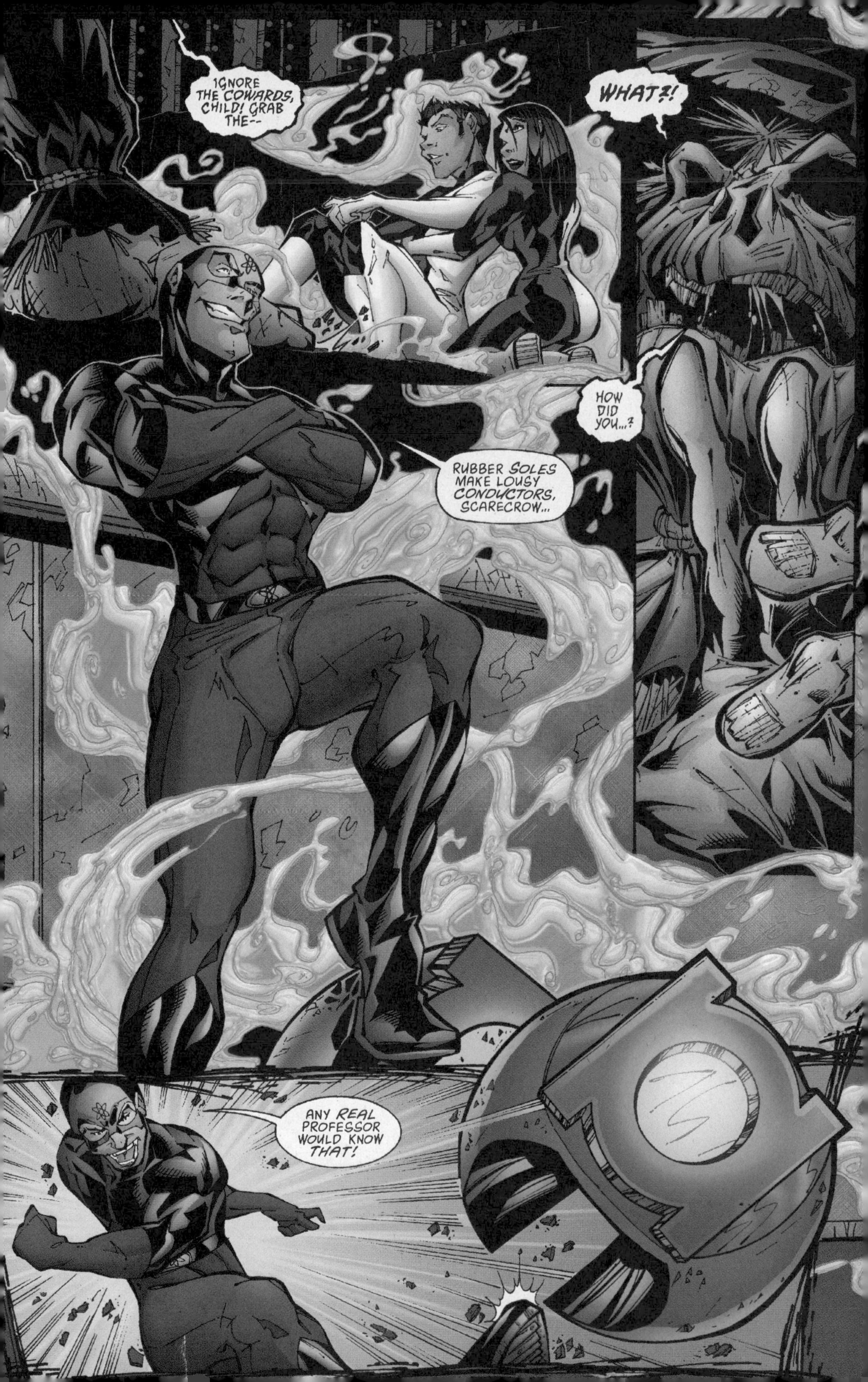
IGNORE THE COWARDS, CHILD! GRAB THE--
WHAT?!
HOW DID YOU...?
RUBBER SOLES MAKE LOUSY CONDUCTORS, SCARECROW...
ANY REAL PROFESSOR WOULD KNOW THAT!

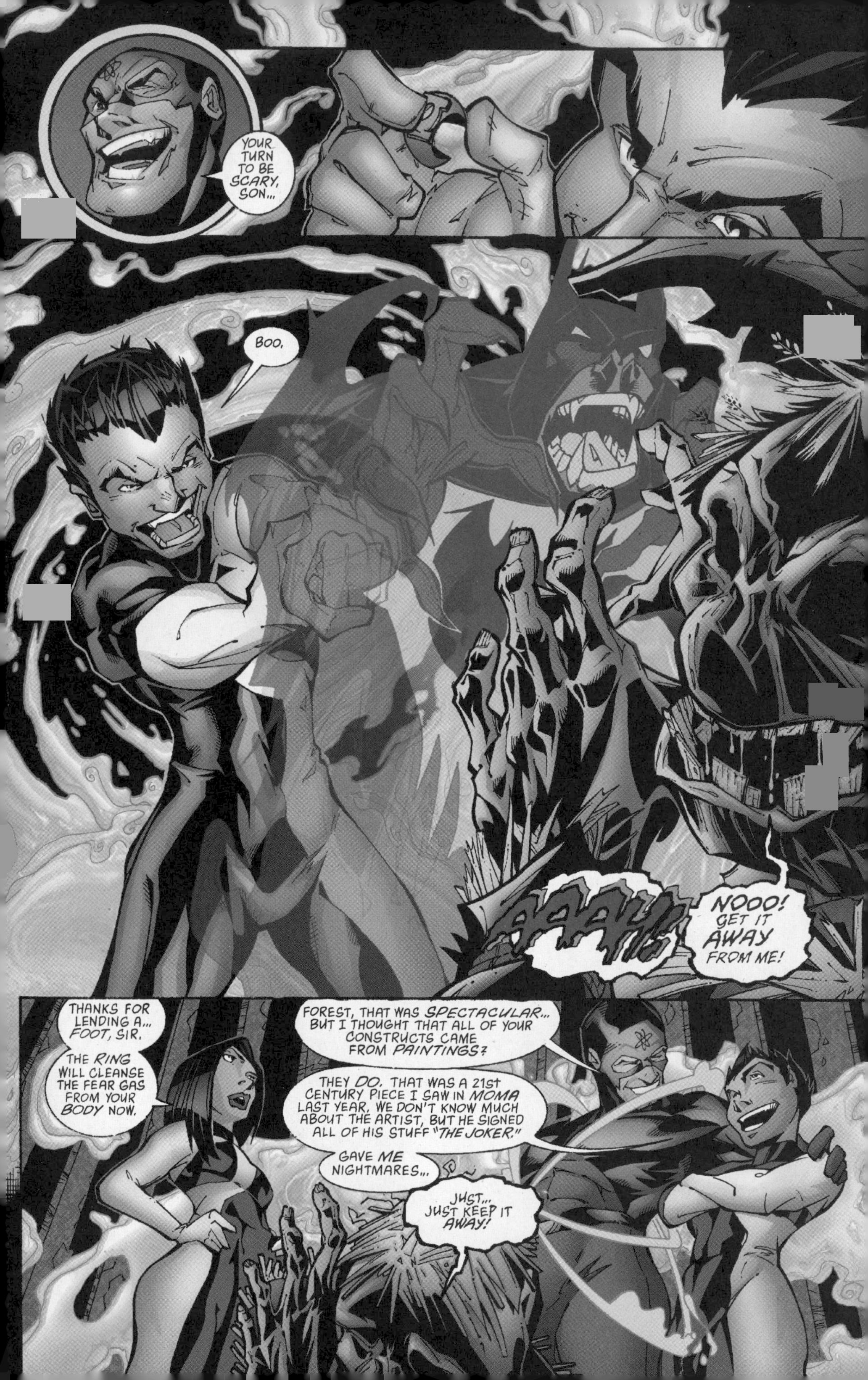
YOUR TURN TO BE SCARY, SON...
BOO.
AAAH!
NOOO! GET IT AWAY FROM ME!
THANKS FOR LENDING A... FOOT, SIR.
THE RING WILL CLEANSE THE FEAR GAS FROM YOUR BODY NOW.
FOREST, THAT WAS SPECTACULAR... BUT I THOUGHT THAT ALL OF YOUR CONSTRUCTS CAME FROM PAINTINGS?
THEY DO. THAT WAS A 21st CENTURY PIECE I SAW IN MOMA LAST YEAR. WE DON'T KNOW MUCH ABOUT THE ARTIST, BUT HE SIGNED ALL OF HIS STUFF "THE JOKER."
GAVE ME NIGHTMARES...
JUST... JUST KEEP IT AWAY!

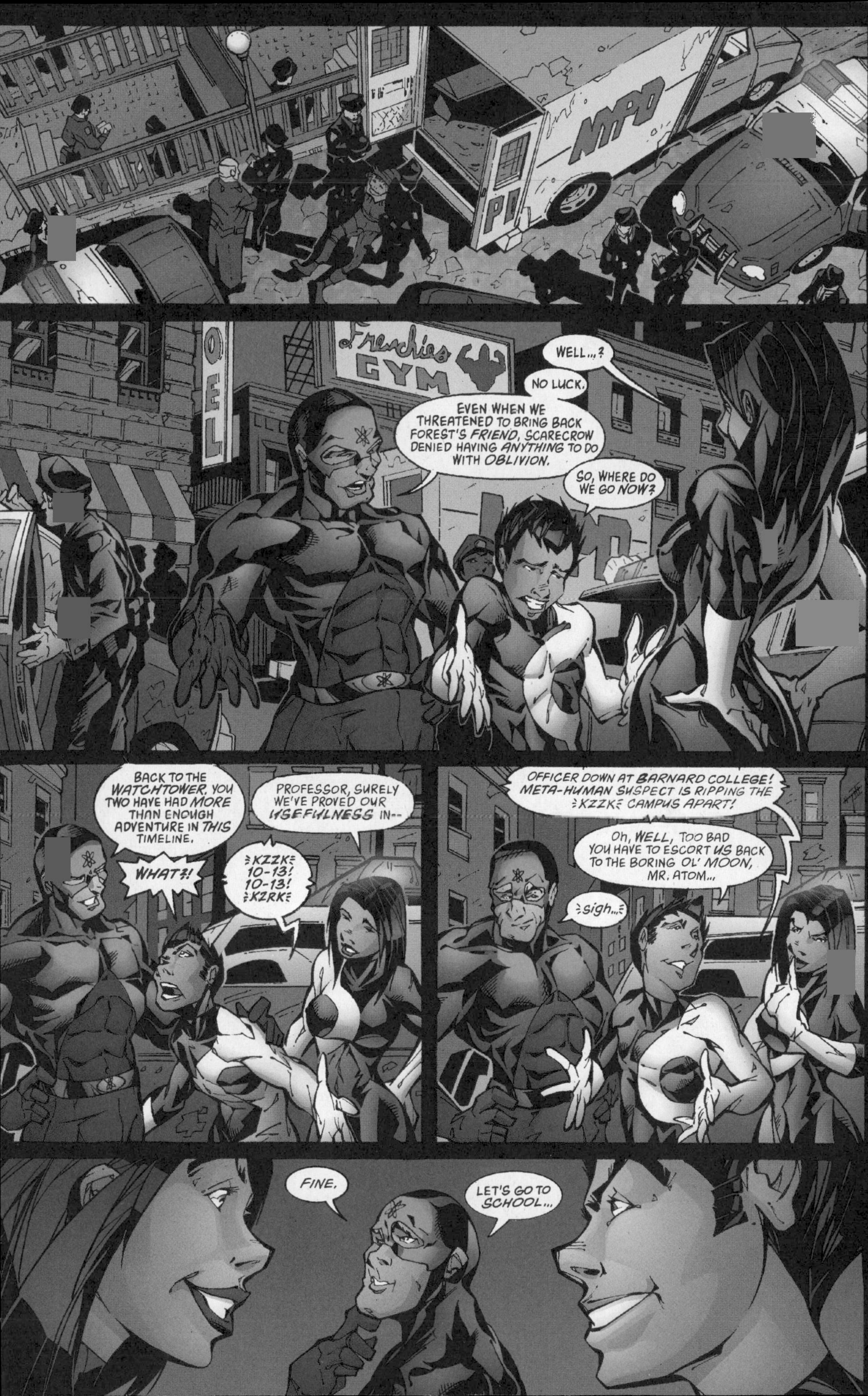
NYPD
Frenchie's GYM
WELL...?
NO LUCK.
EVEN WHEN WE THREATENED TO BRING BACK FOREST'S FRIEND, SCARECROW DENIED HAVING ANYTHING TO DO WITH OBLIVION.
SO, WHERE DO WE GO NOW?
BACK TO THE WATCHTOWER. YOU TWO HAVE HAD MORE THAN ENOUGH ADVENTURE IN THIS TIMELINE.
WHAT?!
PROFESSOR, SURELY WE'VE PROVED OUR USEFULNESS IN--
KZZK 10-13! 10-13! KZRK
OFFICER DOWN AT BARNARD COLLEGE! META-HUMAN SUSPECT IS RIPPING THE KZZK CAMPUS APART!
Oh, WELL, TOO BAD YOU HAVE TO ESCORT US BACK TO THE BORING OL' MOON, MR. ATOM...
sigh...
FINE.
LET'S GO TO SCHOOL...

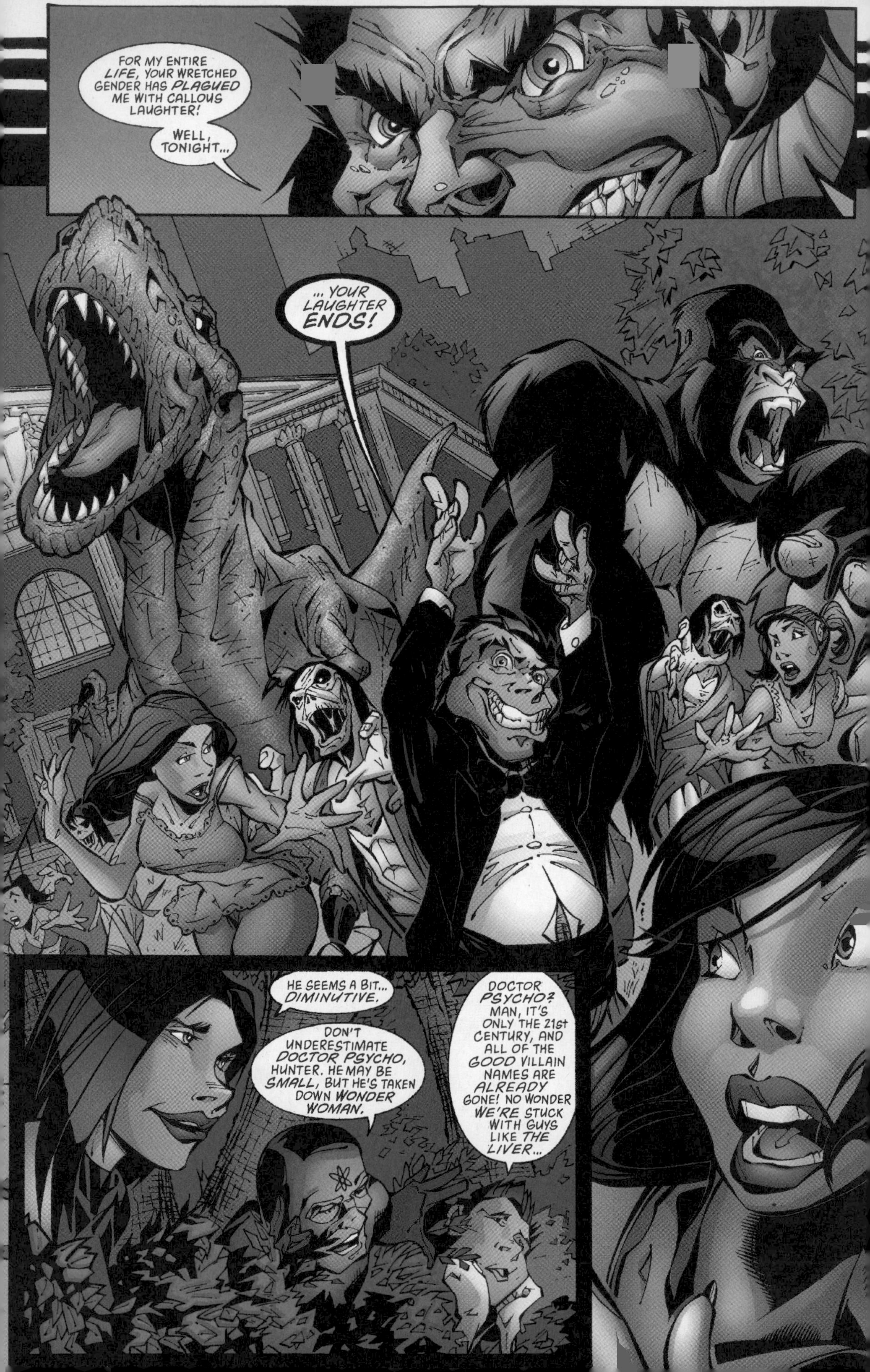
FOR MY ENTIRE LIFE, YOUR WRETCHED GENDER HAS PLAGUED ME WITH CALLOUS LAUGHTER!
WELL, TONIGHT...
...YOUR LAUGHTER ENDS!
HE SEEMS A BIT... DIMINUTIVE.
DON'T UNDERESTIMATE DOCTOR PSYCHO, HUNTER. HE MAY BE SMALL, BUT HE'S TAKEN DOWN WONDER WOMAN.
DOCTOR PSYCHO? MAN, IT'S ONLY THE 21st CENTURY, AND ALL OF THE GOOD VILLAIN NAMES ARE ALREADY GONE! NO WONDER WE'RE STUCK WITH GUYS LIKE THE LIVER...

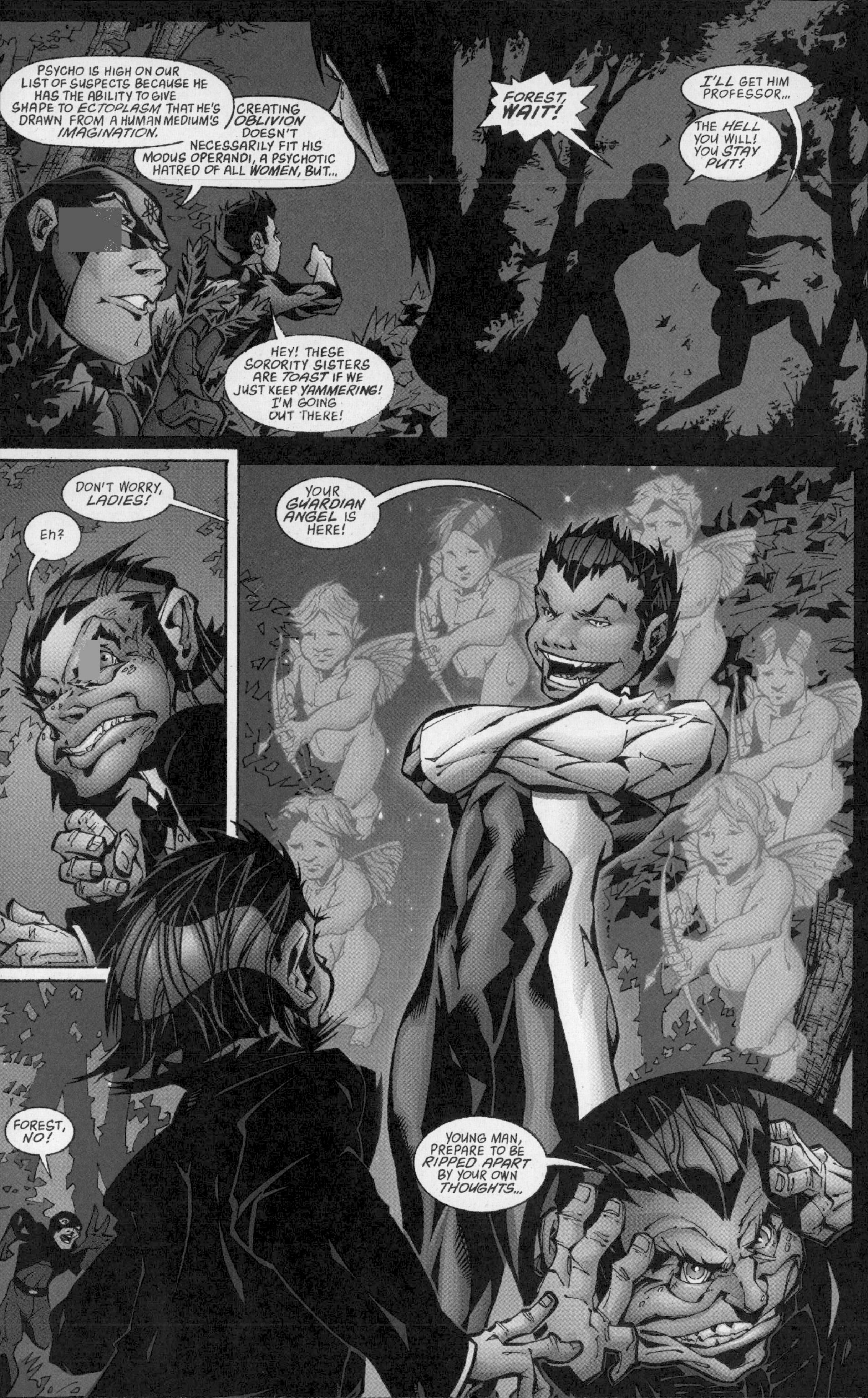
PSYCHO IS HIGH ON OUR LIST OF SUSPECTS BECAUSE HE HAS THE ABILITY TO GIVE SHAPE TO ECTOPLASM THAT HE'S DRAWN FROM A HUMAN MEDIUM'S IMAGINATION.
CREATING OBLIVION DOESN'T NECESSARILY FIT HIS MODUS OPERANDI, A PSYCHOTIC HATRED OF ALL WOMEN, BUT...
HEY! THESE SORORITY SISTERS ARE TOAST IF WE JUST KEEP YAMMERING! I'M GOING OUT THERE!
FOREST, WAIT!
I'LL GET HIM PROFESSOR...
THE HELL YOU WILL! YOU STAY PUT!
DON'T WORRY, LADIES!
Eh?
YOUR GUARDIAN ANGEL IS HERE!
FOREST, NO!
YOUNG MAN, PREPARE TO BE RIPPED APART BY YOUR OWN THOUGHTS...

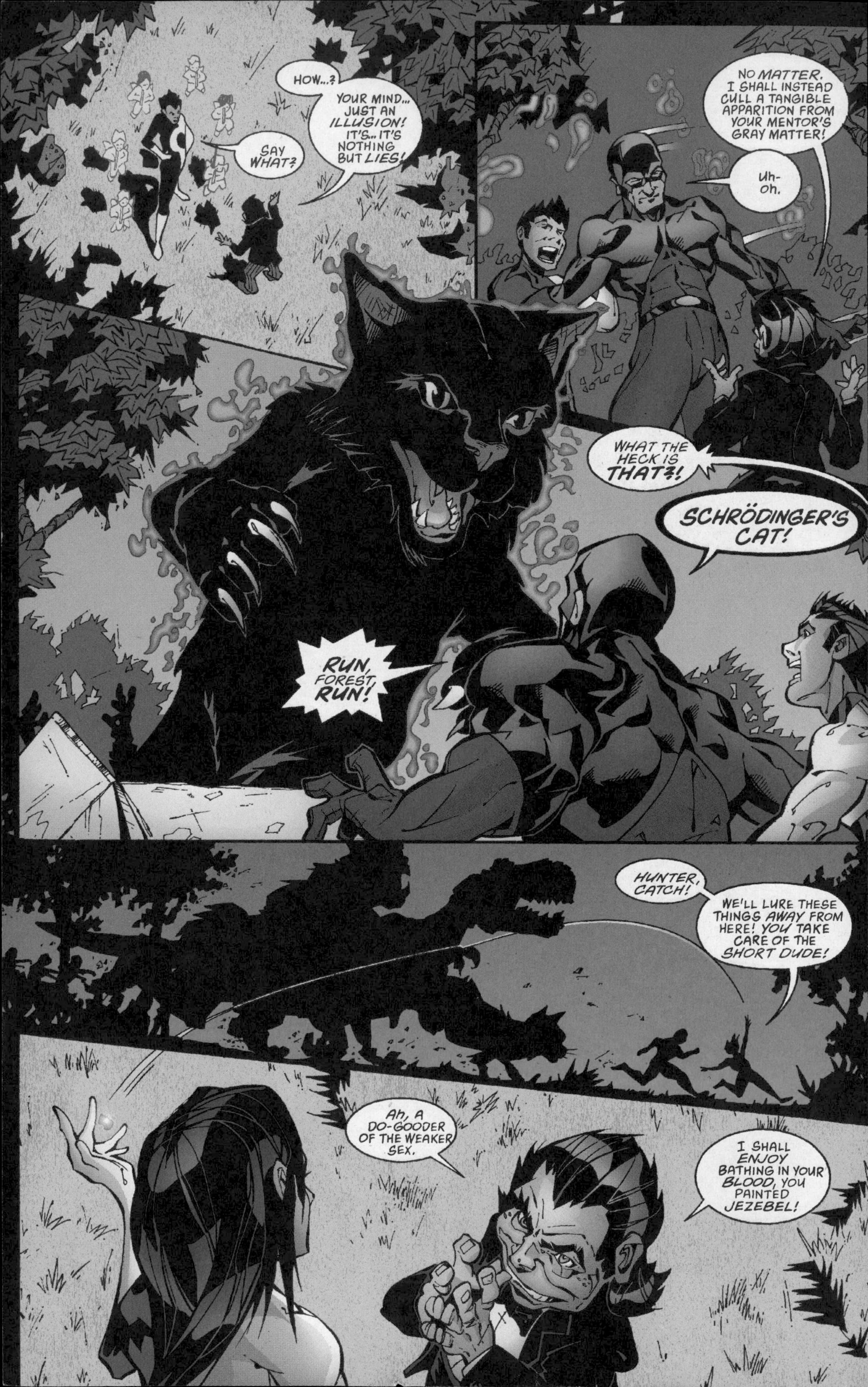
HOW...?
YOUR MIND... JUST AN ILLUSION! IT'S... IT'S NOTHING BUT LIES!
SAY WHAT?
NO MATTER. I SHALL INSTEAD CULL A TANGIBLE APPARITION FROM YOUR MENTOR'S GRAY MATTER!
Uh-oh.
WHAT THE HECK IS THAT?!
SCHRÖDINGER'S CAT!
RUN, FOREST, RUN!
HUNTER, CATCH!
WE'LL LURE THESE THINGS AWAY FROM HERE! YOU TAKE CARE OF THE SHORT DUDE!
Ah, A DO-GOODER OF THE WEAKER SEX.
I SHALL ENJOY BATHING IN YOUR BLOOD, YOU PAINTED JEZEBEL!

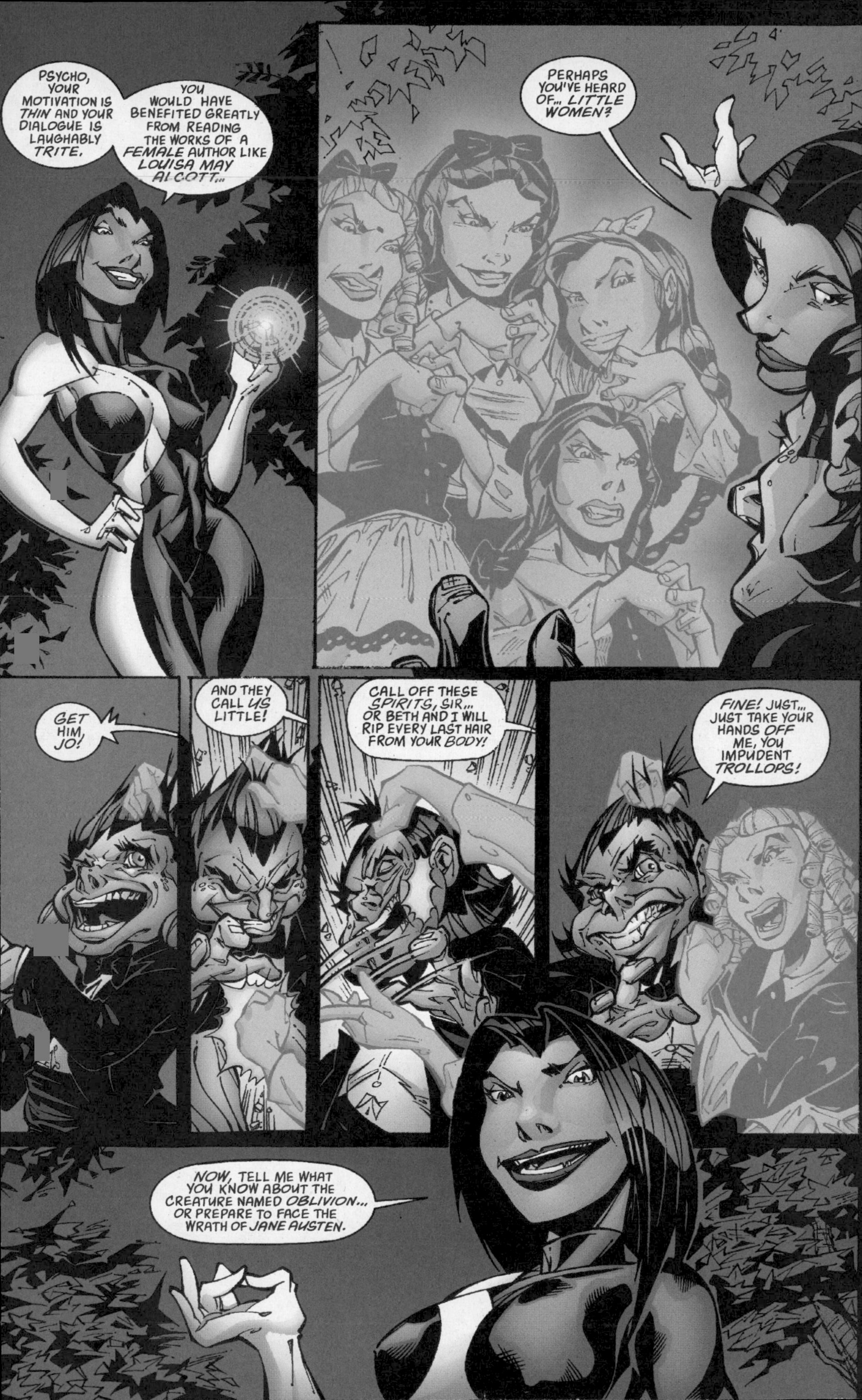
PSYCHO, YOUR MOTIVATION IS THIN AND YOUR DIALOGUE IS LAUGHABLY TRITE.
YOU WOULD HAVE BENEFITED GREATLY FROM READING THE WORKS OF A FEMALE AUTHOR LIKE LOUISA MAY ALCOTT...
PERHAPS YOU'VE HEARD OF... LITTLE WOMEN?
GET HIM, JO!
AND THEY CALL US LITTLE!
CALL OFF THESE SPIRITS, SIR... OR BETH AND I WILL RIP EVERY LAST HAIR FROM YOUR BODY!
FINE! JUST... JUST TAKE YOUR HANDS OFF ME, YOU IMPUDENT TROLLOPS!
NOW, TELL ME WHAT YOU KNOW ABOUT THE CREATURE NAMED OBLIVION... OR PREPARE TO FACE THE WRATH OF JANE AUSTEN.

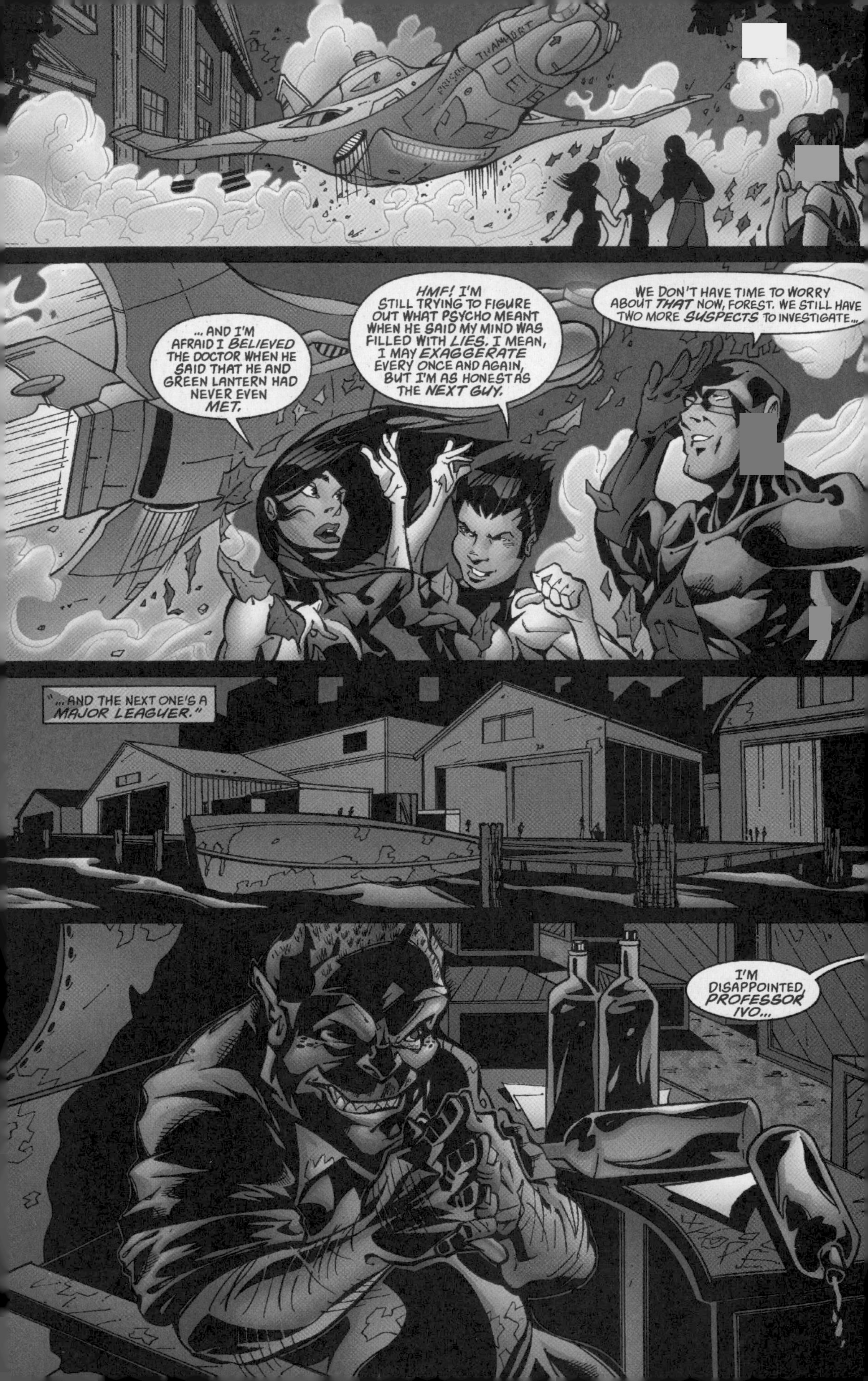
...AND I'M AFRAID I BELIEVED THE DOCTOR WHEN HE SAID THAT HE AND GREEN LANTERN HAD NEVER EVEN MET.
HMF! I'M STILL TRYING TO FIGURE OUT WHAT PSYCHO MEANT WHEN HE SAID MY MIND WAS FILLED WITH LIES. I MEAN, I MAY EXAGGERATE EVERY ONCE AND AGAIN, BUT I'M AS HONEST AS THE NEXT GUY.
WE DON'T HAVE TIME TO WORRY ABOUT THAT NOW, FOREST. WE STILL HAVE TWO MORE SUSPECTS TO INVESTIGATE...
"...AND THE NEXT ONE'S A MAJOR LEAGUER."
I'M DISAPPOINTED, PROFESSOR IVO...

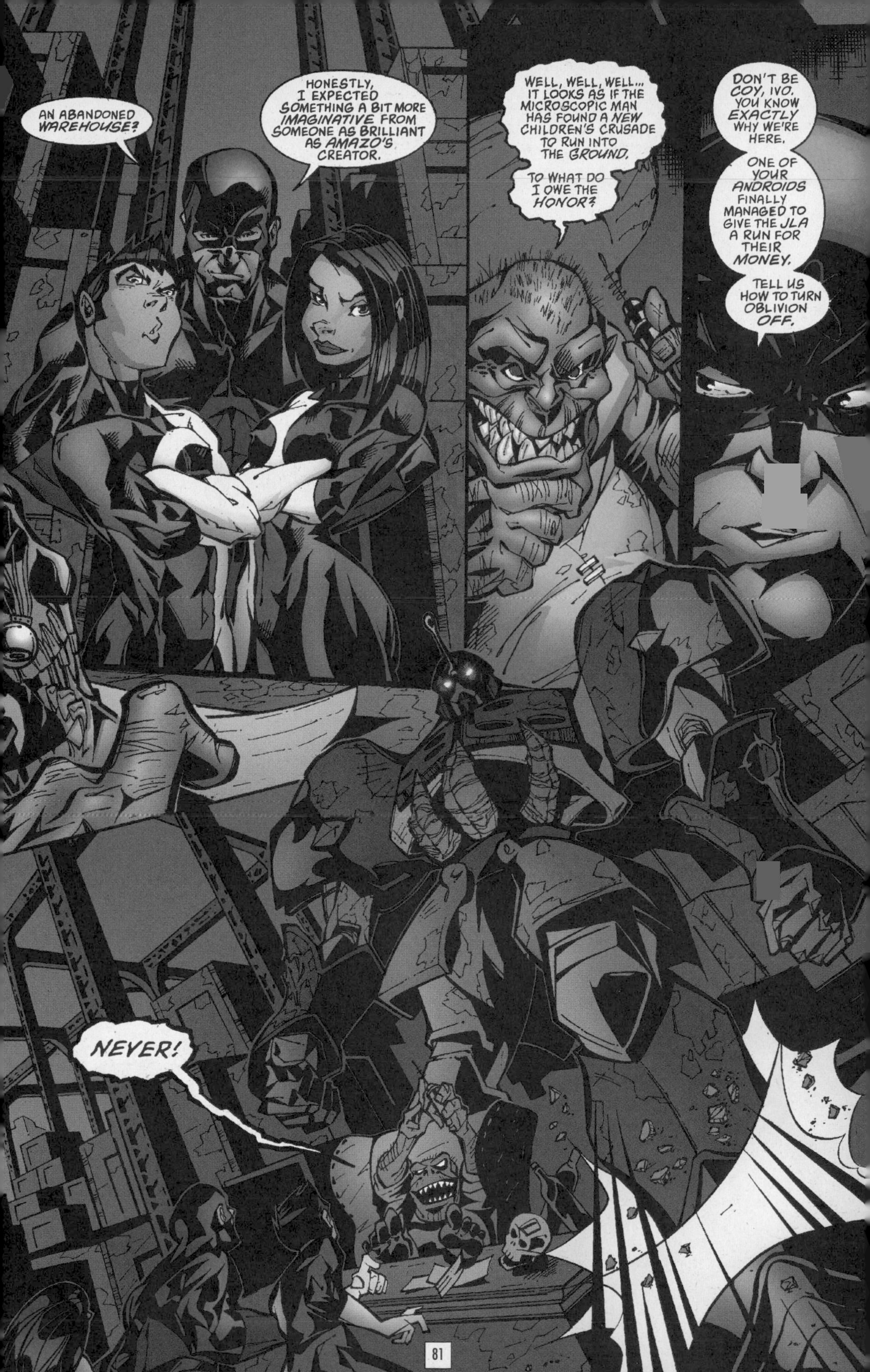

AN ABANDONED WAREHOUSE?
HONESTLY, I EXPECTED SOMETHING A BIT MORE IMAGINATIVE FROM SOMEONE AS BRILLIANT AS AMAZO'S CREATOR.
WELL, WELL, WELL... IT LOOKS AS IF THE MICROSCOPIC MAN HAS FOUND A NEW CHILDREN'S CRUSADE TO RUN INTO THE GROUND.
TO WHAT DO I OWE THE HONOR?
DON'T BE COY, IVO. YOU KNOW EXACTLY WHY WE'RE HERE.
ONE OF YOUR ANDROIDS FINALLY MANAGED TO GIVE THE JLA A RUN FOR THEIR MONEY.
TELL US HOW TO TURN OBLIVION OFF.
NEVER!

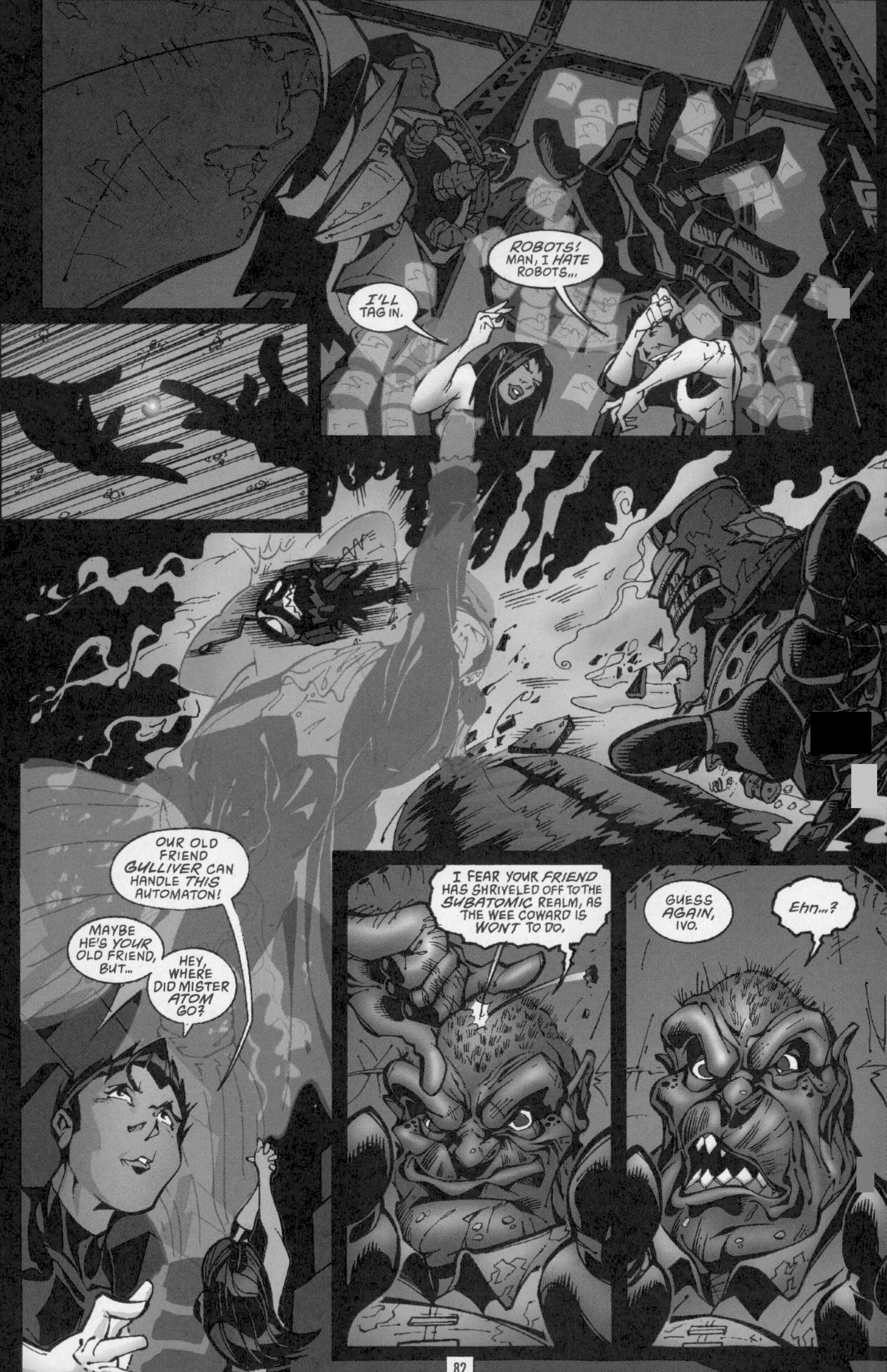
ROBOTS! MAN, I HATE ROBOTS...
I'LL TAG IN.
OUR OLD FRIEND GULLIVER CAN HANDLE THIS AUTOMATON!
MAYBE HE'S YOUR OLD FRIEND, BUT...
HEY, WHERE DID MISTER ATOM GO?
I FEAR YOUR FRIEND HAS SHRIVELED OFF TO THE SUBATOMIC REALM, AS THE WEE COWARD IS WONT TO DO.
GUESS AGAIN, IVO.
Ehn...?

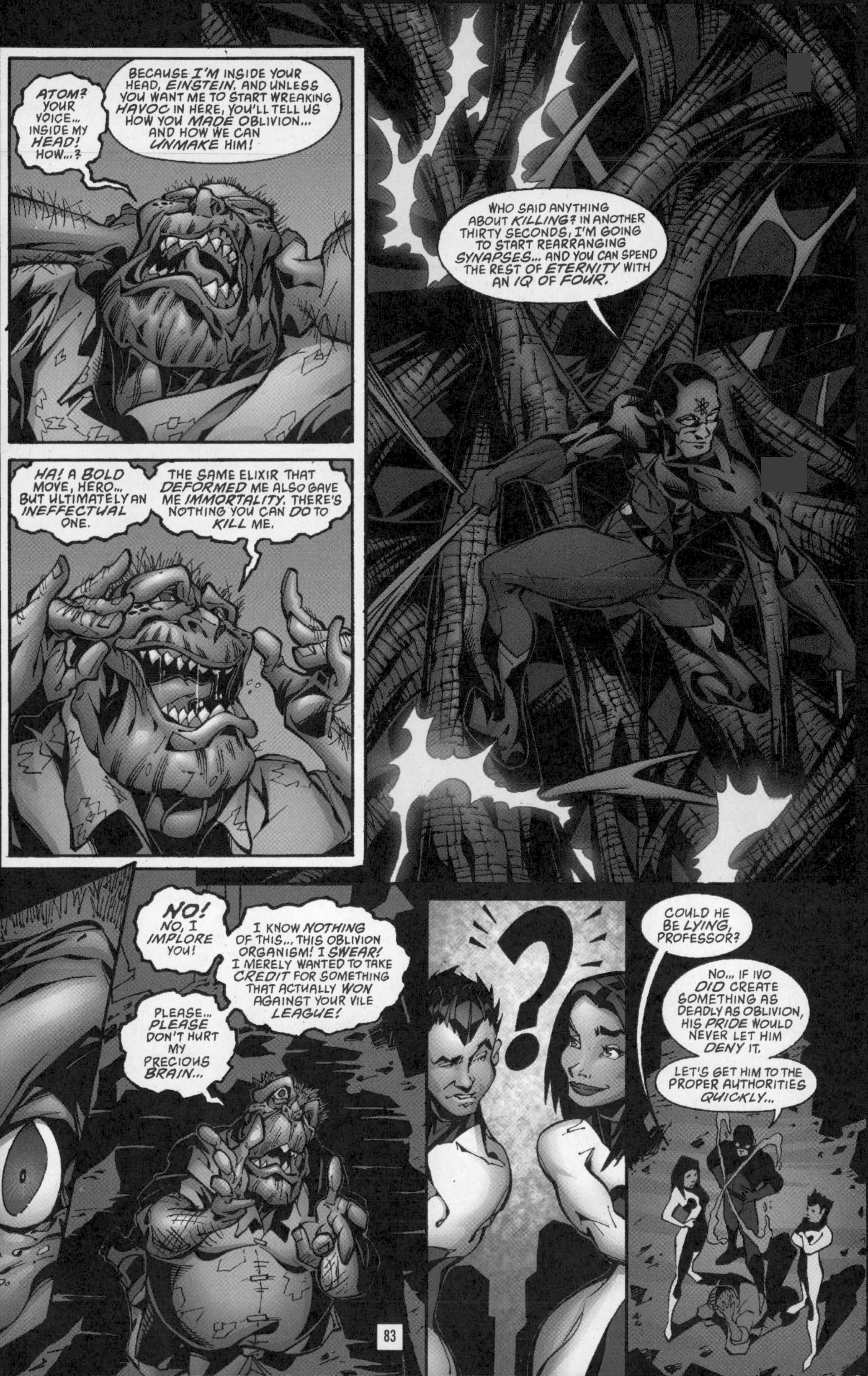
ATOM? YOUR VOICE... INSIDE MY HEAD! HOW...?
BECAUSE I'M INSIDE YOUR HEAD, EINSTEIN, AND UNLESS YOU WANT ME TO START WREAKING HAVOC IN HERE, YOU'LL TELL US HOW YOU MADE OBLIVION... AND HOW WE CAN UNMAKE HIM!
HA! A BOLD MOVE, HERO... BUT ULTIMATELY AN INEFFECTUAL ONE.
THE SAME ELIXIR THAT DEFORMED ME ALSO GAVE ME IMMORTALITY. THERE'S NOTHING YOU CAN DO TO KILL ME.
WHO SAID ANYTHING ABOUT KILLING? IN ANOTHER THIRTY SECONDS, I'M GOING TO START REARRANGING SYNAPSES... AND YOU CAN SPEND THE REST OF ETERNITY WITH AN IQ OF FOUR.
NO! NO, I IMPLORE YOU!
I KNOW NOTHING OF THIS... THIS OBLIVION ORGANISM! I SWEAR! I MERELY WANTED TO TAKE CREDIT FOR SOMETHING THAT ACTUALLY WON AGAINST YOUR VILE LEAGUE!
PLEASE... PLEASE DON'T HURT MY PRECIOUS BRAIN...
?
COULD HE BE LYING, PROFESSOR?
NO... IF IVO DID CREATE SOMETHING AS DEADLY AS OBLIVION, HIS PRIDE WOULD NEVER LET HIM DENY IT.
LET'S GET HIM TO THE PROPER AUTHORITIES QUICKLY...

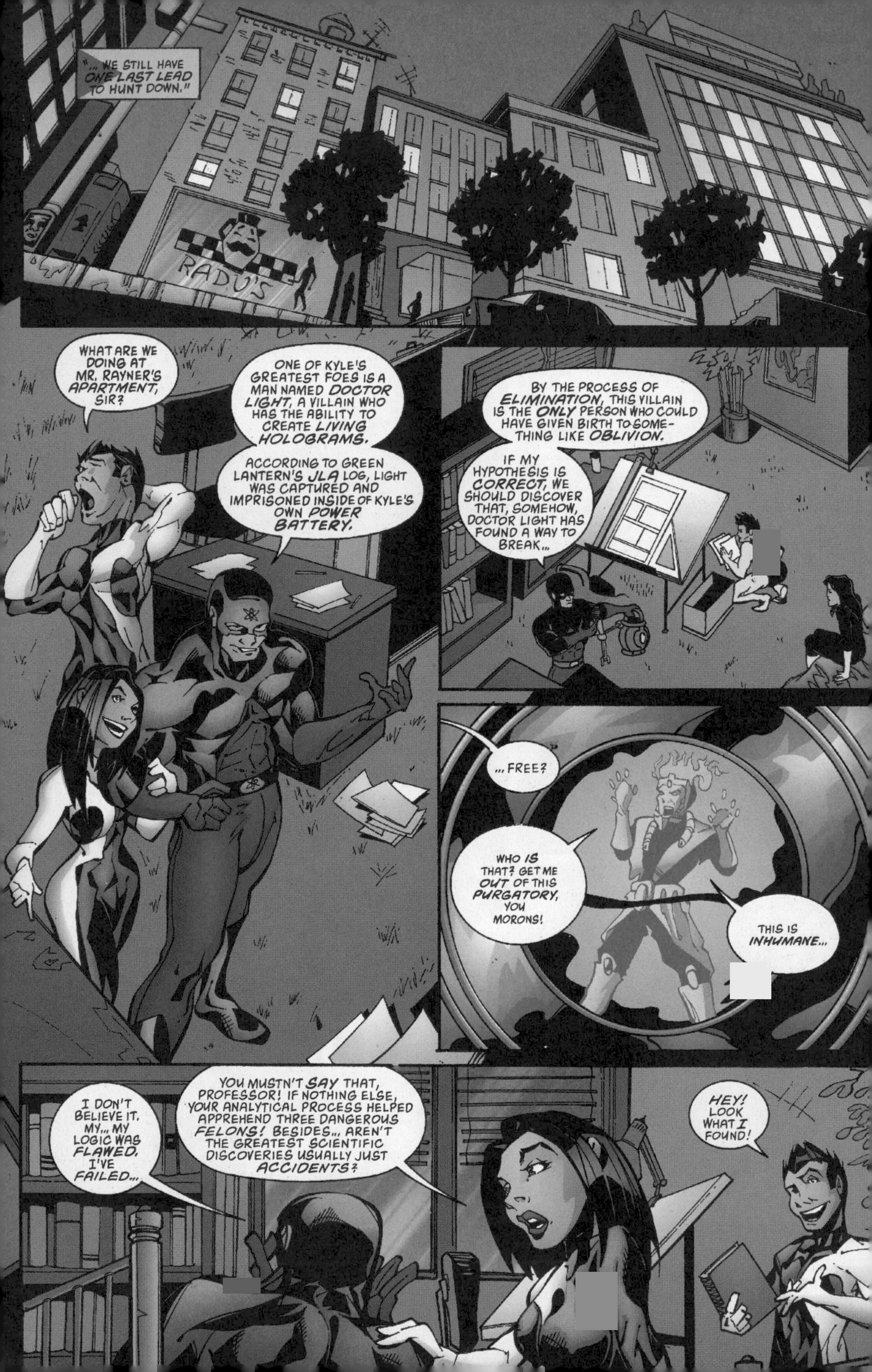
"...WE STILL HAVE ONE LAST LEAD TO HUNT DOWN."
RADU'S
WHAT ARE WE DOING AT MR. RAYNER'S APARTMENT, SIR?
ONE OF KYLE'S GREATEST FOES IS A MAN NAMED DOCTOR LIGHT, A VILLAIN WHO HAS THE ABILITY TO CREATE LIVING HOLOGRAMS.
ACCORDING TO GREEN LANTERN'S JLA LOG, LIGHT WAS CAPTURED AND IMPRISONED INSIDE OF KYLE'S OWN POWER BATTERY.
BY THE PROCESS OF ELIMINATION, THIS VILLAIN IS THE ONLY PERSON WHO COULD HAVE GIVEN BIRTH TO SOME-THING LIKE OBLIVION.
IF MY HYPOTHESIS IS CORRECT, WE SHOULD DISCOVER THAT, SOMEHOW, DOCTOR LIGHT HAS FOUND A WAY TO BREAK...
...FREE?
WHO IS THAT? GET ME OUT OF THIS PURGATORY, YOU MORONS!
THIS IS INHUMANE...
I DON'T BELIEVE IT. MY... MY LOGIC WAS FLAWED. I'VE FAILED...
YOU MUSTN'T SAY THAT, PROFESSOR! IF NOTHING ELSE, YOUR ANALYTICAL PROCESS HELPED APPREHEND THREE DANGEROUS FELONS! BESIDES... AREN'T THE GREATEST SCIENTIFIC DISCOVERIES USUALLY JUST ACCIDENTS?
HEY! LOOK WHAT I FOUND!

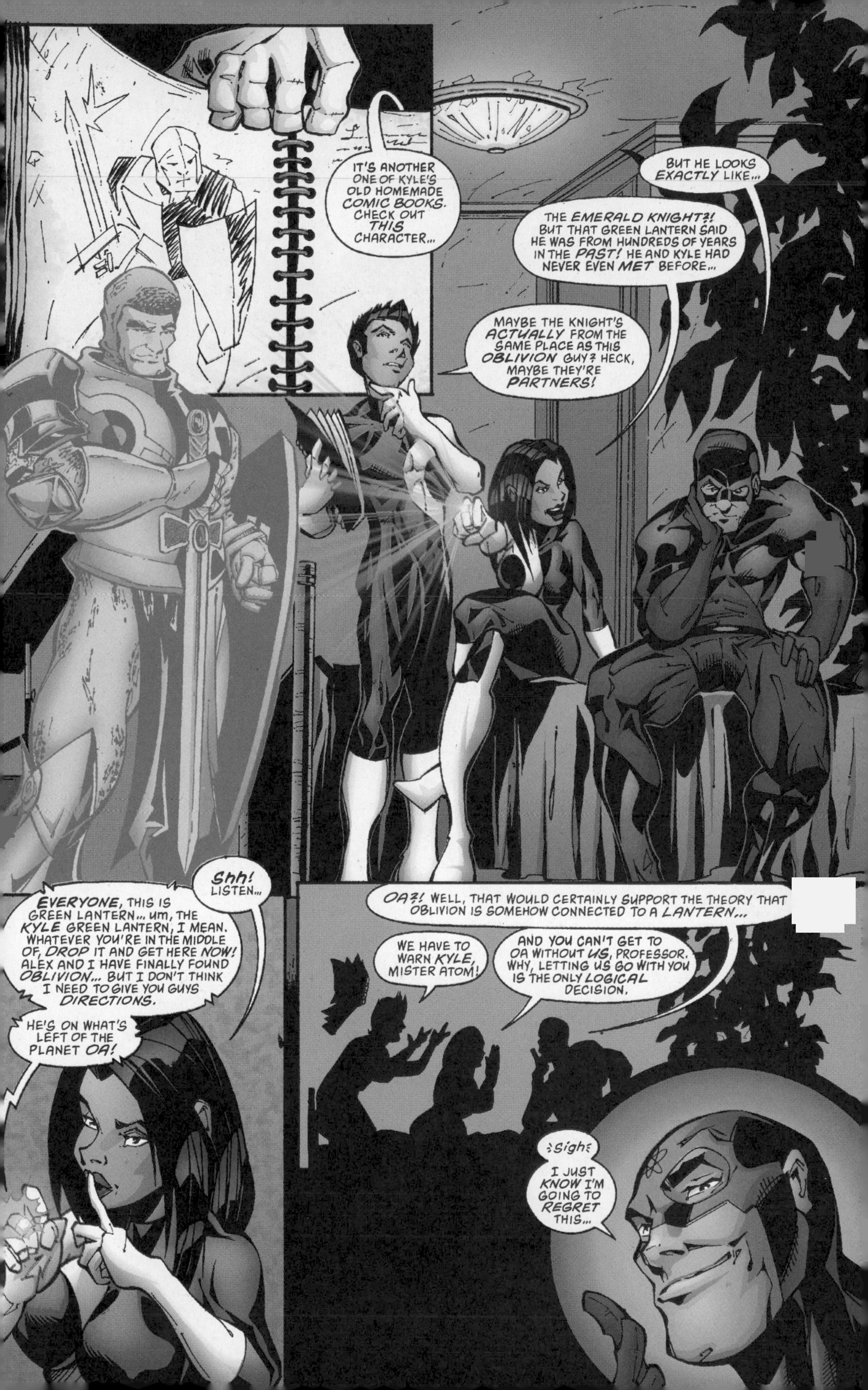
IT'S ANOTHER ONE OF KYLE'S OLD HOMEMADE COMIC BOOKS. CHECK OUT THIS CHARACTER...
BUT HE LOOKS EXACTLY LIKE...
THE EMERALD KNIGHT?! BUT THAT GREEN LANTERN SAID HE WAS FROM HUNDREDS OF YEARS IN THE PAST! HE AND KYLE HAD NEVER EVEN MET BEFORE...
MAYBE THE KNIGHT'S ACTUALLY FROM THE SAME PLACE AS THIS OBLIVION GUY? HECK, MAYBE THEY'RE PARTNERS!
Shh! LISTEN...
EVERYONE, THIS IS GREEN LANTERN... um, THE KYLE GREEN LANTERN, I MEAN. WHATEVER YOU'RE IN THE MIDDLE OF, DROP IT AND GET HERE NOW! ALEX AND I HAVE FINALLY FOUND OBLIVION... BUT I DON'T THINK I NEED TO GIVE YOU GUYS DIRECTIONS.
HE'S ON WHAT'S LEFT OF THE PLANET OA!
OA?! WELL, THAT WOULD CERTAINLY SUPPORT THE THEORY THAT OBLIVION IS SOMEHOW CONNECTED TO A LANTERN...
WE HAVE TO WARN KYLE, MISTER ATOM!
AND YOU CAN'T GET TO OA WITHOUT US, PROFESSOR. WHY, LETTING US GO WITH YOU IS THE ONLY LOGICAL DECISION.
Sigh
I JUST KNOW I'M GOING TO REGRET THIS...

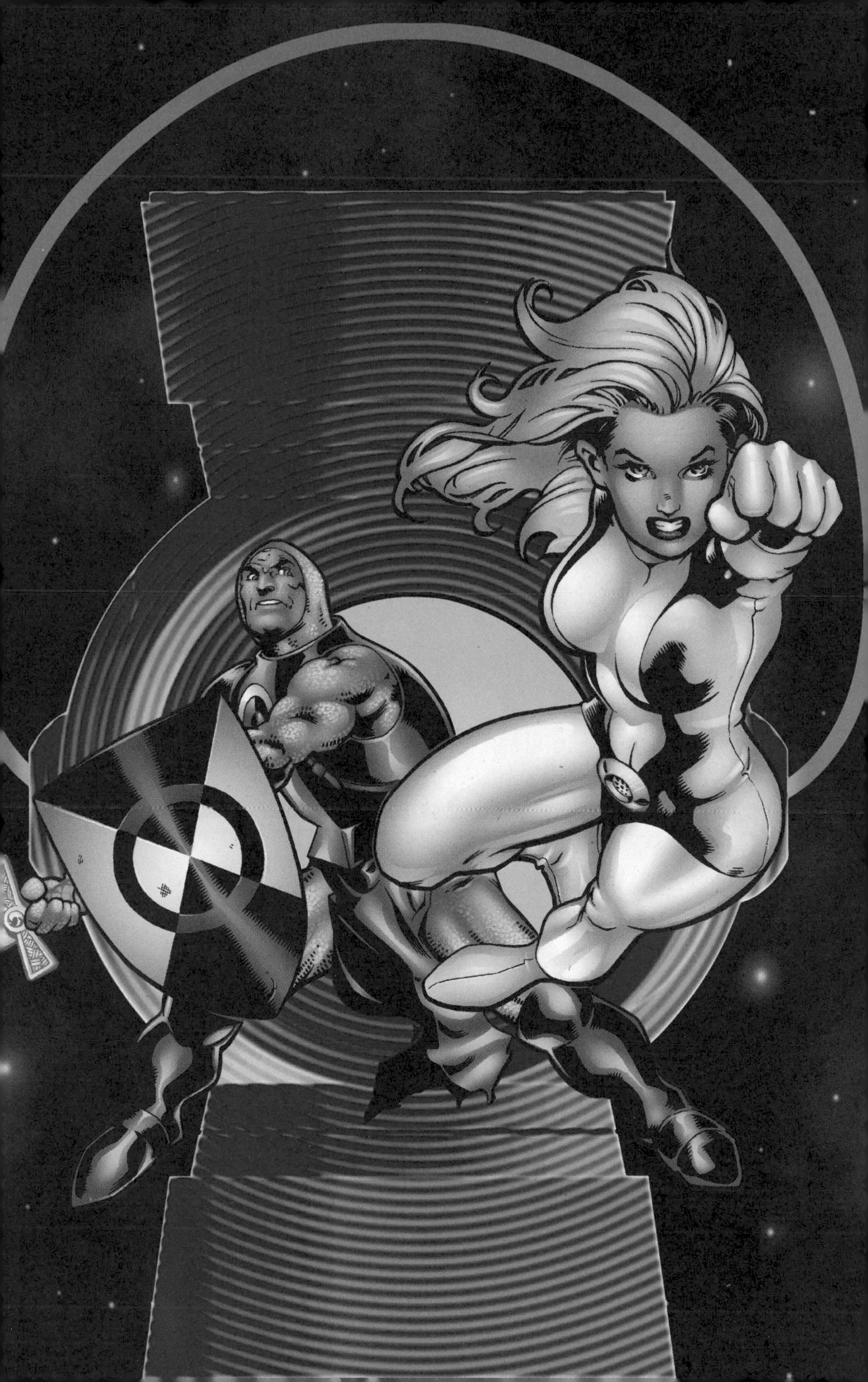

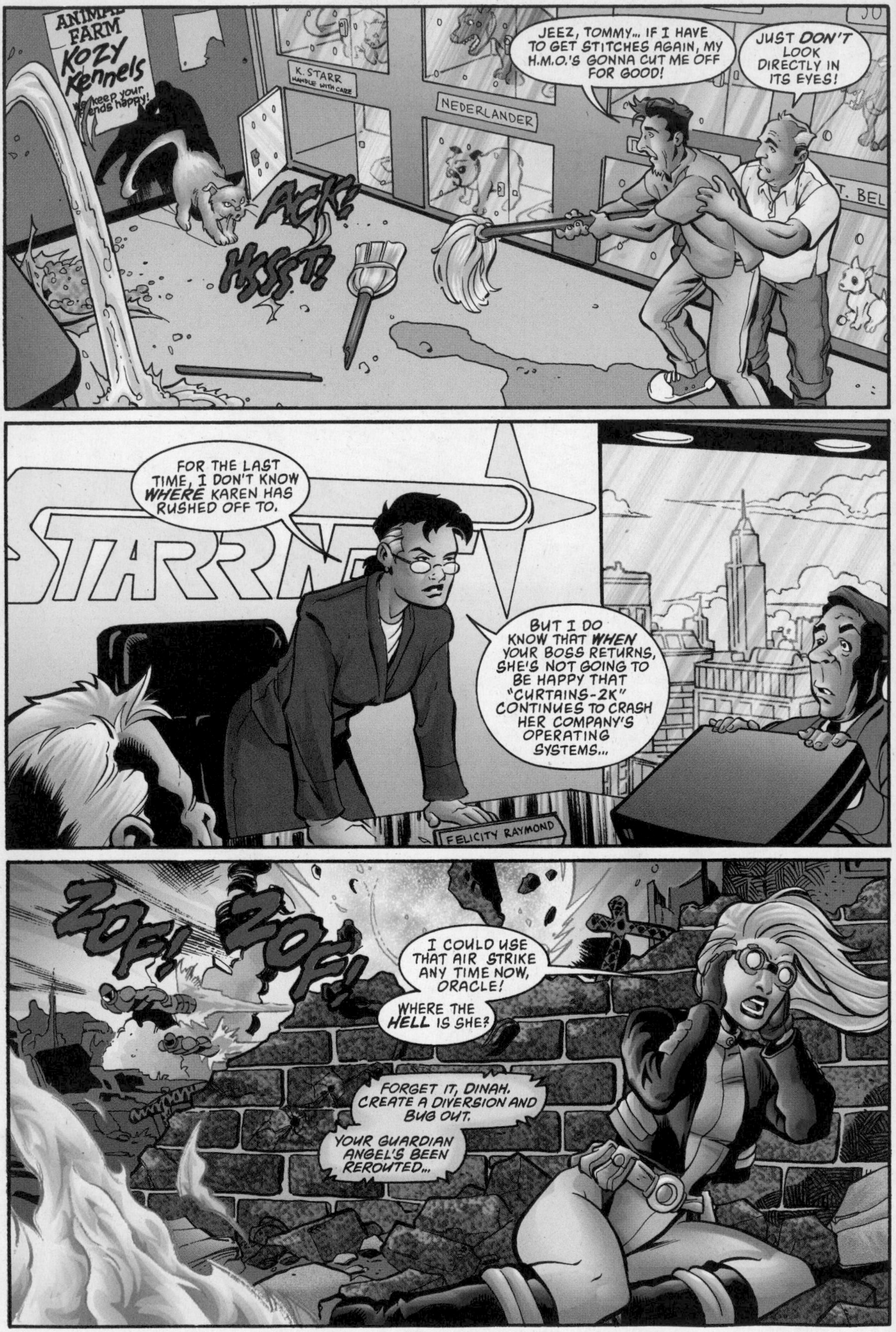
ANIMAL FARM
KOZY Kennels
We keep your friends happy!
K. STARR HANDLE WITH CARE
NEDERLANDER
JEEZ, TOMMY... IF I HAVE TO GET STITCHES AGAIN, MY H.M.O.'S GONNA CUT ME OFF FOR GOOD!
JUST DON'T LOOK DIRECTLY IN ITS EYES!
ACK!
HSSST!
FOR THE LAST TIME, I DON'T KNOW WHERE KAREN HAS RUSHED OFF TO.
BUT I DO KNOW THAT WHEN YOUR BOSS RETURNS, SHE'S NOT GOING TO BE HAPPY THAT "CURTAINS-2K" CONTINUES TO CRASH HER COMPANY'S OPERATING SYSTEMS...
FELICITY RAYMOND
ZOF! ZOF!
I COULD USE THAT AIR STRIKE ANY TIME NOW, ORACLE!
WHERE THE HELL IS SHE?
FORGET IT, DINAH. CREATE A DIVERSION AND BUG OUT.
YOUR GUARDIAN ANGEL'S BEEN REROUTED...

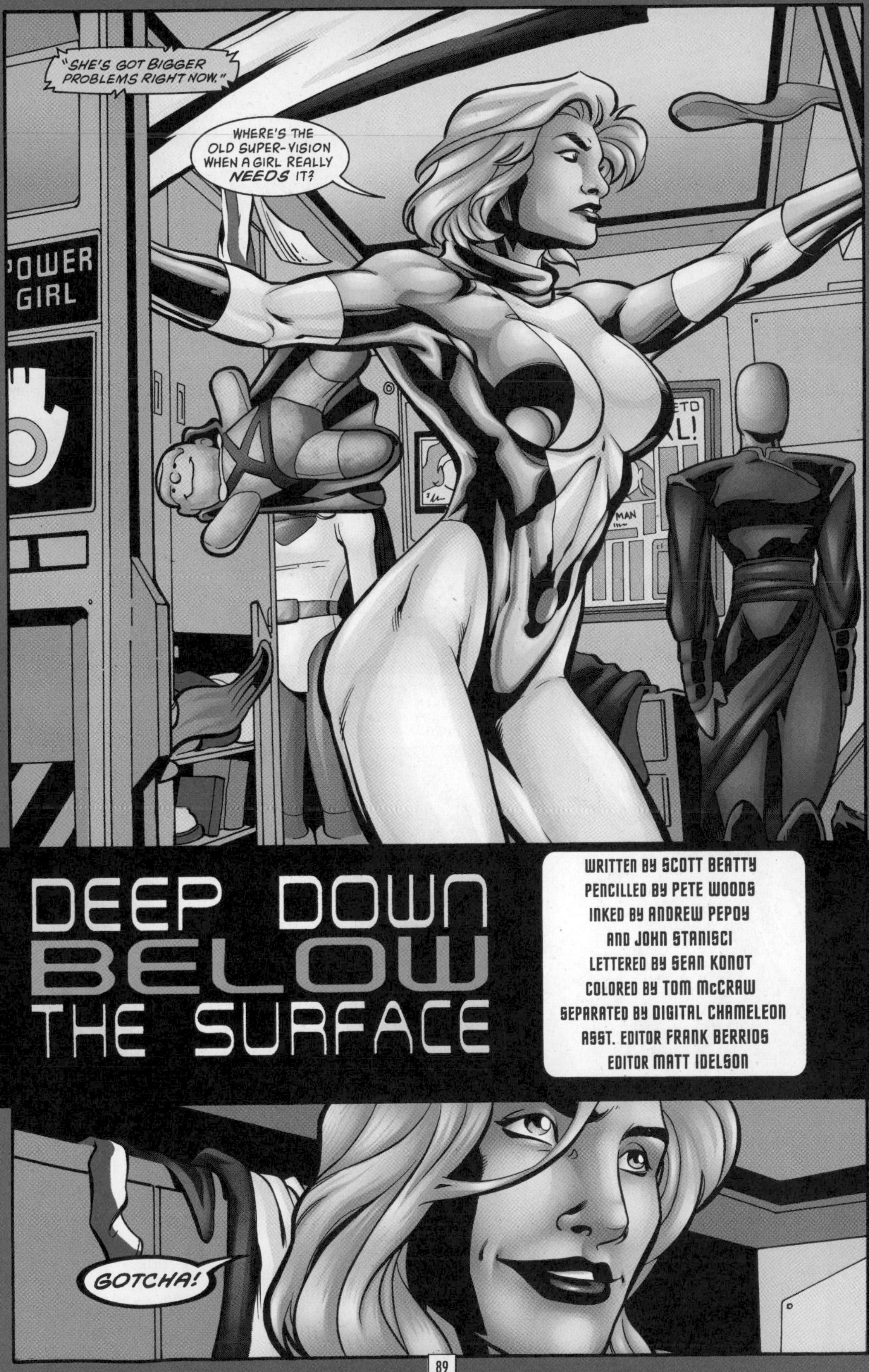
"SHE'S GOT BIGGER PROBLEMS RIGHT NOW."
WHERE'S THE OLD SUPER-VISION WHEN A GIRL REALLY NEEDS IT?
POWER GIRL
DEEP DOWN BELOW THE SURFACE
WRITTEN BY SCOTT BEATTY
PENCILLED BY PETE WOODS
INKED BY ANDREW PEPOY AND JOHN STANISCI
LETTERED BY SEAN KONOT
COLORED BY TOM McCRAW
SEPARATED BY DIGITAL CHAMELEON
ASST. EDITOR FRANK BERRIOS
EDITOR MATT IDELSON
GOTCHA!

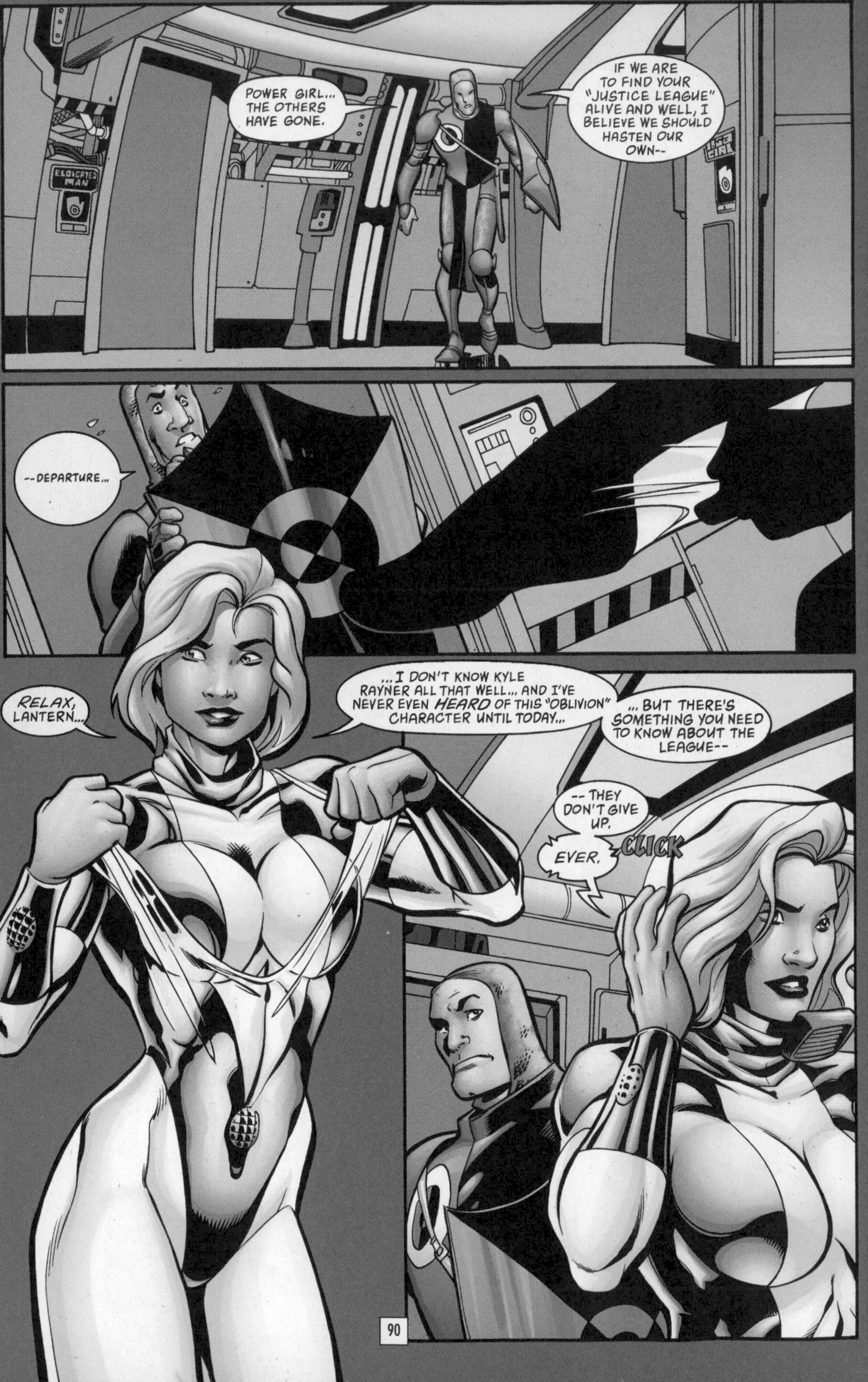
POWER GIRL... THE OTHERS HAVE GONE.
IF WE ARE TO FIND YOUR "JUSTICE LEAGUE" ALIVE AND WELL, I BELIEVE WE SHOULD HASTEN OUR OWN--
ELONGATED MAN
--DEPARTURE...
RELAX, LANTERN...
...I DON'T KNOW KYLE RAYNER ALL THAT WELL... AND I'VE NEVER EVEN HEARD OF THIS "OBLIVION" CHARACTER UNTIL TODAY...
...BUT THERE'S SOMETHING YOU NEED TO KNOW ABOUT THE LEAGUE--
--THEY DON'T GIVE UP.
EVER.
CLICK

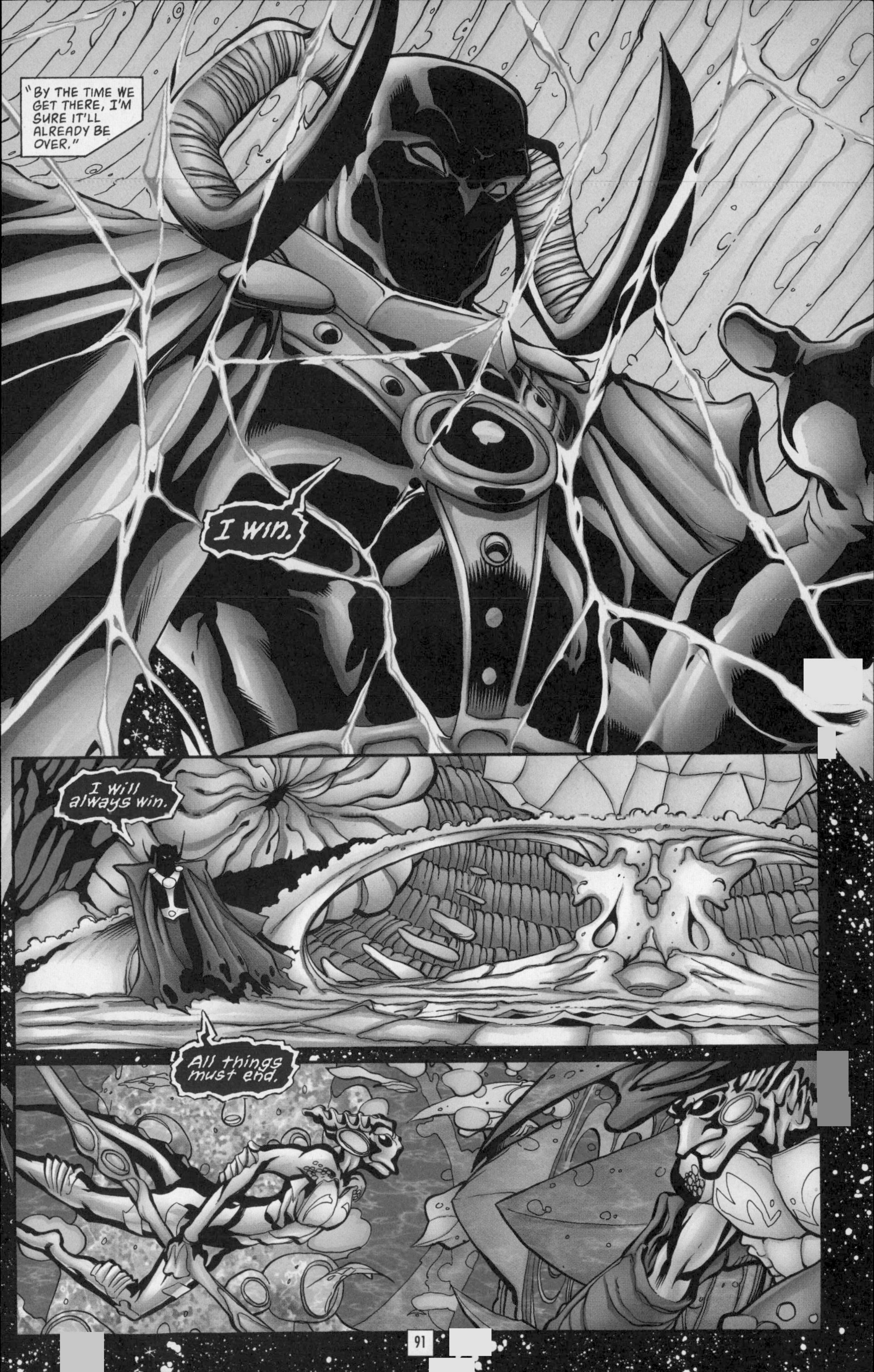
"BY THE TIME WE GET THERE, I'M SURE IT'LL ALREADY BE OVER."
I win.
I will always win.
All things must end.

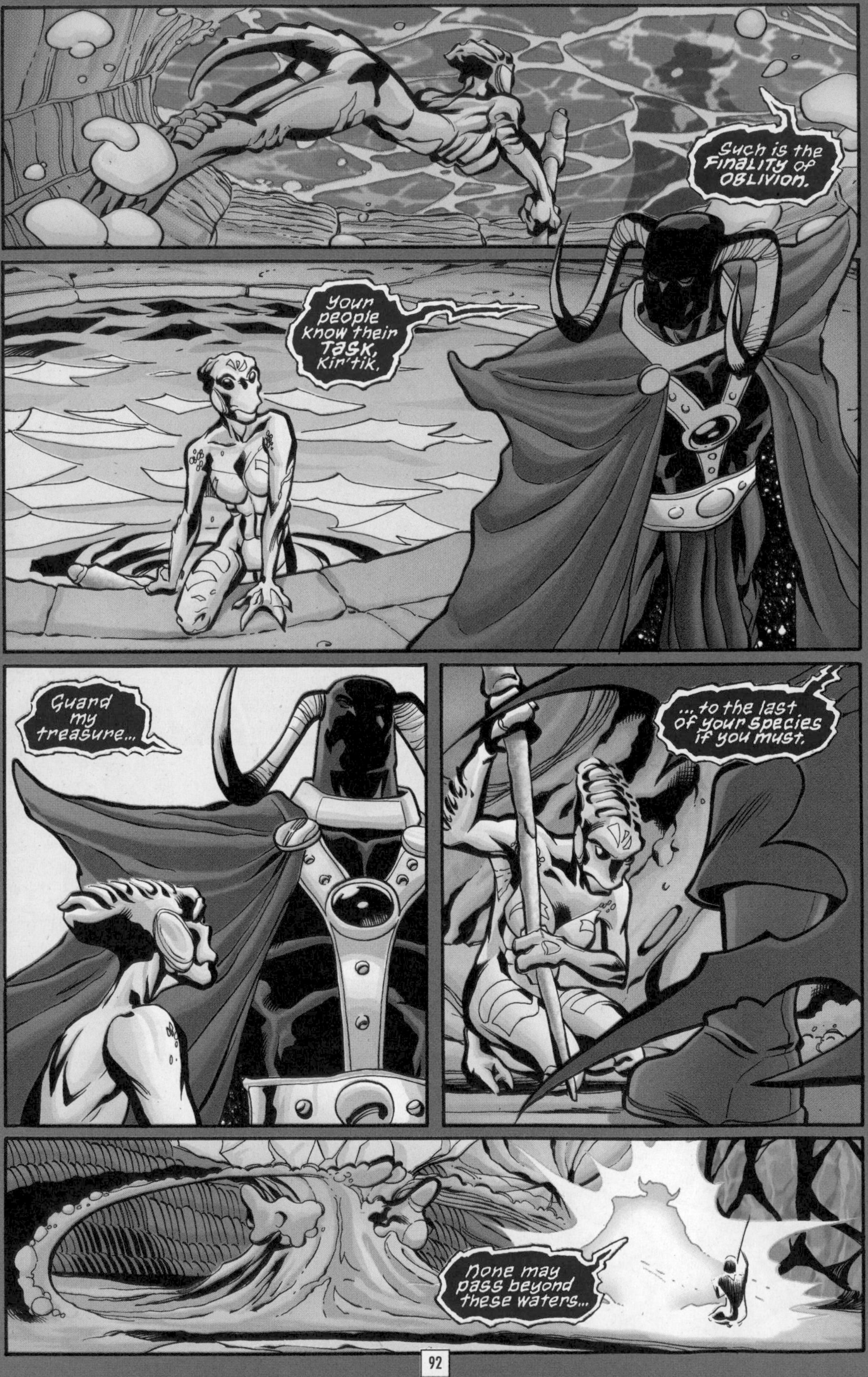
Such is the FINALITY of OBLIVION.
Your people know their TASK, Kir'tik.
Guard my treasure...
...to the last of your species if you must.
None may pass beyond these waters...

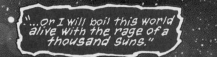

"...Or I will boil this world alive with the rage of a thousand suns."

CATCH SOME RAYS ON YOUR *OWN* TIME, LANTERN. WE NEED TO MAKE TRACKS.

I THOUGHT IT BEST TO... *RECHARGE.*

DON'T YOU NEED A *POWER BATTERY* FOR THAT?

THE SOLAR WIND OF YOUR YELLOW STAR GIVES ME ADDED STRENGTH.

RIGHT. YOU'RE A DAXAMITE *AND* A GREEN LANTERN. THERE'S GOTTA BE A *PUNCH-LINE* IN THAT.

EITHER WAY, YOU'RE GOING TO HAVE TO GIVE ME A LIFT OUT TO DEEP SPACE, OR I'LL USE UP ALL *MY* POWER JUST GETTING THERE.

AND I'M *NOT* RELYING ON ANY *COLOR-BIASED* COSTUME JEWELRY TO KEEP ME FROM BREATHING IN A VACUUM.

SO FORGET THE GREEN BUBBLES.

I DON'T DO ENCLOSED SPACES REAL WELL.

EARLY CHILDHOOD TRAUMA AND ALL THAT.

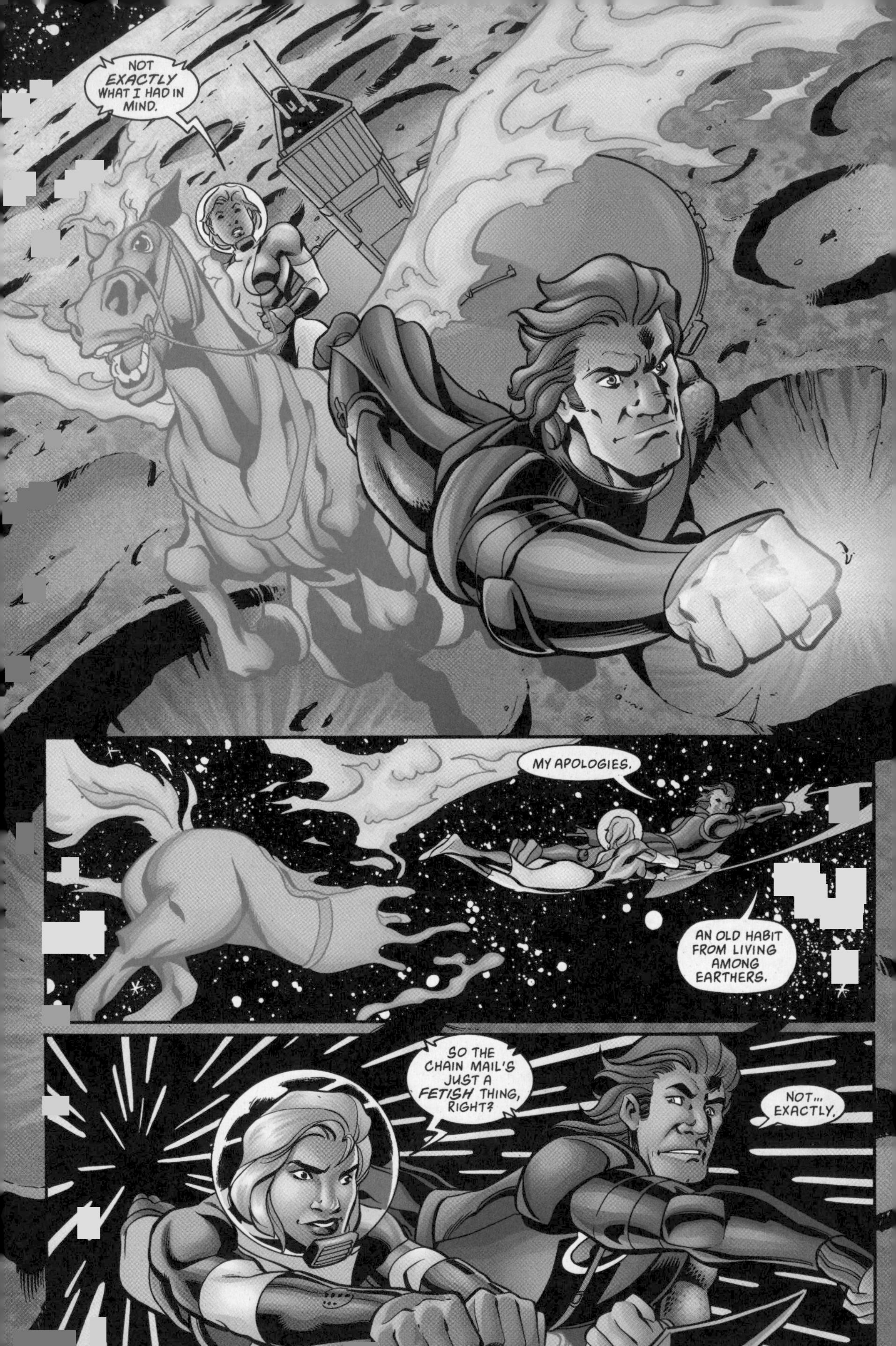
NOT EXACTLY WHAT I HAD IN MIND.
MY APOLOGIES.
AN OLD HABIT FROM LIVING AMONG EARTHERS.
SO THE CHAIN MAIL'S JUST A FETISH THING, RIGHT?
NOT... EXACTLY.

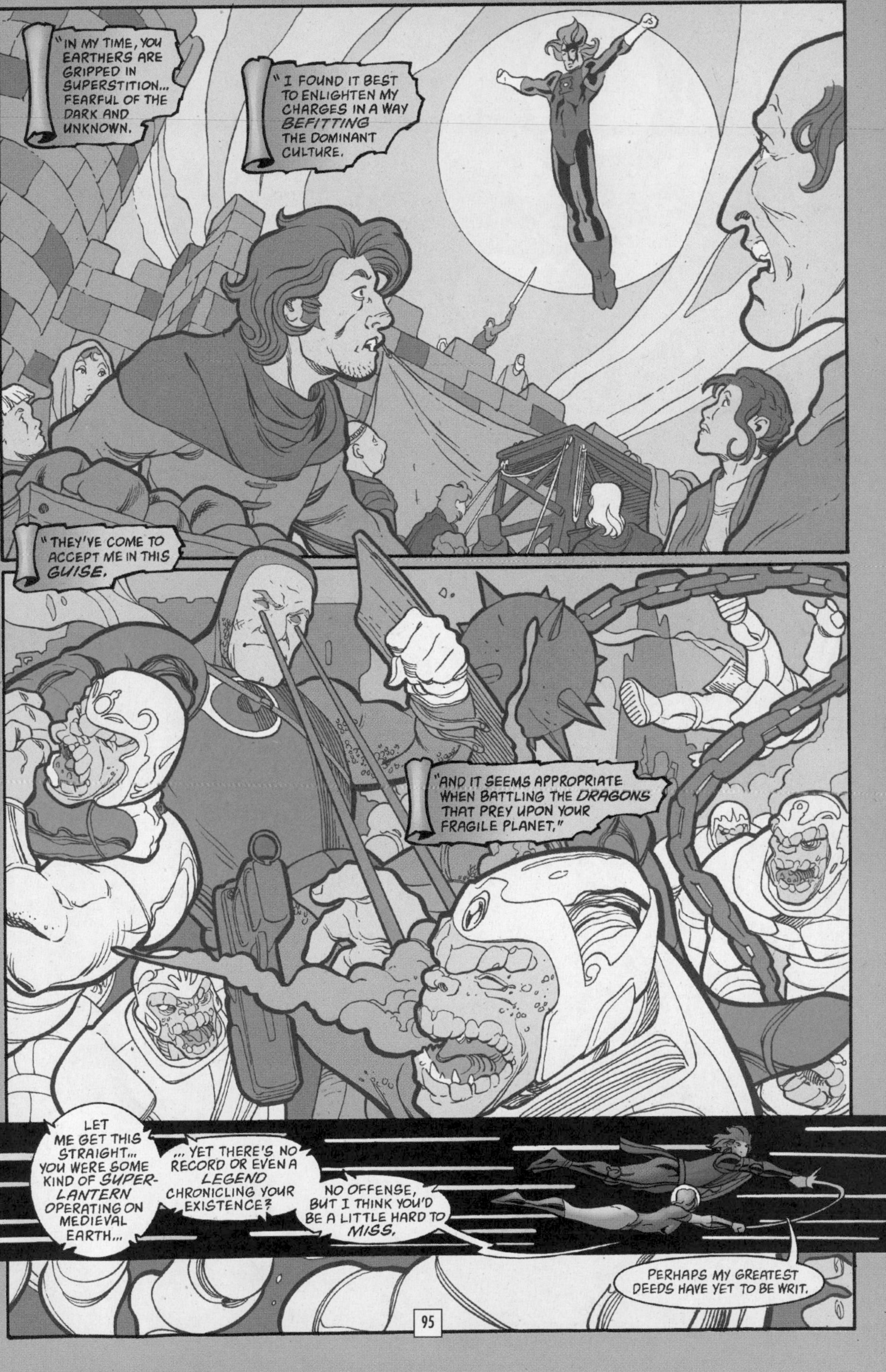
"IN MY TIME, YOU EARTHERS ARE GRIPPED IN SUPERSTITION... FEARFUL OF THE DARK AND UNKNOWN.
"I FOUND IT BEST TO ENLIGHTEN MY CHARGES IN A WAY BEFITTING THE DOMINANT CULTURE.
"THEY'VE COME TO ACCEPT ME IN THIS GUISE.
"AND IT SEEMS APPROPRIATE WHEN BATTLING THE DRAGONS THAT PREY UPON YOUR FRAGILE PLANET."
LET ME GET THIS STRAIGHT... YOU WERE SOME KIND OF SUPER-LANTERN OPERATING ON MEDIEVAL EARTH...
...YET THERE'S NO RECORD OR EVEN A LEGEND CHRONICLING YOUR EXISTENCE?
NO OFFENSE, BUT I THINK YOU'D BE A LITTLE HARD TO MISS.
PERHAPS MY GREATEST DEEDS HAVE YET TO BE WRIT.

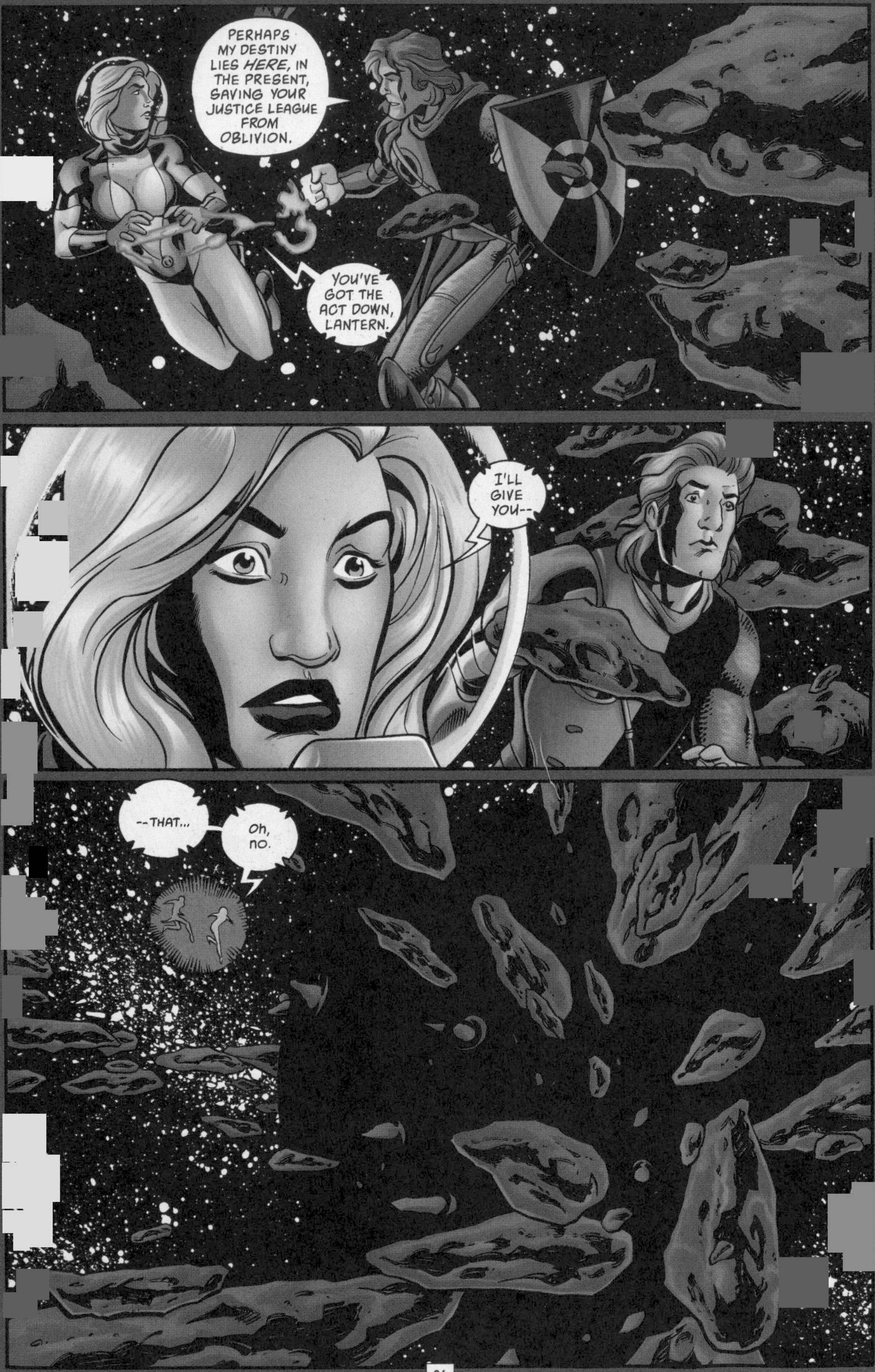
PERHAPS MY DESTINY LIES *HERE*, IN THE PRESENT, SAVING YOUR JUSTICE LEAGUE FROM OBLIVION.
YOU'VE GOT THE ACT DOWN, LANTERN.
I'LL GIVE YOU--
--THAT...
Oh, no.

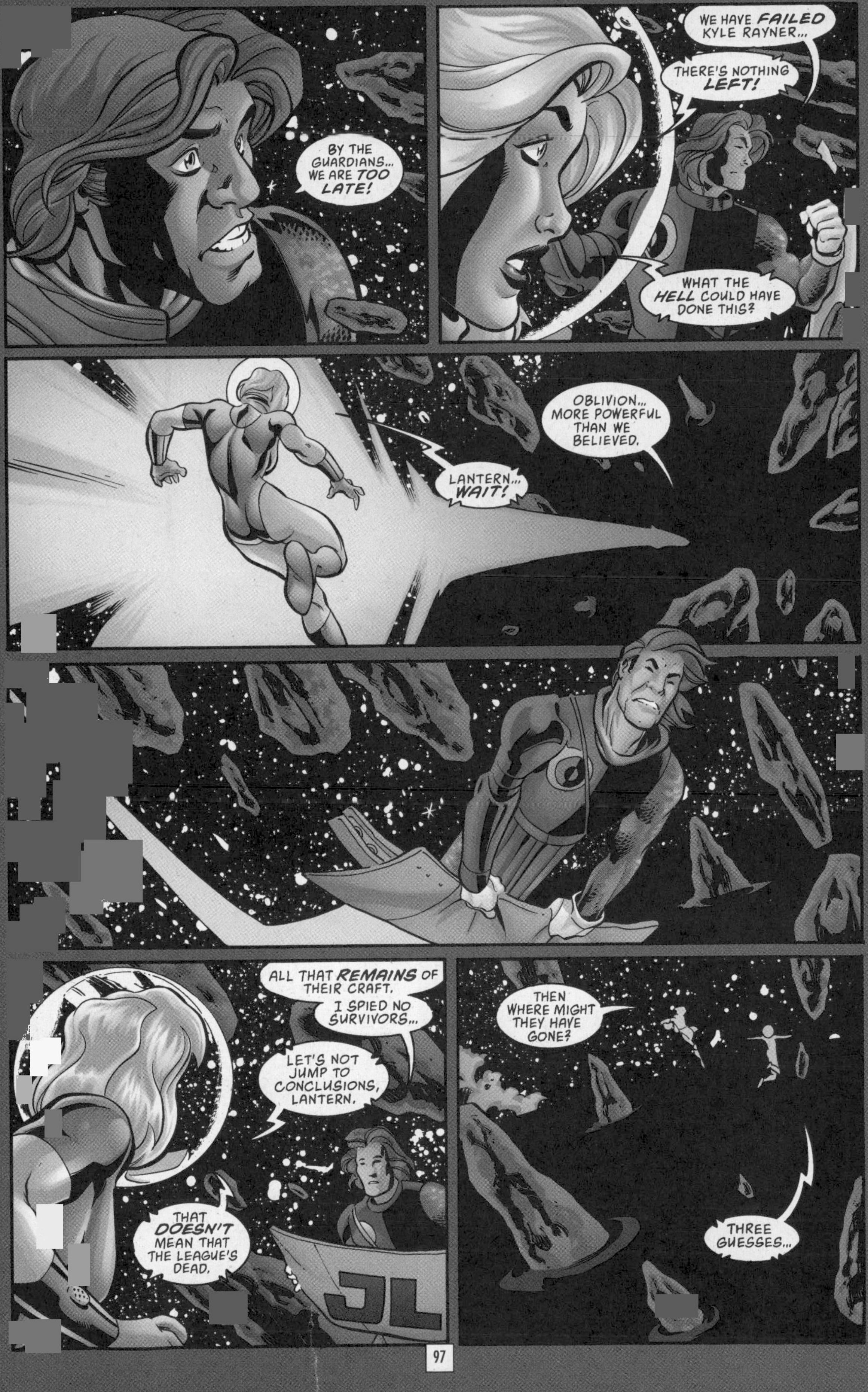
BY THE GUARDIANS... WE ARE *TOO LATE!*
WE HAVE *FAILED* KYLE RAYNER...
THERE'S NOTHING *LEFT!*
WHAT THE *HELL* COULD HAVE DONE THIS?
OBLIVION... MORE POWERFUL THAN WE BELIEVED.
LANTERN... *WAIT!*
ALL THAT *REMAINS* OF THEIR CRAFT.
I SPIED NO SURVIVORS...
LET'S NOT JUMP TO CONCLUSIONS, LANTERN.
THAT *DOESN'T* MEAN THAT THE LEAGUE'S DEAD.
JL
THEN WHERE MIGHT THEY HAVE GONE?
THREE GUESSES...

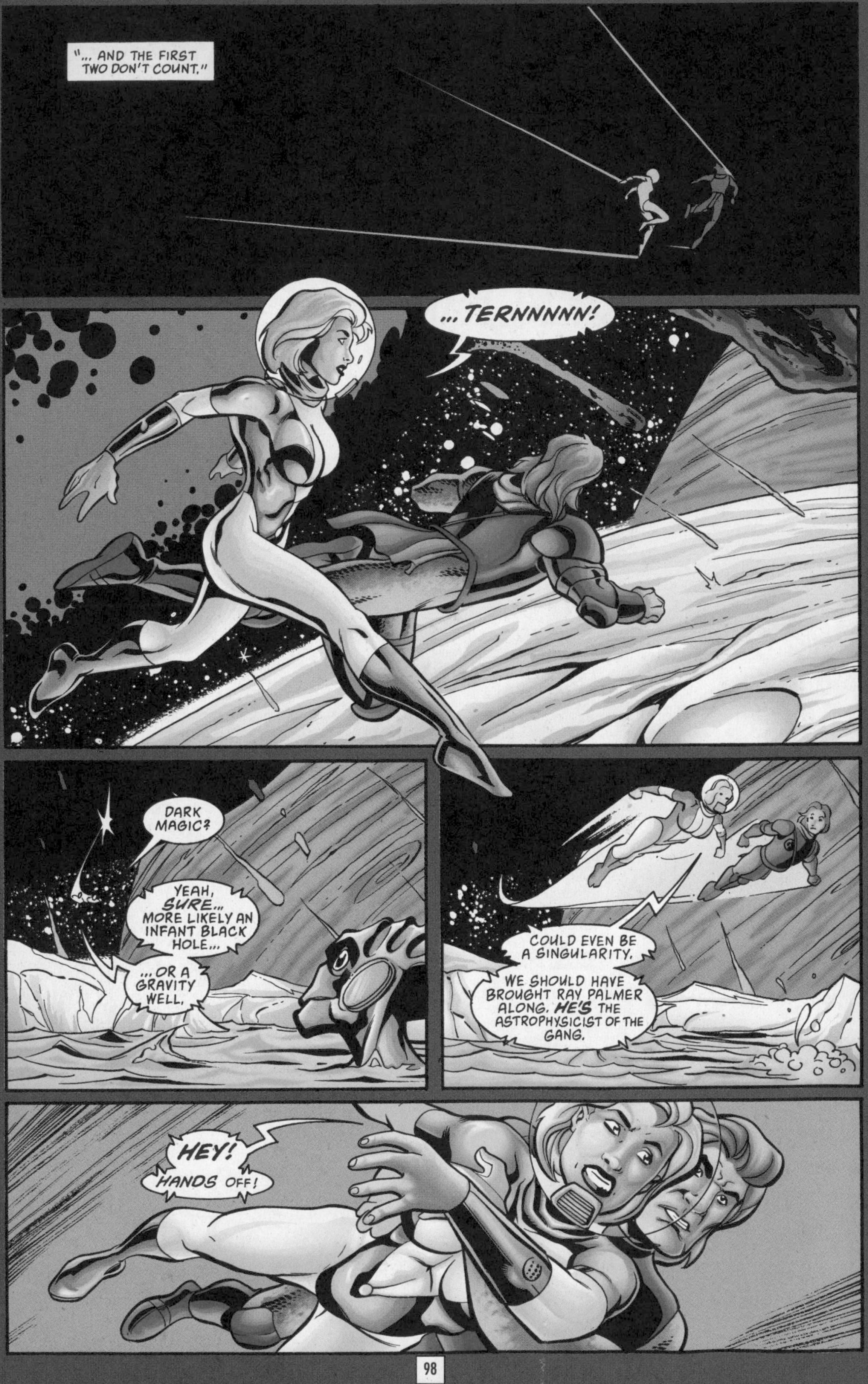
"... AND THE FIRST TWO DON'T COUNT."
... TERNNNNN!
DARK MAGIC?
YEAH, SURE... MORE LIKELY AN INFANT BLACK HOLE...
... OR A GRAVITY WELL.
COULD EVEN BE A SINGULARITY.
WE SHOULD HAVE BROUGHT RAY PALMER ALONG. HE'S THE ASTROPHYSICIST OF THE GANG.
HEY! HANDS OFF!

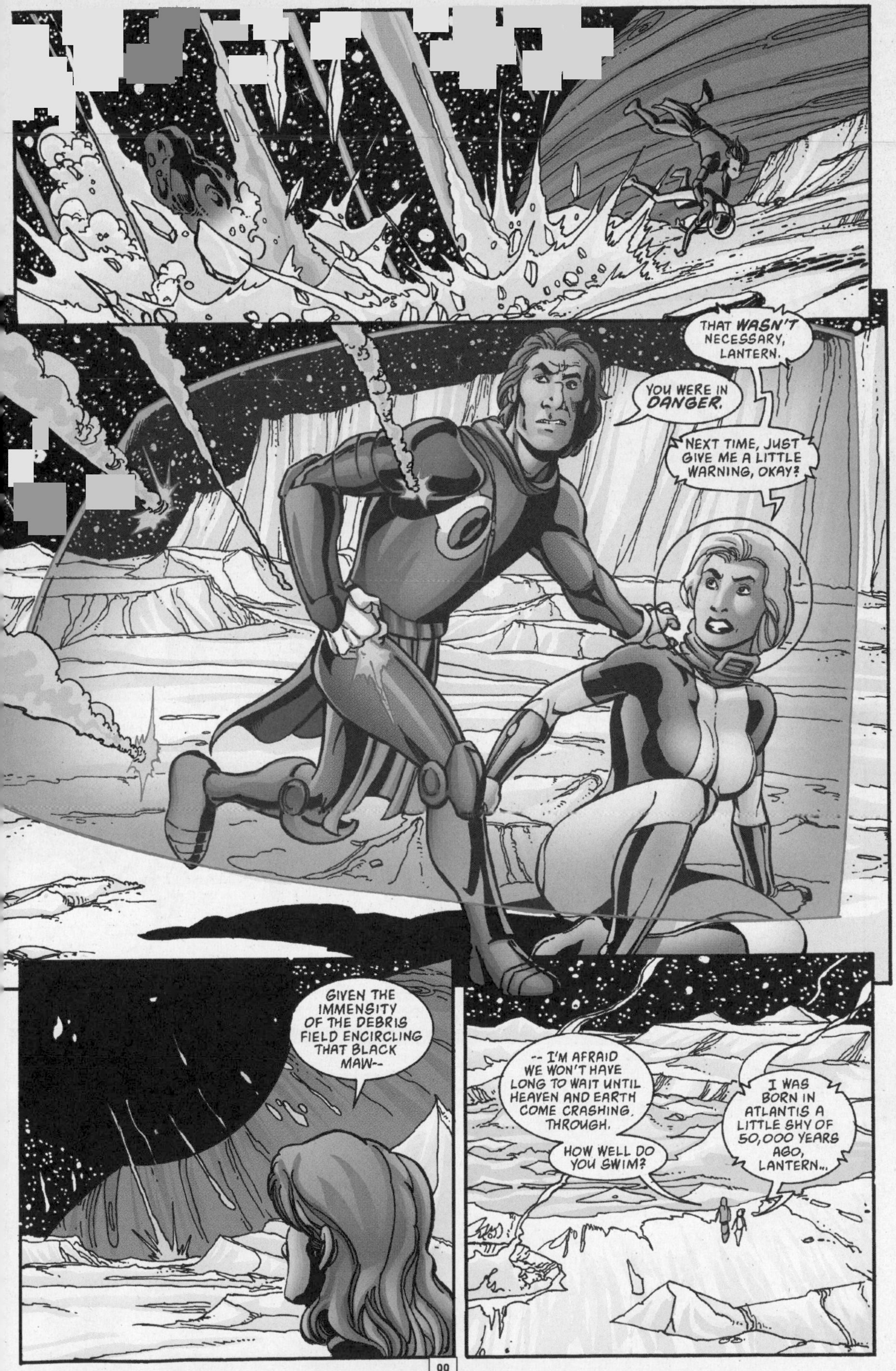
THAT WASN'T NECESSARY, LANTERN.
YOU WERE IN DANGER.
NEXT TIME, JUST GIVE ME A LITTLE WARNING, OKAY?
GIVEN THE IMMENSITY OF THE DEBRIS FIELD ENCIRCLING THAT BLACK MAW--
-- I'M AFRAID WE WON'T HAVE LONG TO WAIT UNTIL HEAVEN AND EARTH COME CRASHING THROUGH.
HOW WELL DO YOU SWIM?
I WAS BORN IN ATLANTIS A LITTLE SHY OF 50,000 YEARS AGO, LANTERN...

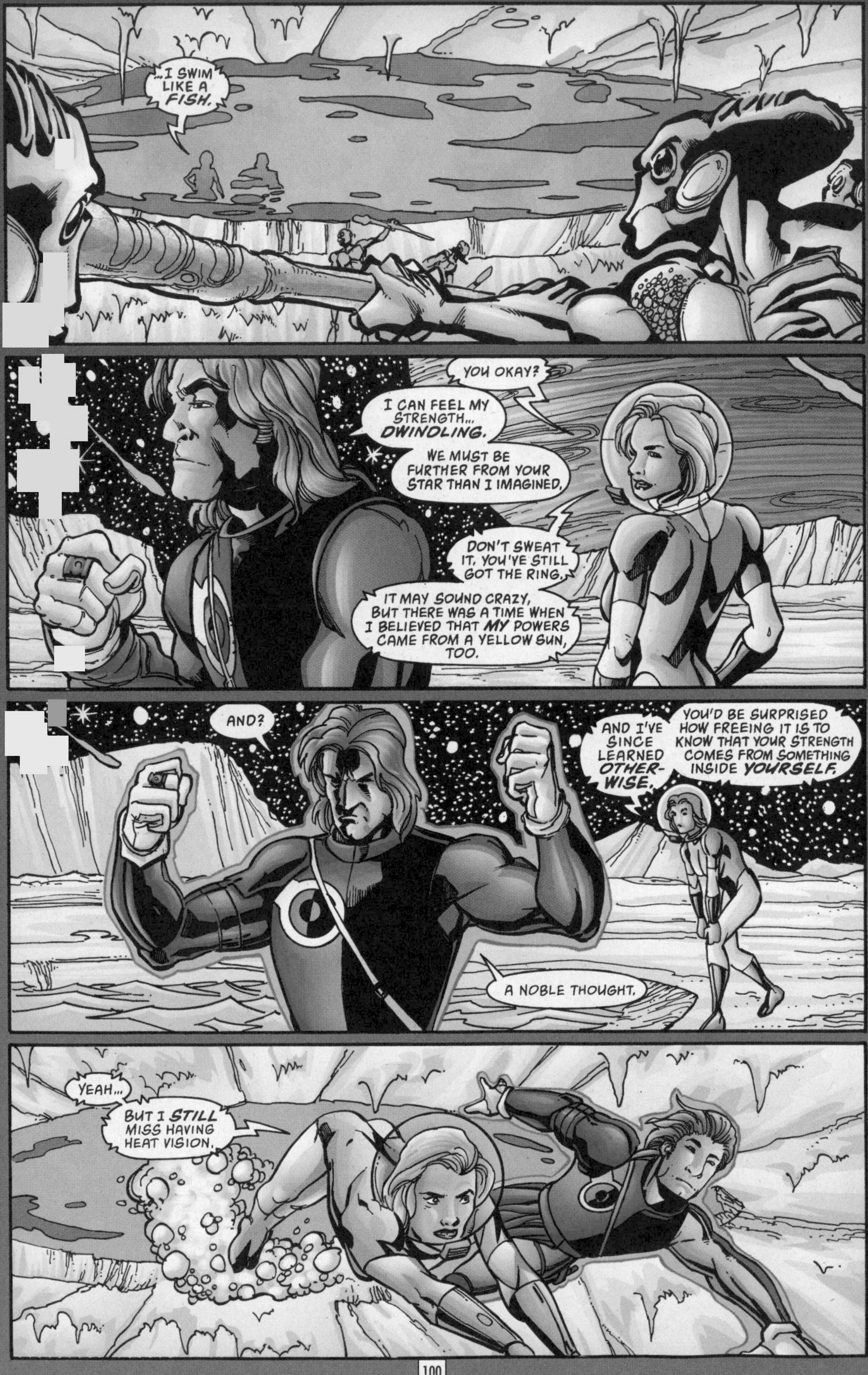
...I SWIM LIKE A FISH.
YOU OKAY?
I CAN FEEL MY STRENGTH... DWINDLING.
WE MUST BE FURTHER FROM YOUR STAR THAN I IMAGINED.
DON'T SWEAT IT. YOU'VE STILL GOT THE RING.
IT MAY SOUND CRAZY, BUT THERE WAS A TIME WHEN I BELIEVED THAT MY POWERS CAME FROM A YELLOW SUN, TOO.
AND?
AND I'VE SINCE LEARNED OTHER-WISE.
YOU'D BE SURPRISED HOW FREEING IT IS TO KNOW THAT YOUR STRENGTH COMES FROM SOMETHING INSIDE YOURSELF.
A NOBLE THOUGHT.
YEAH...
BUT I STILL MISS HAVING HEAT VISION.

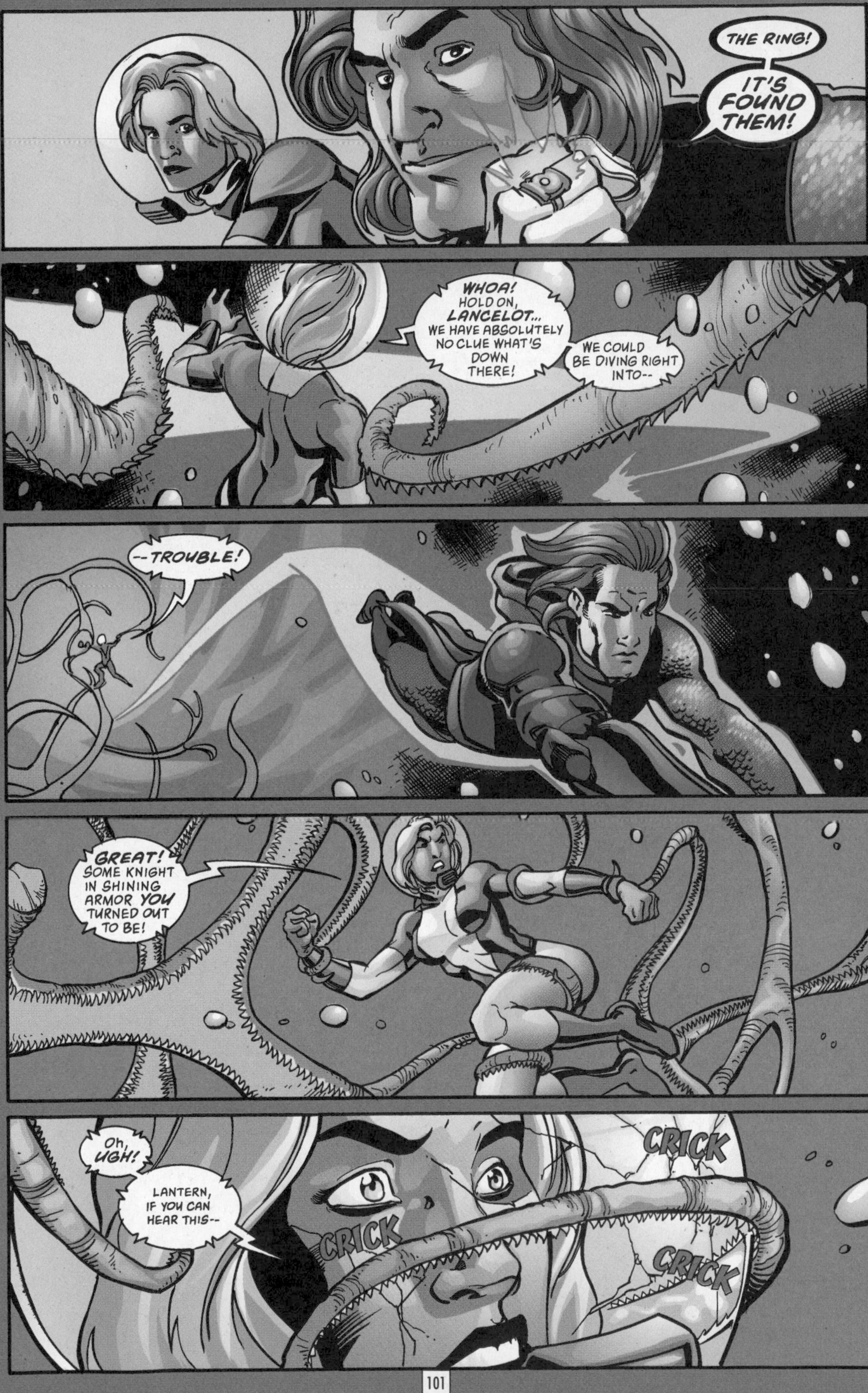
THE RING!
IT'S FOUND THEM!
WHOA! HOLD ON, LANCELOT... WE HAVE ABSOLUTELY NO CLUE WHAT'S DOWN THERE!
WE COULD BE DIVING RIGHT INTO--
--TROUBLE!
GREAT! SOME KNIGHT IN SHINING ARMOR YOU TURNED OUT TO BE!
Oh, UGH!
LANTERN, IF YOU CAN HEAR THIS--
CRICK
CRICK
CRICK

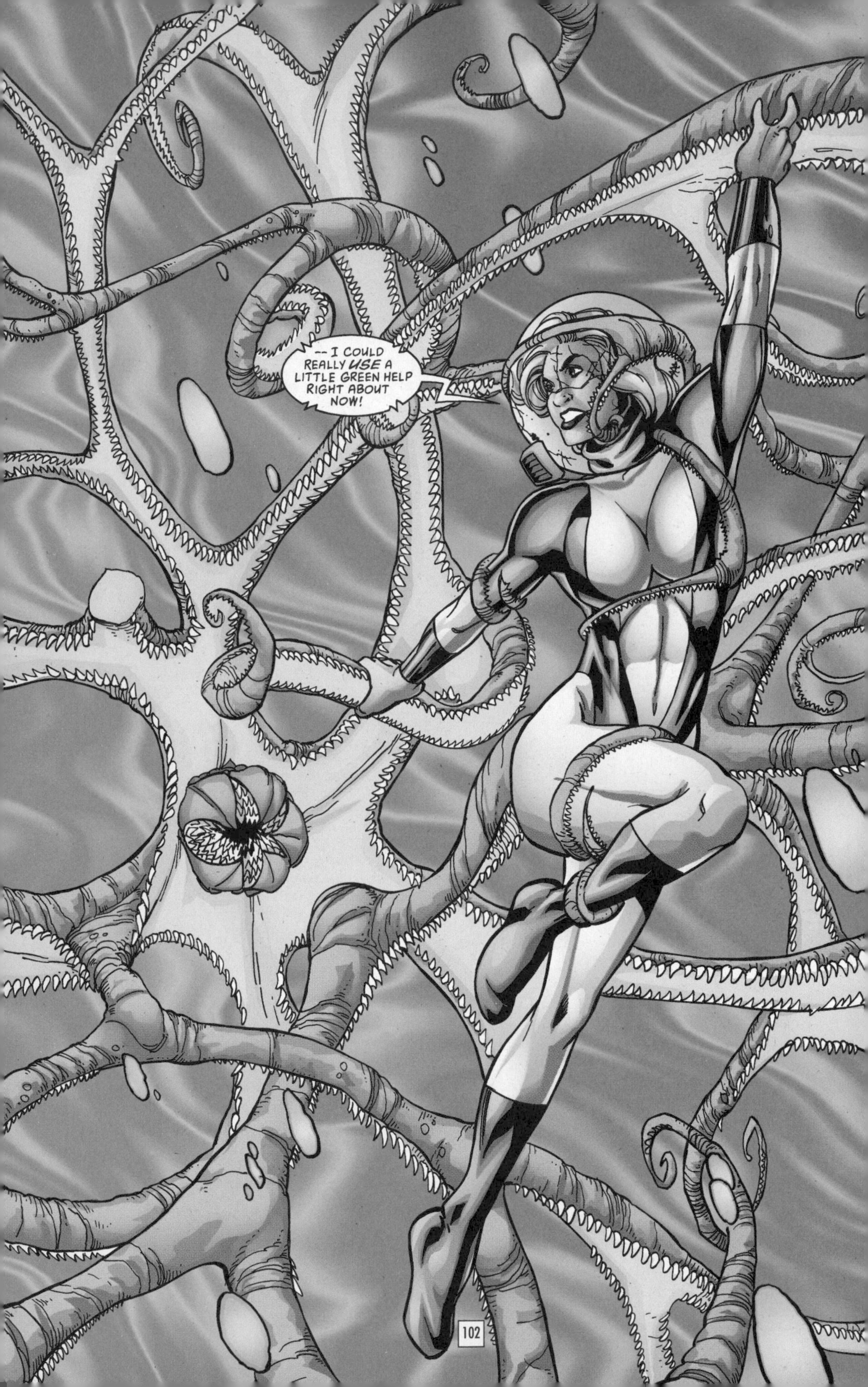
--I COULD REALLY USE A LITTLE GREEN HELP RIGHT ABOUT NOW!

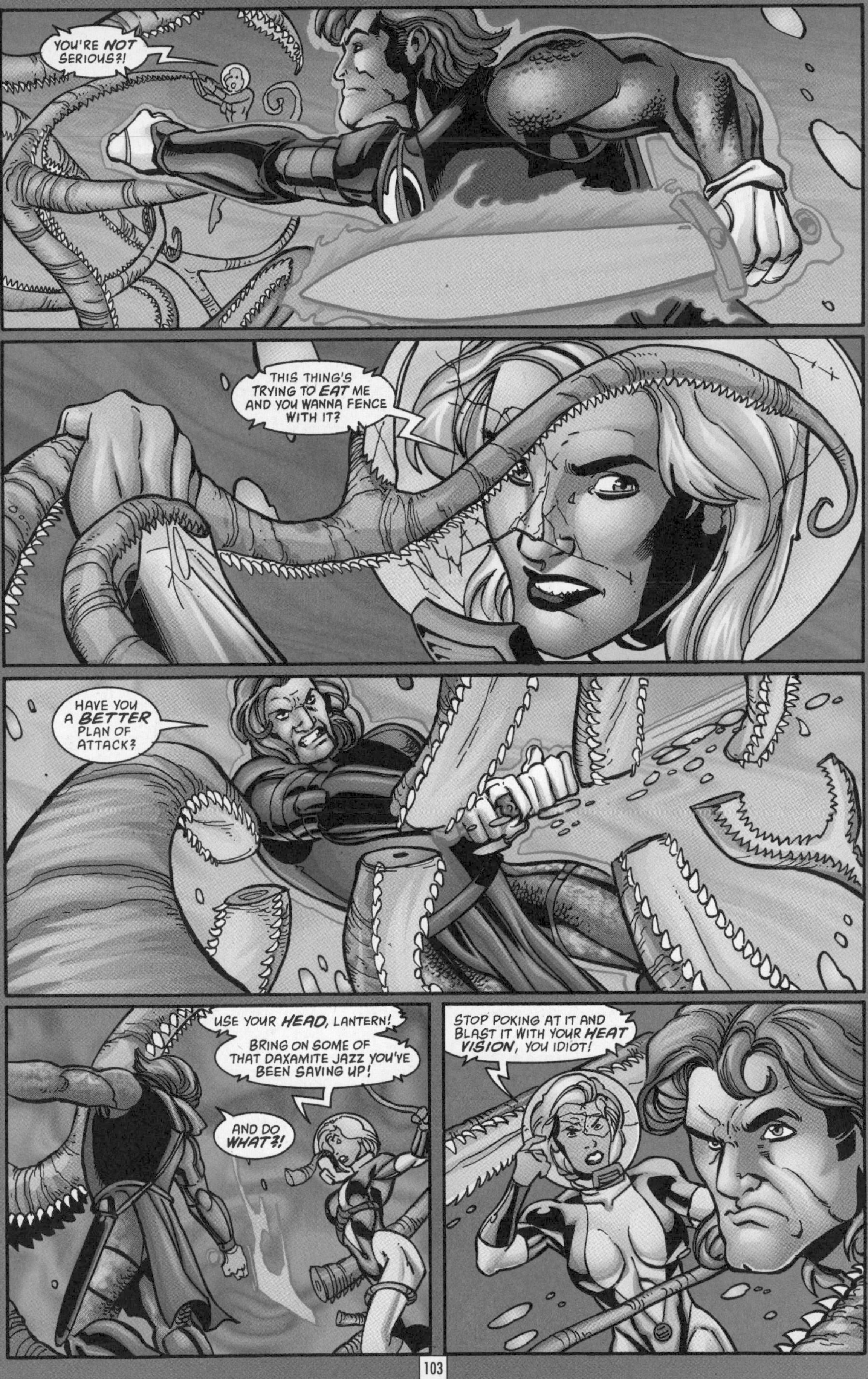
YOU'RE NOT SERIOUS?!
THIS THING'S TRYING TO EAT ME AND YOU WANNA FENCE WITH IT?
HAVE YOU A BETTER PLAN OF ATTACK?
USE YOUR HEAD, LANTERN!
BRING ON SOME OF THAT DAXAMITE JAZZ YOU'VE BEEN SAVING UP!
AND DO WHAT?!
STOP POKING AT IT AND BLAST IT WITH YOUR HEAT VISION, YOU IDIOT!

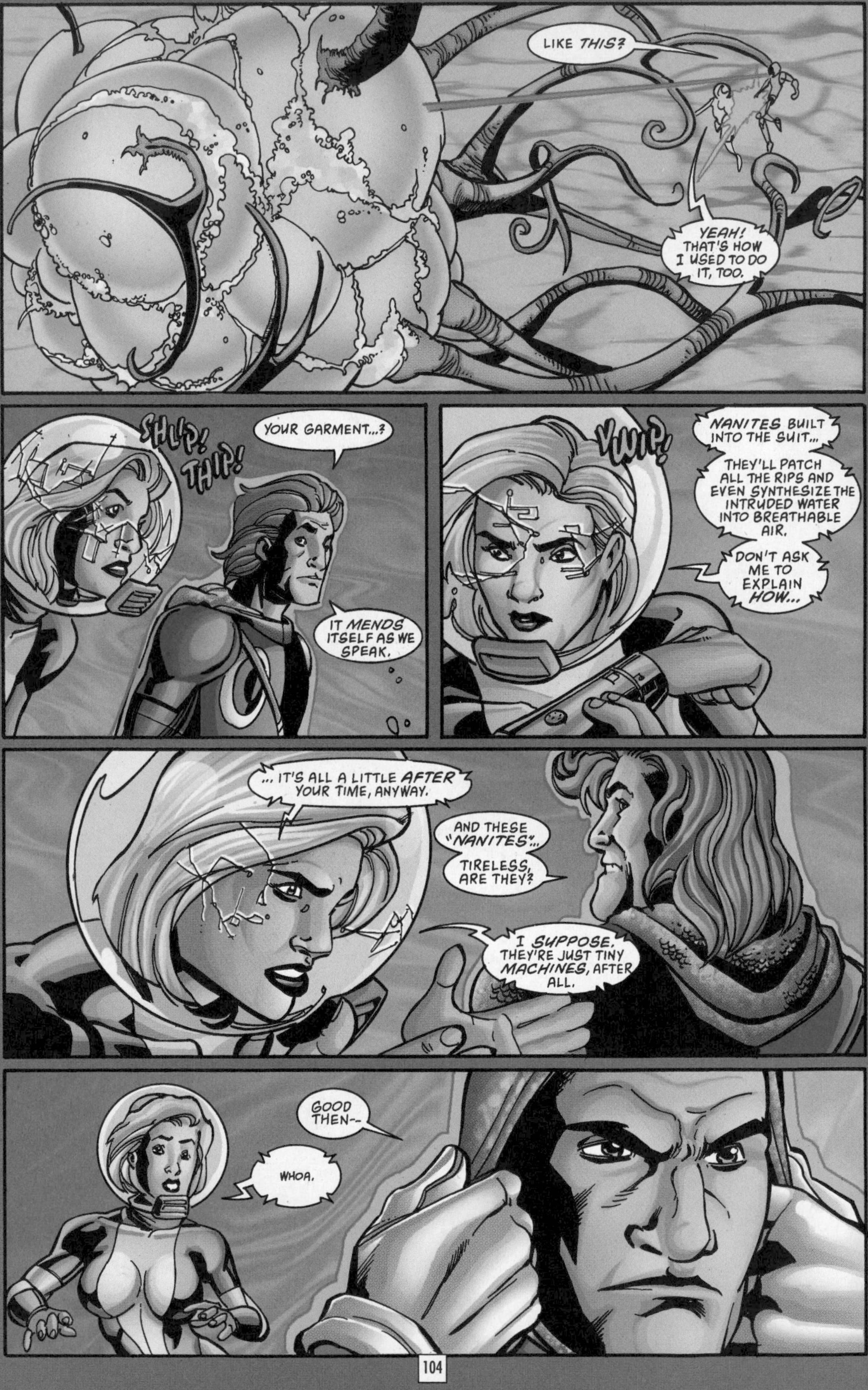
LIKE THIS?
YEAH! THAT'S HOW I USED TO DO IT, TOO.
SHLIP! THIP!
YOUR GARMENT...?
IT MENDS ITSELF AS WE SPEAK.
VWIP!
NANITES BUILT INTO THE SUIT...
THEY'LL PATCH ALL THE RIPS AND EVEN SYNTHESIZE THE INTRUDED WATER INTO BREATHABLE AIR.
DON'T ASK ME TO EXPLAIN HOW...
... IT'S ALL A LITTLE AFTER YOUR TIME, ANYWAY.
AND THESE "NANITES"... TIRELESS, ARE THEY?
I SUPPOSE. THEY'RE JUST TINY MACHINES, AFTER ALL.
GOOD THEN--
WHOA.

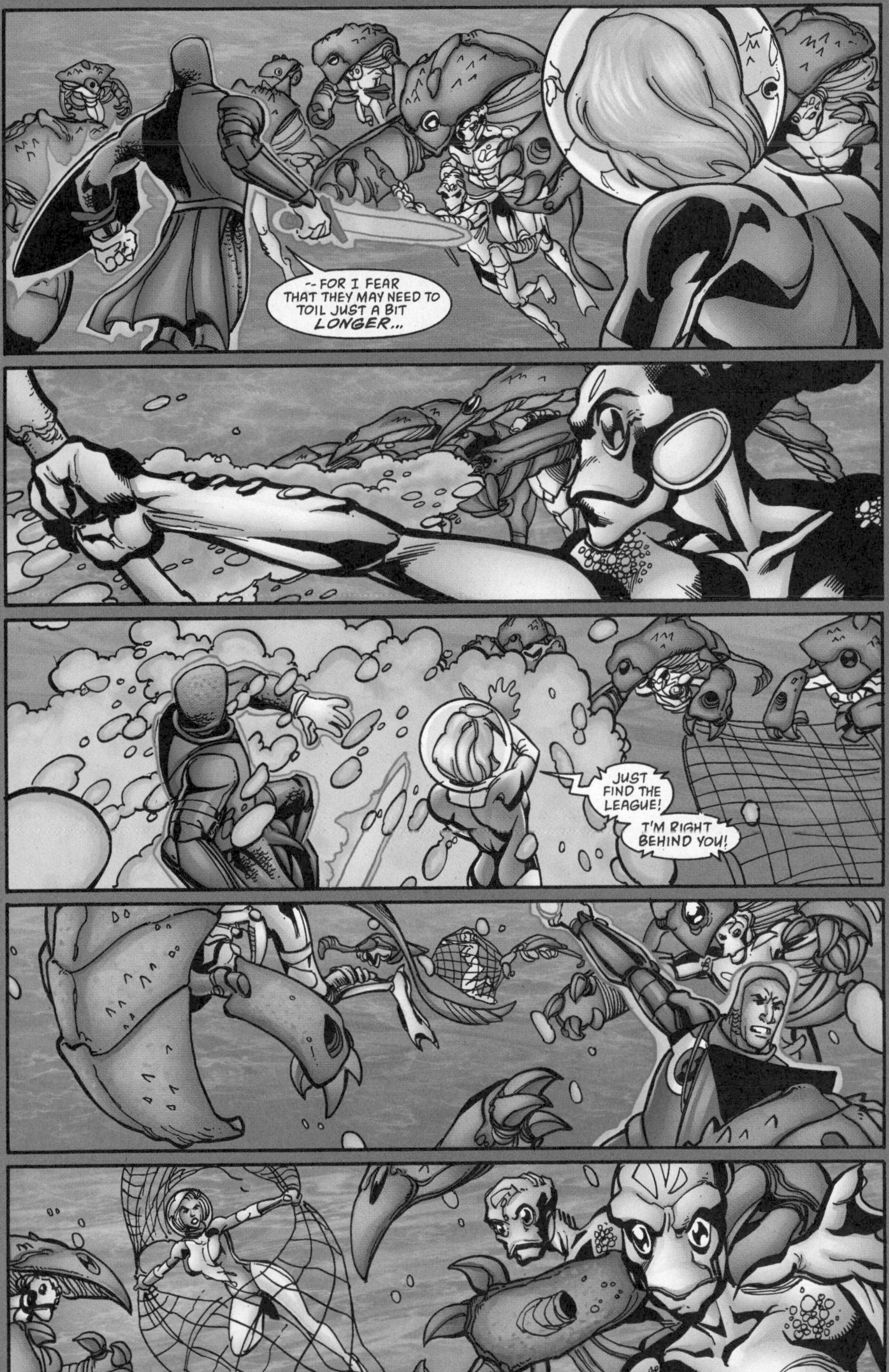
--FOR I FEAR THAT THEY MAY NEED TO TOIL JUST A BIT LONGER...
JUST FIND THE LEAGUE!
I'M RIGHT BEHIND YOU!

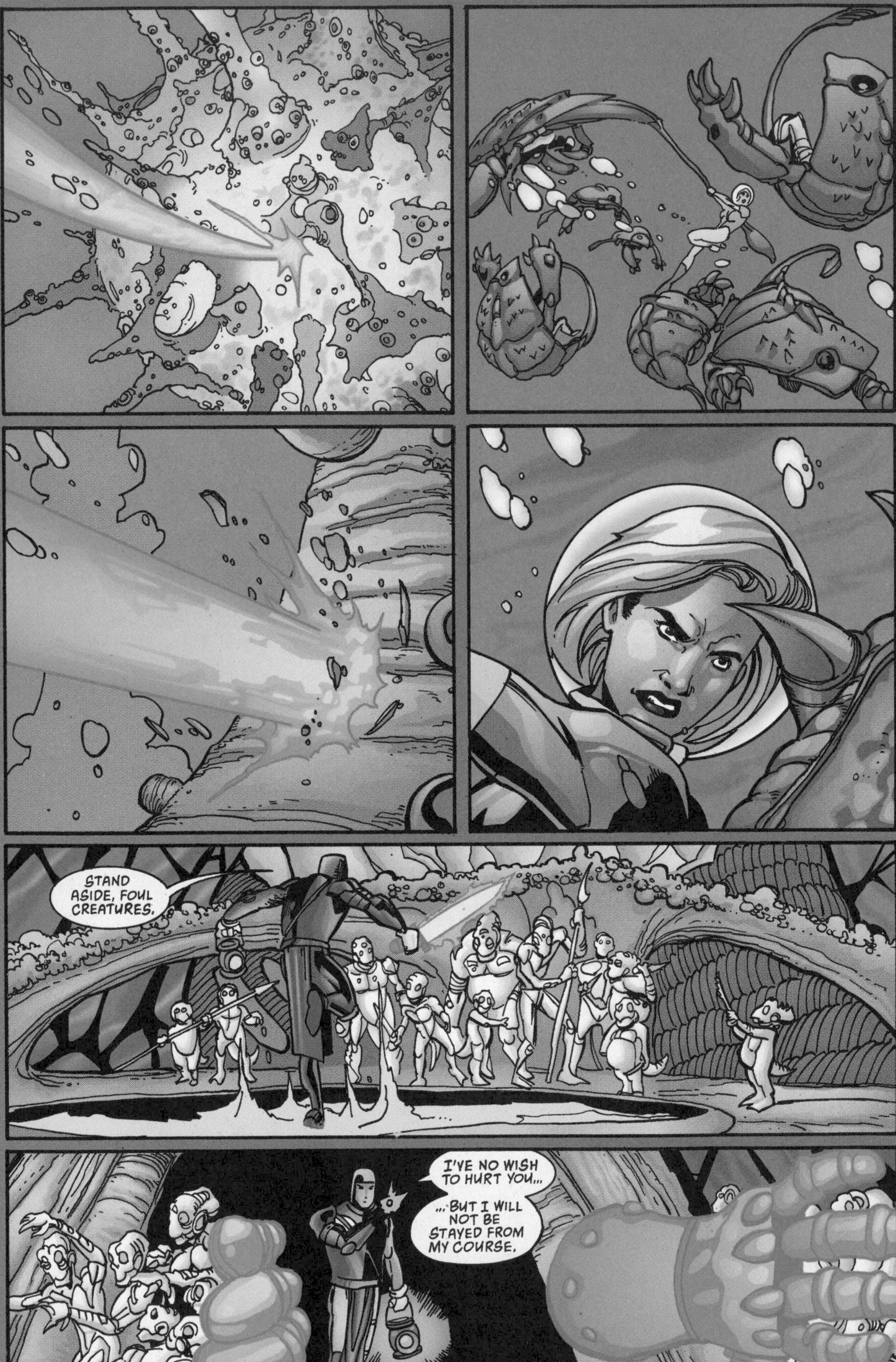
STAND ASIDE, FOUL CREATURES.
I'VE NO WISH TO HURT YOU...
...BUT I WILL NOT BE STAYED FROM MY COURSE.

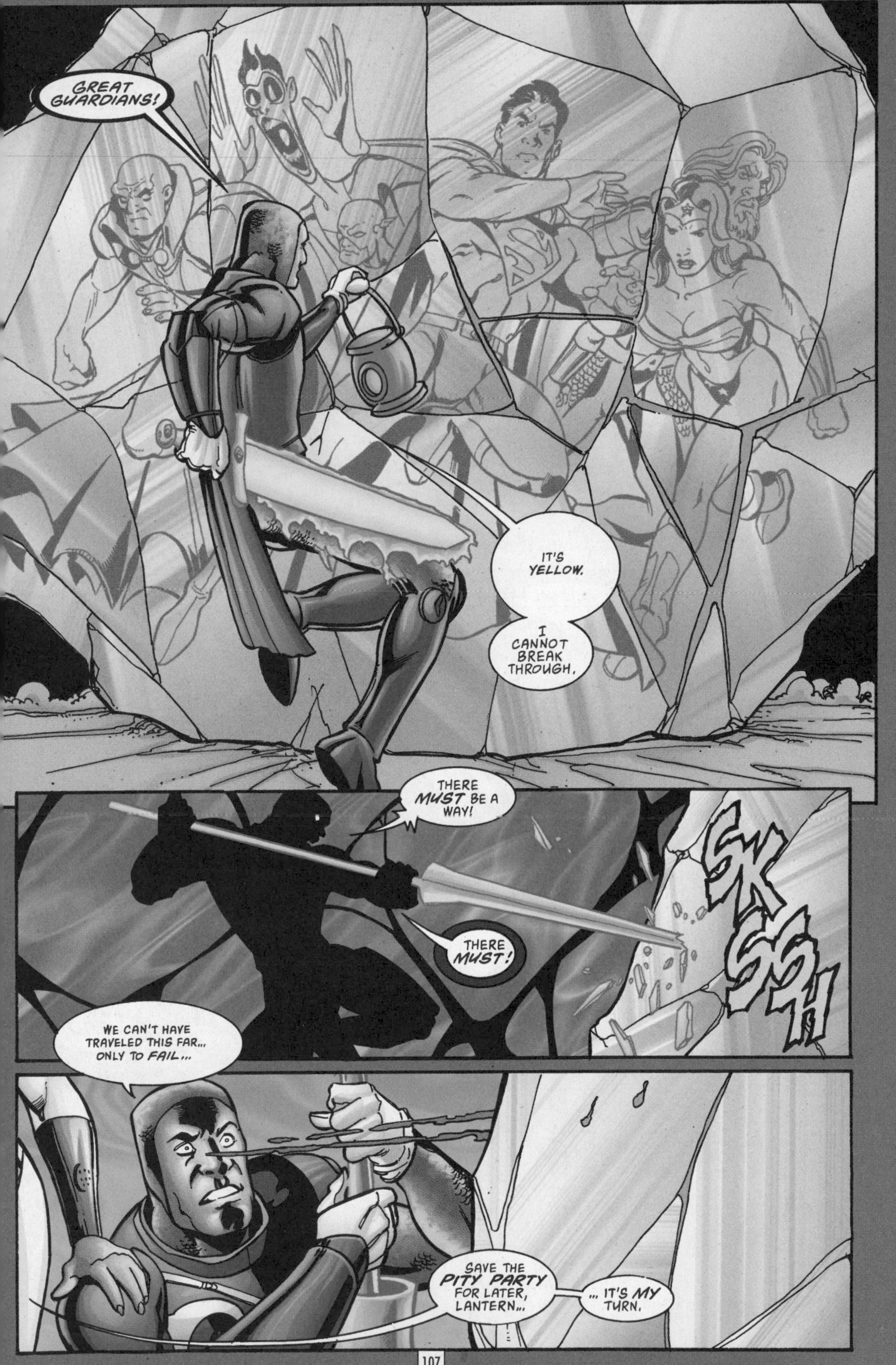
GREAT GUARDIANS!
IT'S YELLOW.
I CANNOT BREAK THROUGH.
THERE MUST BE A WAY!
THERE MUST!
SKSSH
WE CAN'T HAVE TRAVELED THIS FAR... ONLY TO FAIL...
SAVE THE PITY PARTY FOR LATER, LANTERN...
... IT'S MY TURN.

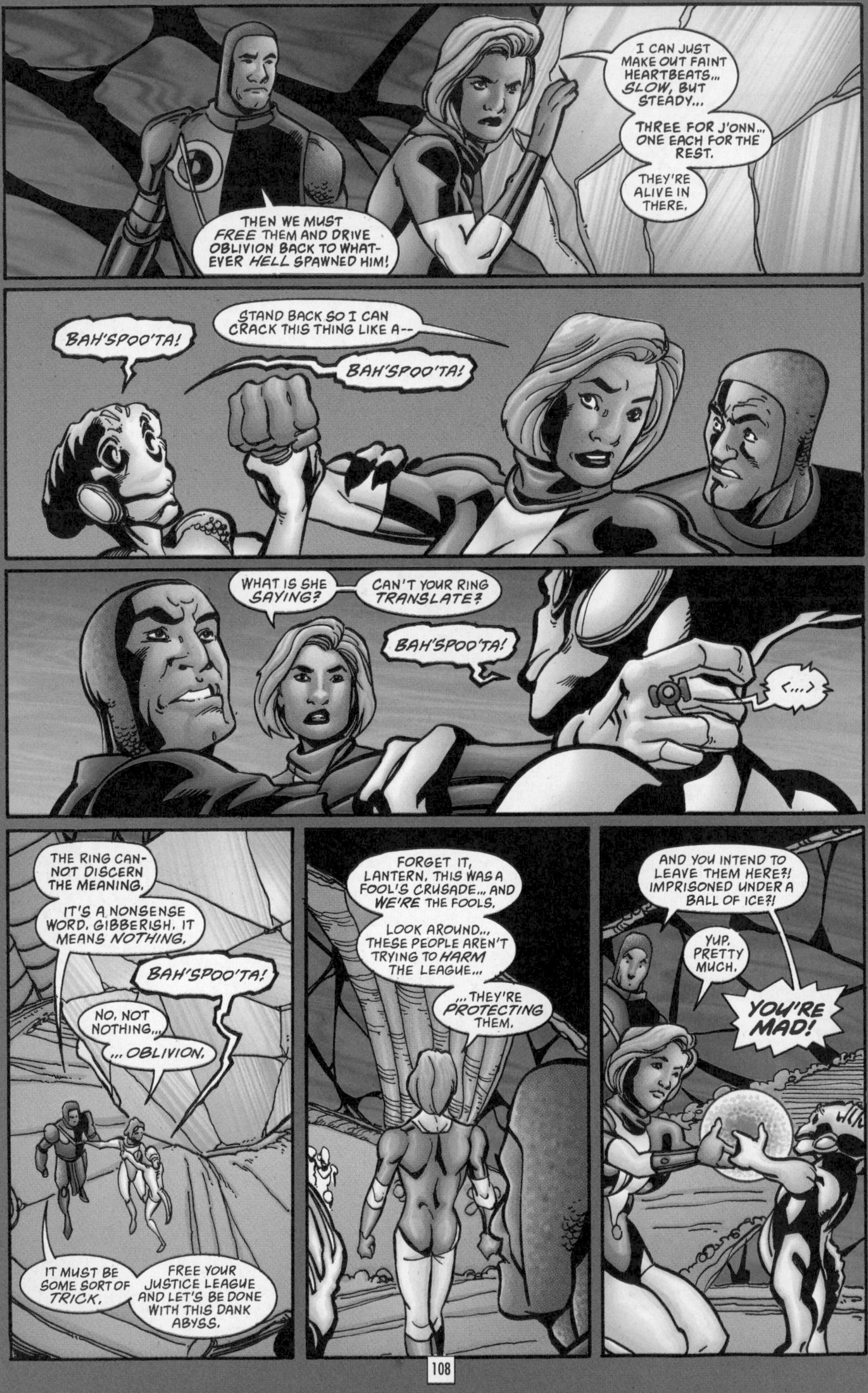
I CAN JUST MAKE OUT FAINT HEARTBEATS... SLOW, BUT STEADY...
THREE FOR J'ONN... ONE EACH FOR THE REST.
THEY'RE ALIVE IN THERE.
THEN WE MUST FREE THEM AND DRIVE OBLIVION BACK TO WHATEVER HELL SPAWNED HIM!
BAH'SPOO'TA!
STAND BACK SO I CAN CRACK THIS THING LIKE A--
BAH'SPOO'TA!
WHAT IS SHE SAYING?
CAN'T YOUR RING TRANSLATE?
BAH'SPOO'TA!
<...>
THE RING CANNOT DISCERN THE MEANING.
IT'S A NONSENSE WORD. GIBBERISH. IT MEANS NOTHING.
BAH'SPOO'TA!
NO, NOT NOTHING...
...OBLIVION.
IT MUST BE SOME SORT OF TRICK.
FREE YOUR JUSTICE LEAGUE AND LET'S BE DONE WITH THIS DANK ABYSS.
FORGET IT, LANTERN. THIS WAS A FOOL'S CRUSADE... AND WE'RE THE FOOLS.
LOOK AROUND... THESE PEOPLE AREN'T TRYING TO HARM THE LEAGUE...
...THEY'RE PROTECTING THEM.
AND YOU INTEND TO LEAVE THEM HERE?! IMPRISONED UNDER A BALL OF ICE?!
YUP. PRETTY MUCH.
YOU'RE MAD!

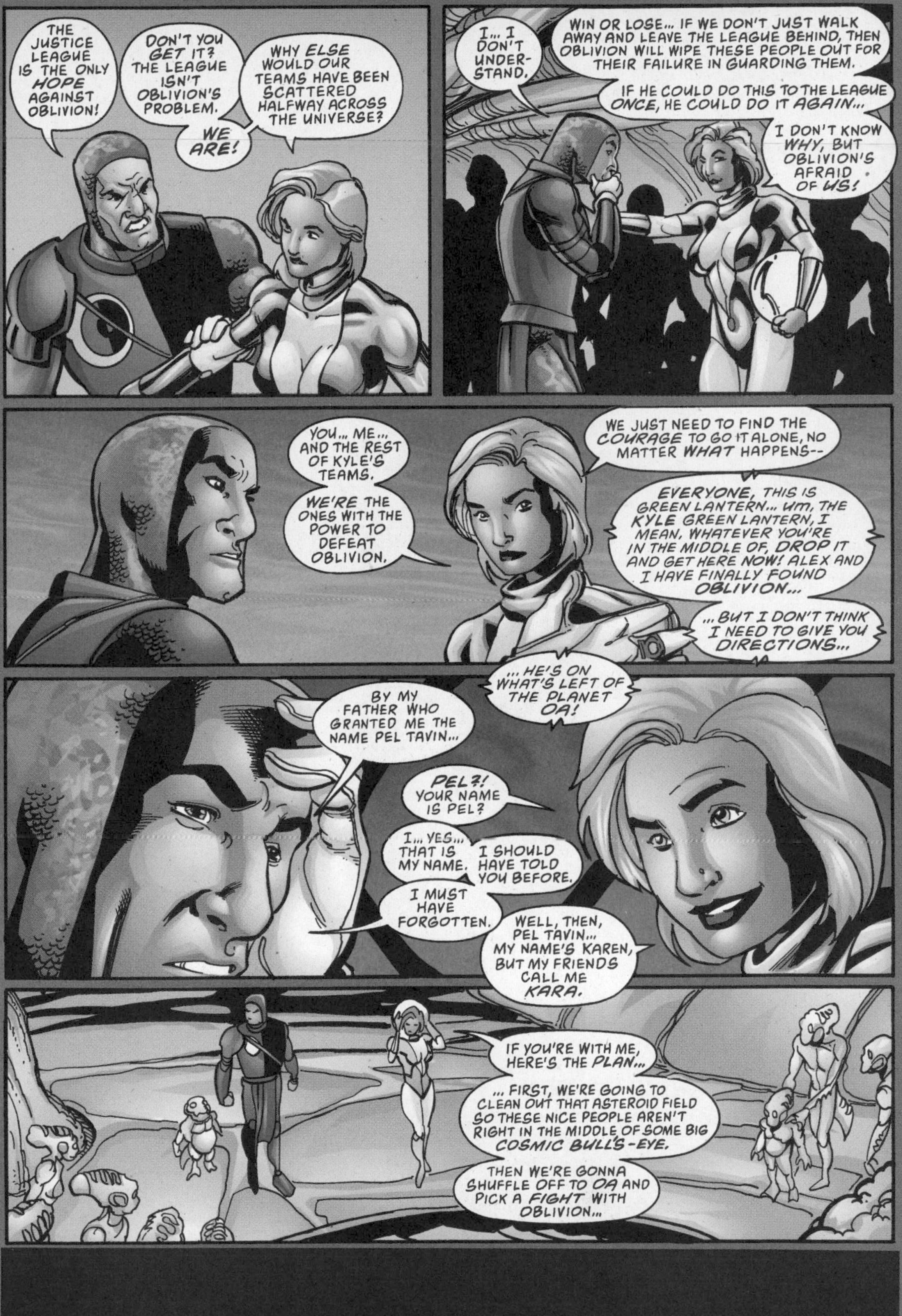

THE JUSTICE LEAGUE IS THE ONLY HOPE AGAINST OBLIVION!
DON'T YOU GET IT? THE LEAGUE ISN'T OBLIVION'S PROBLEM.
WE ARE!
WHY ELSE WOULD OUR TEAMS HAVE BEEN SCATTERED HALFWAY ACROSS THE UNIVERSE?
I... I DON'T UNDER-STAND.
WIN OR LOSE... IF WE DON'T JUST WALK AWAY AND LEAVE THE LEAGUE BEHIND, THEN OBLIVION WILL WIPE THESE PEOPLE OUT FOR THEIR FAILURE IN GUARDING THEM.
IF HE COULD DO THIS TO THE LEAGUE ONCE, HE COULD DO IT AGAIN...
I DON'T KNOW WHY, BUT OBLIVION'S AFRAID OF US!
YOU... ME... AND THE REST OF KYLE'S TEAMS.
WE'RE THE ONES WITH THE POWER TO DEFEAT OBLIVION.
WE JUST NEED TO FIND THE COURAGE TO GO IT ALONE, NO MATTER WHAT HAPPENS--
EVERYONE, THIS IS GREEN LANTERN... UM, THE KYLE GREEN LANTERN, I MEAN. WHATEVER YOU'RE IN THE MIDDLE OF, DROP IT AND GET HERE NOW! ALEX AND I HAVE FINALLY FOUND OBLIVION...
...BUT I DON'T THINK I NEED TO GIVE YOU DIRECTIONS...
...HE'S ON WHAT'S LEFT OF THE PLANET OA!
BY MY FATHER WHO GRANTED ME THE NAME PEL TAVIN...
PEL?! YOUR NAME IS PEL?
I... YES... THAT IS MY NAME.
I SHOULD HAVE TOLD YOU BEFORE.
I MUST HAVE FORGOTTEN.
WELL, THEN, PEL TAVIN... MY NAME'S KAREN, BUT MY FRIENDS CALL ME KARA.
IF YOU'RE WITH ME, HERE'S THE PLAN...
...FIRST, WE'RE GOING TO CLEAN OUT THAT ASTEROID FIELD SO THESE NICE PEOPLE AREN'T RIGHT IN THE MIDDLE OF SOME BIG COSMIC BULL'S-EYE.
THEN WE'RE GONNA SHUFFLE OFF TO OA AND PICK A FIGHT WITH OBLIVION...

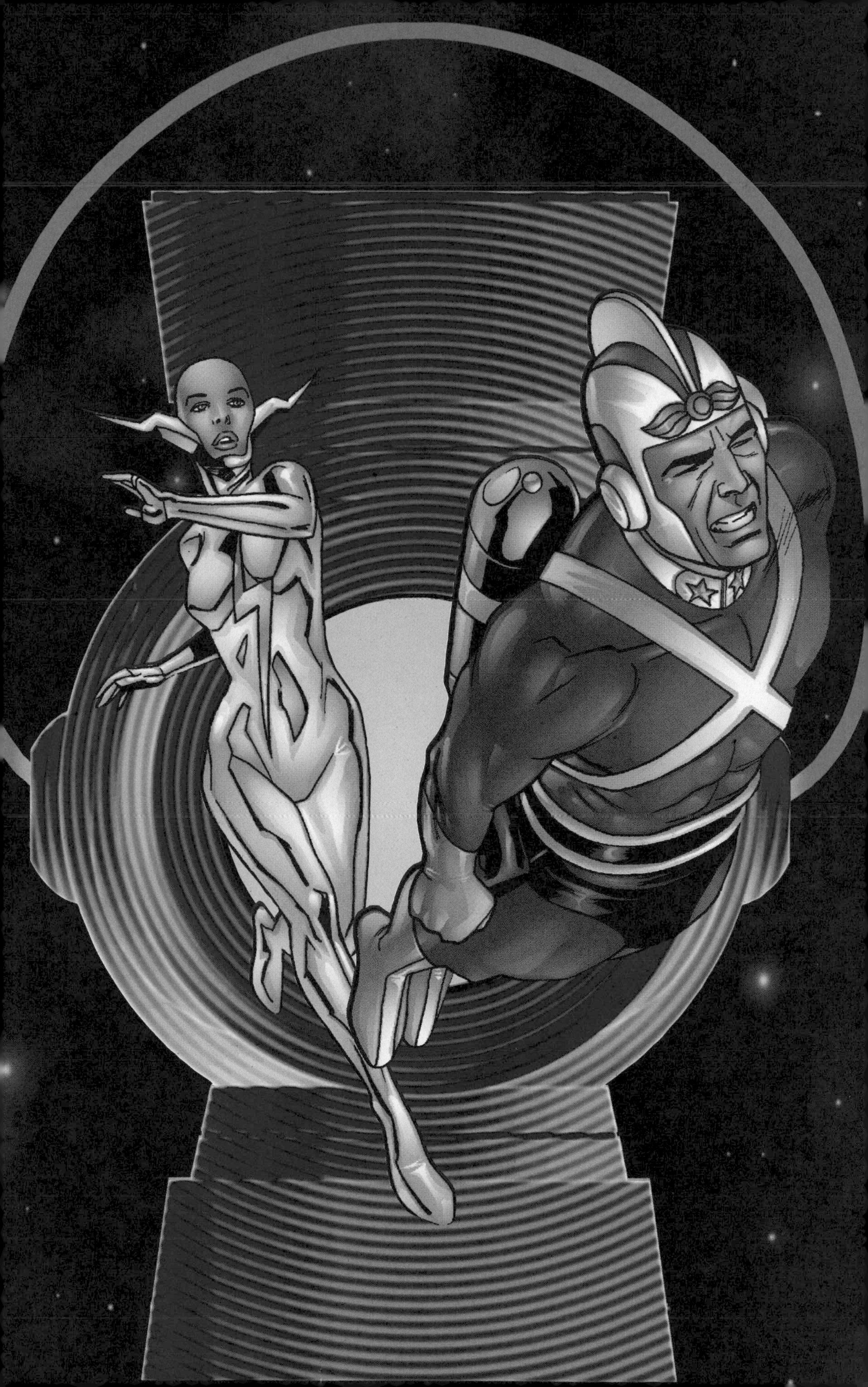

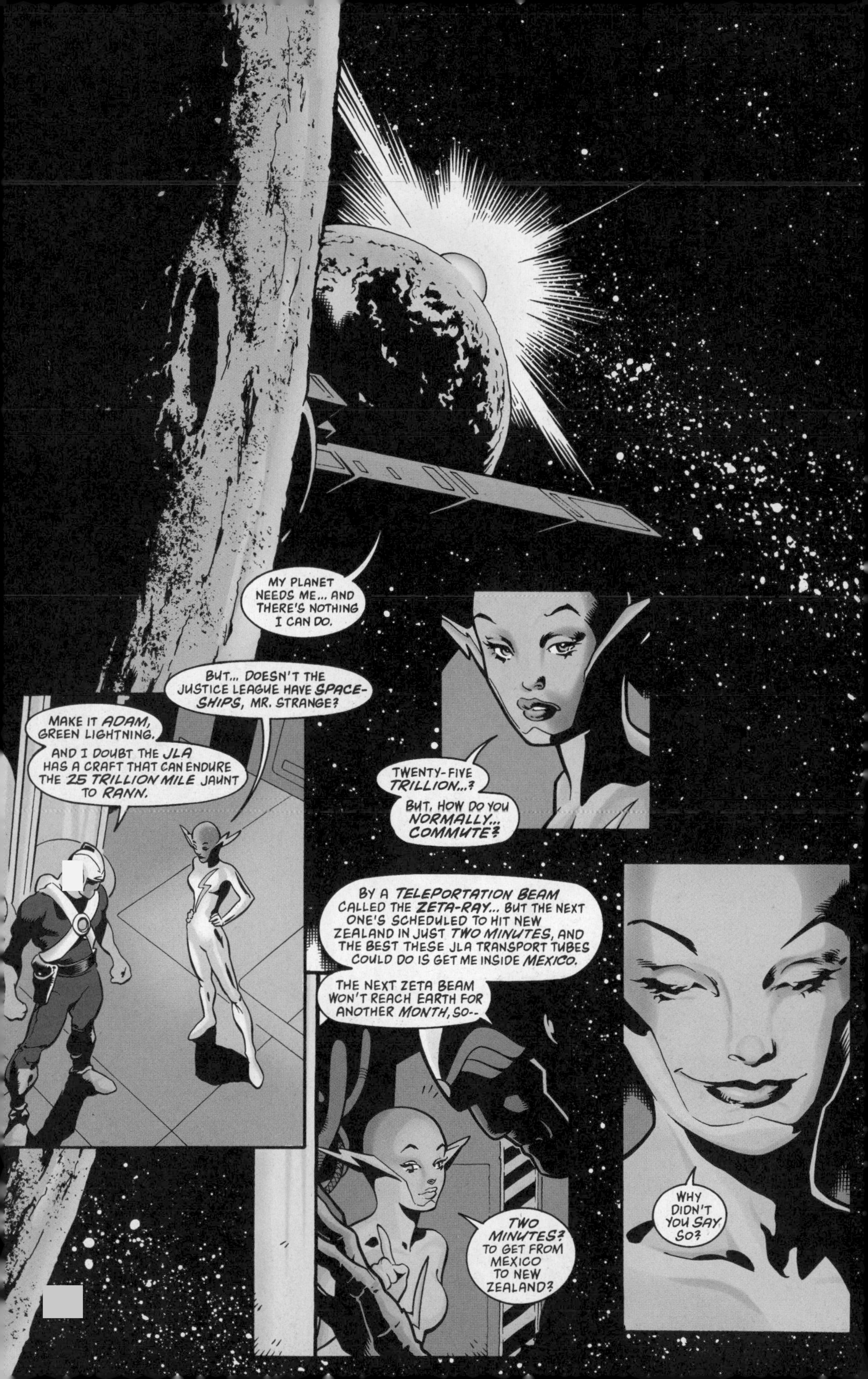
MY PLANET NEEDS ME... AND THERE'S NOTHING I CAN DO.
BUT... DOESN'T THE JUSTICE LEAGUE HAVE SPACE-SHIPS, MR. STRANGE?
MAKE IT ADAM, GREEN LIGHTNING.
AND I DOUBT THE JLA HAS A CRAFT THAT CAN ENDURE THE 25 TRILLION MILE JAUNT TO RANN.
TWENTY-FIVE TRILLION...?
BUT, HOW DO YOU NORMALLY... COMMUTE?
BY A TELEPORTATION BEAM CALLED THE ZETA-RAY... BUT THE NEXT ONE'S SCHEDULED TO HIT NEW ZEALAND IN JUST TWO MINUTES, AND THE BEST THESE JLA TRANSPORT TUBES COULD DO IS GET ME INSIDE MEXICO.
THE NEXT ZETA BEAM WON'T REACH EARTH FOR ANOTHER MONTH, SO--
TWO MINUTES? TO GET FROM MEXICO TO NEW ZEALAND?
WHY DIDN'T YOU SAY SO?

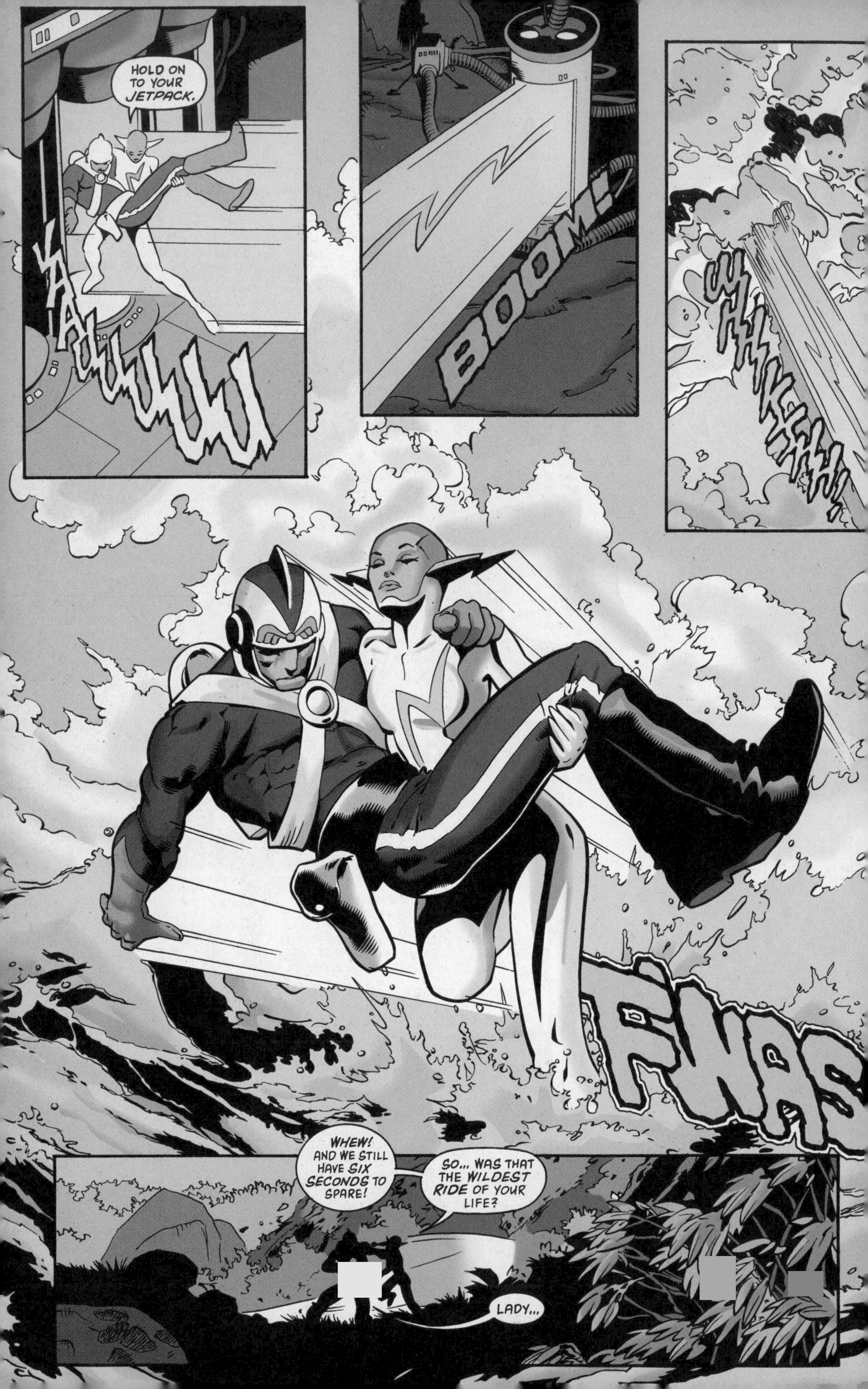
HOLD ON TO YOUR *JETPACK.*
BOOM!
*WHEW!* AND WE STILL HAVE *SIX SECONDS* TO SPARE!
SO... WAS THAT THE *WILDEST RIDE* OF YOUR LIFE?
LADY...

# WE R ANN ALL NIGHT

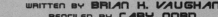

WRITTEN BY BRIAN K. VAUGHAN
PENCILED BY CARY NORD
INKED BY MARK LIPKA    LETTERED BY SEAN KONOT
COLORED BY TOM McCRAW    SEPARATED BY JAMISON
FRANK BERRIOS ASST. EDITOR   MATT IDELSON EDITOR

...YOU AIN'T SEEN NOTHING YET...

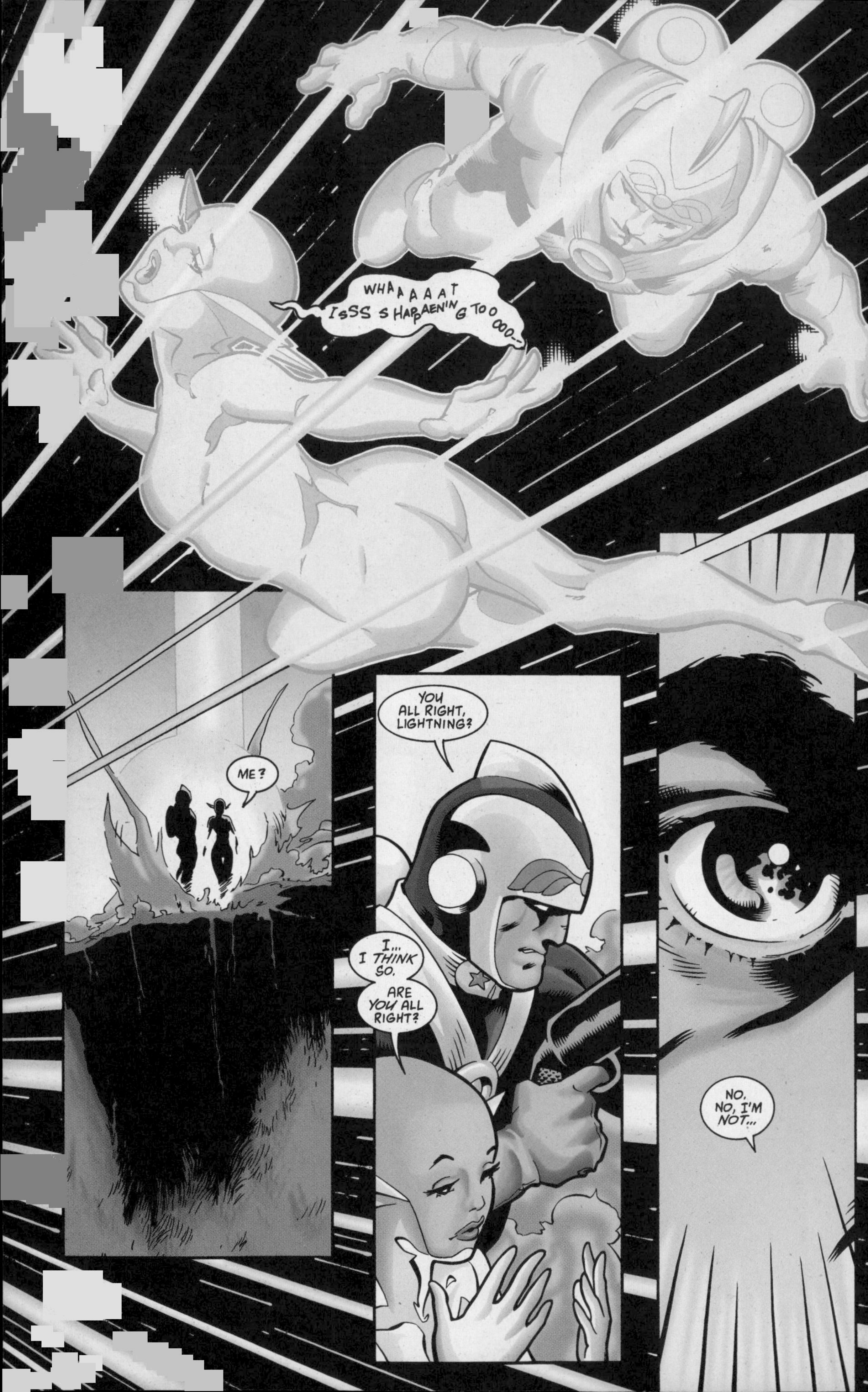
WHAAAAAT IsSS sHAPPAENING TOOOOO--
ME?
YOU ALL RIGHT, LIGHTNING?
I... I THINK SO. ARE YOU ALL RIGHT?
NO. NO, I'M NOT...

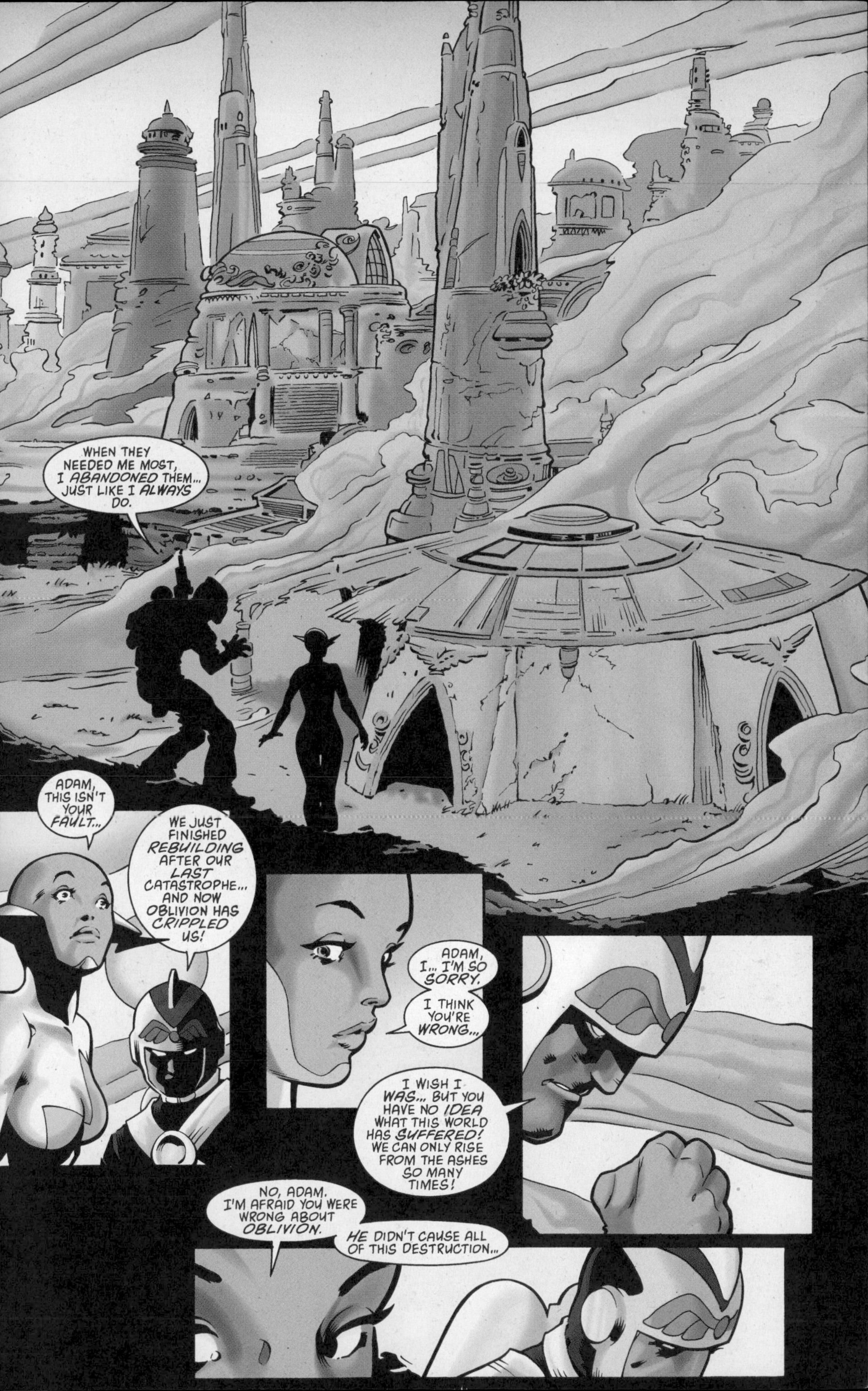
WHEN THEY NEEDED ME MOST, I ABANDONED THEM... JUST LIKE I ALWAYS DO.
ADAM, THIS ISN'T YOUR FAULT...
WE JUST FINISHED REBUILDING AFTER OUR LAST CATASTROPHE... AND NOW OBLIVION HAS CRIPPLED US!
ADAM, I... I'M SO SORRY.
I THINK YOU'RE WRONG...
I WISH I WAS... BUT YOU HAVE NO IDEA WHAT THIS WORLD HAS SUFFERED! WE CAN ONLY RISE FROM THE ASHES SO MANY TIMES!
NO, ADAM. I'M AFRAID YOU WERE WRONG ABOUT OBLIVION.
HE DIDN'T CAUSE ALL OF THIS DESTRUCTION...

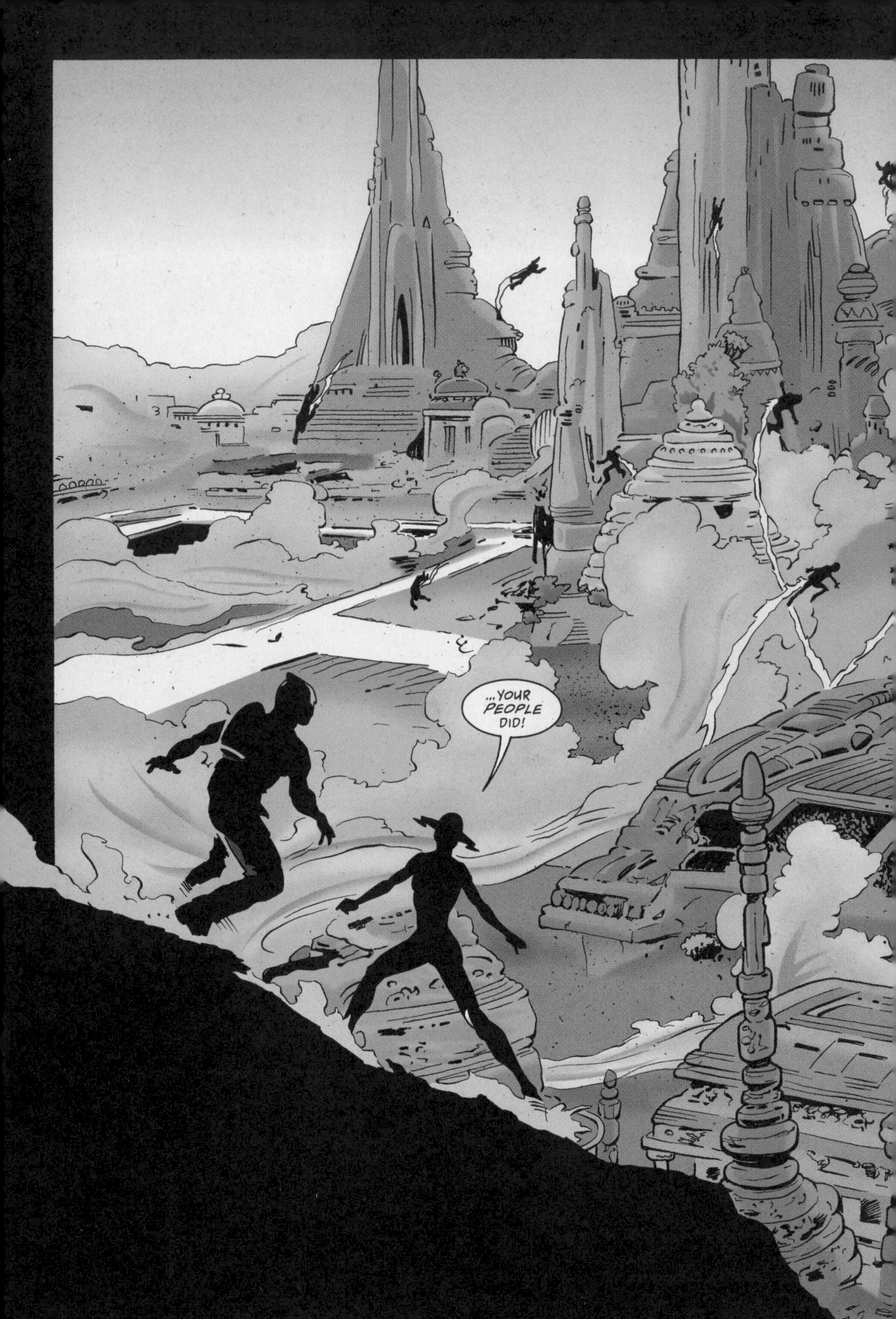
...YOUR PEOPLE DID!

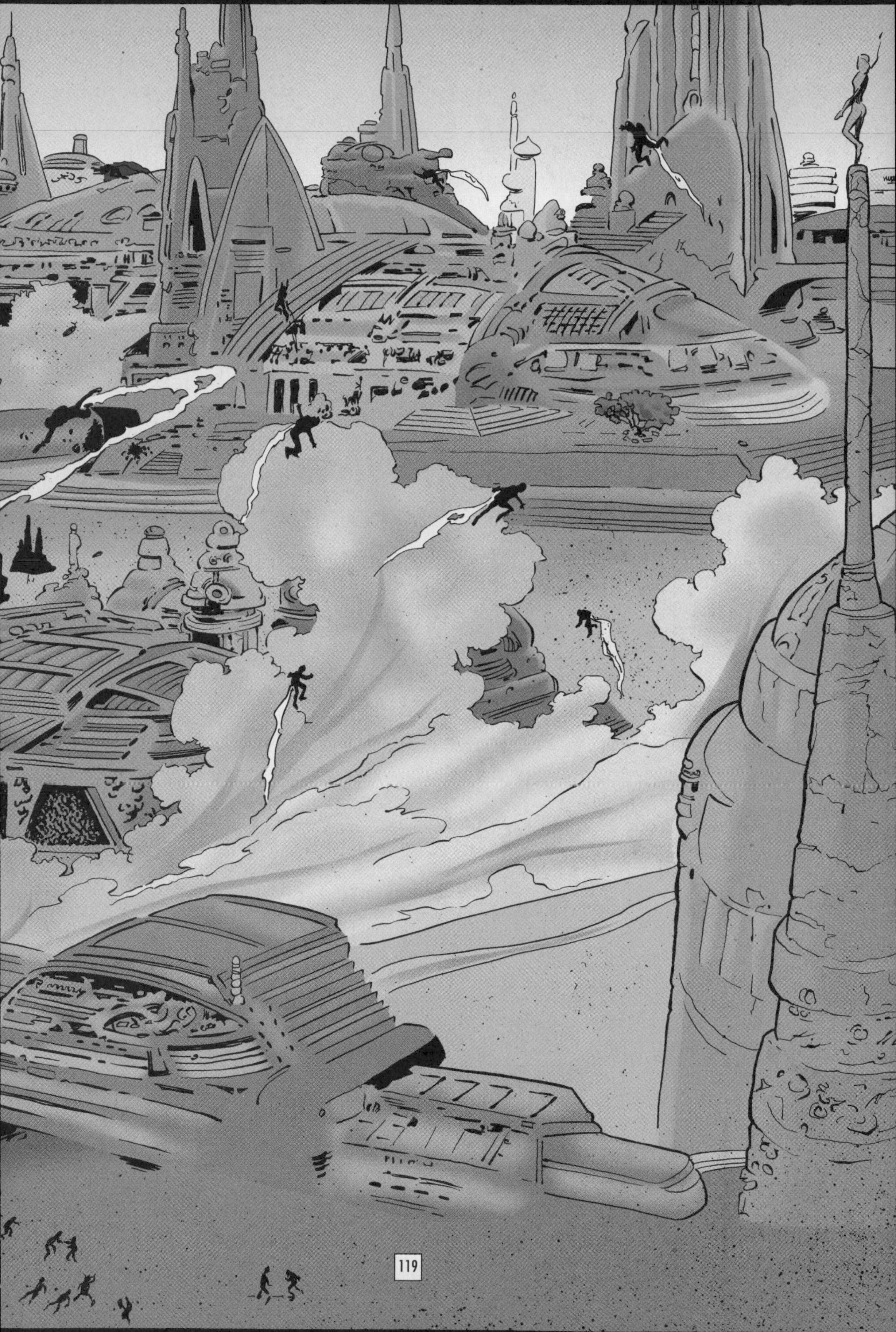

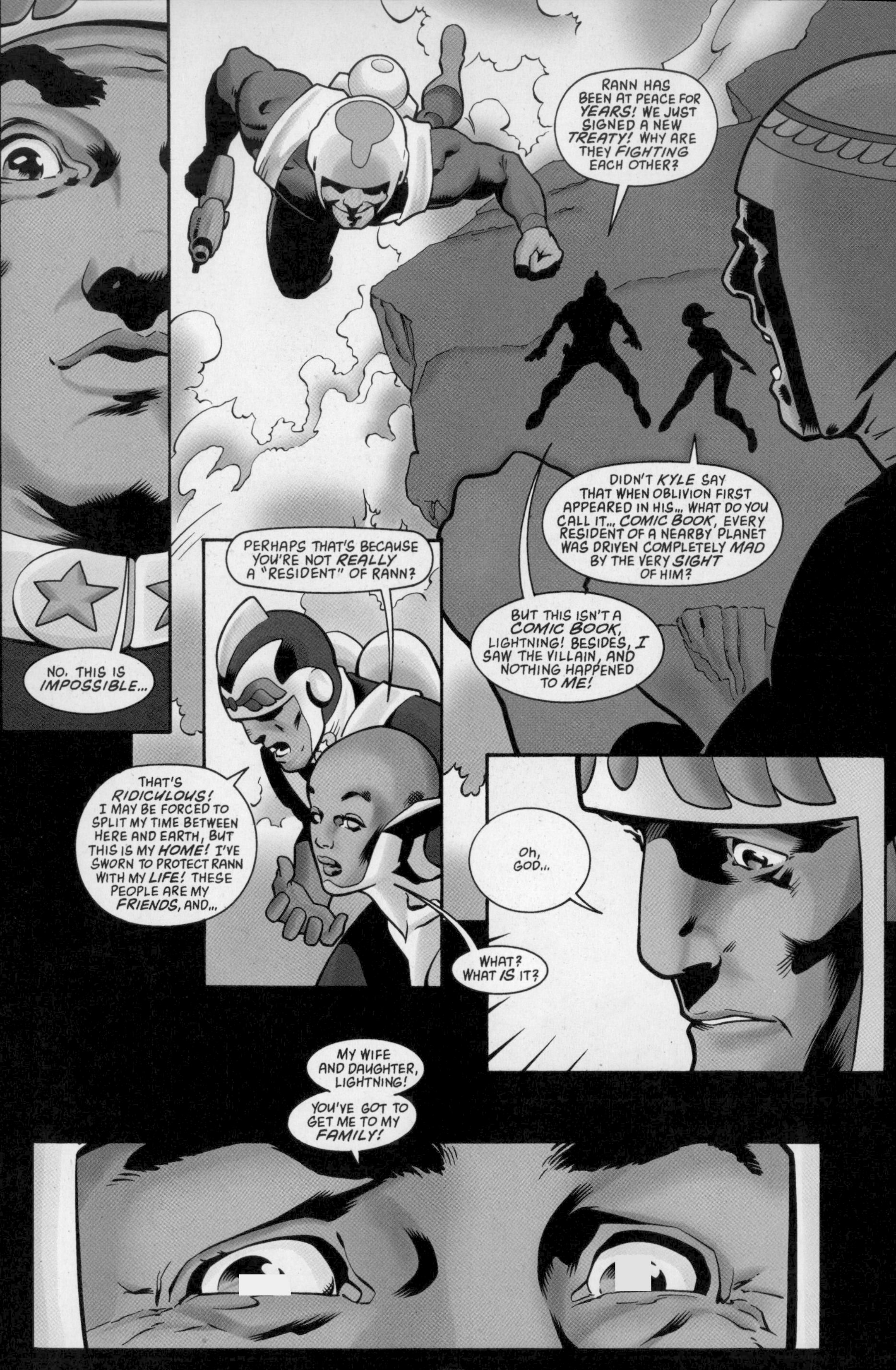
RANN HAS BEEN AT PEACE FOR YEARS! WE JUST SIGNED A NEW TREATY! WHY ARE THEY FIGHTING EACH OTHER?
DIDN'T KYLE SAY THAT WHEN OBLIVION FIRST APPEARED IN HIS... WHAT DO YOU CALL IT... COMIC BOOK, EVERY RESIDENT OF A NEARBY PLANET WAS DRIVEN COMPLETELY MAD BY THE VERY SIGHT OF HIM?
BUT THIS ISN'T A COMIC BOOK, LIGHTNING! BESIDES, I SAW THE VILLAIN, AND NOTHING HAPPENED TO ME!
PERHAPS THAT'S BECAUSE YOU'RE NOT REALLY A "RESIDENT" OF RANN?
THAT'S RIDICULOUS! I MAY BE FORCED TO SPLIT MY TIME BETWEEN HERE AND EARTH, BUT THIS IS MY HOME! I'VE SWORN TO PROTECT RANN WITH MY LIFE! THESE PEOPLE ARE MY FRIENDS, AND...
NO. THIS IS IMPOSSIBLE...
Oh, GOD...
WHAT? WHAT IS IT?
MY WIFE AND DAUGHTER, LIGHTNING!
YOU'VE GOT TO GET ME TO MY FAMILY!

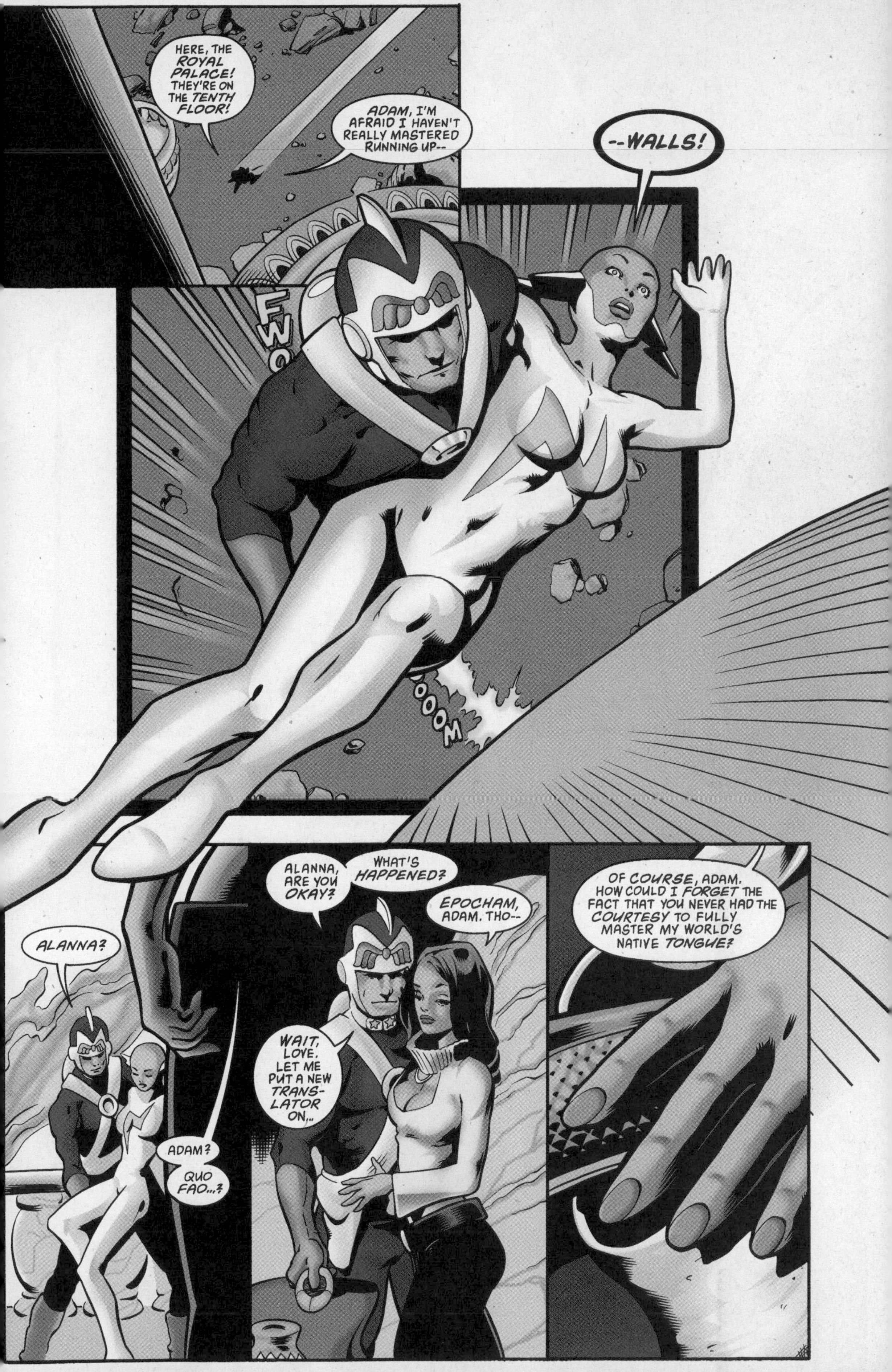
HERE, THE ROYAL PALACE! THEY'RE ON THE TENTH FLOOR!
ADAM, I'M AFRAID I HAVEN'T REALLY MASTERED RUNNING UP--
--WALLS!
FWOOOOOM
ALANNA?
ADAM?
QUO FAO...?
ALANNA, ARE YOU OKAY?
WHAT'S HAPPENED?
EPOCHAM, ADAM. THO--
WAIT, LOVE. LET ME PUT A NEW TRANSLATOR ON...
OF COURSE, ADAM. HOW COULD I FORGET THE FACT THAT YOU NEVER HAD THE COURTESY TO FULLY MASTER MY WORLD'S NATIVE TONGUE?

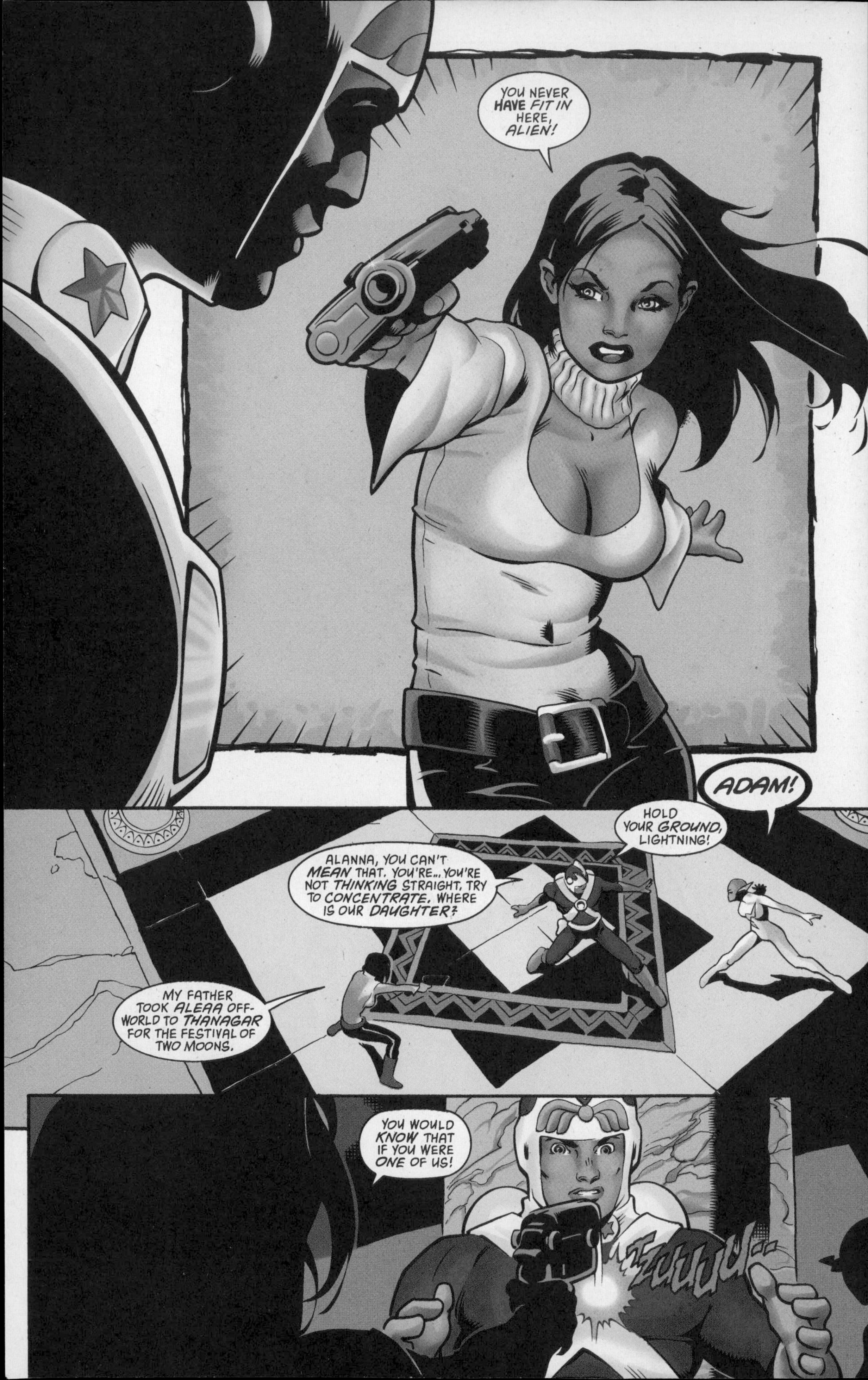
YOU NEVER HAVE FIT IN HERE, ALIEN!
ADAM!
HOLD YOUR GROUND, LIGHTNING!
ALANNA, YOU CAN'T MEAN THAT. YOU'RE... YOU'RE NOT THINKING STRAIGHT. TRY TO CONCENTRATE. WHERE IS OUR DAUGHTER?
MY FATHER TOOK ALEAA OFF-WORLD TO THANAGAR FOR THE FESTIVAL OF TWO MOONS.
YOU WOULD KNOW THAT IF YOU WERE ONE OF US!

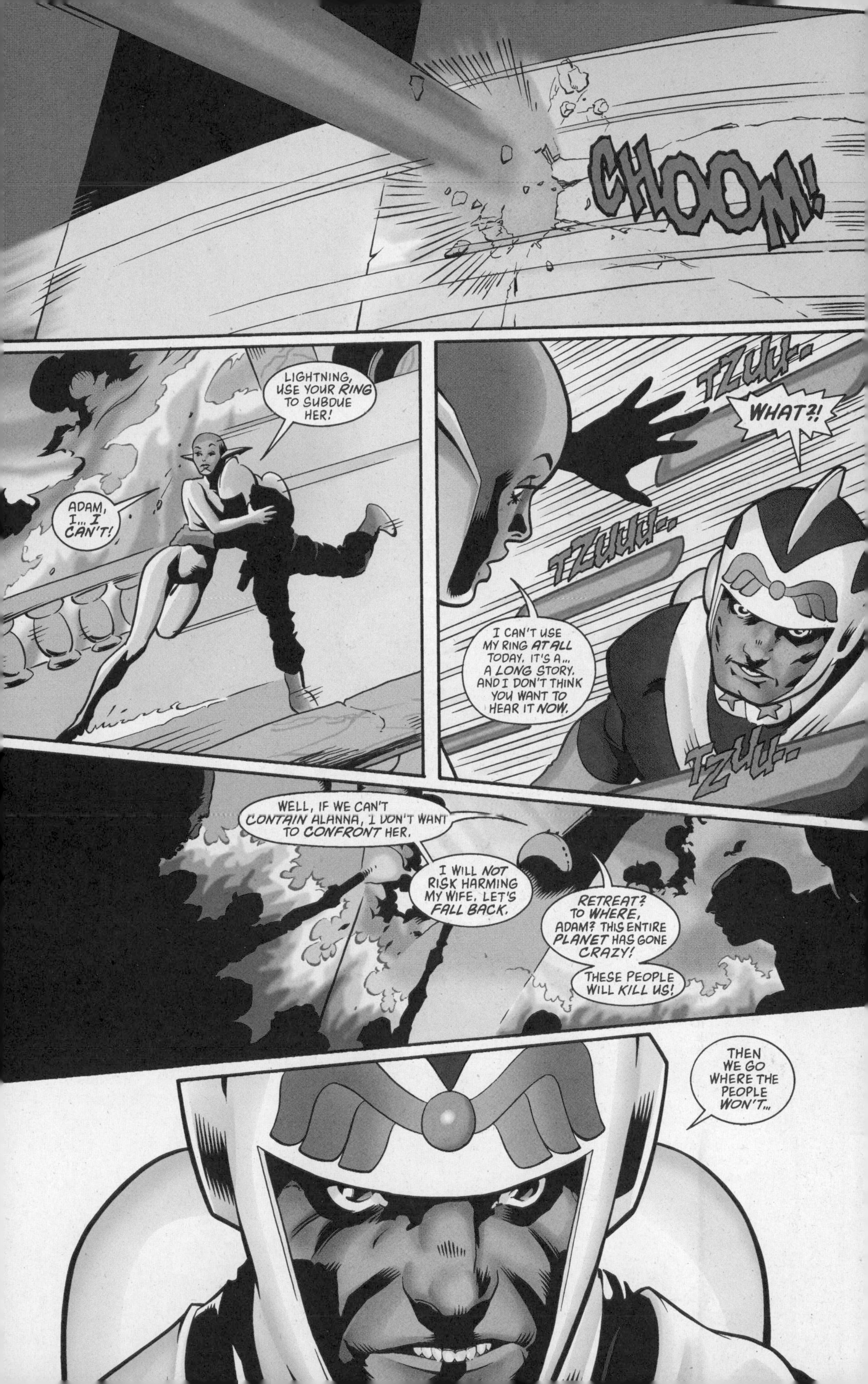
CHOOM!
LIGHTNING, USE YOUR RING TO SUBDUE HER!
ADAM, I... I CAN'T!
TZUU-
WHAT?!
TZUUU-
I CAN'T USE MY RING AT ALL TODAY. IT'S A... A LONG STORY. AND I DON'T THINK YOU WANT TO HEAR IT NOW.
TZUU-
WELL, IF WE CAN'T CONTAIN ALANNA, I DON'T WANT TO CONFRONT HER.
I WILL NOT RISK HARMING MY WIFE. LET'S FALL BACK.
RETREAT? TO WHERE, ADAM? THIS ENTIRE PLANET HAS GONE CRAZY!
THESE PEOPLE WILL KILL US!
THEN WE GO WHERE THE PEOPLE WON'T...

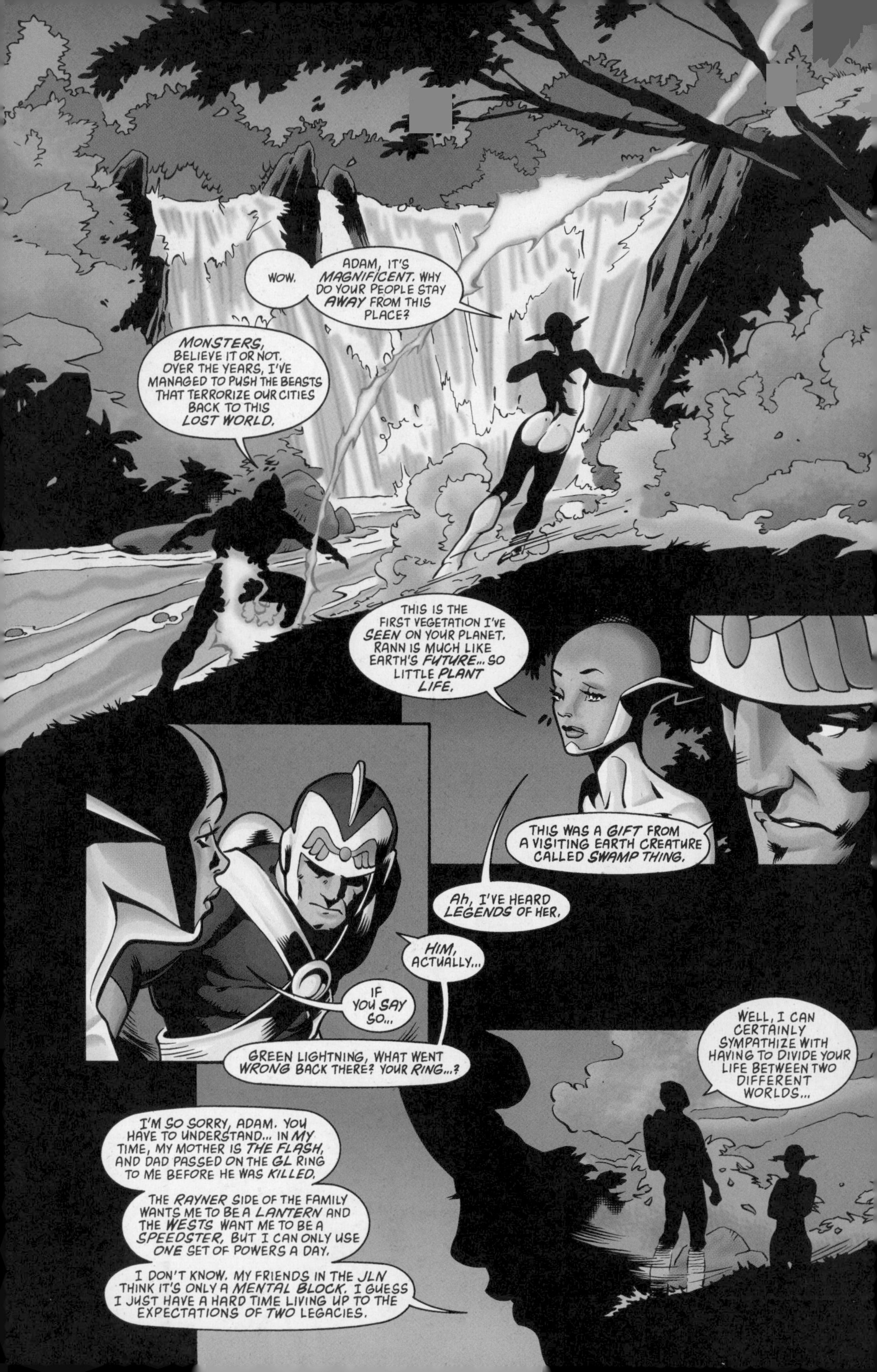

WOW.
ADAM, IT'S MAGNIFICENT. WHY DO YOUR PEOPLE STAY AWAY FROM THIS PLACE?
MONSTERS, BELIEVE IT OR NOT. OVER THE YEARS, I'VE MANAGED TO PUSH THE BEASTS THAT TERRORIZE OUR CITIES BACK TO THIS LOST WORLD.
THIS IS THE FIRST VEGETATION I'VE SEEN ON YOUR PLANET. RANN IS MUCH LIKE EARTH'S FUTURE... SO LITTLE PLANT LIFE.
THIS WAS A GIFT FROM A VISITING EARTH CREATURE CALLED SWAMP THING.
Ah, I'VE HEARD LEGENDS OF HER.
HIM, ACTUALLY...
IF YOU SAY SO...
GREEN LIGHTNING, WHAT WENT WRONG BACK THERE? YOUR RING...?
WELL, I CAN CERTAINLY SYMPATHIZE WITH HAVING TO DIVIDE YOUR LIFE BETWEEN TWO DIFFERENT WORLDS...
I'M SO SORRY, ADAM. YOU HAVE TO UNDERSTAND... IN MY TIME, MY MOTHER IS THE FLASH, AND DAD PASSED ON THE GL RING TO ME BEFORE HE WAS KILLED.
THE RAYNER SIDE OF THE FAMILY WANTS ME TO BE A LANTERN AND THE WESTS WANT ME TO BE A SPEEDSTER, BUT I CAN ONLY USE ONE SET OF POWERS A DAY.
I DON'T KNOW. MY FRIENDS IN THE JLN THINK IT'S ONLY A MENTAL BLOCK. I GUESS I JUST HAVE A HARD TIME LIVING UP TO THE EXPECTATIONS OF TWO LEGACIES.

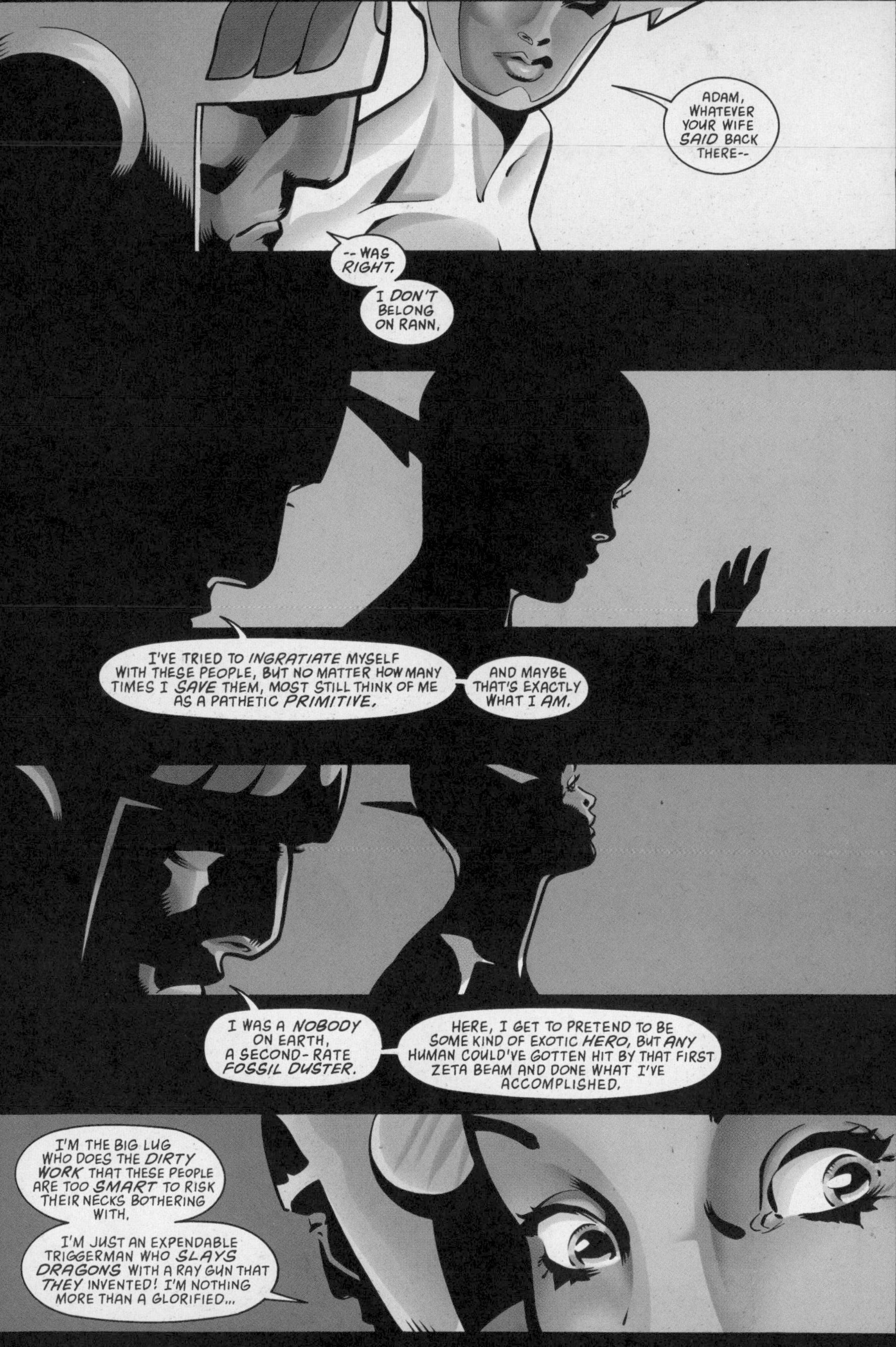
ADAM, WHATEVER YOUR WIFE SAID BACK THERE--
--WAS RIGHT.
I DON'T BELONG ON RANN.
I'VE TRIED TO INGRATIATE MYSELF WITH THESE PEOPLE, BUT NO MATTER HOW MANY TIMES I SAVE THEM, MOST STILL THINK OF ME AS A PATHETIC PRIMITIVE.
AND MAYBE THAT'S EXACTLY WHAT I AM.
I WAS A NOBODY ON EARTH, A SECOND-RATE FOSSIL DUSTER.
HERE, I GET TO PRETEND TO BE SOME KIND OF EXOTIC HERO, BUT ANY HUMAN COULD'VE GOTTEN HIT BY THAT FIRST ZETA BEAM AND DONE WHAT I'VE ACCOMPLISHED.
I'M THE BIG LUG WHO DOES THE DIRTY WORK THAT THESE PEOPLE ARE TOO SMART TO RISK THEIR NECKS BOTHERING WITH.
I'M JUST AN EXPENDABLE TRIGGERMAN WHO SLAYS DRAGONS WITH A RAY GUN THAT THEY INVENTED! I'M NOTHING MORE THAN A GLORIFIED...

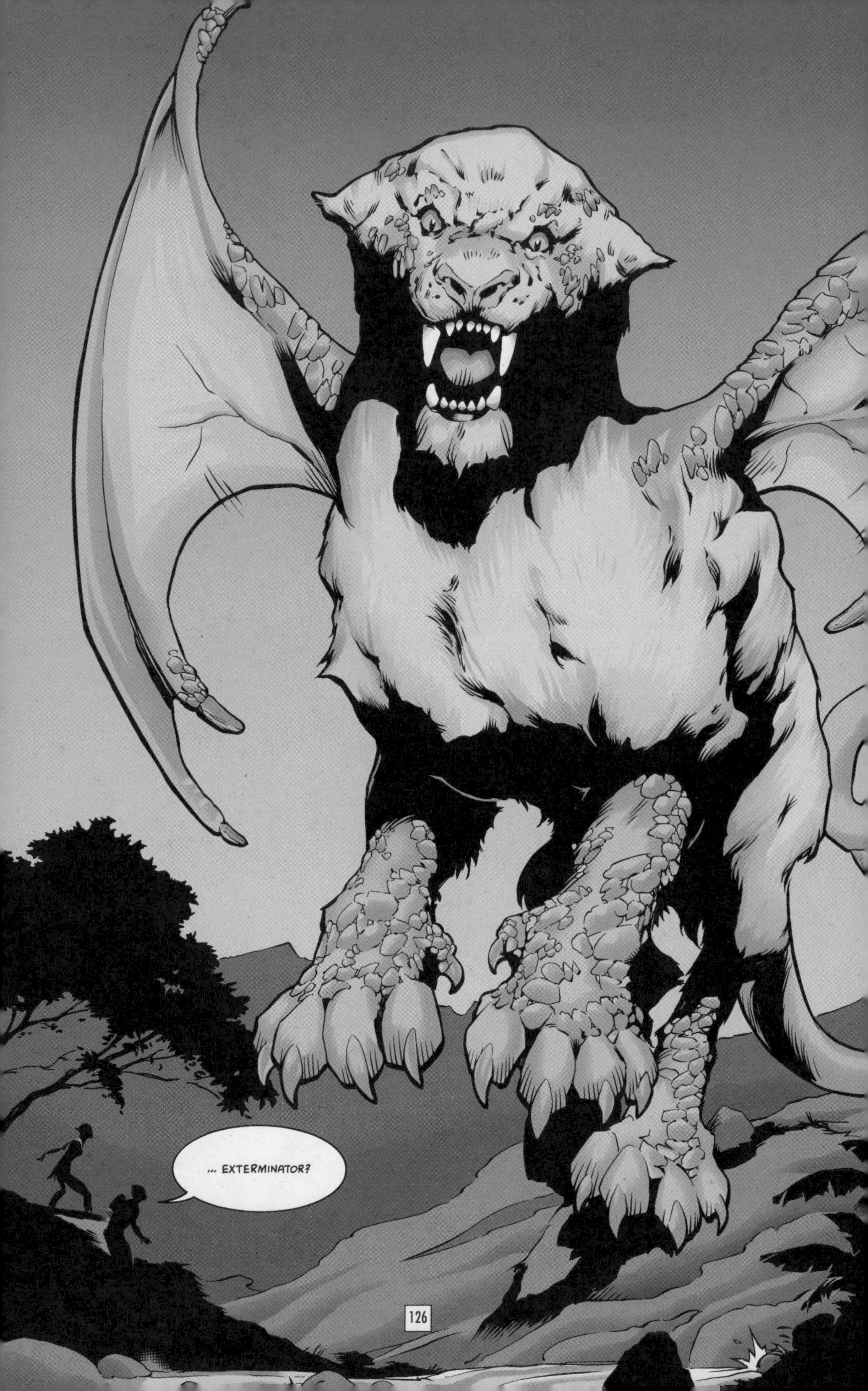
... EXTERMINATOR?

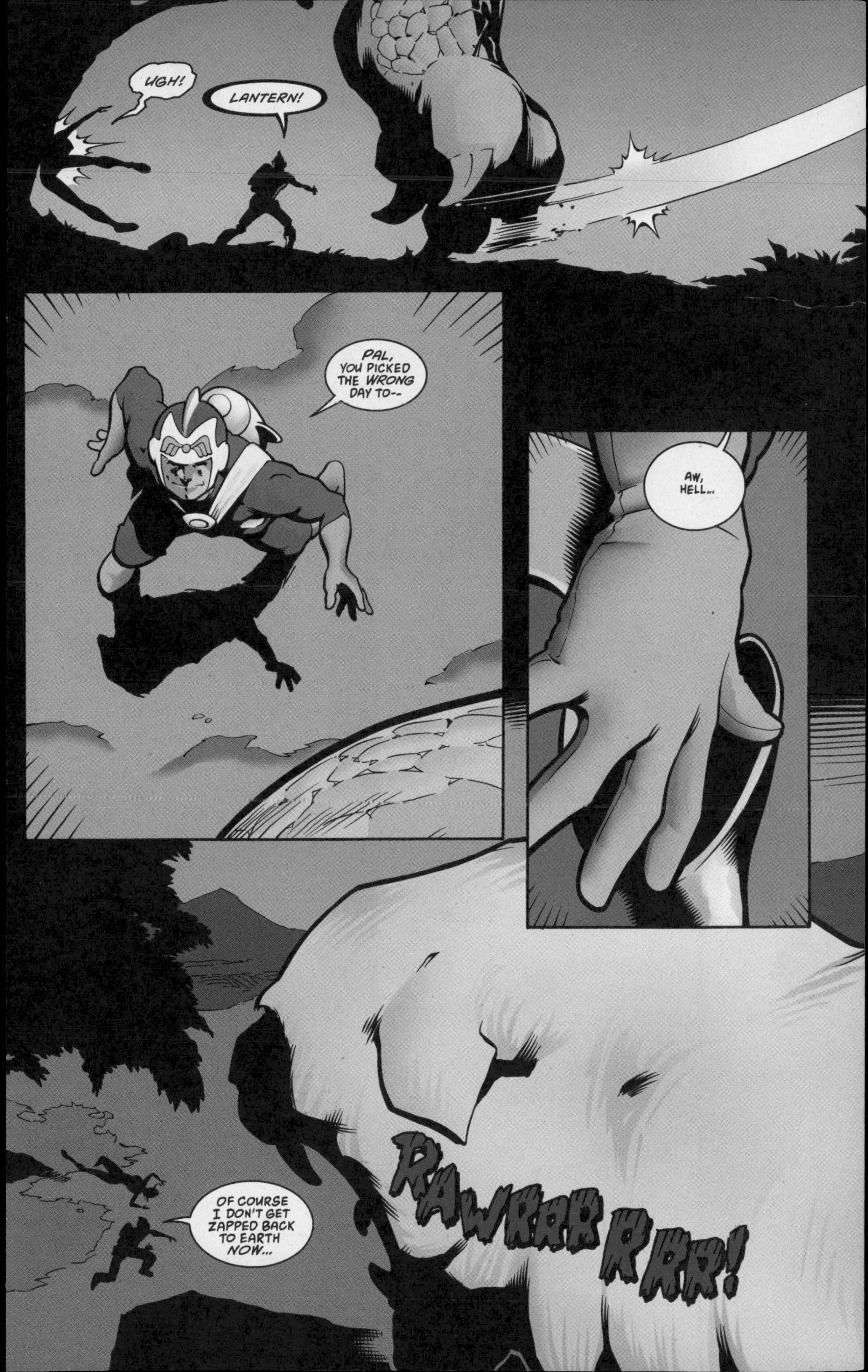
UGH!
LANTERN!
PAL, YOU PICKED THE WRONG DAY TO--
AW, HELL...
OF COURSE I DON'T GET ZAPPED BACK TO EARTH NOW...
RAWRRRRRRR!

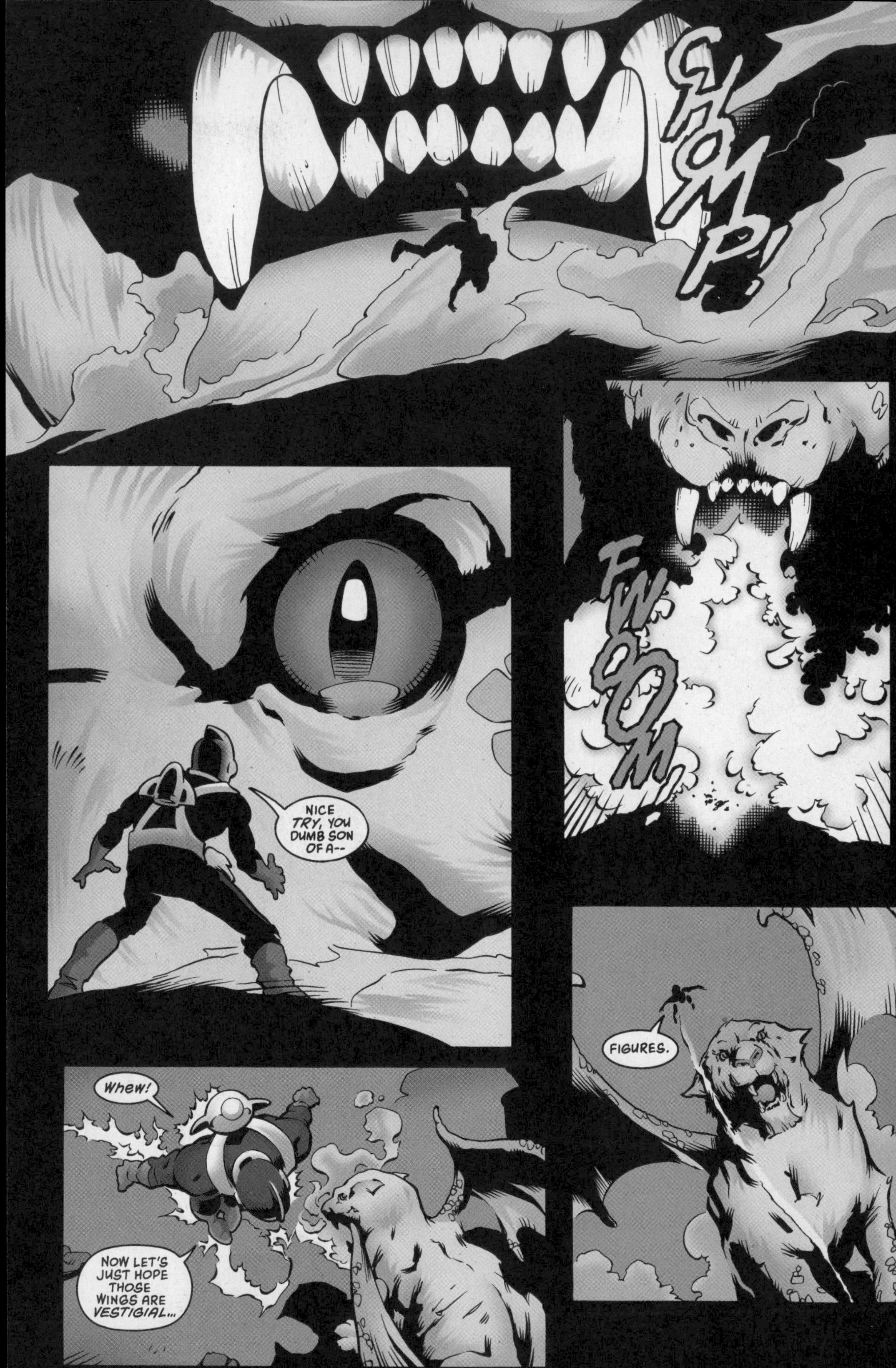
CHOMP!
FWOOM
NICE TRY, YOU DUMB SON OF A--
FIGURES.
Whew!
NOW LET'S JUST HOPE THOSE WINGS ARE VESTIGIAL...

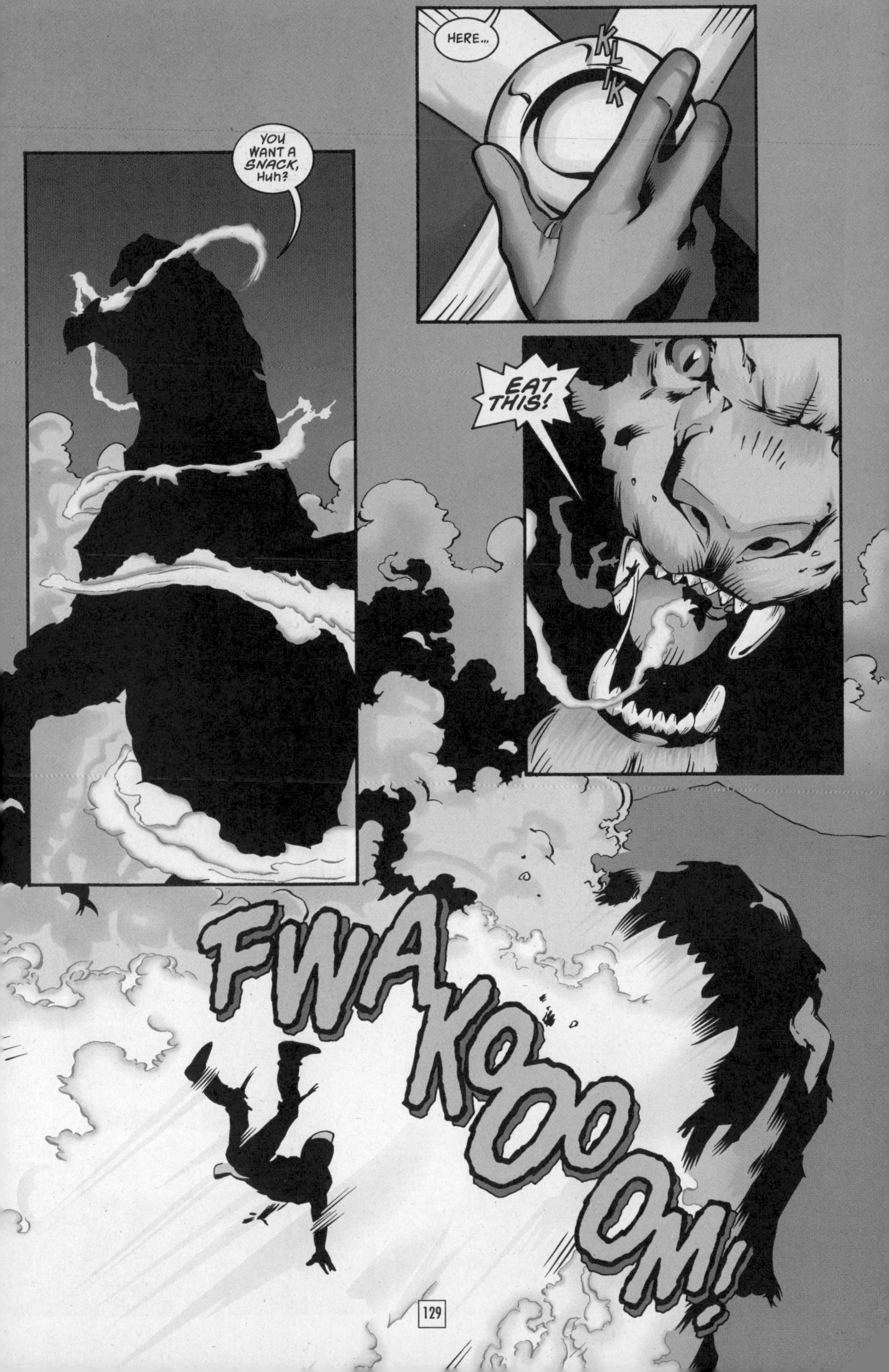
HERE...
KLIK
YOU WANT A SNACK, Huh?
EAT THIS!
FWAKOOOOM!!

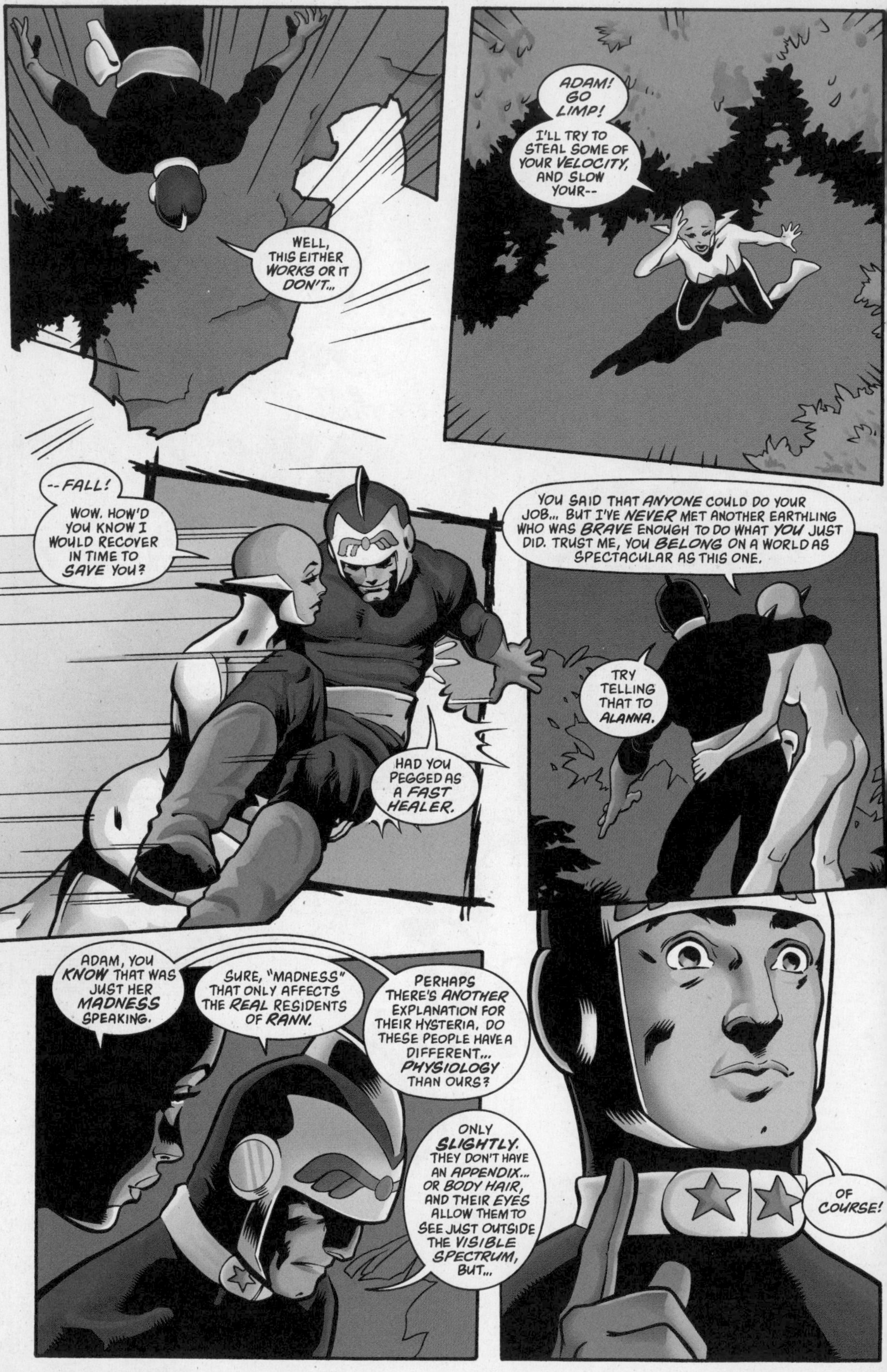
WELL, THIS EITHER WORKS OR IT DON'T...
ADAM! GO LIMP!
I'LL TRY TO STEAL SOME OF YOUR VELOCITY, AND SLOW YOUR--
--FALL!
WOW. HOW'D YOU KNOW I WOULD RECOVER IN TIME TO SAVE YOU?
HAD YOU PEGGED AS A FAST HEALER.
YOU SAID THAT ANYONE COULD DO YOUR JOB... BUT I'VE NEVER MET ANOTHER EARTHLING WHO WAS BRAVE ENOUGH TO DO WHAT YOU JUST DID. TRUST ME, YOU BELONG ON A WORLD AS SPECTACULAR AS THIS ONE.
TRY TELLING THAT TO ALANNA.
ADAM, YOU KNOW THAT WAS JUST HER MADNESS SPEAKING.
SURE, "MADNESS" THAT ONLY AFFECTS THE REAL RESIDENTS OF RANN.
PERHAPS THERE'S ANOTHER EXPLANATION FOR THEIR HYSTERIA. DO THESE PEOPLE HAVE A DIFFERENT... PHYSIOLOGY THAN OURS?
ONLY SLIGHTLY. THEY DON'T HAVE AN APPENDIX... OR BODY HAIR, AND THEIR EYES ALLOW THEM TO SEE JUST OUTSIDE THE VISIBLE SPECTRUM, BUT...
OF COURSE!

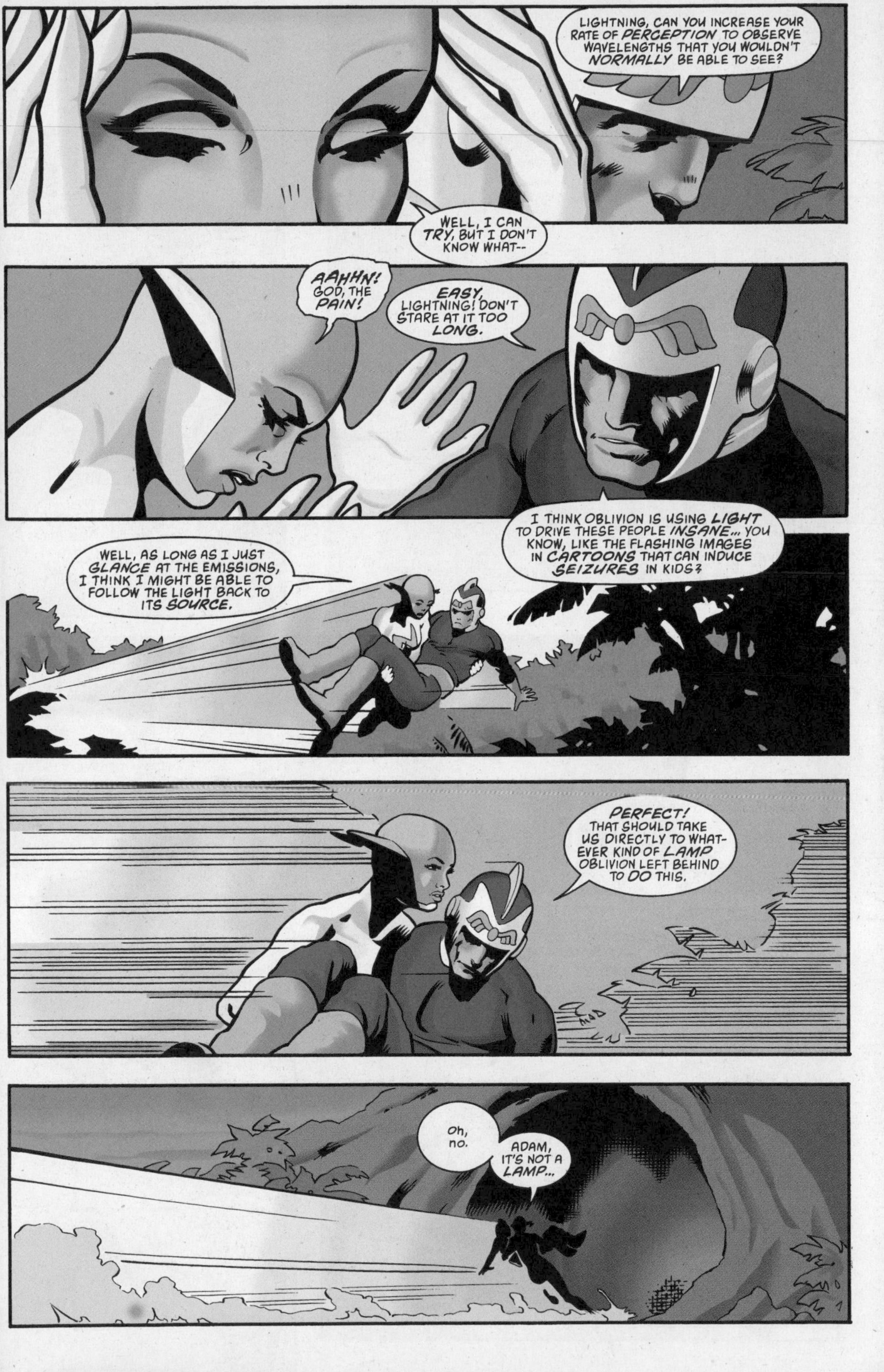
LIGHTNING, CAN YOU INCREASE YOUR RATE OF PERCEPTION TO OBSERVE WAVELENGTHS THAT YOU WOULDN'T NORMALLY BE ABLE TO SEE?
WELL, I CAN TRY, BUT I DON'T KNOW WHAT--
AAHHN! GOD, THE PAIN!
EASY, LIGHTNING! DON'T STARE AT IT TOO LONG.
I THINK OBLIVION IS USING LIGHT TO DRIVE THESE PEOPLE INSANE... YOU KNOW, LIKE THE FLASHING IMAGES IN CARTOONS THAT CAN INDUCE SEIZURES IN KIDS?
WELL, AS LONG AS I JUST GLANCE AT THE EMISSIONS, I THINK I MIGHT BE ABLE TO FOLLOW THE LIGHT BACK TO ITS SOURCE.
PERFECT! THAT SHOULD TAKE US DIRECTLY TO WHATEVER KIND OF LAMP OBLIVION LEFT BEHIND TO DO THIS.
Oh, no.
ADAM, IT'S NOT A LAMP...

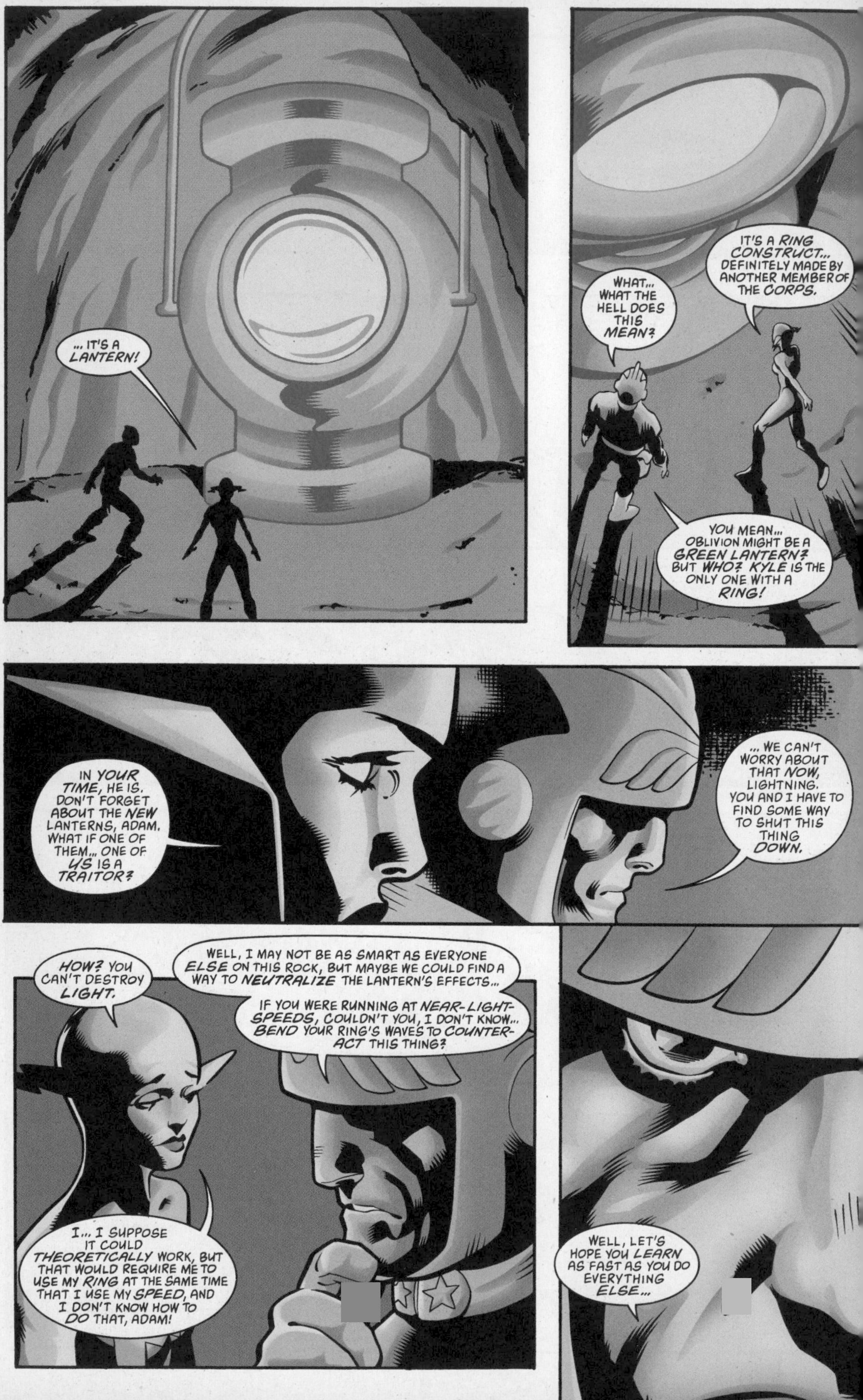
... IT'S A LANTERN!
WHAT... WHAT THE HELL DOES THIS MEAN?
IT'S A RING CONSTRUCT... DEFINITELY MADE BY ANOTHER MEMBER OF THE CORPS.
YOU MEAN... OBLIVION MIGHT BE A GREEN LANTERN? BUT WHO? KYLE IS THE ONLY ONE WITH A RING!
IN YOUR TIME, HE IS. DON'T FORGET ABOUT THE NEW LANTERNS, ADAM. WHAT IF ONE OF THEM... ONE OF US IS A TRAITOR?
... WE CAN'T WORRY ABOUT THAT NOW, LIGHTNING. YOU AND I HAVE TO FIND SOME WAY TO SHUT THIS THING DOWN.
HOW? YOU CAN'T DESTROY LIGHT.
WELL, I MAY NOT BE AS SMART AS EVERYONE ELSE ON THIS ROCK, BUT MAYBE WE COULD FIND A WAY TO NEUTRALIZE THE LANTERN'S EFFECTS...
IF YOU WERE RUNNING AT NEAR-LIGHT-SPEEDS, COULDN'T YOU, I DON'T KNOW... BEND YOUR RING'S WAVES TO COUNTER-ACT THIS THING?
I... I SUPPOSE IT COULD THEORETICALLY WORK, BUT THAT WOULD REQUIRE ME TO USE MY RING AT THE SAME TIME THAT I USE MY SPEED, AND I DON'T KNOW HOW TO DO THAT, ADAM!
WELL, LET'S HOPE YOU LEARN AS FAST AS YOU DO EVERYTHING ELSE...

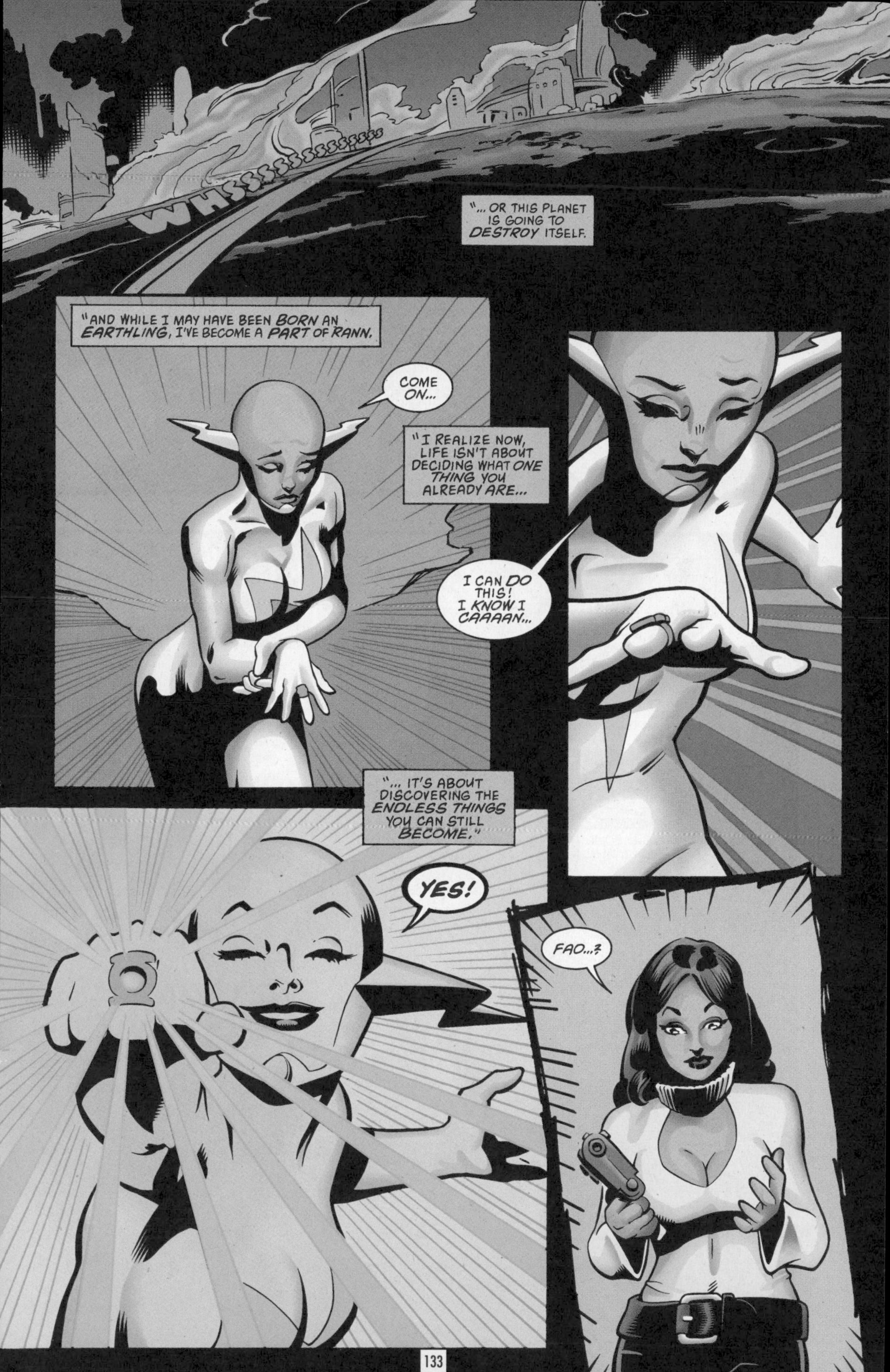
WHSSSSSSSSSSSSSSSS
"... OR THIS PLANET IS GOING TO DESTROY ITSELF.
"AND WHILE I MAY HAVE BEEN BORN AN EARTHLING, I'VE BECOME A PART OF RANN.
COME ON...
"I REALIZE NOW, LIFE ISN'T ABOUT DECIDING WHAT ONE THING YOU ALREADY ARE...
I CAN DO THIS! I KNOW I CAAAAN...
"... IT'S ABOUT DISCOVERING THE ENDLESS THINGS YOU CAN STILL BECOME."
YES!
FAO...?

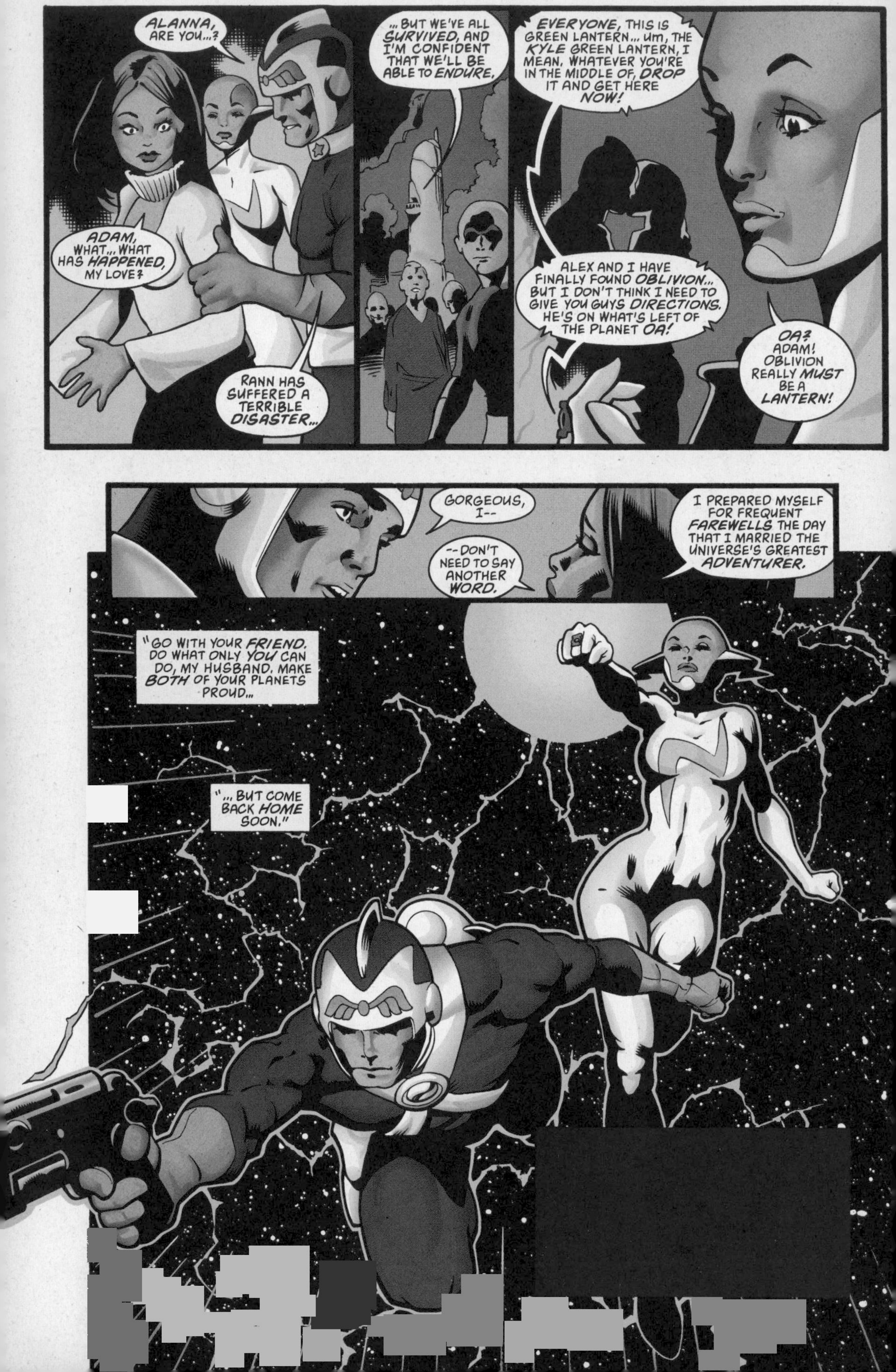
ALANNA, ARE YOU...?
ADAM, WHAT... WHAT HAS HAPPENED, MY LOVE?
RANN HAS SUFFERED A TERRIBLE DISASTER...
...BUT WE'VE ALL SURVIVED, AND I'M CONFIDENT THAT WE'LL BE ABLE TO ENDURE.
EVERYONE, THIS IS GREEN LANTERN... UM, THE KYLE GREEN LANTERN, I MEAN. WHATEVER YOU'RE IN THE MIDDLE OF, DROP IT AND GET HERE NOW!
ALEX AND I HAVE FINALLY FOUND OBLIVION... BUT I DON'T THINK I NEED TO GIVE YOU GUYS DIRECTIONS. HE'S ON WHAT'S LEFT OF THE PLANET OA!
OA? ADAM! OBLIVION REALLY MUST BE A LANTERN!
GORGEOUS, I--
--DON'T NEED TO SAY ANOTHER WORD.
I PREPARED MYSELF FOR FREQUENT FAREWELLS THE DAY THAT I MARRIED THE UNIVERSE'S GREATEST ADVENTURER.
"GO WITH YOUR FRIEND. DO WHAT ONLY YOU CAN DO, MY HUSBAND. MAKE BOTH OF YOUR PLANETS PROUD...
"...BUT COME BACK HOME SOON."
[redacted]

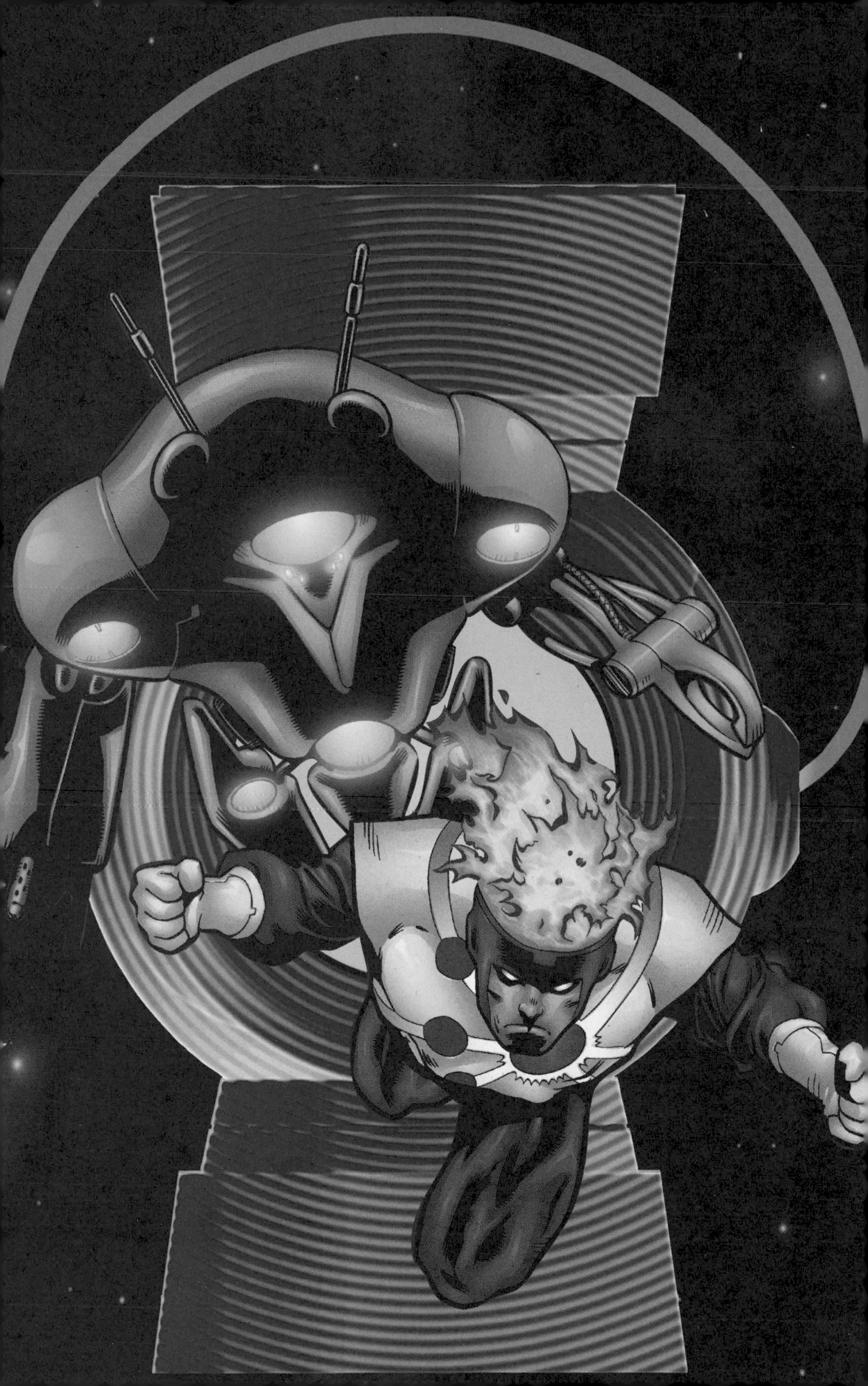

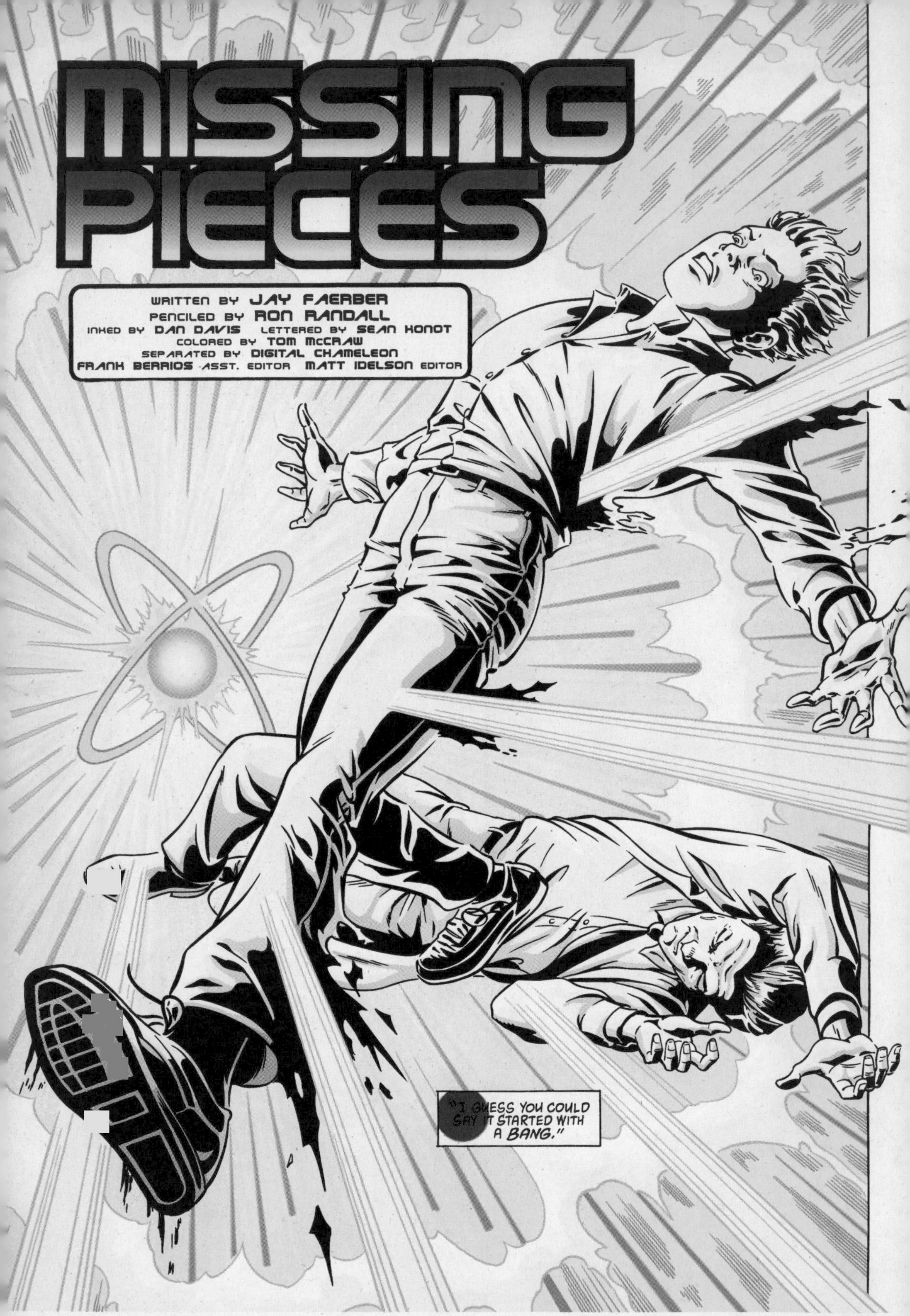

MISSING PIECES
WRITTEN BY JAY FAERBER
PENCILED BY RON RANDALL
INKED BY DAN DAVIS LETTERED BY SEAN KONOT
COLORED BY TOM McCRAW
SEPARATED BY DIGITAL CHAMELEON
FRANK BERRIOS ASST. EDITOR MATT IDELSON EDITOR
"I GUESS YOU COULD SAY IT STARTED WITH A BANG."

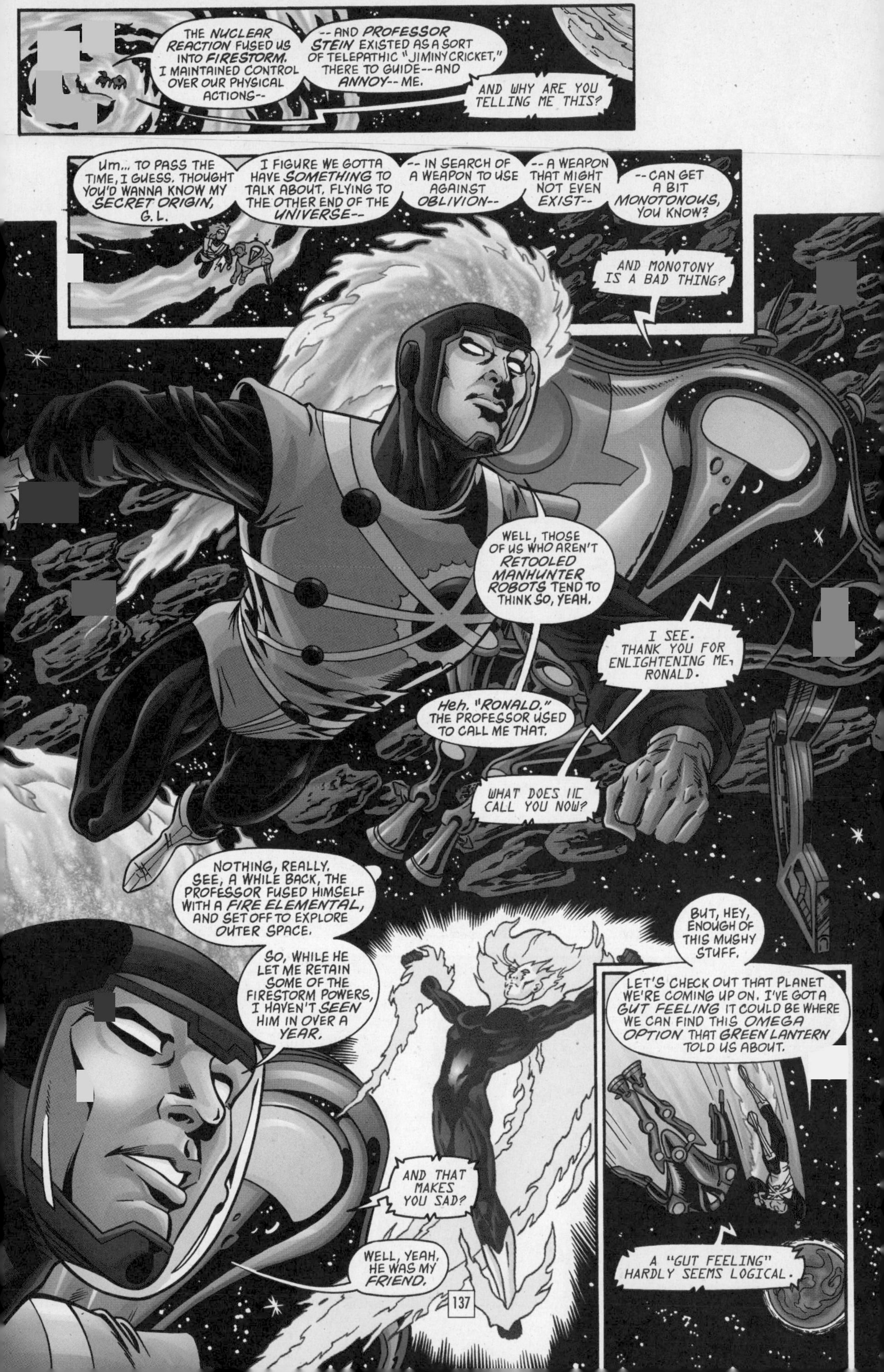

THE NUCLEAR REACTION FUSED US INTO FIRESTORM. I MAINTAINED CONTROL OVER OUR PHYSICAL ACTIONS--
--AND PROFESSOR STEIN EXISTED AS A SORT OF TELEPATHIC "JIMINY CRICKET," THERE TO GUIDE--AND ANNOY--ME.
AND WHY ARE YOU TELLING ME THIS?
UM... TO PASS THE TIME, I GUESS. THOUGHT YOU'D WANNA KNOW MY SECRET ORIGIN, G.L.
I FIGURE WE GOTTA HAVE SOMETHING TO TALK ABOUT, FLYING TO THE OTHER END OF THE UNIVERSE--
--IN SEARCH OF A WEAPON TO USE AGAINST OBLIVION--
--A WEAPON THAT MIGHT NOT EVEN EXIST--
--CAN GET A BIT MONOTONOUS, YOU KNOW?
AND MONOTONY IS A BAD THING?
WELL, THOSE OF US WHO AREN'T RETOOLED MANHUNTER ROBOTS TEND TO THINK SO, YEAH.
I SEE. THANK YOU FOR ENLIGHTENING ME, RONALD.
Heh. "RONALD." THE PROFESSOR USED TO CALL ME THAT.
WHAT DOES HE CALL YOU NOW?
NOTHING, REALLY. SEE, A WHILE BACK, THE PROFESSOR FUSED HIMSELF WITH A FIRE ELEMENTAL, AND SET OFF TO EXPLORE OUTER SPACE.
SO, WHILE HE LET ME RETAIN SOME OF THE FIRESTORM POWERS, I HAVEN'T SEEN HIM IN OVER A YEAR.
AND THAT MAKES YOU SAD?
WELL, YEAH, HE WAS MY FRIEND.
BUT, HEY, ENOUGH OF THIS MUSHY STUFF.
LET'S CHECK OUT THAT PLANET WE'RE COMING UP ON. I'VE GOT A GUT FEELING IT COULD BE WHERE WE CAN FIND THIS OMEGA OPTION THAT GREEN LANTERN TOLD US ABOUT.
A "GUT FEELING" HARDLY SEEMS LOGICAL.

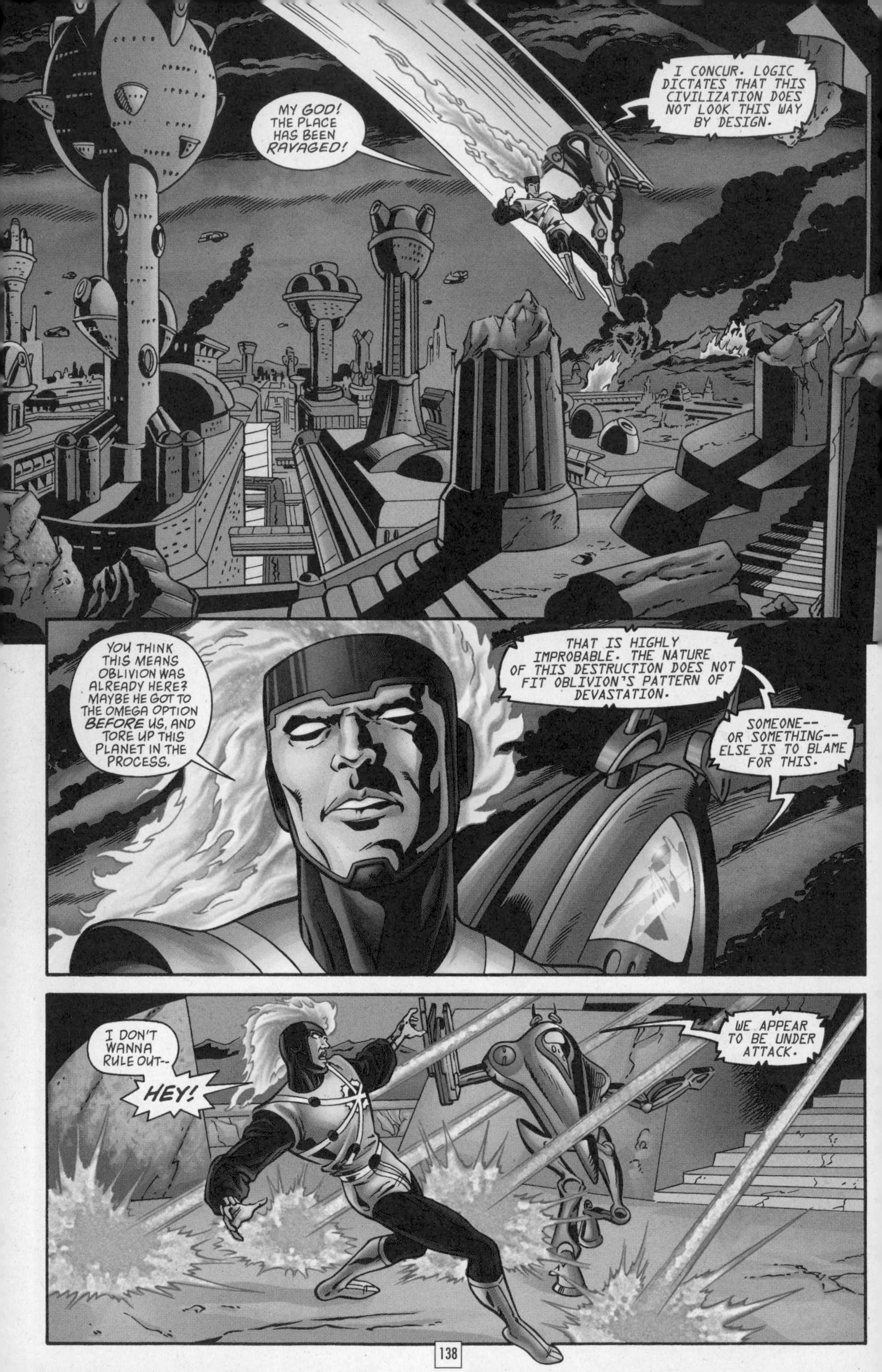
MY GOD! THE PLACE HAS BEEN RAVAGED!
I CONCUR. LOGIC DICTATES THAT THIS CIVILIZATION DOES NOT LOOK THIS WAY BY DESIGN.
YOU THINK THIS MEANS OBLIVION WAS ALREADY HERE? MAYBE HE GOT TO THE OMEGA OPTION BEFORE US, AND TORE UP THIS PLANET IN THE PROCESS.
THAT IS HIGHLY IMPROBABLE. THE NATURE OF THIS DESTRUCTION DOES NOT FIT OBLIVION'S PATTERN OF DEVASTATION.
SOMEONE-- OR SOMETHING-- ELSE IS TO BLAME FOR THIS.
I DON'T WANNA RULE OUT--
HEY!
WE APPEAR TO BE UNDER ATTACK.

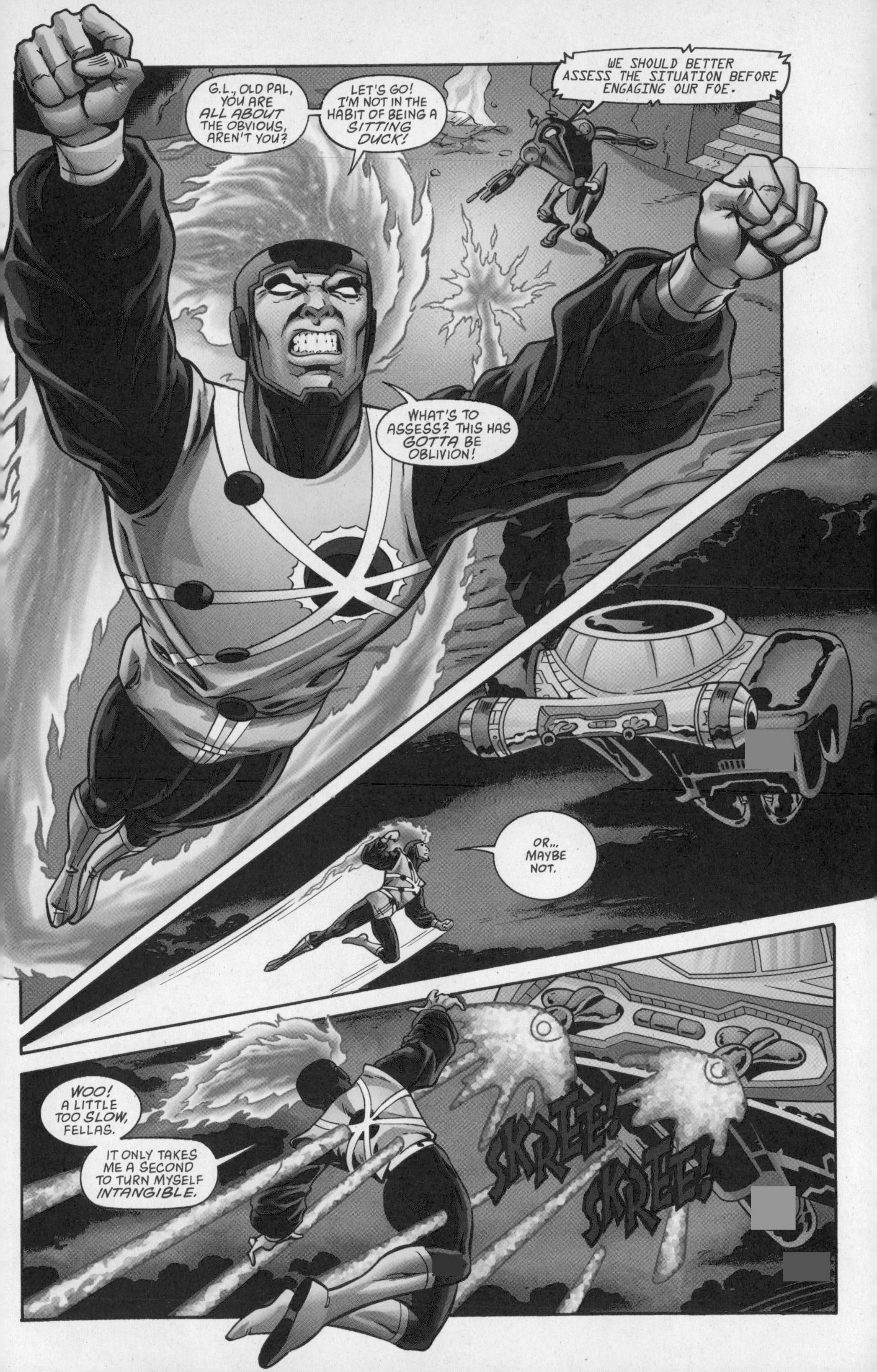
G.L., OLD PAL, YOU ARE ALL ABOUT THE OBVIOUS, AREN'T YOU?
LET'S GO! I'M NOT IN THE HABIT OF BEING A SITTING DUCK!
WE SHOULD BETTER ASSESS THE SITUATION BEFORE ENGAGING OUR FOE.
WHAT'S TO ASSESS? THIS HAS GOTTA BE OBLIVION!
OR... MAYBE NOT.
WOO! A LITTLE TOO SLOW, FELLAS.
IT ONLY TAKES ME A SECOND TO TURN MYSELF INTANGIBLE.
SKREEE! SKREEE!

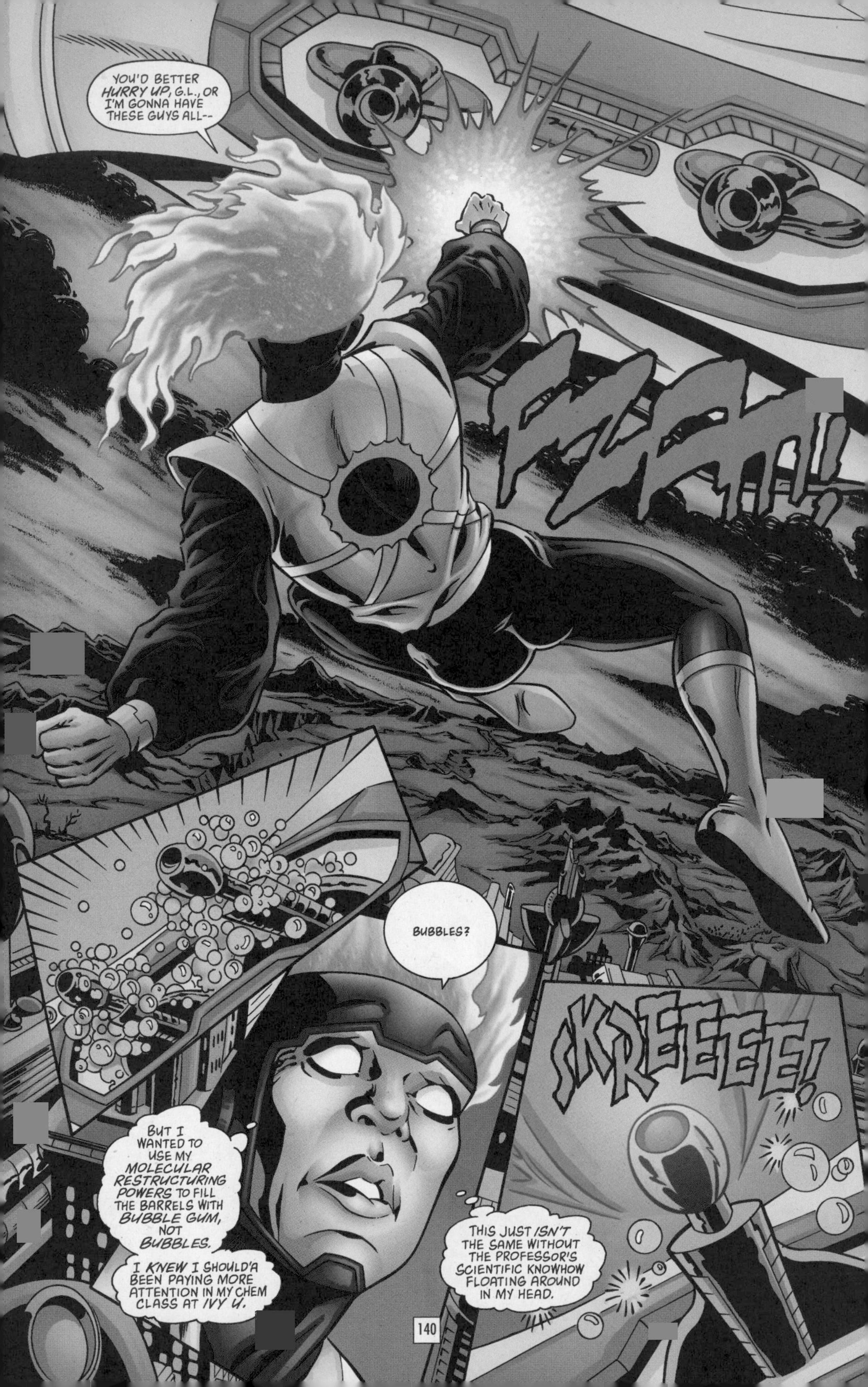
YOU'D BETTER HURRY UP, G.L., OR I'M GONNA HAVE THESE GUYS ALL--
FZZAT!!
BUBBLES?
BUT I WANTED TO USE MY MOLECULAR RESTRUCTURING POWERS TO FILL THE BARRELS WITH BUBBLE GUM, NOT BUBBLES.
I KNEW I SHOULD'A BEEN PAYING MORE ATTENTION IN MY CHEM CLASS AT IVY U.
SKREEEE!
THIS JUST ISN'T THE SAME WITHOUT THE PROFESSOR'S SCIENTIFIC KNOWHOW FLOATING AROUND IN MY HEAD.

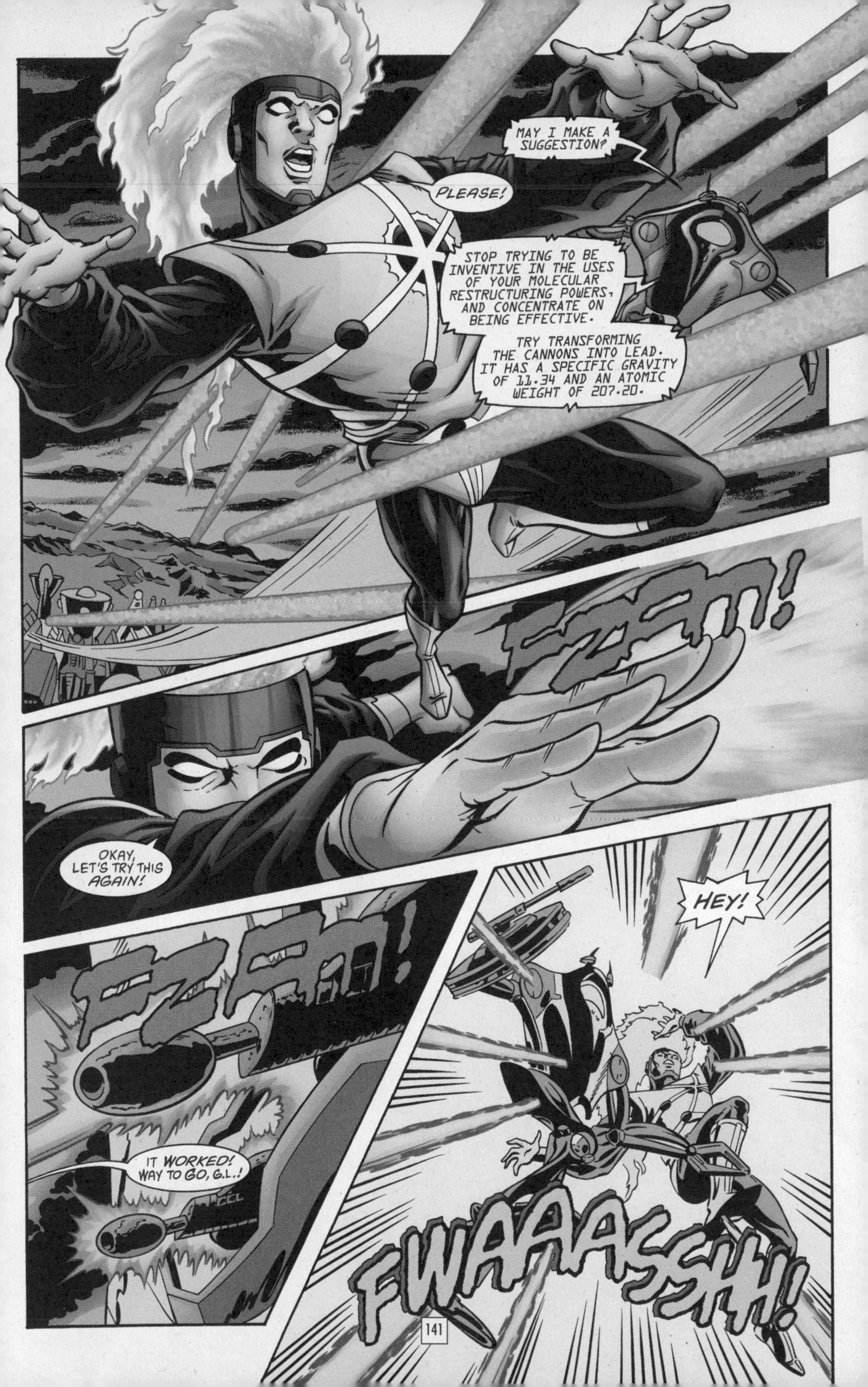
MAY I MAKE A SUGGESTION?
PLEASE!
STOP TRYING TO BE INVENTIVE IN THE USES OF YOUR MOLECULAR RESTRUCTURING POWERS, AND CONCENTRATE ON BEING EFFECTIVE.
TRY TRANSFORMING THE CANNONS INTO LEAD. IT HAS A SPECIFIC GRAVITY OF 11.34 AND AN ATOMIC WEIGHT OF 207.20.
FZZAM!
OKAY, LET'S TRY THIS AGAIN!
FZZAM!
IT WORKED! WAY TO GO, G.L.!
HEY!
FWAAASSH!

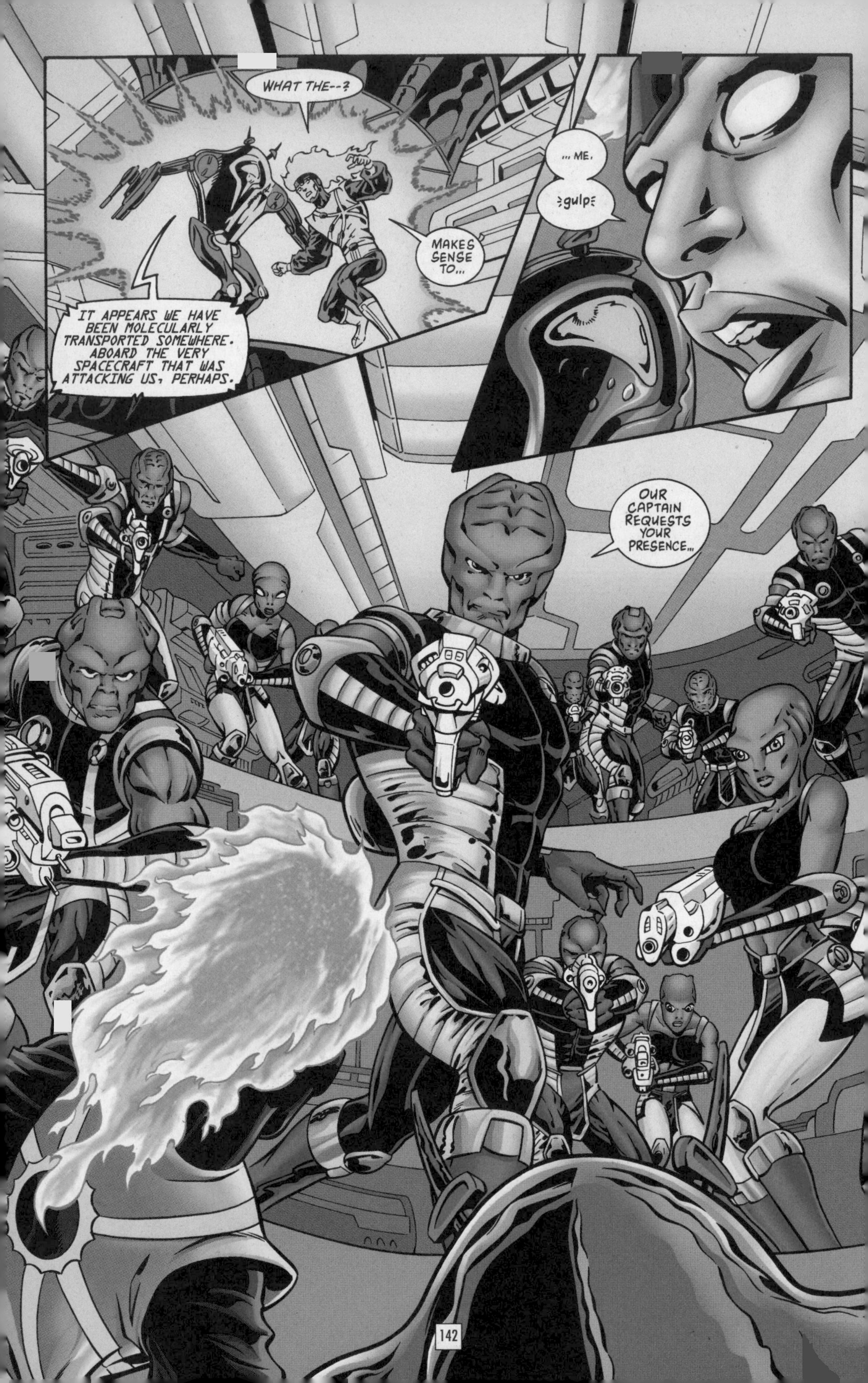
WHAT THE--?
IT APPEARS WE HAVE BEEN MOLECULARLY TRANSPORTED SOMEWHERE. ABOARD THE VERY SPACECRAFT THAT WAS ATTACKING US, PERHAPS.
MAKES SENSE TO...
...ME.
≥gulp≤
OUR CAPTAIN REQUESTS YOUR PRESENCE...

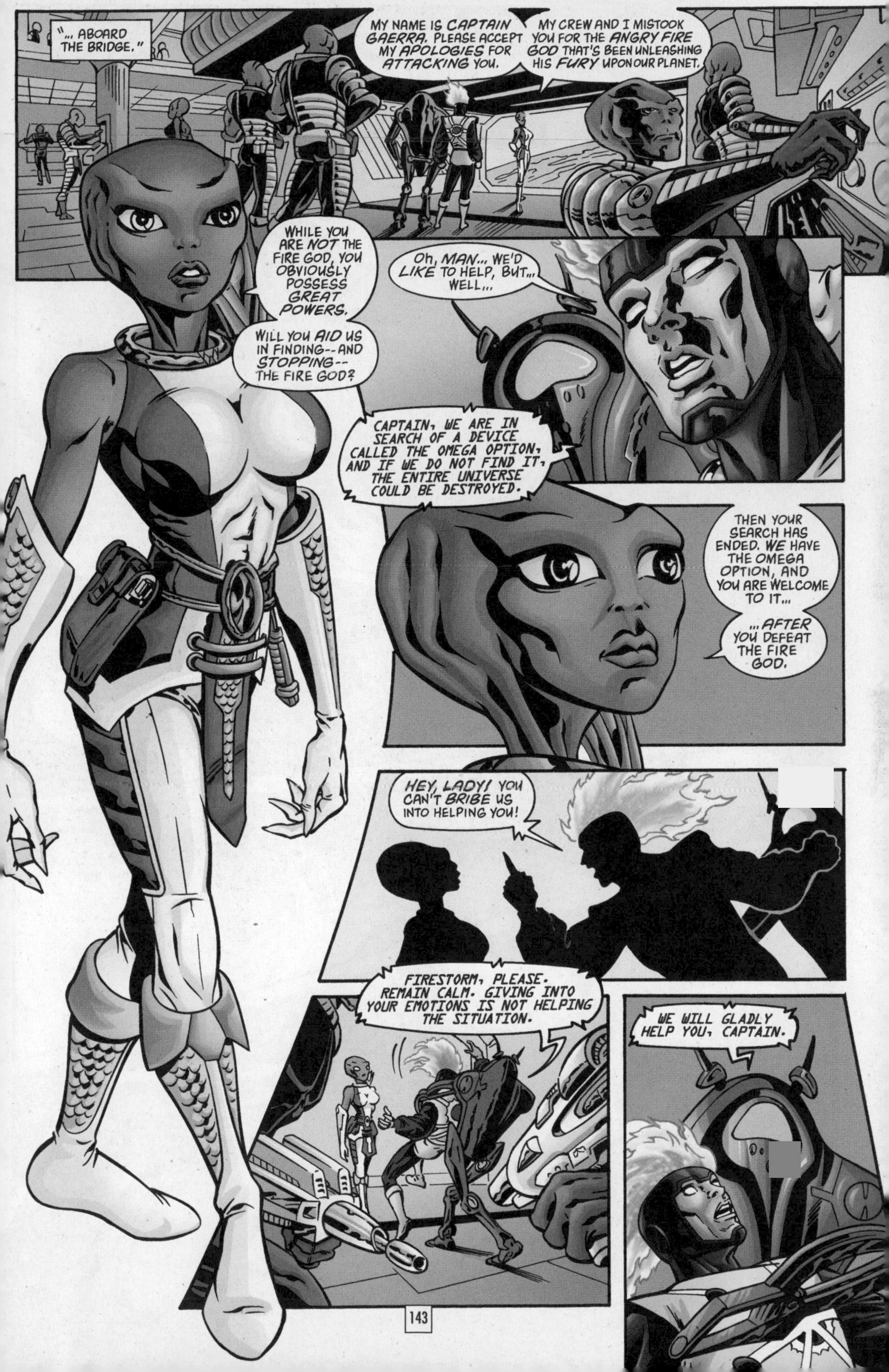
"... ABOARD THE BRIDGE."
MY NAME IS CAPTAIN GAERRA. PLEASE ACCEPT MY APOLOGIES FOR ATTACKING YOU.
MY CREW AND I MISTOOK YOU FOR THE ANGRY FIRE GOD THAT'S BEEN UNLEASHING HIS FURY UPON OUR PLANET.
WHILE YOU ARE NOT THE FIRE GOD, YOU OBVIOUSLY POSSESS GREAT POWERS.
WILL YOU AID US IN FINDING-- AND STOPPING-- THE FIRE GOD?
Oh, MAN... WE'D LIKE TO HELP, BUT... WELL...
CAPTAIN, WE ARE IN SEARCH OF A DEVICE CALLED THE OMEGA OPTION, AND IF WE DO NOT FIND IT, THE ENTIRE UNIVERSE COULD BE DESTROYED.
THEN YOUR SEARCH HAS ENDED. WE HAVE THE OMEGA OPTION, AND YOU ARE WELCOME TO IT...
...AFTER YOU DEFEAT THE FIRE GOD.
HEY, LADY! YOU CAN'T BRIBE US INTO HELPING YOU!
FIRESTORM, PLEASE. REMAIN CALM. GIVING INTO YOUR EMOTIONS IS NOT HELPING THE SITUATION.
WE WILL GLADLY HELP YOU, CAPTAIN.

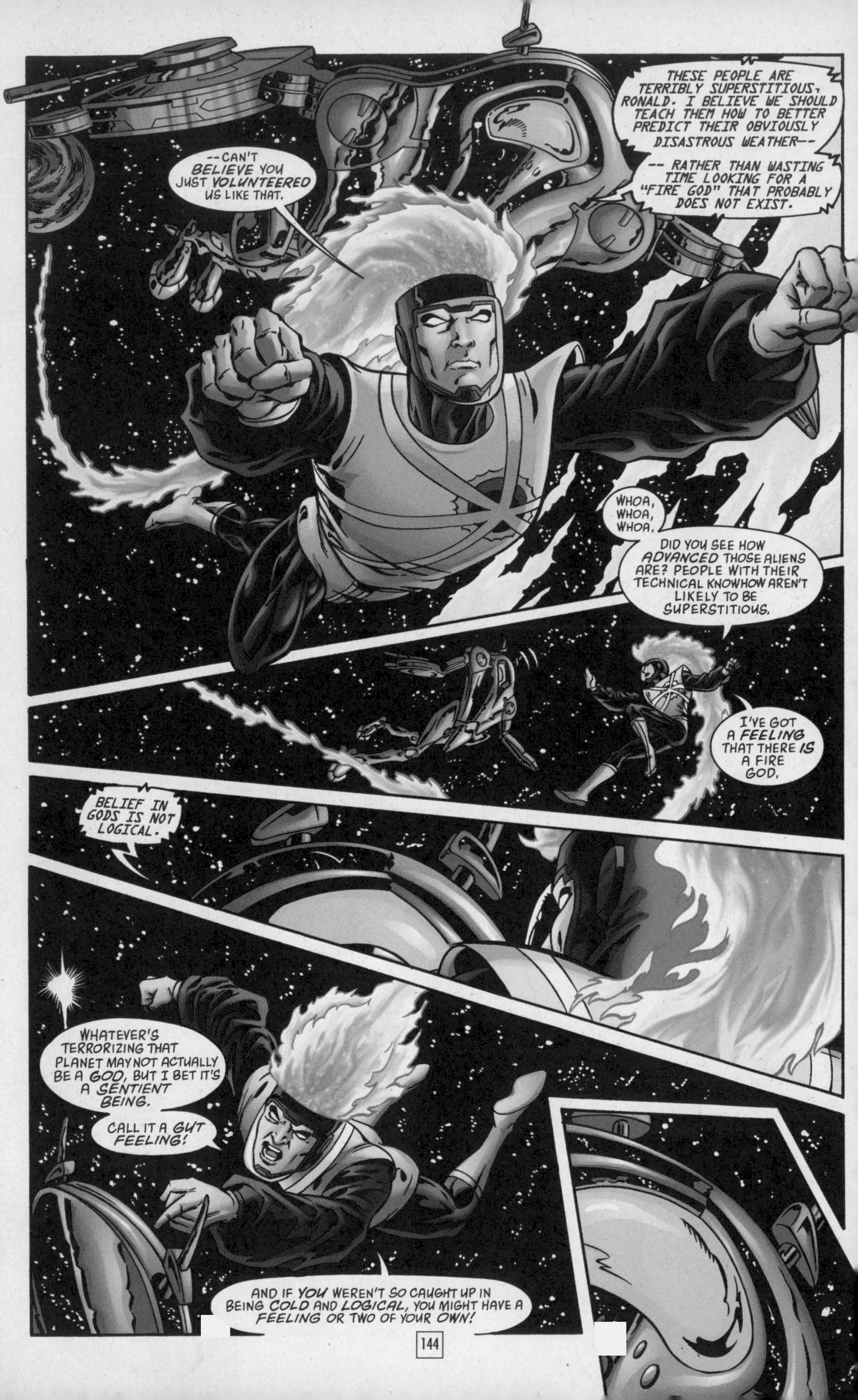
--CAN'T BELIEVE YOU JUST VOLUNTEERED US LIKE THAT.
THESE PEOPLE ARE TERRIBLY SUPERSTITIOUS, RONALD. I BELIEVE WE SHOULD TEACH THEM HOW TO BETTER PREDICT THEIR OBVIOUSLY DISASTROUS WEATHER--
--RATHER THAN WASTING TIME LOOKING FOR A "FIRE GOD" THAT PROBABLY DOES NOT EXIST.
WHOA, WHOA, WHOA.
DID YOU SEE HOW ADVANCED THOSE ALIENS ARE? PEOPLE WITH THEIR TECHNICAL KNOWHOW AREN'T LIKELY TO BE SUPERSTITIOUS.
I'VE GOT A FEELING THAT THERE IS A FIRE GOD.
BELIEF IN GODS IS NOT LOGICAL.
WHATEVER'S TERRORIZING THAT PLANET MAY NOT ACTUALLY BE A GOD, BUT I BET IT'S A SENTIENT BEING.
CALL IT A GUT FEELING!
AND IF YOU WEREN'T SO CAUGHT UP IN BEING COLD AND LOGICAL, YOU MIGHT HAVE A FEELING OR TWO OF YOUR OWN!

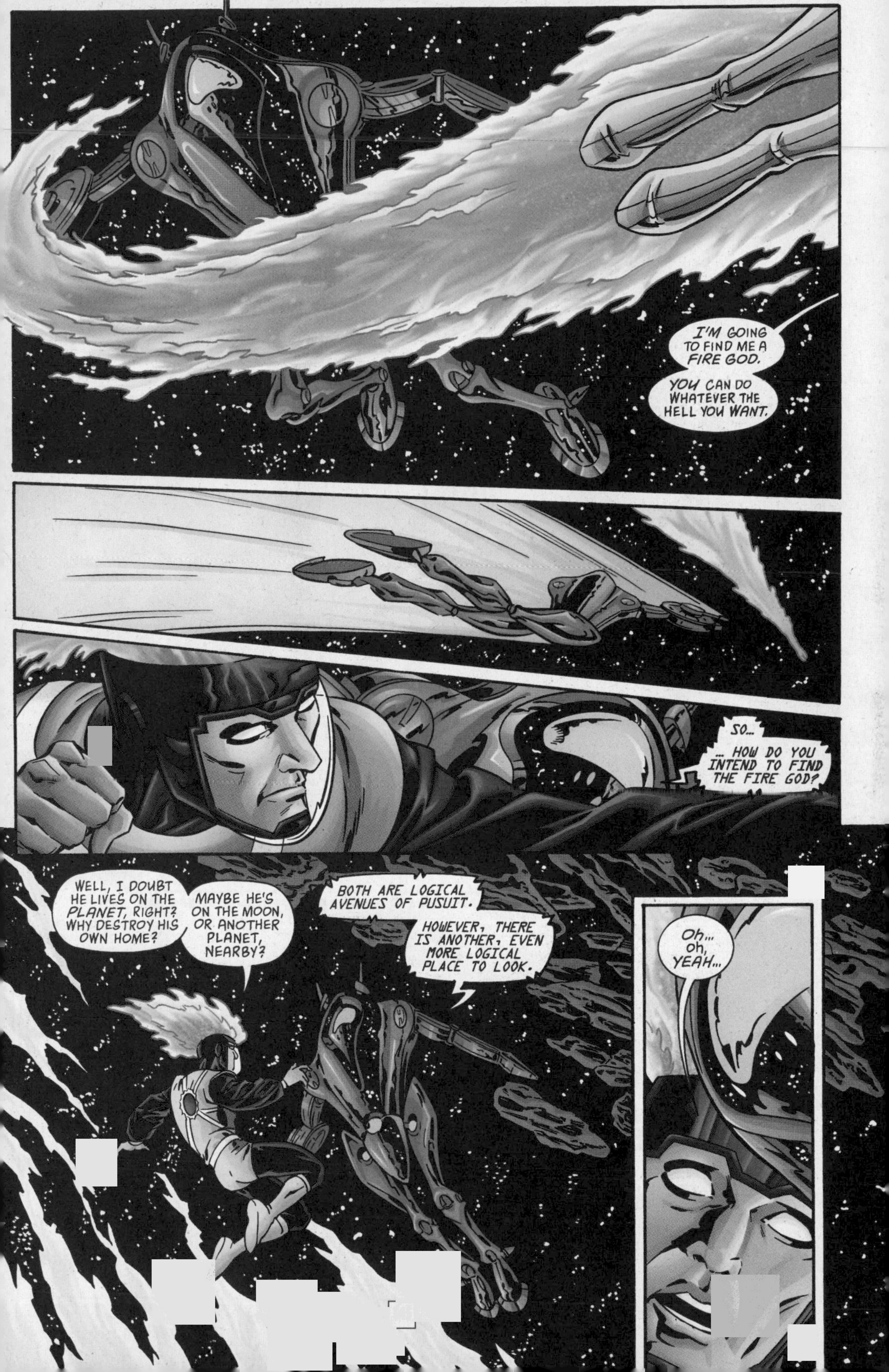

I'M GOING TO FIND ME A FIRE GOD.
YOU CAN DO WHATEVER THE HELL YOU WANT.
SO...
... HOW DO YOU INTEND TO FIND THE FIRE GOD?
WELL, I DOUBT HE LIVES ON THE PLANET, RIGHT? WHY DESTROY HIS OWN HOME?
MAYBE HE'S ON THE MOON, OR ANOTHER PLANET, NEARBY?
BOTH ARE LOGICAL AVENUES OF PUSUIT.
HOWEVER, THERE IS ANOTHER, EVEN MORE LOGICAL PLACE TO LOOK.
Oh... oh, YEAH...

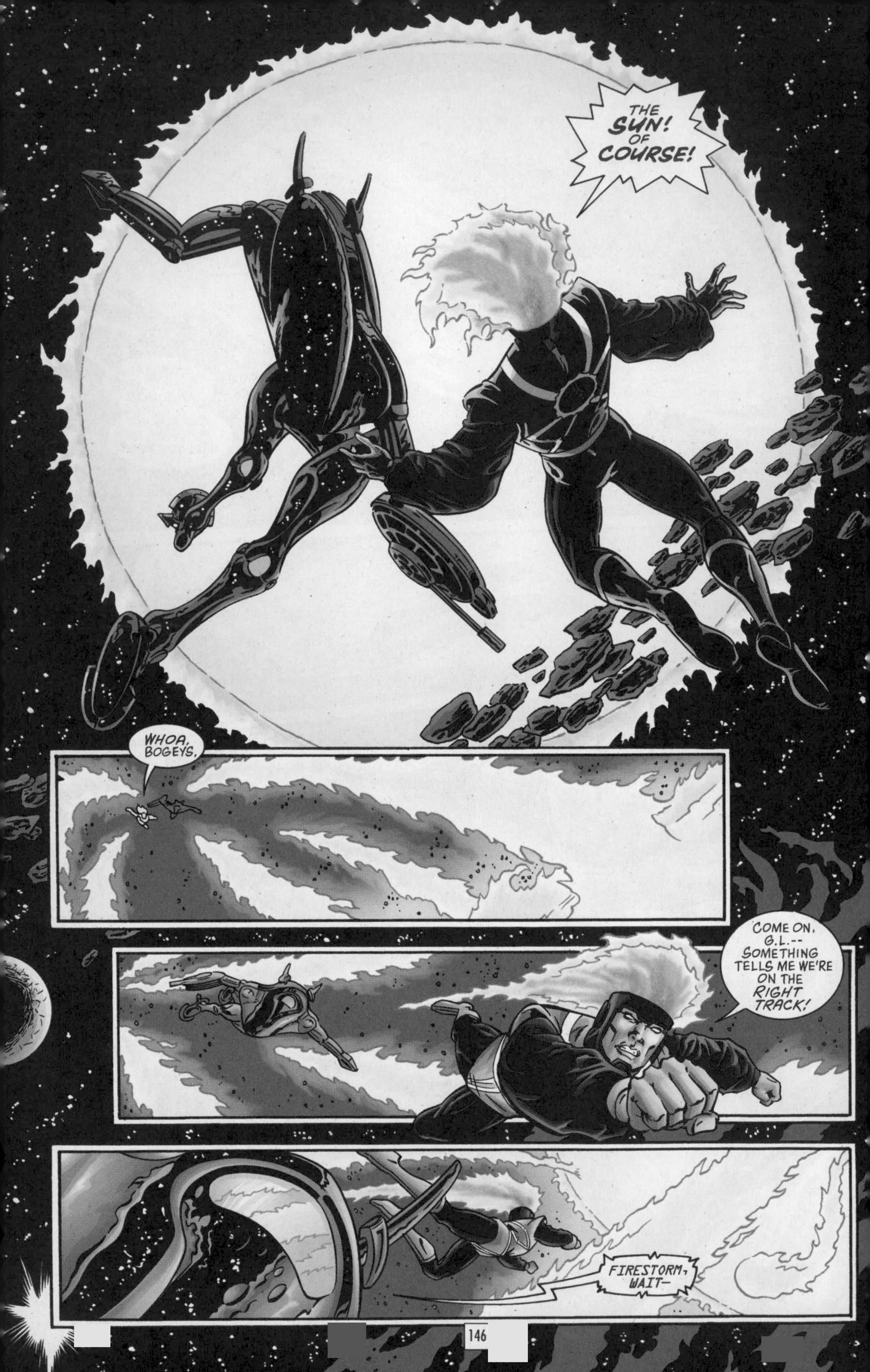
THE SUN! OF COURSE!
WHOA, BOGEYS.
COME ON, G.L.-- SOMETHING TELLS ME WE'RE ON THE RIGHT TRACK!
FIRESTORM, WAIT--

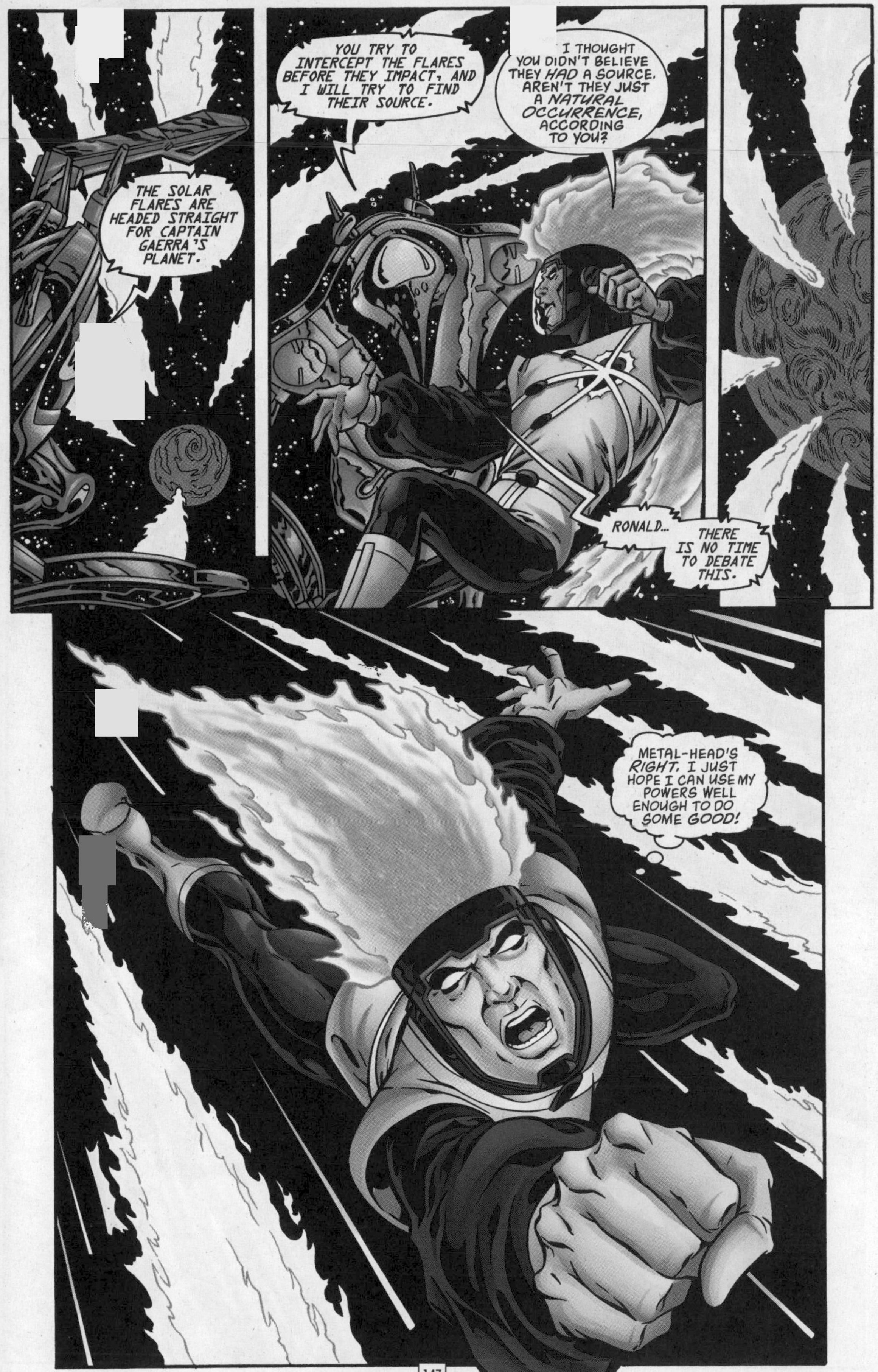
THE SOLAR FLARES ARE HEADED STRAIGHT FOR CAPTAIN GAERRA'S PLANET.
YOU TRY TO INTERCEPT THE FLARES BEFORE THEY IMPACT, AND I WILL TRY TO FIND THEIR SOURCE.
I THOUGHT YOU DIDN'T BELIEVE THEY HAD A SOURCE. AREN'T THEY JUST A NATURAL OCCURRENCE, ACCORDING TO YOU?
RONALD...
THERE IS NO TIME TO DEBATE THIS.
METAL-HEAD'S RIGHT. I JUST HOPE I CAN USE MY POWERS WELL ENOUGH TO DO SOME GOOD!

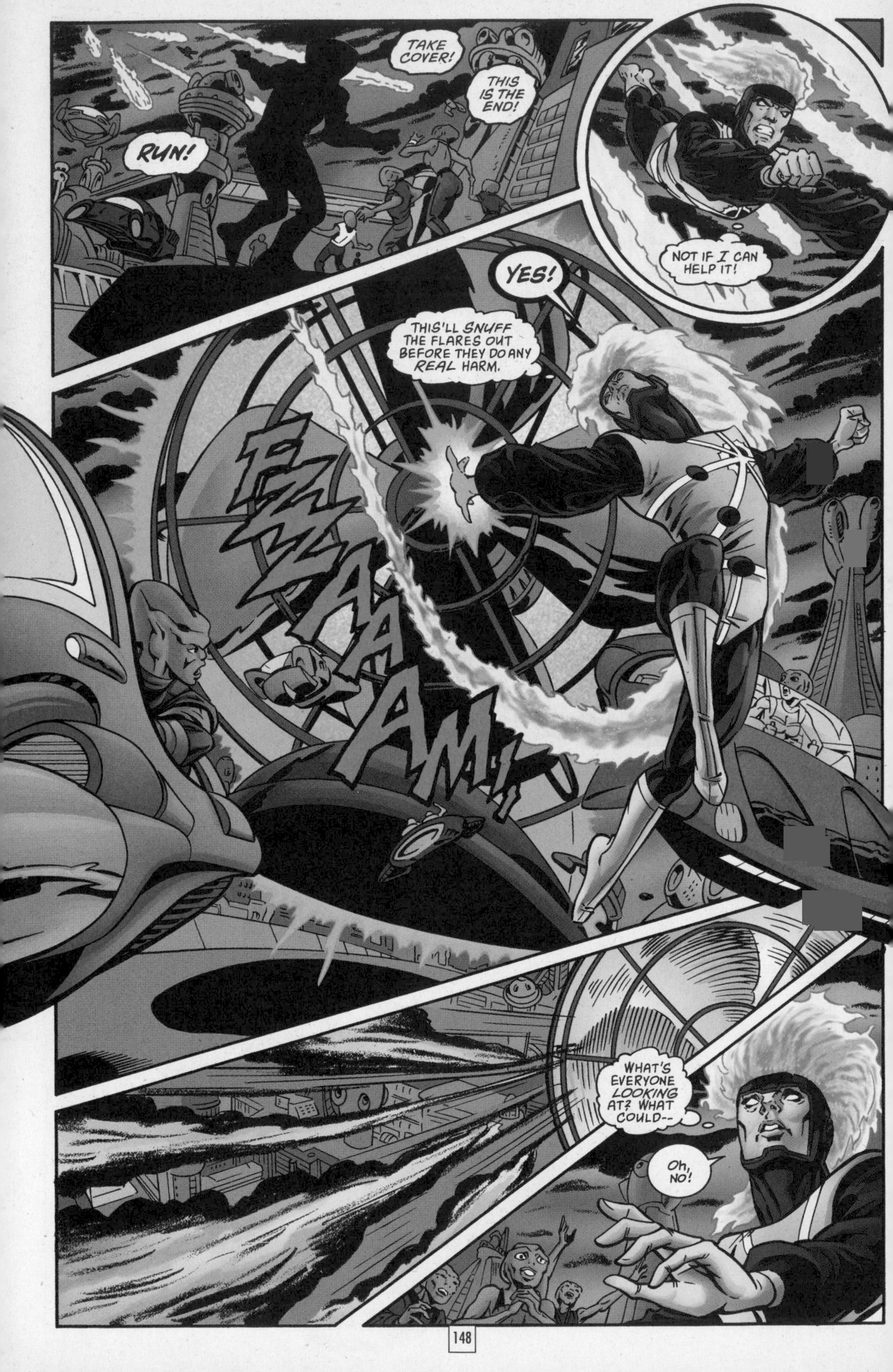
TAKE COVER!
THIS IS THE END!
RUN!
NOT IF I CAN HELP IT!
YES!
THIS'LL SNUFF THE FLARES OUT BEFORE THEY DO ANY REAL HARM.
FZWAAAAM!!
WHAT'S EVERYONE LOOKING AT? WHAT COULD--
Oh, NO!

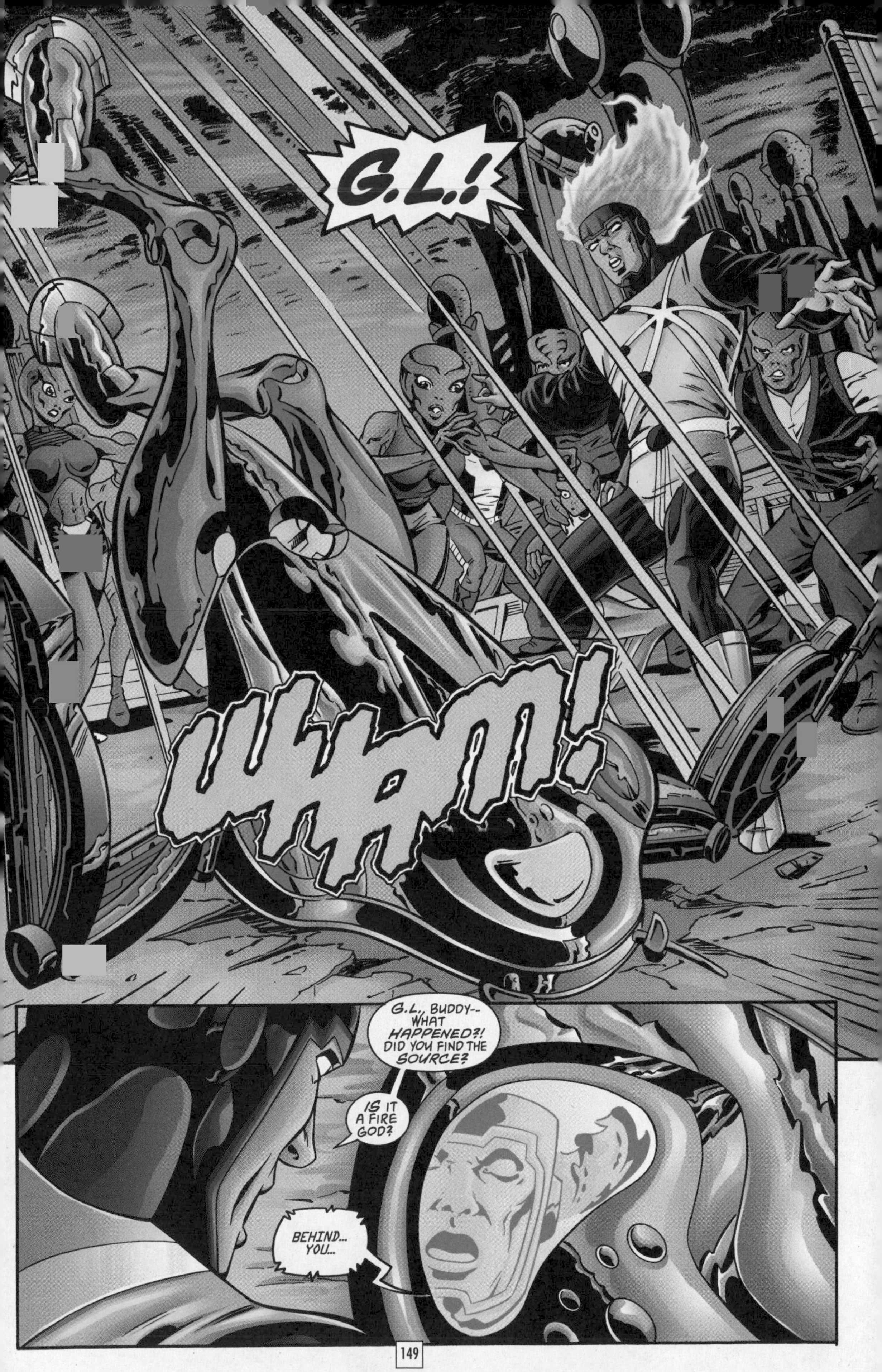
G.L.!
WHAM!
G.L., BUDDY--WHAT HAPPENED?! DID YOU FIND THE SOURCE?
IS IT A FIRE GOD?
BEHIND... YOU...

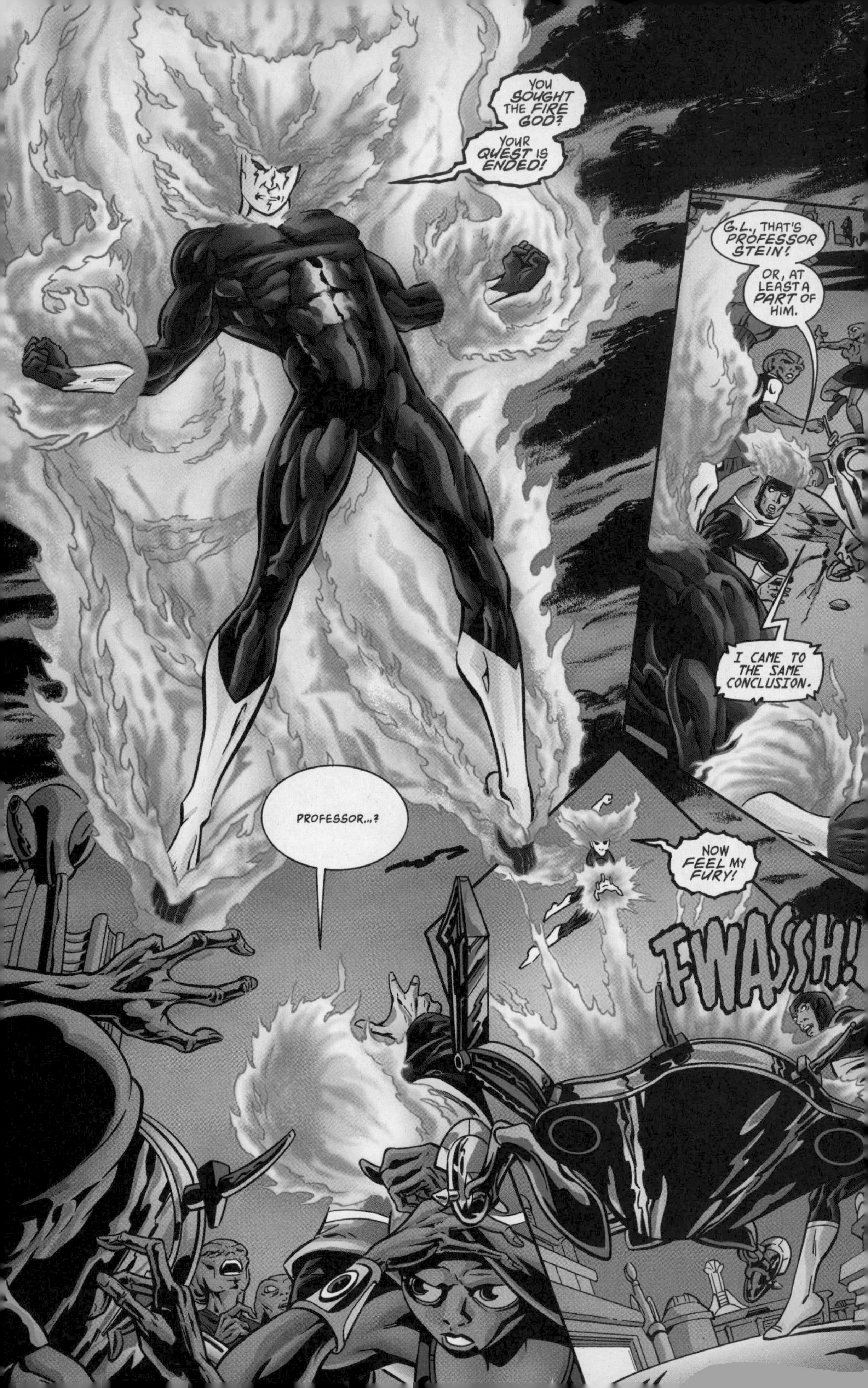
YOU SOUGHT THE FIRE GOD?
YOUR QUEST IS ENDED!
G.L., THAT'S PROFESSOR STEIN!
OR, AT LEAST A PART OF HIM.
I CAME TO THE SAME CONCLUSION.
PROFESSOR...?
NOW FEEL MY FURY!
FWASSH!

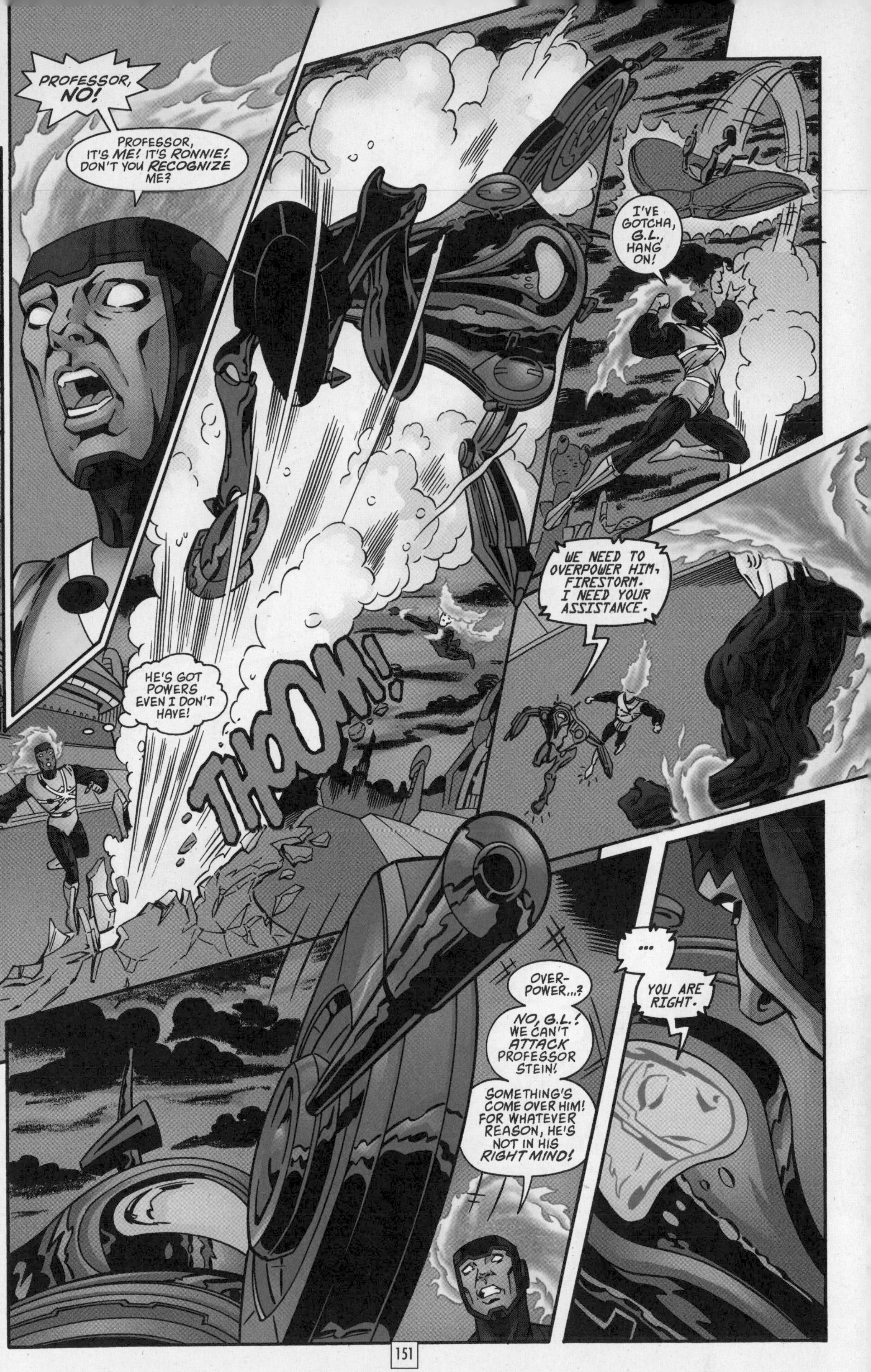
PROFESSOR, NO!
PROFESSOR, IT'S ME! IT'S RONNIE! DON'T YOU RECOGNIZE ME?
I'VE GOTCHA, G.L., HANG ON!
HE'S GOT POWERS EVEN I DON'T HAVE!
THOOM!!
WE NEED TO OVERPOWER HIM, FIRESTORM. I NEED YOUR ASSISTANCE.
OVER-POWER...?
NO, G.L.! WE CAN'T ATTACK PROFESSOR STEIN!
SOMETHING'S COME OVER HIM! FOR WHATEVER REASON, HE'S NOT IN HIS RIGHT MIND!
...
YOU ARE RIGHT.

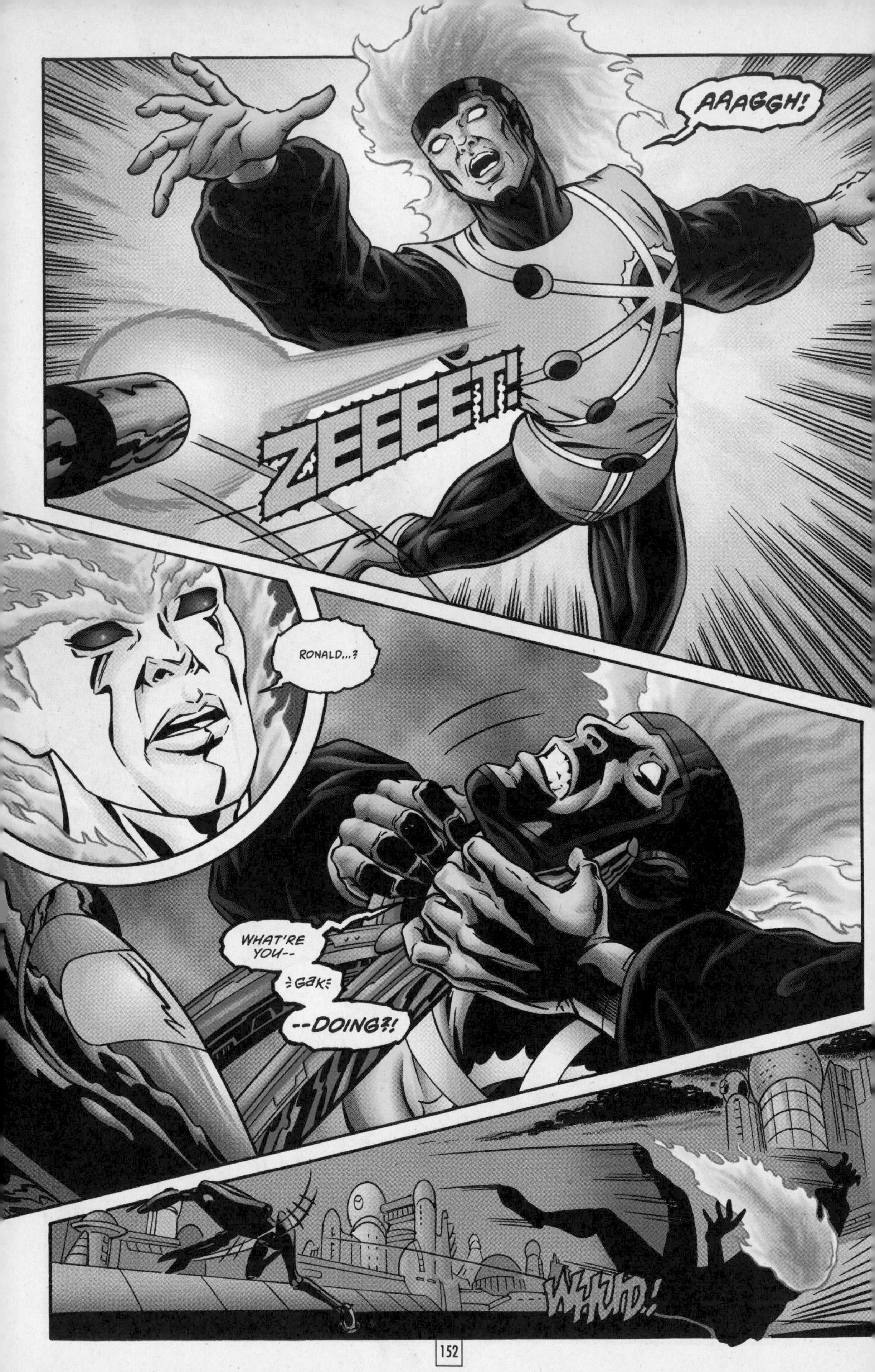
AAAGGH!
ZEEEEET!
RONALD...?
WHAT'RE YOU--
GAK
--DOING?!
WHUD!

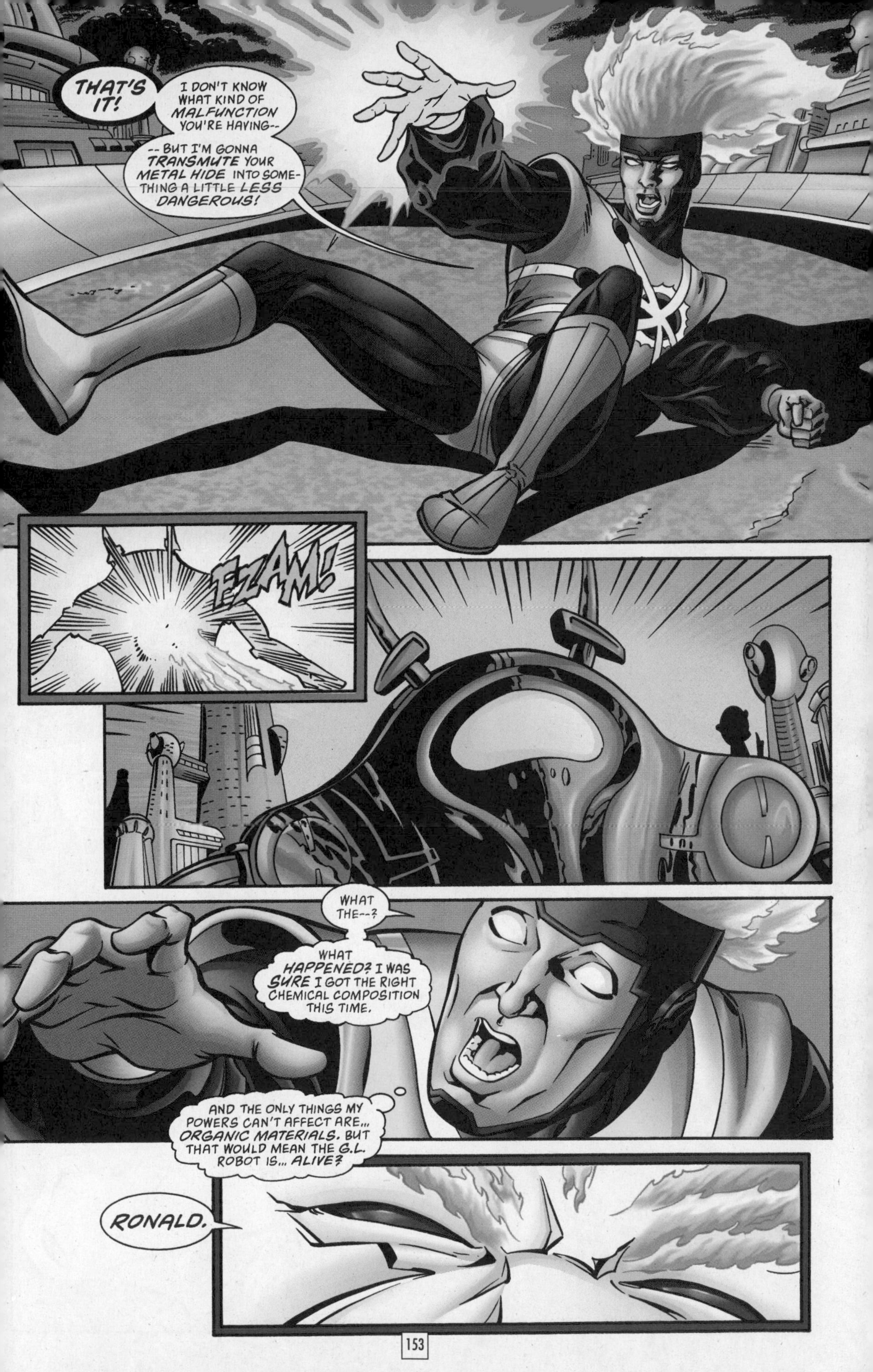
THAT'S IT!
I DON'T KNOW WHAT KIND OF MALFUNCTION YOU'RE HAVING--
-- BUT I'M GONNA TRANSMUTE YOUR METAL HIDE INTO SOMETHING A LITTLE LESS DANGEROUS!
FZAM!
WHAT THE--?
WHAT HAPPENED? I WAS SURE I GOT THE RIGHT CHEMICAL COMPOSITION THIS TIME.
AND THE ONLY THINGS MY POWERS CAN'T AFFECT ARE... ORGANIC MATERIALS. BUT THAT WOULD MEAN THE G.L. ROBOT IS... ALIVE?
RONALD.

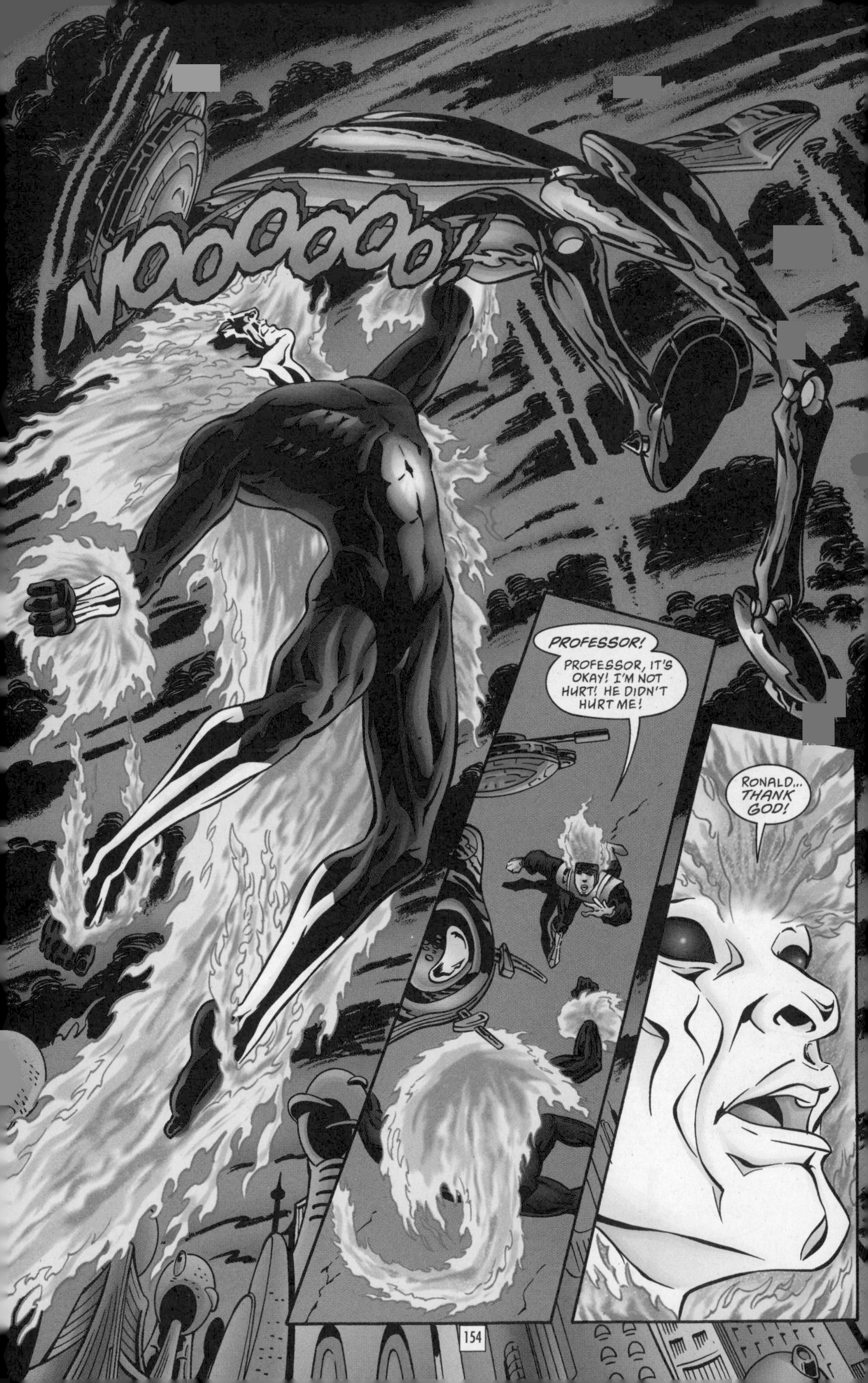
NOOOOOO!!
PROFESSOR!
PROFESSOR, IT'S OKAY! I'M NOT HURT! HE DIDN'T HURT ME!
RONALD... THANK GOD!

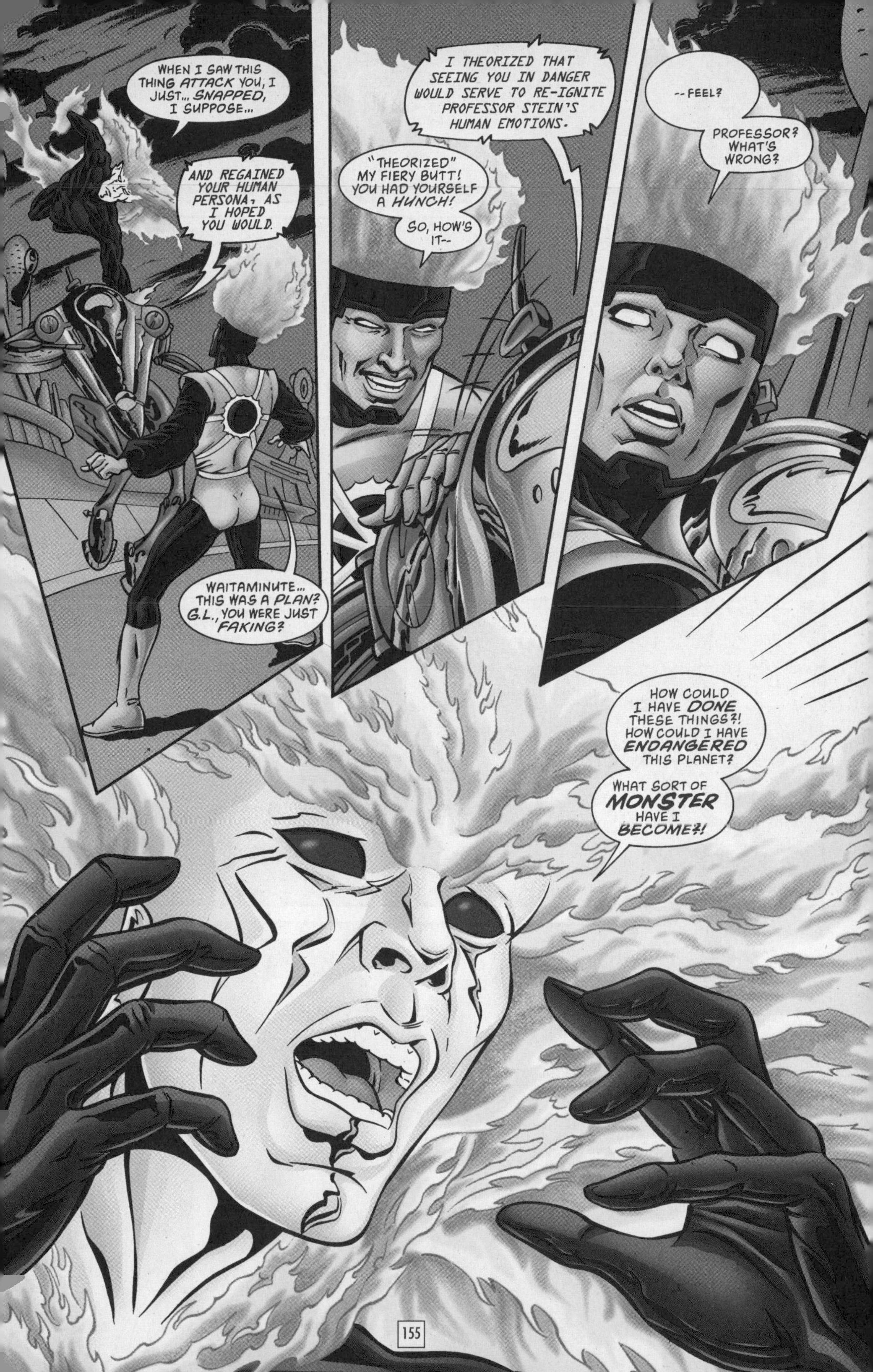
WHEN I SAW THIS THING ATTACK YOU, I JUST... SNAPPED, I SUPPOSE...
AND REGAINED YOUR HUMAN PERSONA, AS I HOPED YOU WOULD.
WAITAMINUTE... THIS WAS A PLAN? G.L., YOU WERE JUST FAKING?
I THEORIZED THAT SEEING YOU IN DANGER WOULD SERVE TO RE-IGNITE PROFESSOR STEIN'S HUMAN EMOTIONS.
"THEORIZED" MY FIERY BUTT! YOU HAD YOURSELF A HUNCH!
SO, HOW'S IT--
--FEEL?
PROFESSOR? WHAT'S WRONG?
HOW COULD I HAVE DONE THESE THINGS?! HOW COULD I HAVE ENDANGERED THIS PLANET?
WHAT SORT OF MONSTER HAVE I BECOME?!

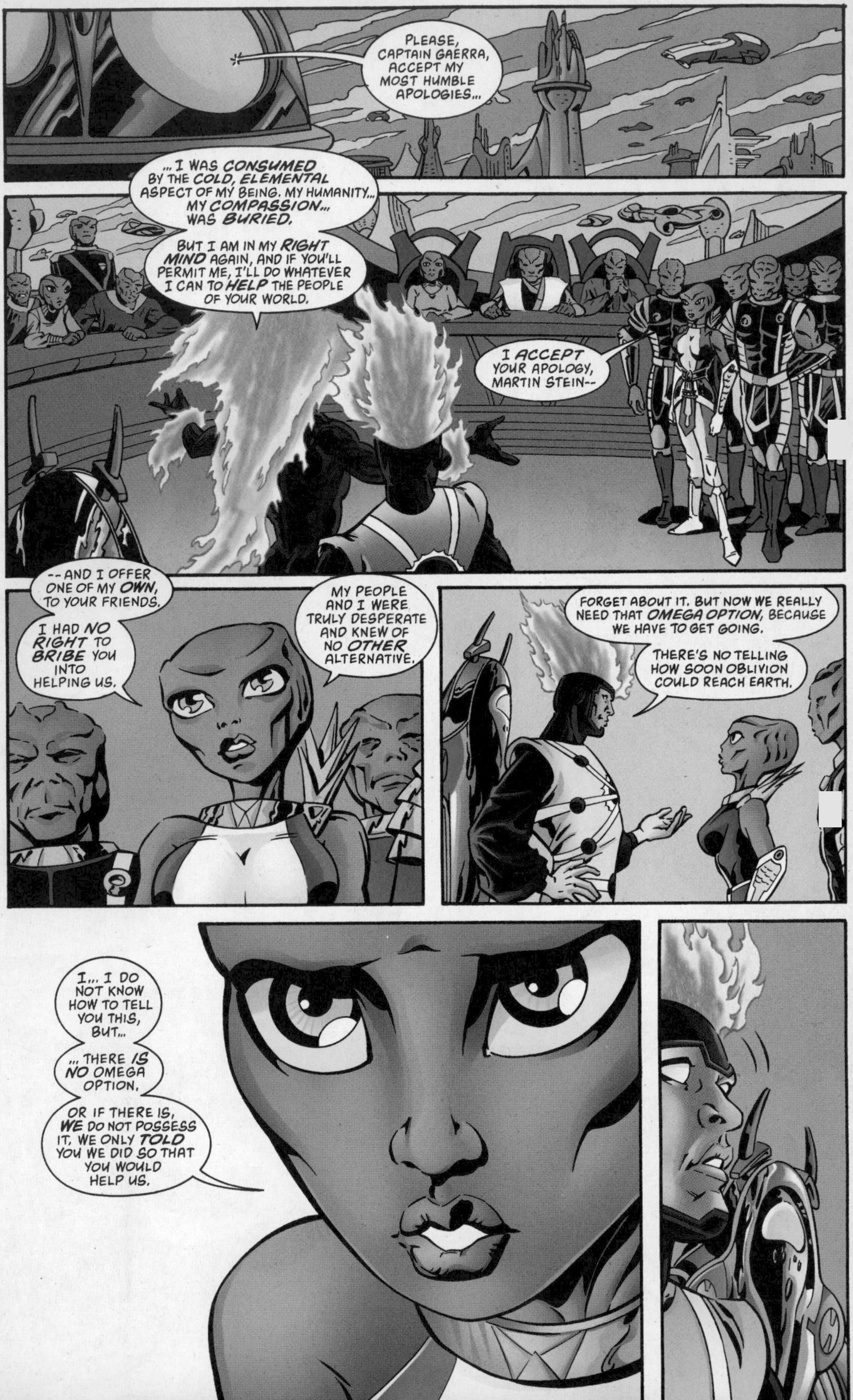
PLEASE, CAPTAIN GAERRA, ACCEPT MY MOST HUMBLE APOLOGIES...
...I WAS CONSUMED BY THE COLD, ELEMENTAL ASPECT OF MY BEING. MY HUMANITY... MY COMPASSION... WAS BURIED.
BUT I AM IN MY RIGHT MIND AGAIN, AND IF YOU'LL PERMIT ME, I'LL DO WHATEVER I CAN TO HELP THE PEOPLE OF YOUR WORLD.
I ACCEPT YOUR APOLOGY, MARTIN STEIN--
--AND I OFFER ONE OF MY OWN, TO YOUR FRIENDS.
I HAD NO RIGHT TO BRIBE YOU INTO HELPING US.
MY PEOPLE AND I WERE TRULY DESPERATE AND KNEW OF NO OTHER ALTERNATIVE.
FORGET ABOUT IT. BUT NOW WE REALLY NEED THAT OMEGA OPTION, BECAUSE WE HAVE TO GET GOING.
THERE'S NO TELLING HOW SOON OBLIVION COULD REACH EARTH.
I... I DO NOT KNOW HOW TO TELL YOU THIS, BUT...
...THERE IS NO OMEGA OPTION.
OR IF THERE IS, WE DO NOT POSSESS IT. WE ONLY TOLD YOU WE DID SO THAT YOU WOULD HELP US.

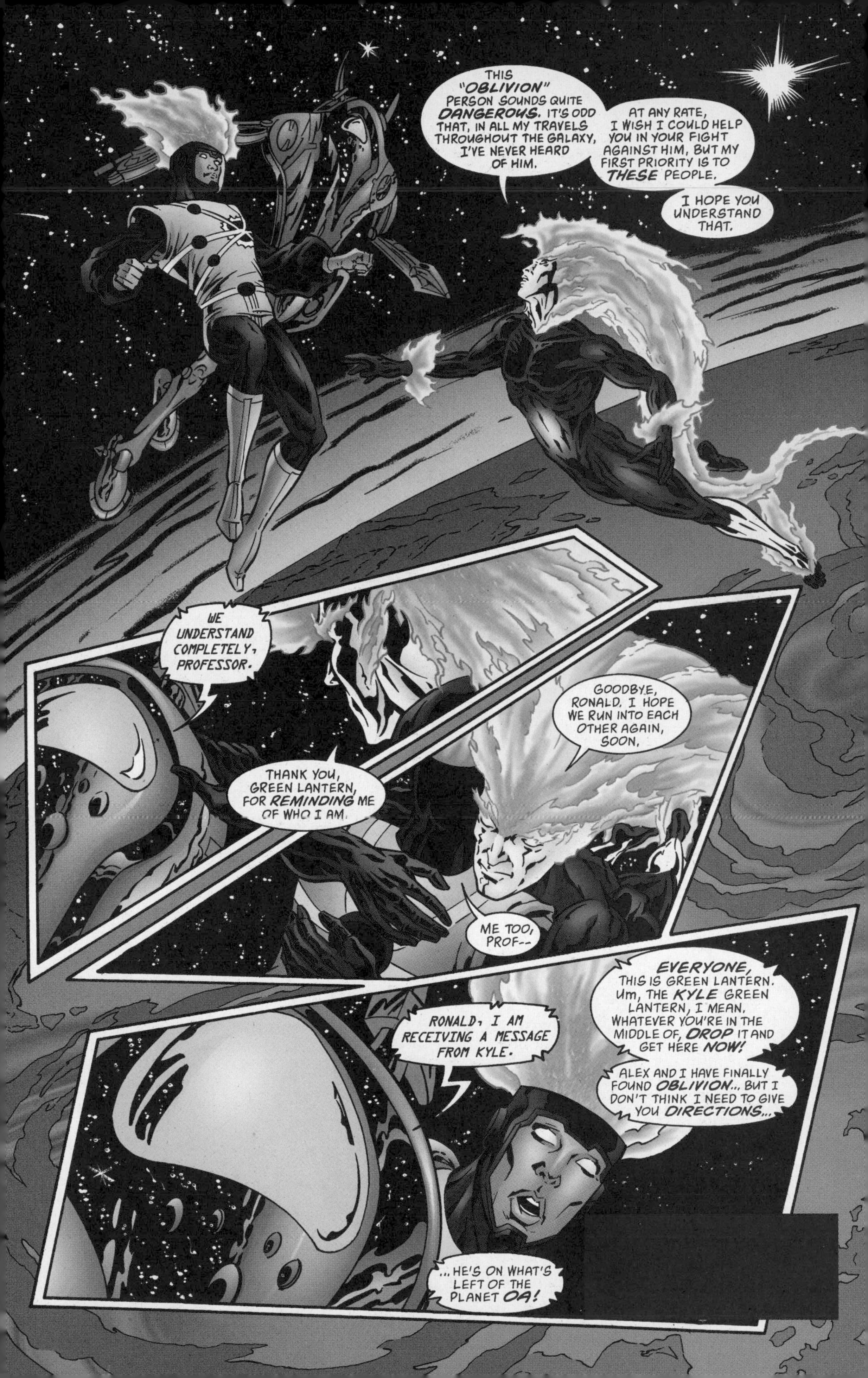
THIS "OBLIVION" PERSON SOUNDS QUITE DANGEROUS. IT'S ODD THAT, IN ALL MY TRAVELS THROUGHOUT THE GALAXY, I'VE NEVER HEARD OF HIM.
AT ANY RATE, I WISH I COULD HELP YOU IN YOUR FIGHT AGAINST HIM, BUT MY FIRST PRIORITY IS TO THESE PEOPLE.
I HOPE YOU UNDERSTAND THAT.
WE UNDERSTAND COMPLETELY, PROFESSOR.
GOODBYE, RONALD. I HOPE WE RUN INTO EACH OTHER AGAIN, SOON.
THANK YOU, GREEN LANTERN, FOR REMINDING ME OF WHO I AM.
ME TOO, PROF--
RONALD, I AM RECEIVING A MESSAGE FROM KYLE.
EVERYONE, THIS IS GREEN LANTERN. Um, THE KYLE GREEN LANTERN, I MEAN. WHATEVER YOU'RE IN THE MIDDLE OF, DROP IT AND GET HERE NOW!
ALEX AND I HAVE FINALLY FOUND OBLIVION... BUT I DON'T THINK I NEED TO GIVE YOU DIRECTIONS...
...HE'S ON WHAT'S LEFT OF THE PLANET OA!

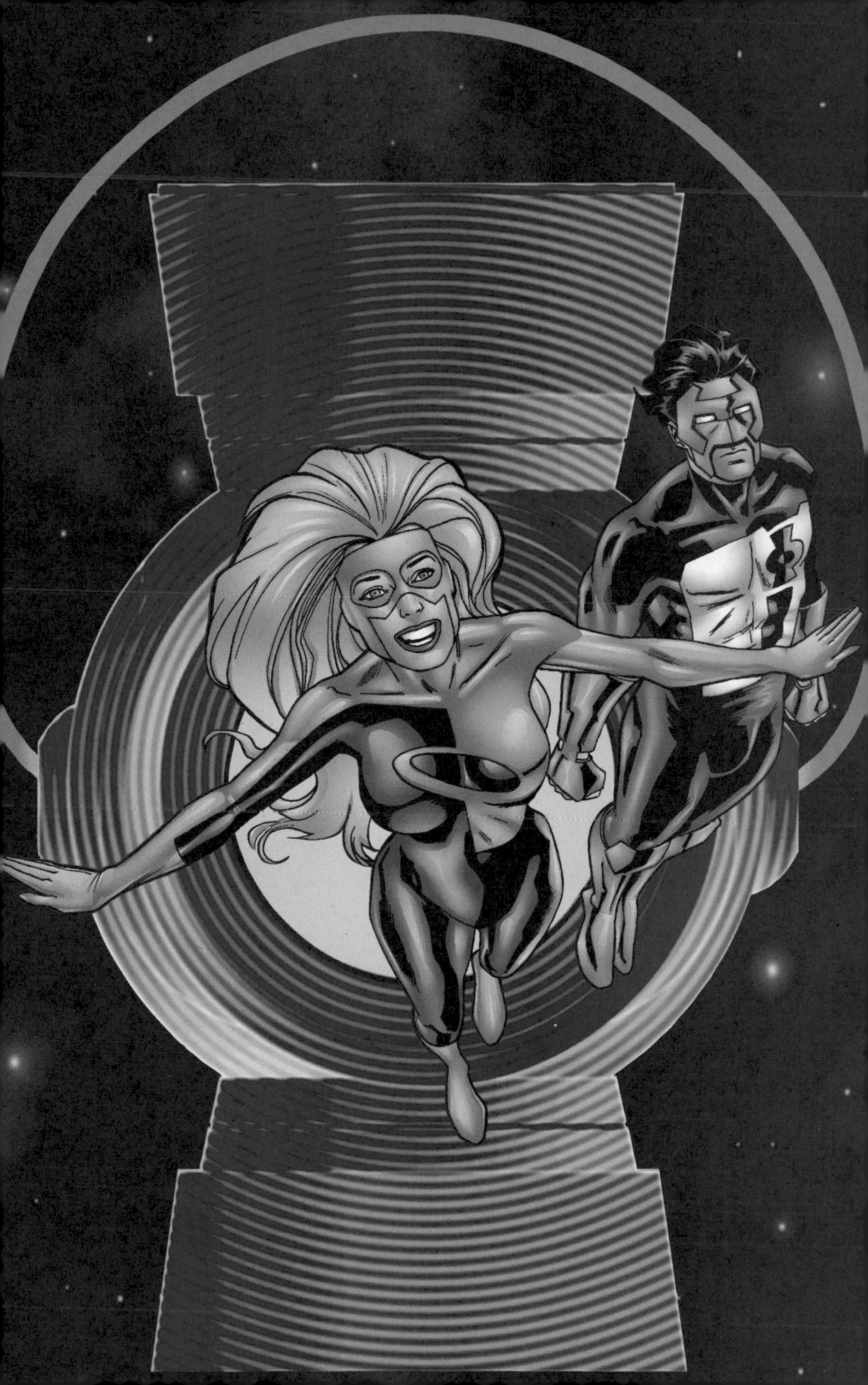

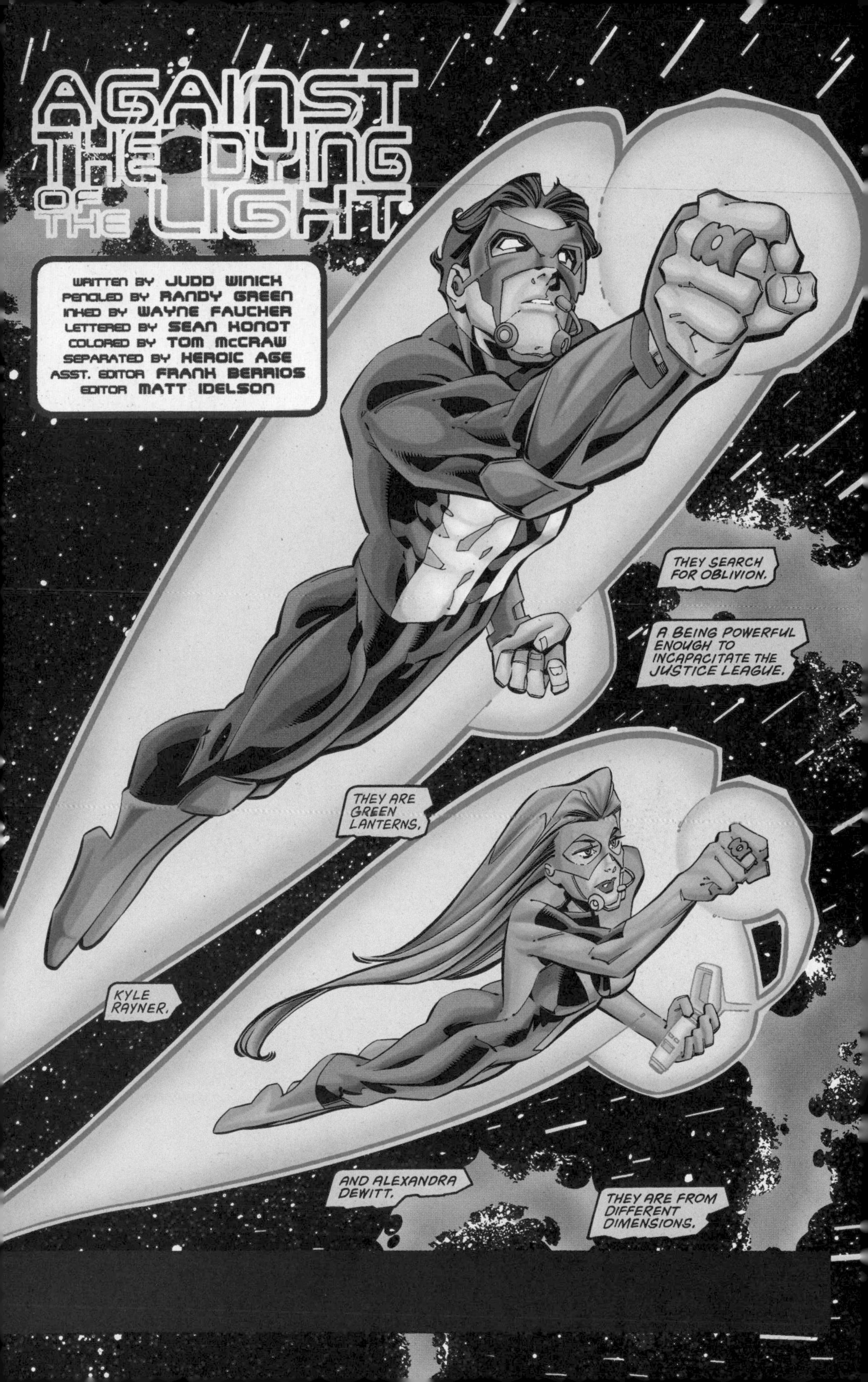
AGAINST THE DYING OF THE LIGHT
WRITTEN BY JUDD WINICK
PENCILED BY RANDY GREEN
INKED BY WAYNE FAUCHER
LETTERED BY SEAN KONOT
COLORED BY TOM McCRAW
SEPARATED BY HEROIC AGE
ASST. EDITOR FRANK BERRIOS
EDITOR MATT IDELSON
THEY SEARCH FOR OBLIVION.
A BEING POWERFUL ENOUGH TO INCAPACITATE THE JUSTICE LEAGUE.
THEY ARE GREEN LANTERNS.
KYLE RAYNER.
AND ALEXANDRA DEWITT.
THEY ARE FROM DIFFERENT DIMENSIONS.
[redacted]

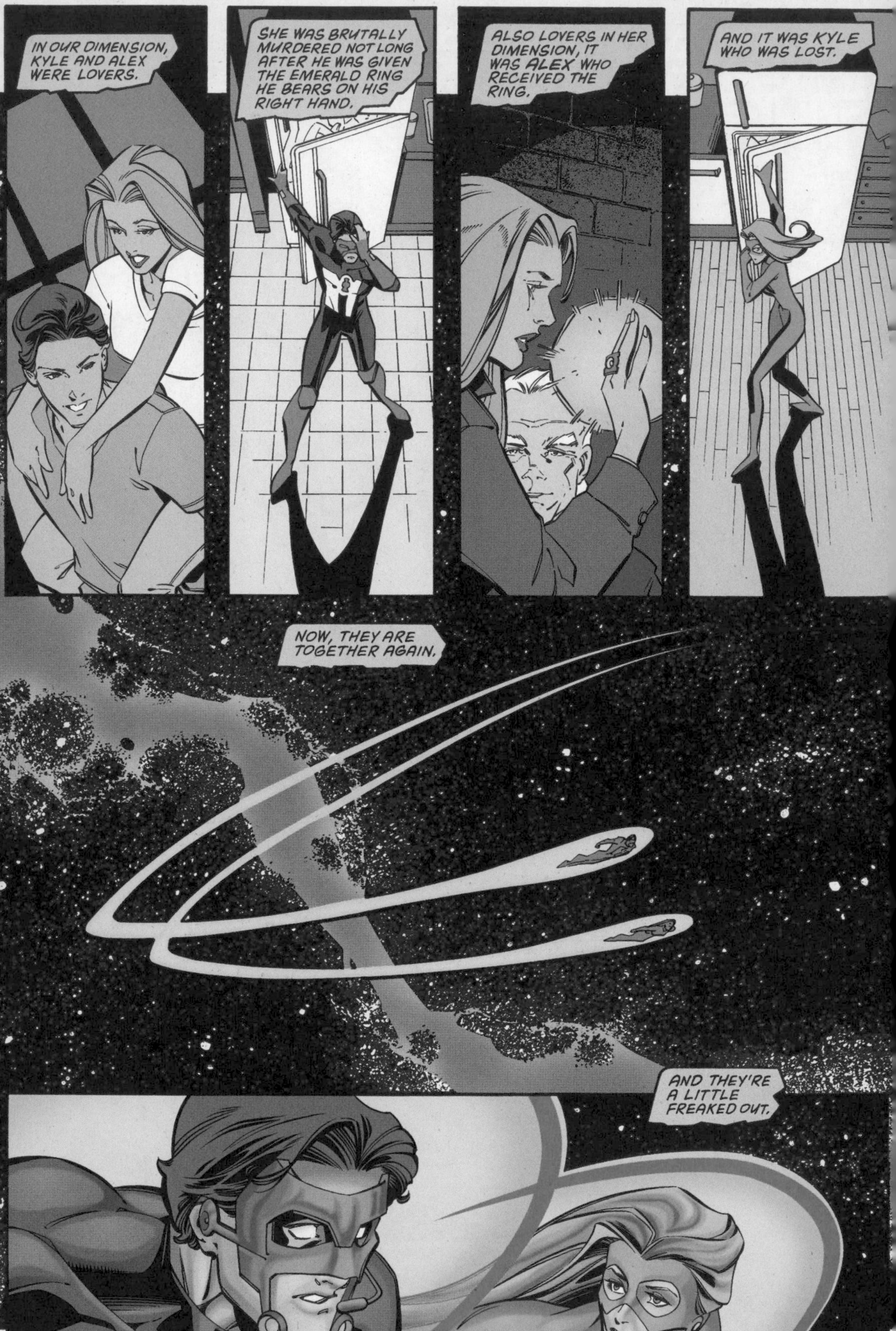

IN OUR DIMENSION, KYLE AND ALEX WERE LOVERS.
SHE WAS BRUTALLY MURDERED NOT LONG AFTER HE WAS GIVEN THE EMERALD RING HE BEARS ON HIS RIGHT HAND.
ALSO LOVERS IN HER DIMENSION, IT WAS ALEX WHO RECEIVED THE RING.
AND IT WAS KYLE WHO WAS LOST.
NOW, THEY ARE TOGETHER AGAIN.
AND THEY'RE A LITTLE FREAKED OUT.

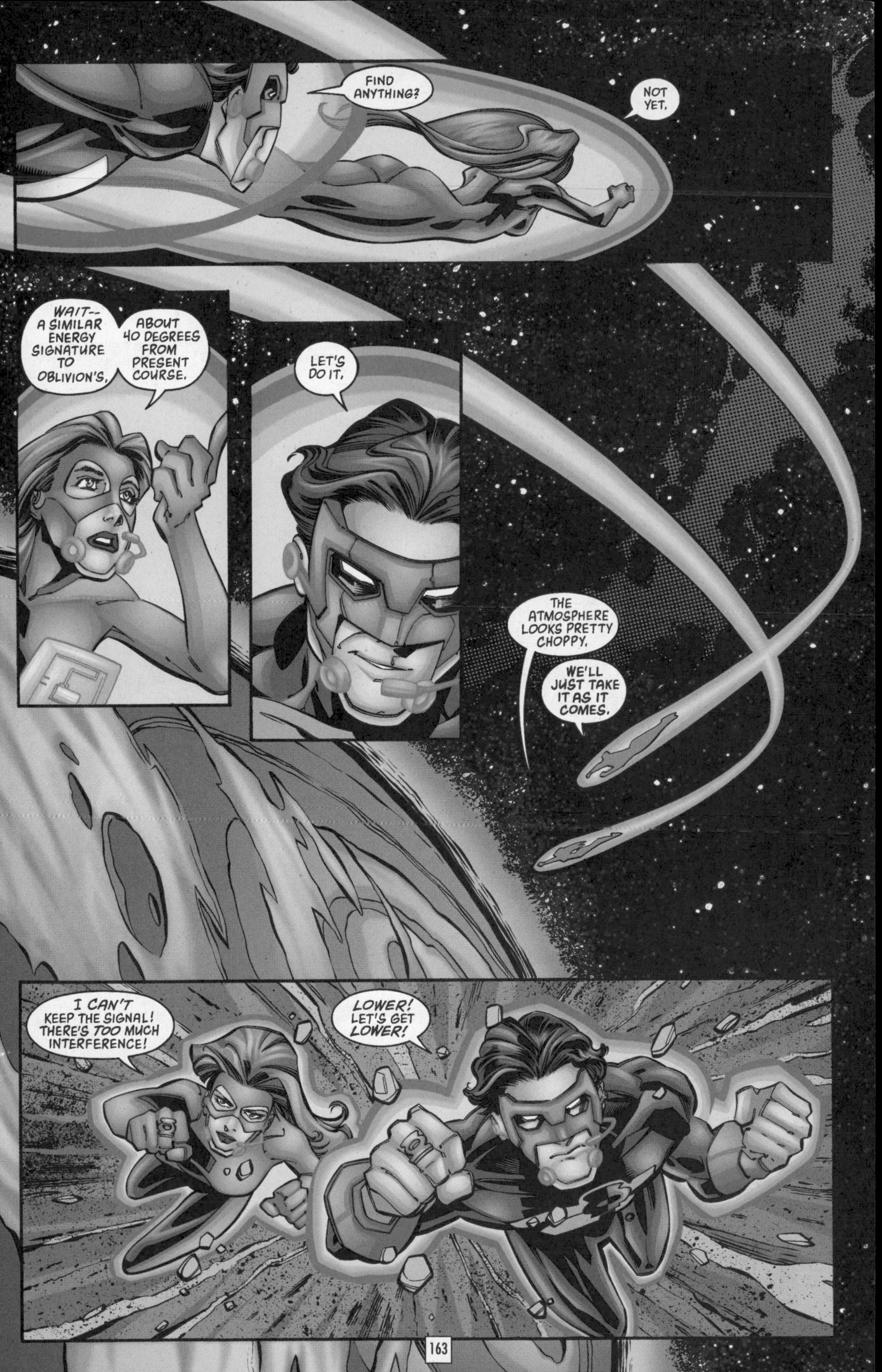
FIND ANYTHING?
NOT YET.
WAIT-- A SIMILAR ENERGY SIGNATURE TO OBLIVION'S.
ABOUT 40 DEGREES FROM PRESENT COURSE.
LET'S DO IT.
THE ATMOSPHERE LOOKS PRETTY CHOPPY.
WE'LL JUST TAKE IT AS IT COMES.
I CAN'T KEEP THE SIGNAL! THERE'S TOO MUCH INTERFERENCE!
LOWER! LET'S GET LOWER!

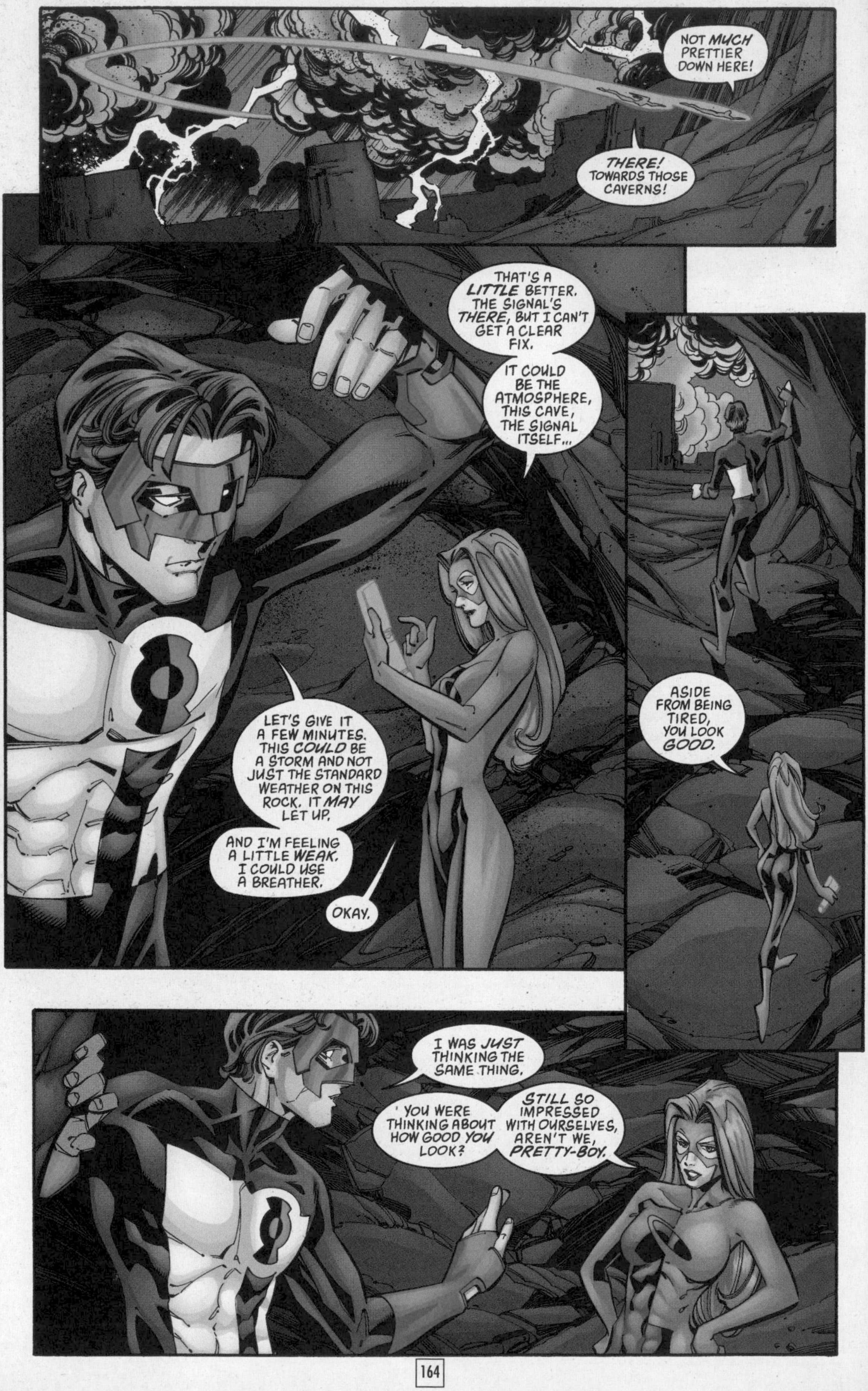
NOT MUCH PRETTIER DOWN HERE!
THERE! TOWARDS THOSE CAVERNS!
THAT'S A LITTLE BETTER. THE SIGNAL'S THERE, BUT I CAN'T GET A CLEAR FIX.
IT COULD BE THE ATMOSPHERE, THIS CAVE, THE SIGNAL ITSELF...
LET'S GIVE IT A FEW MINUTES. THIS COULD BE A STORM AND NOT JUST THE STANDARD WEATHER ON THIS ROCK. IT MAY LET UP.
AND I'M FEELING A LITTLE WEAK. I COULD USE A BREATHER.
OKAY.
ASIDE FROM BEING TIRED, YOU LOOK GOOD.
I WAS JUST THINKING THE SAME THING.
YOU WERE THINKING ABOUT HOW GOOD YOU LOOK?
STILL SO IMPRESSED WITH OURSELVES, AREN'T WE, PRETTY-BOY.

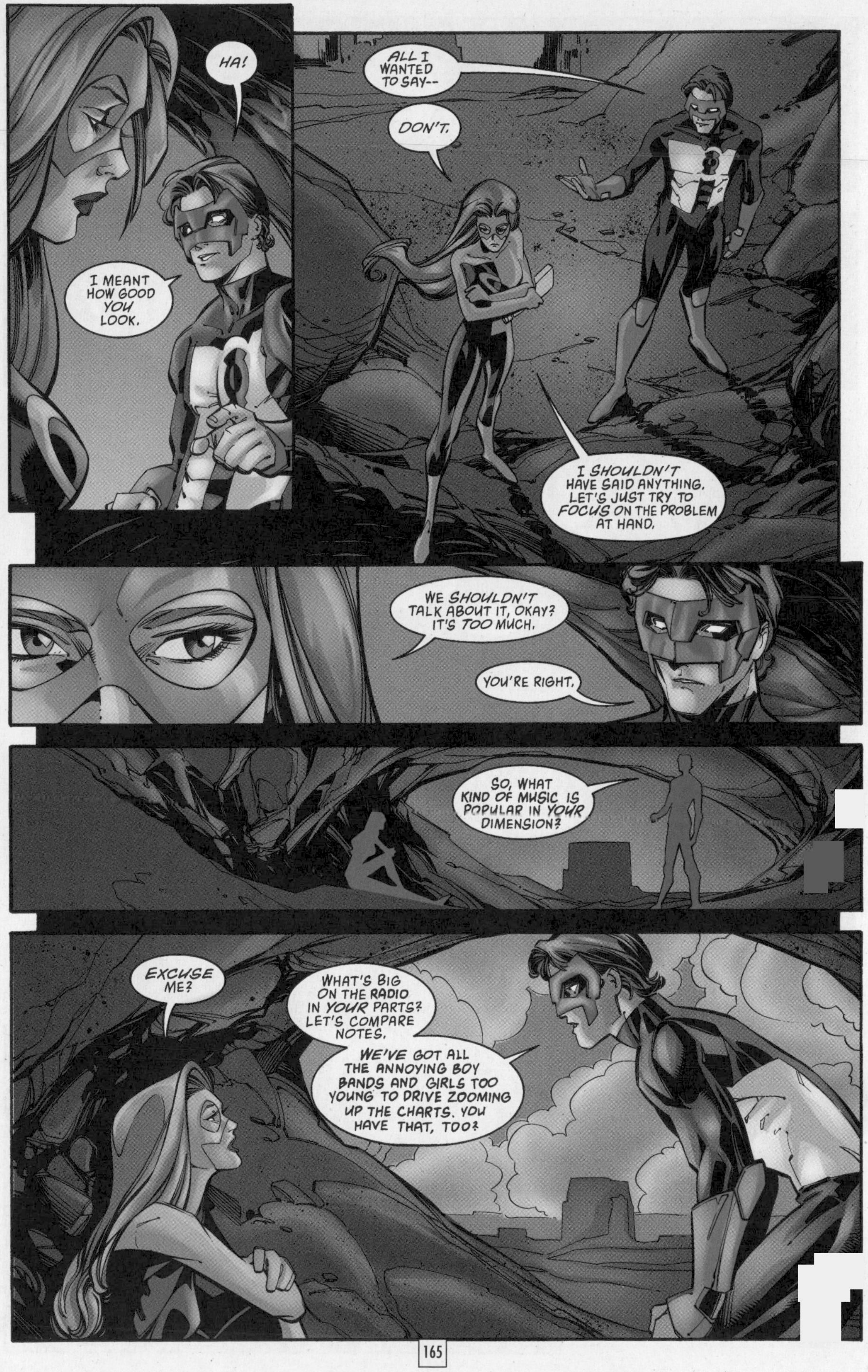
HA!
I MEANT HOW GOOD YOU LOOK.
ALL I WANTED TO SAY--
DON'T.
I SHOULDN'T HAVE SAID ANYTHING. LET'S JUST TRY TO FOCUS ON THE PROBLEM AT HAND.
WE SHOULDN'T TALK ABOUT IT, OKAY? IT'S TOO MUCH.
YOU'RE RIGHT.
SO, WHAT KIND OF MUSIC IS POPULAR IN YOUR DIMENSION?
EXCUSE ME?
WHAT'S BIG ON THE RADIO IN YOUR PARTS? LET'S COMPARE NOTES.
WE'VE GOT ALL THE ANNOYING BOY BANDS AND GIRLS TOO YOUNG TO DRIVE ZOOMING UP THE CHARTS. YOU HAVE THAT, TOO?

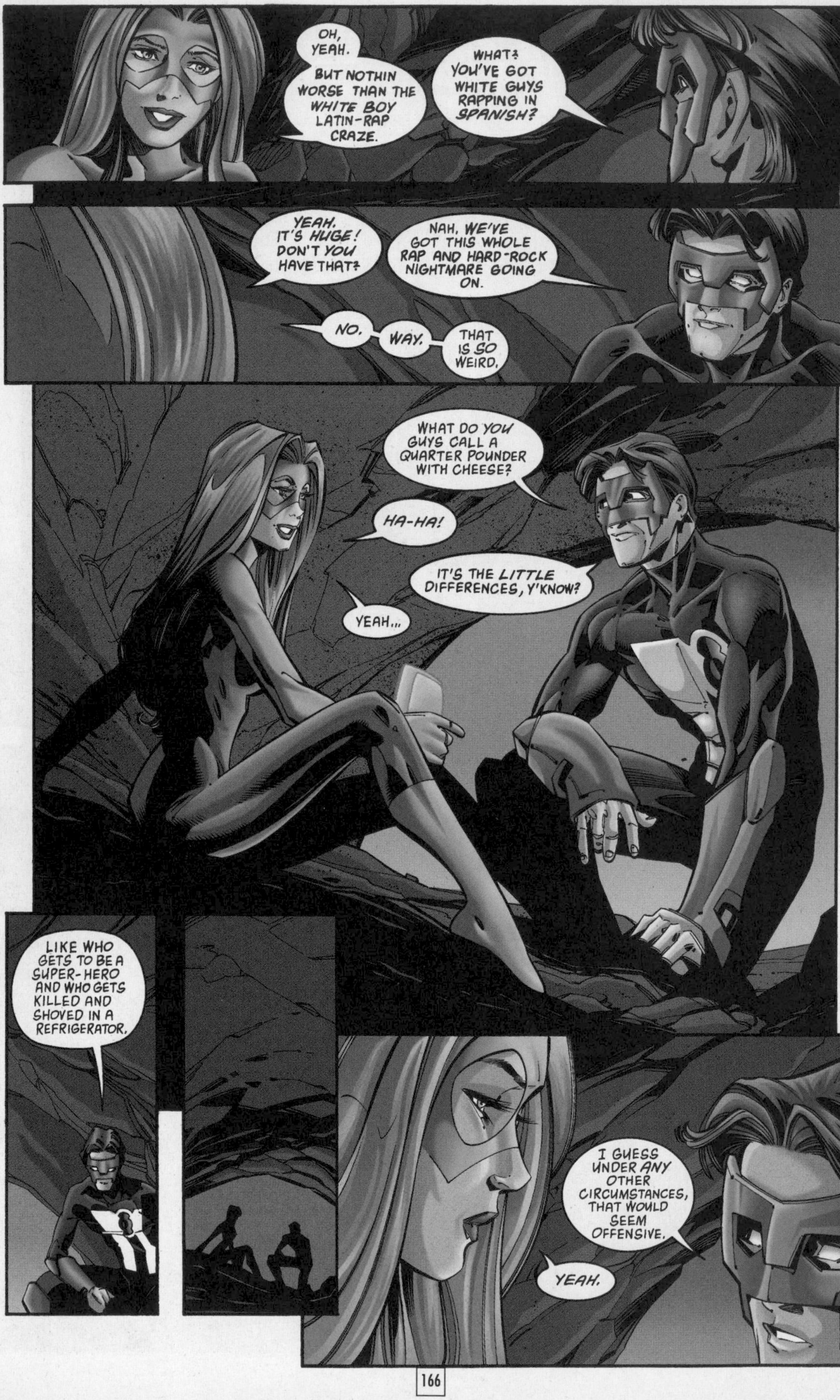
OH, YEAH.
BUT NOTHIN WORSE THAN THE WHITE BOY LATIN-RAP CRAZE.
WHAT? YOU'VE GOT WHITE GUYS RAPPING IN SPANISH?
YEAH. IT'S HUGE! DON'T YOU HAVE THAT?
NAH, WE'VE GOT THIS WHOLE RAP AND HARD-ROCK NIGHTMARE GOING ON.
NO.
WAY.
THAT IS SO WEIRD.
WHAT DO YOU GUYS CALL A QUARTER POUNDER WITH CHEESE?
HA-HA!
IT'S THE LITTLE DIFFERENCES, Y'KNOW?
YEAH...
LIKE WHO GETS TO BE A SUPER-HERO AND WHO GETS KILLED AND SHOVED IN A REFRIGERATOR.
I GUESS UNDER ANY OTHER CIRCUMSTANCES, THAT WOULD SEEM OFFENSIVE.
YEAH.

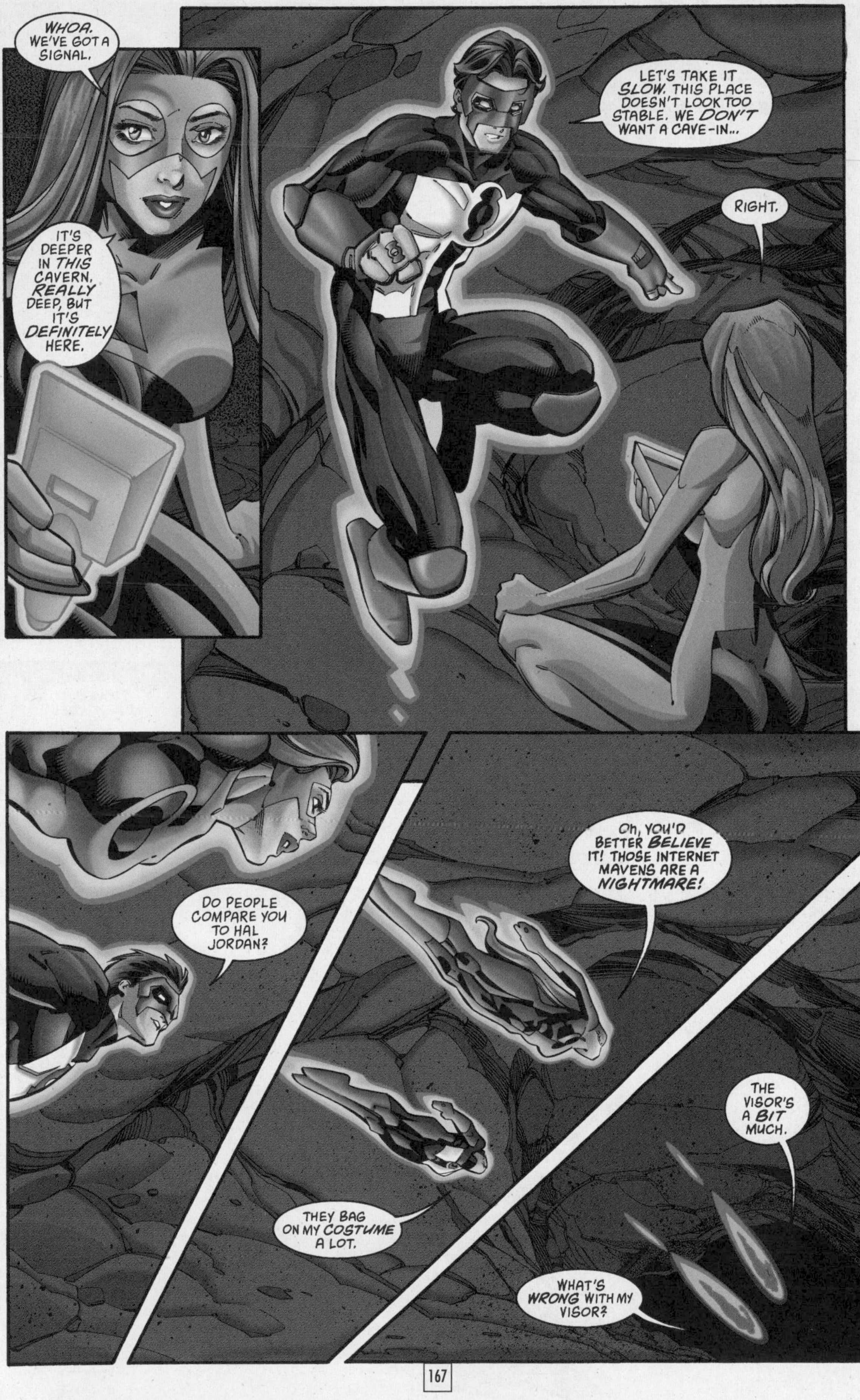

WHOA. WE'VE GOT A SIGNAL.
IT'S DEEPER IN THIS CAVERN. REALLY DEEP, BUT IT'S DEFINITELY HERE.
LET'S TAKE IT SLOW. THIS PLACE DOESN'T LOOK TOO STABLE. WE DON'T WANT A CAVE-IN...
RIGHT.
DO PEOPLE COMPARE YOU TO HAL JORDAN?
THEY BAG ON MY COSTUME A LOT.
Oh, YOU'D BETTER BELIEVE IT! THOSE INTERNET MAVENS ARE A NIGHTMARE!
THE VISOR'S A BIT MUCH.
WHAT'S WRONG WITH MY VISOR?

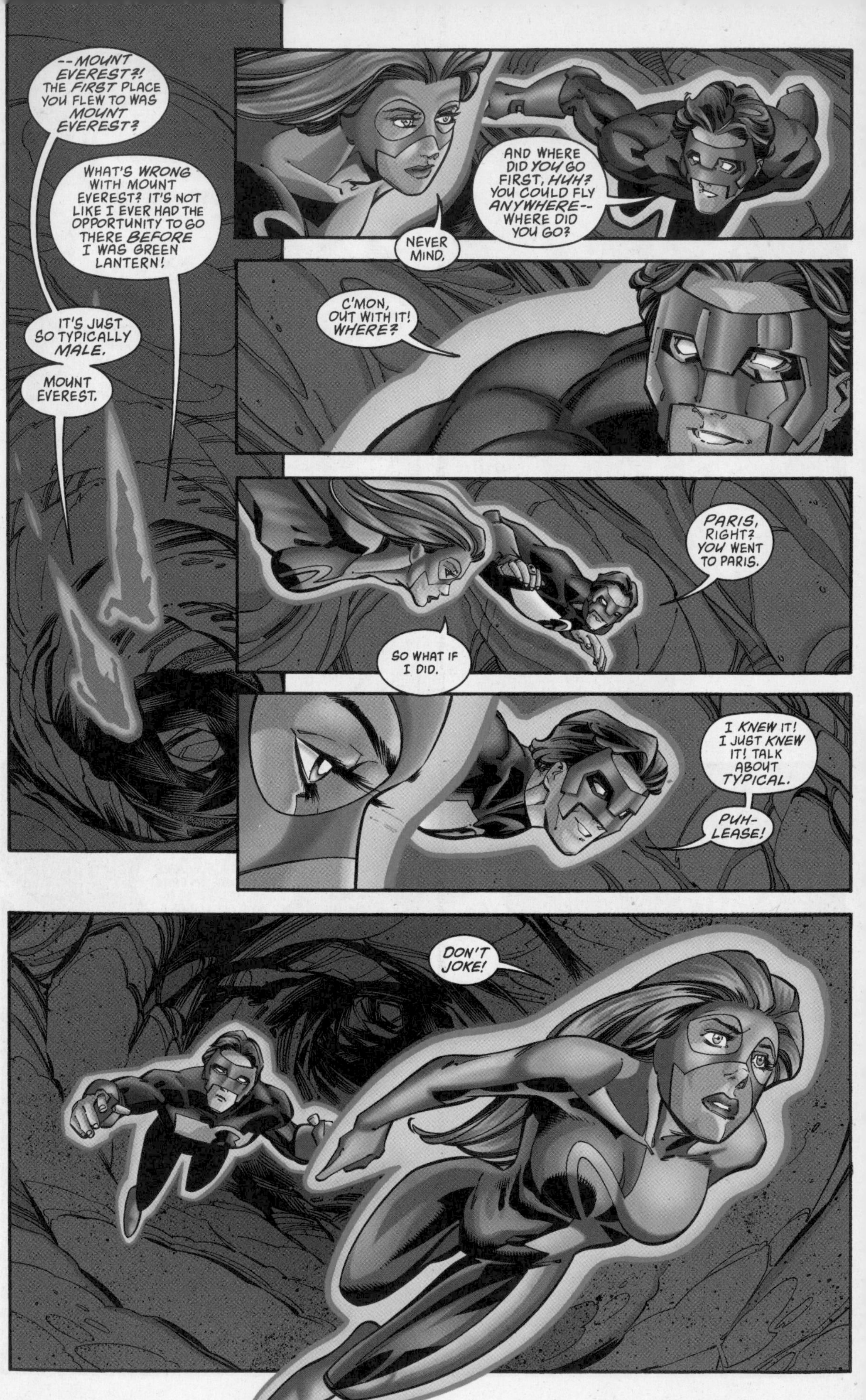
--MOUNT EVEREST?! THE FIRST PLACE YOU FLEW TO WAS MOUNT EVEREST?
WHAT'S WRONG WITH MOUNT EVEREST? IT'S NOT LIKE I EVER HAD THE OPPORTUNITY TO GO THERE BEFORE I WAS GREEN LANTERN!
IT'S JUST SO TYPICALLY MALE.
MOUNT EVEREST.
AND WHERE DID YOU GO FIRST, HUH? YOU COULD FLY ANYWHERE-- WHERE DID YOU GO?
NEVER MIND.
C'MON, OUT WITH IT! WHERE?
PARIS, RIGHT? YOU WENT TO PARIS.
SO WHAT IF I DID.
I KNEW IT! I JUST KNEW IT! TALK ABOUT TYPICAL.
PUH-LEASE!
DON'T JOKE!

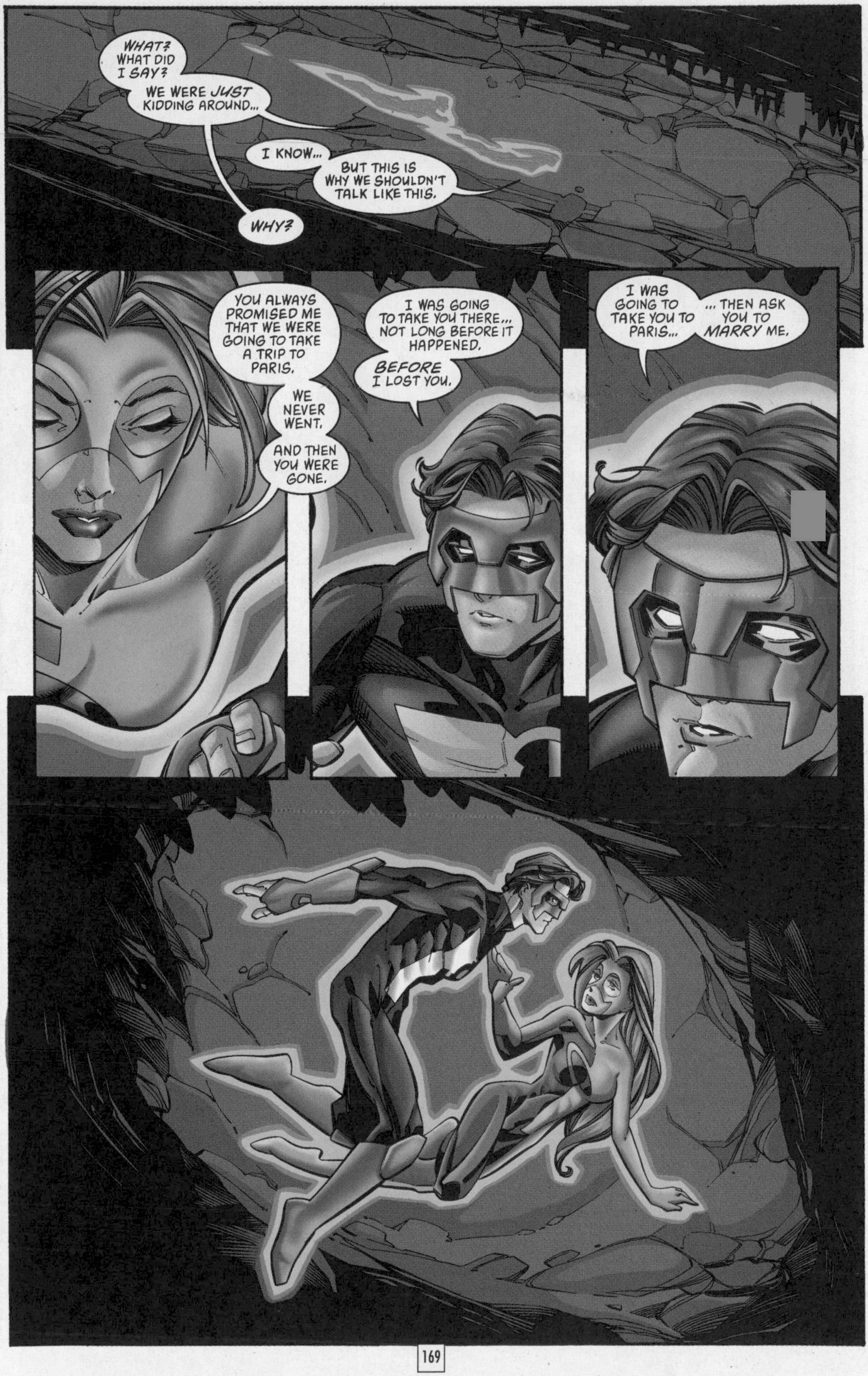
WHAT? WHAT DID I SAY?
WE WERE JUST KIDDING AROUND...
I KNOW...
BUT THIS IS WHY WE SHOULDN'T TALK LIKE THIS.
WHY?
YOU ALWAYS PROMISED ME THAT WE WERE GOING TO TAKE A TRIP TO PARIS.
WE NEVER WENT.
AND THEN YOU WERE GONE.
I WAS GOING TO TAKE YOU THERE... NOT LONG BEFORE IT HAPPENED.
BEFORE I LOST YOU.
I WAS GOING TO TAKE YOU TO PARIS...
... THEN ASK YOU TO MARRY ME.

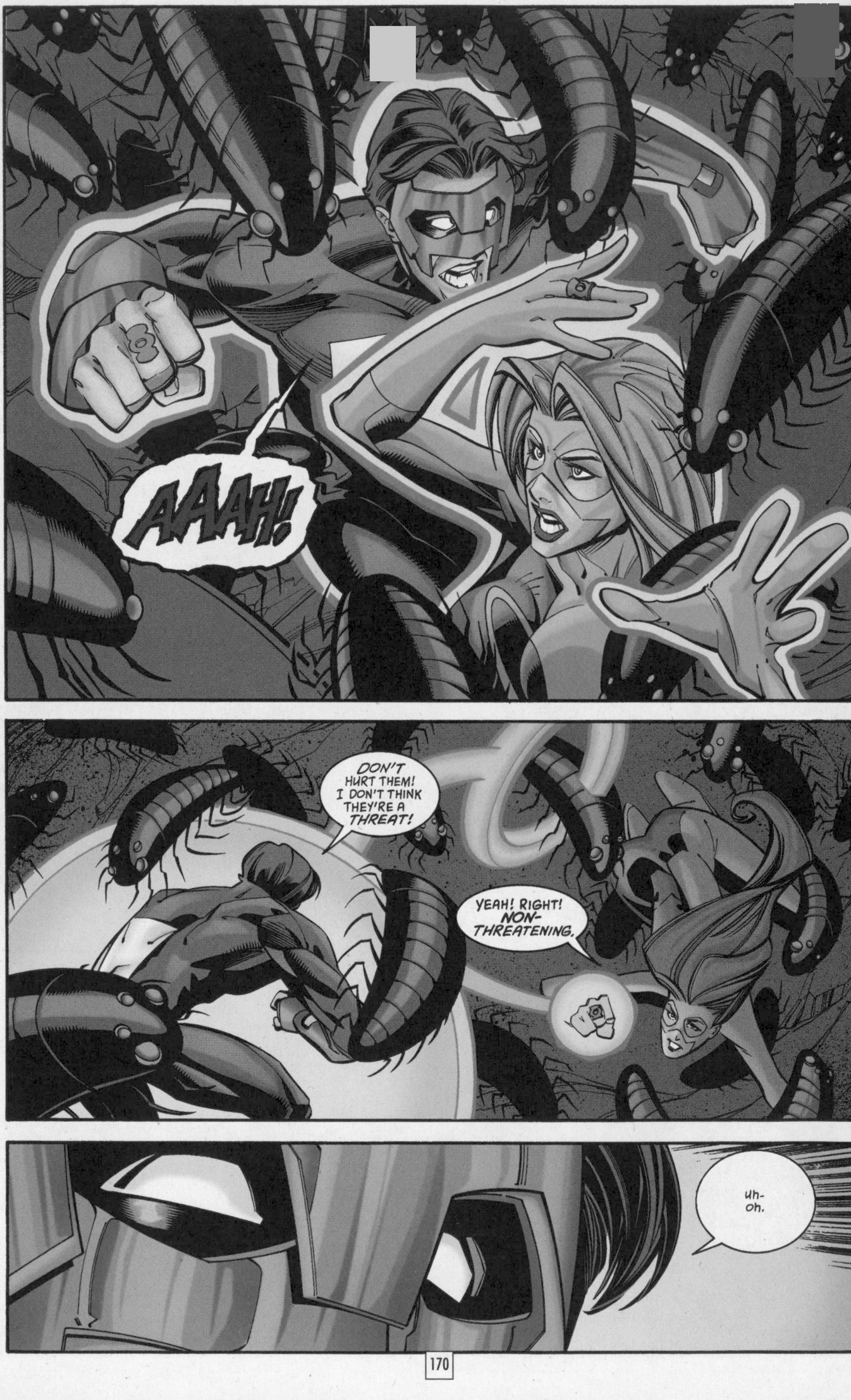
AAAH!
DON'T HURT THEM! I DON'T THINK THEY'RE A THREAT!
YEAH! RIGHT! NON-THREATENING.
UH-OH.

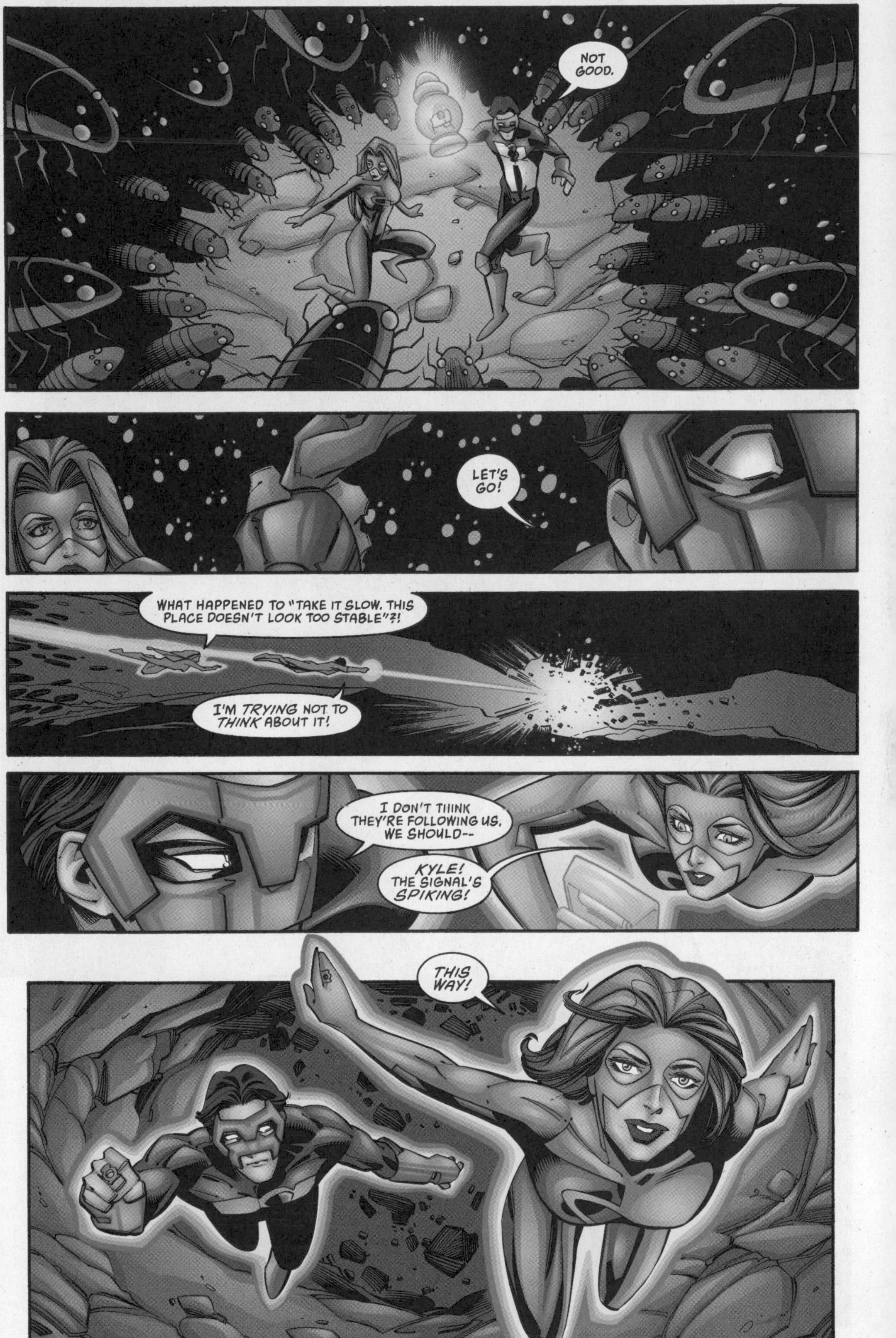
NOT GOOD.
LET'S GO!
WHAT HAPPENED TO "TAKE IT SLOW. THIS PLACE DOESN'T LOOK TOO STABLE"?!
I'M TRYING NOT TO THINK ABOUT IT!
I DON'T TIIINK THEY'RE FOLLOWING US. WE SHOULD--
KYLE! THE SIGNAL'S SPIKING!
THIS WAY!

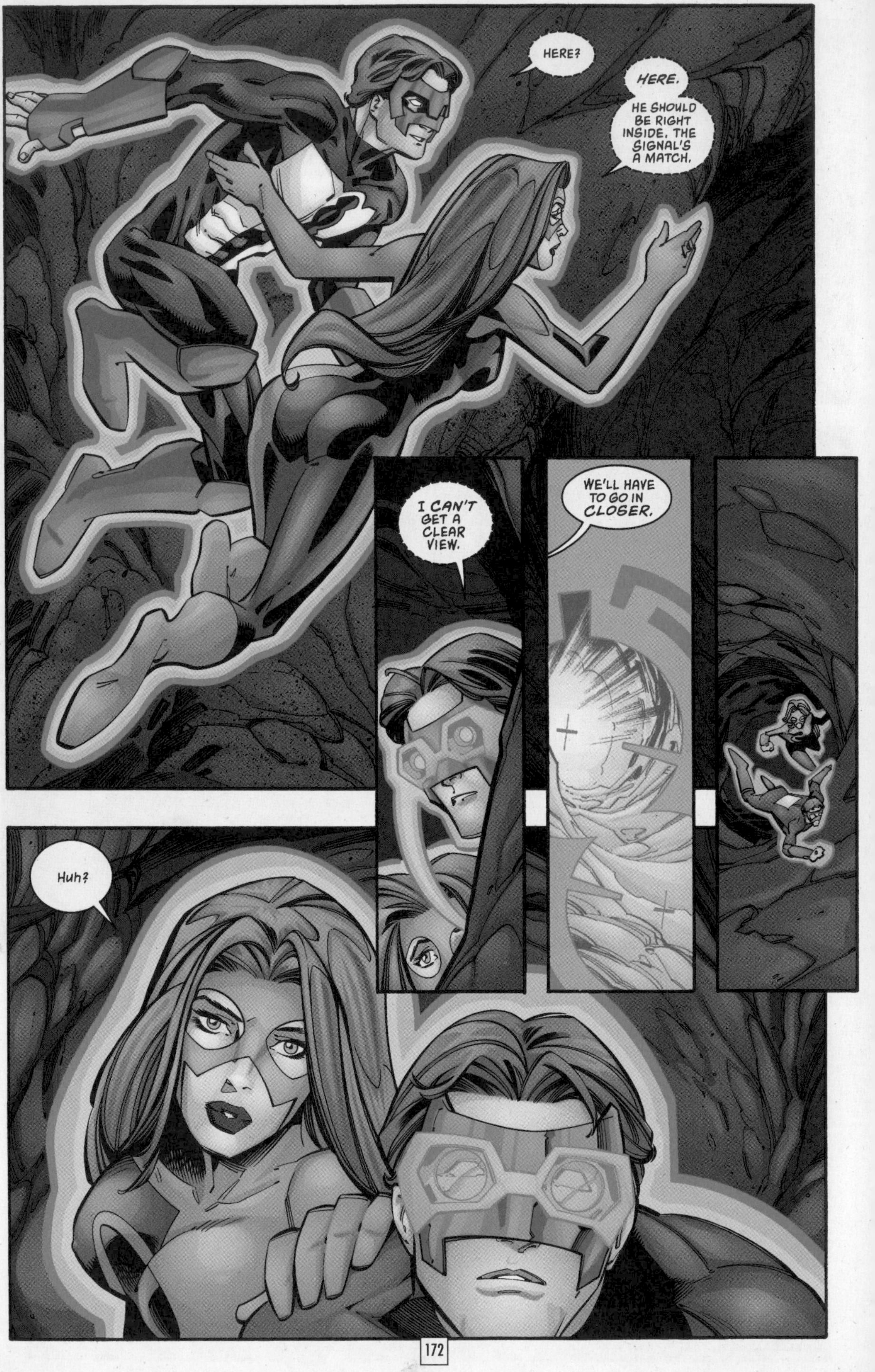
HERE?
HERE.
HE SHOULD BE RIGHT INSIDE. THE SIGNAL'S A MATCH.
I CAN'T GET A CLEAR VIEW.
WE'LL HAVE TO GO IN CLOSER.
Huh?

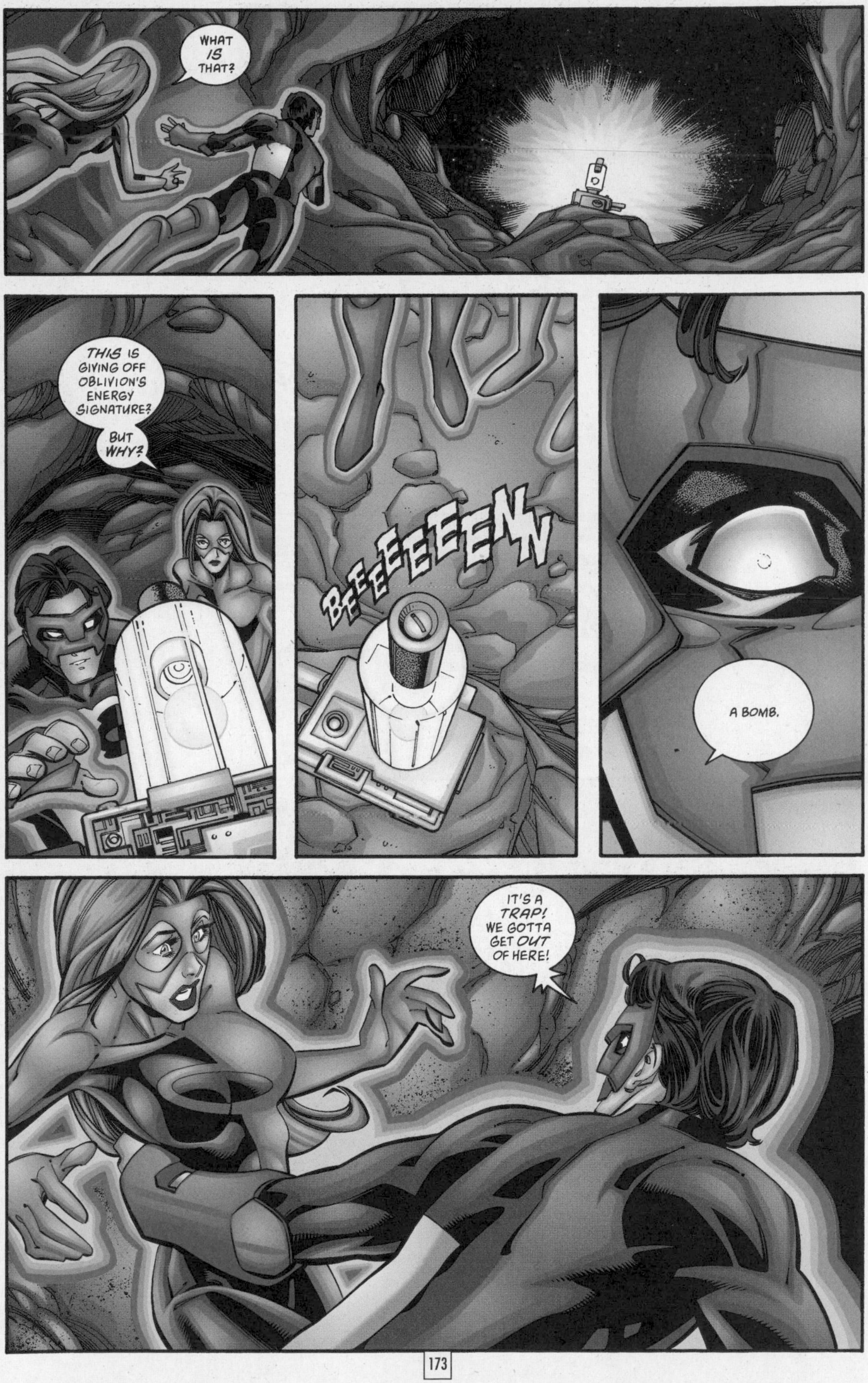
WHAT IS THAT?
THIS IS GIVING OFF OBLIVION'S ENERGY SIGNATURE?
BUT WHY?
BEEEEEEENNN
A BOMB.
IT'S A TRAP! WE GOTTA GET OUT OF HERE!

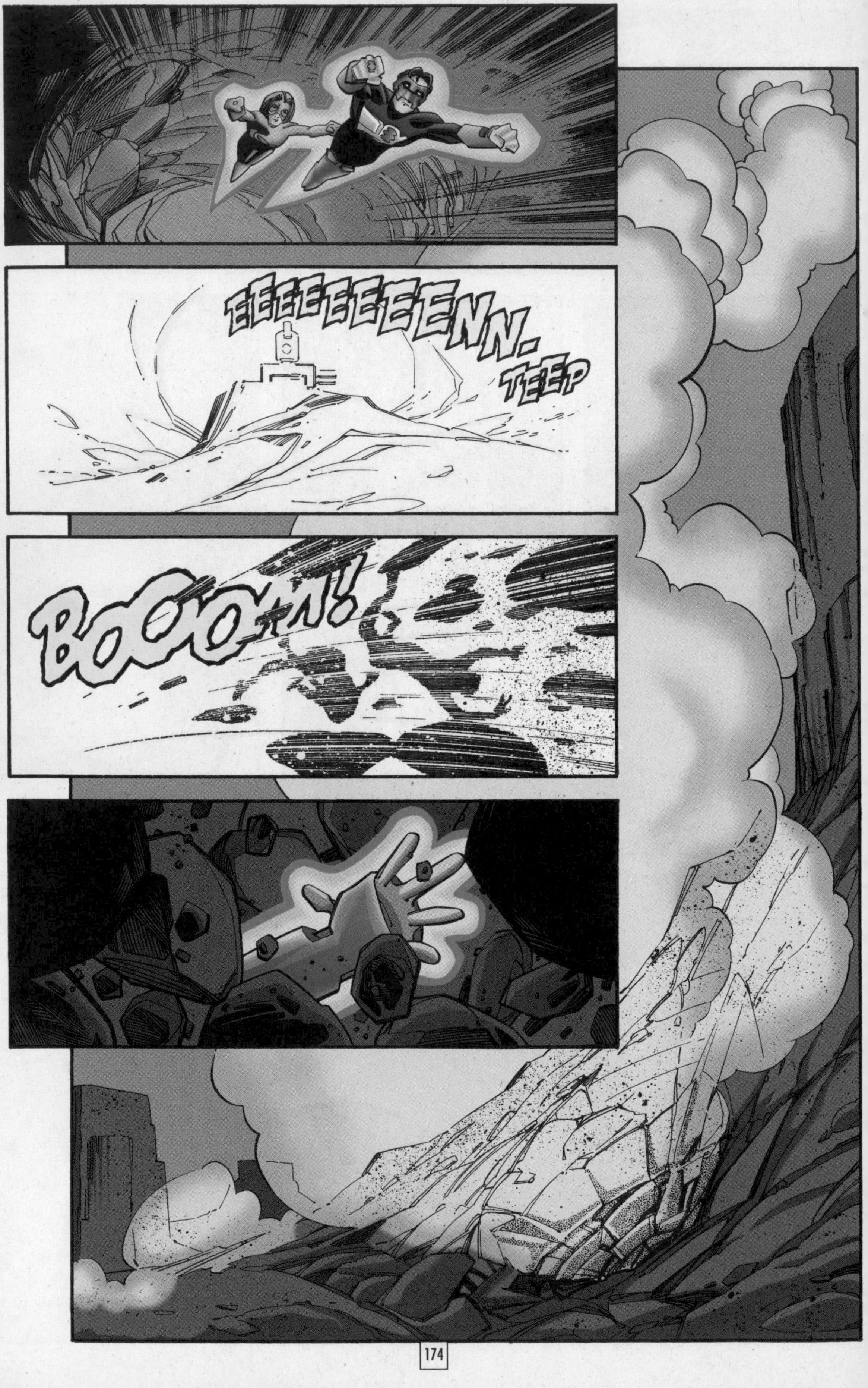
EEEEEEEENN.
TEEP
BOOOM!

ARE YOU OKAY?

I THINK I NEED TO LAND... THAT TOOK *A LOT* OUT OF ME.

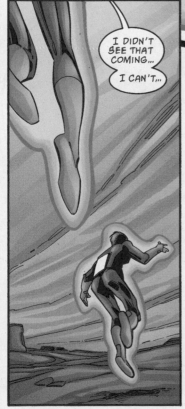

I DIDN'T SEE THAT COMING... I CAN'T...

KYLE? ARE YOU OKAY?

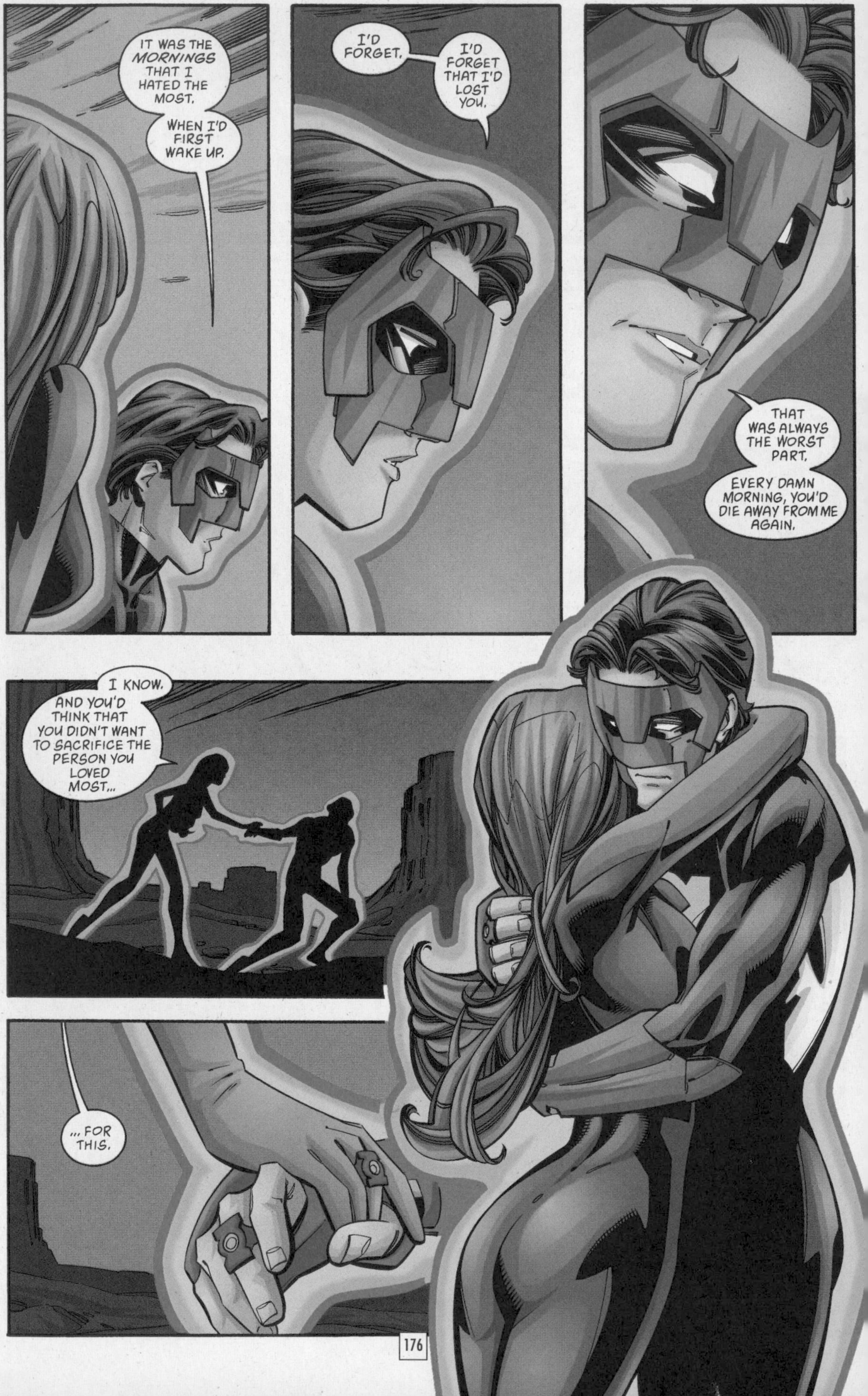
IT WAS THE *MORNINGS* THAT I HATED THE MOST.
WHEN I'D FIRST WAKE UP.
I'D FORGET.
I'D FORGET THAT I'D LOST YOU.
THAT WAS ALWAYS THE WORST PART.
EVERY DAMN MORNING, YOU'D DIE AWAY FROM ME AGAIN.
I KNOW.
AND YOU'D THINK THAT YOU DIDN'T WANT TO SACRIFICE THE PERSON YOU LOVED MOST...
...FOR THIS.

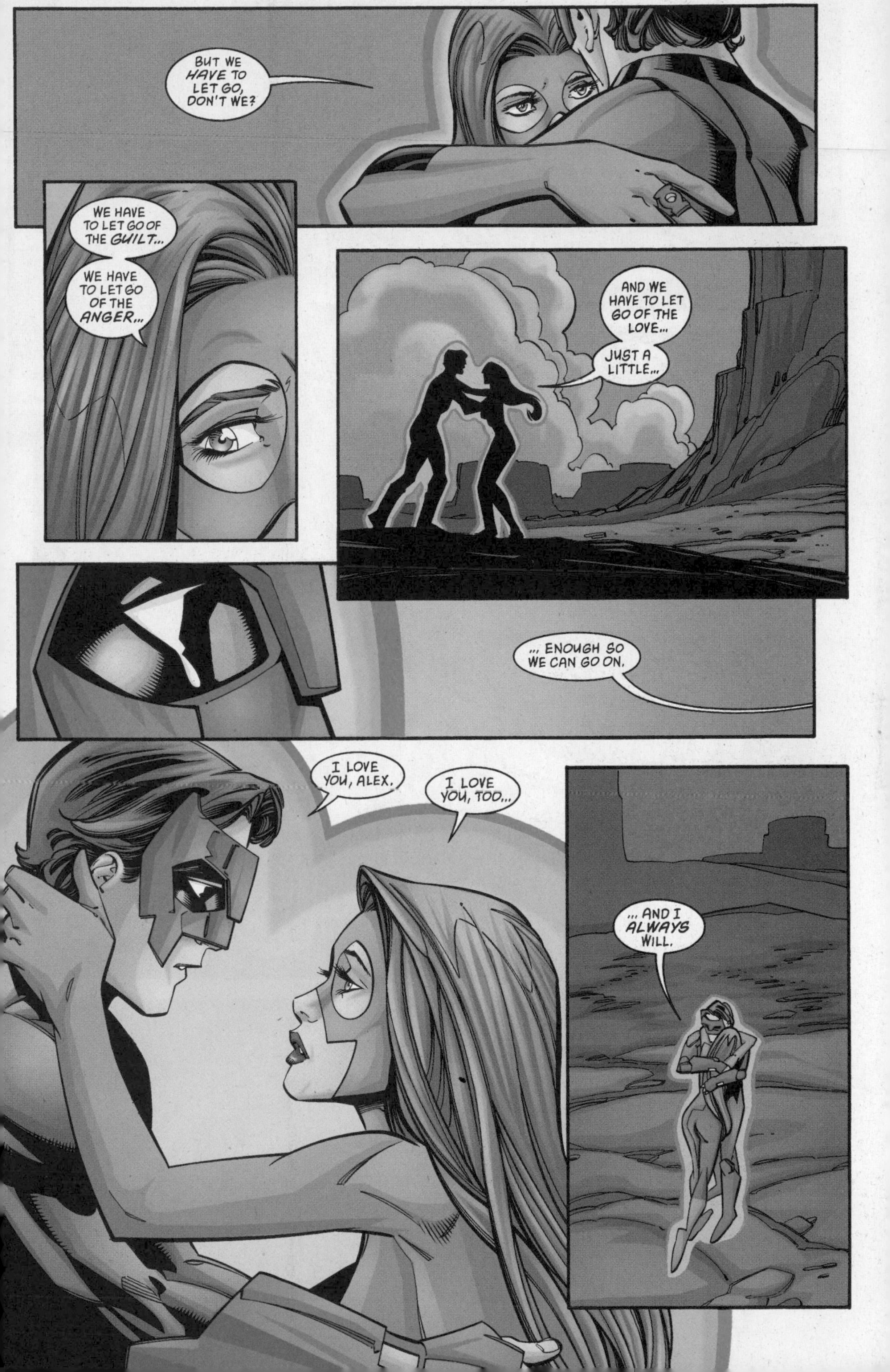
BUT WE HAVE TO LET GO, DON'T WE?
WE HAVE TO LET GO OF THE GUILT...
WE HAVE TO LET GO OF THE ANGER...
AND WE HAVE TO LET GO OF THE LOVE...
JUST A LITTLE...
..., ENOUGH SO WE CAN GO ON.
I LOVE YOU, ALEX.
I LOVE YOU, TOO...
... AND I ALWAYS WILL.

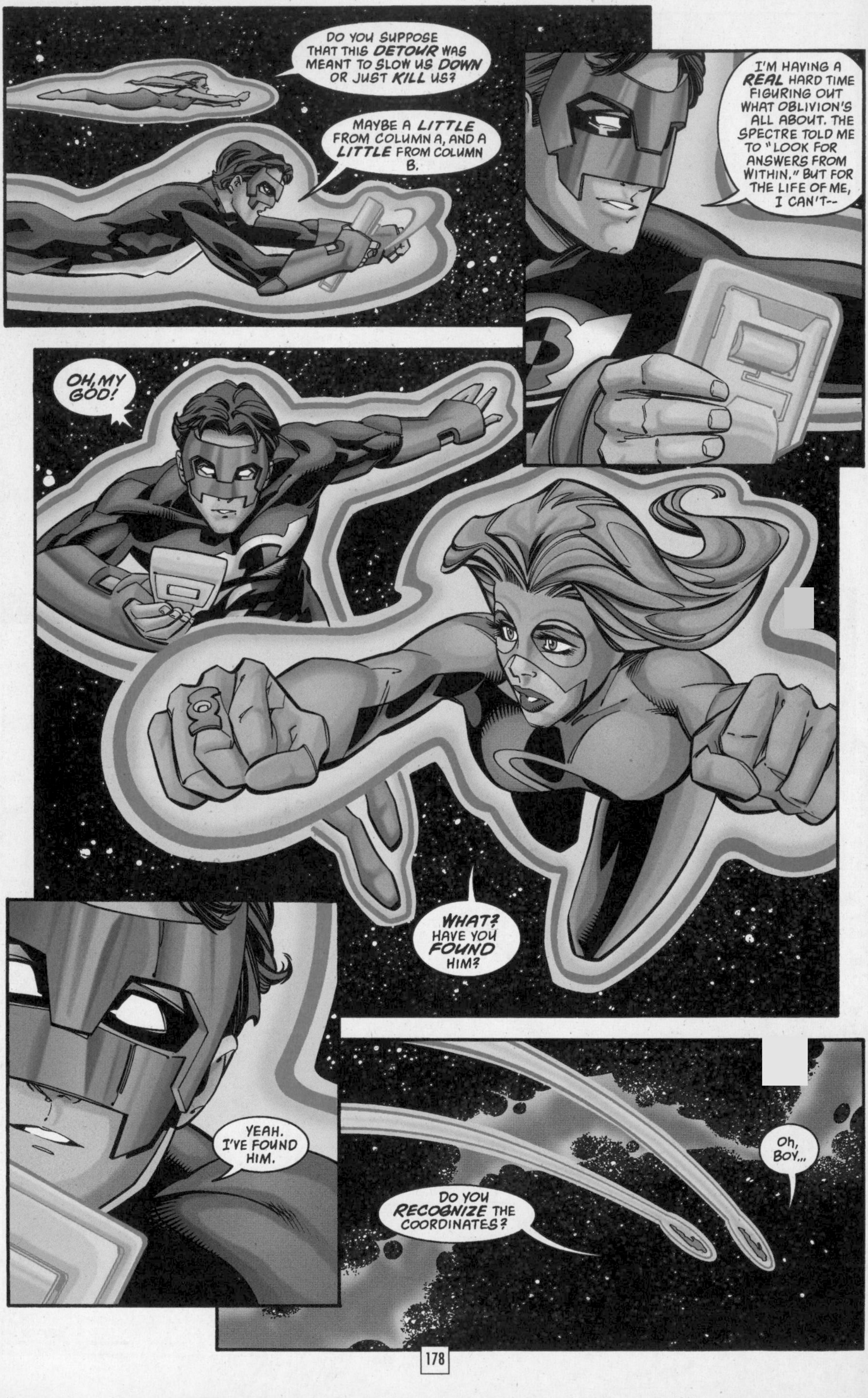
DO YOU SUPPOSE THAT THIS DETOUR WAS MEANT TO SLOW US DOWN OR JUST KILL US?
MAYBE A LITTLE FROM COLUMN A, AND A LITTLE FROM COLUMN B.
I'M HAVING A REAL HARD TIME FIGURING OUT WHAT OBLIVION'S ALL ABOUT. THE SPECTRE TOLD ME TO "LOOK FOR ANSWERS FROM WITHIN," BUT FOR THE LIFE OF ME, I CAN'T--
OH, MY GOD!
WHAT? HAVE YOU FOUND HIM?
YEAH. I'VE FOUND HIM.
DO YOU RECOGNIZE THE COORDINATES?
OH, BOY...

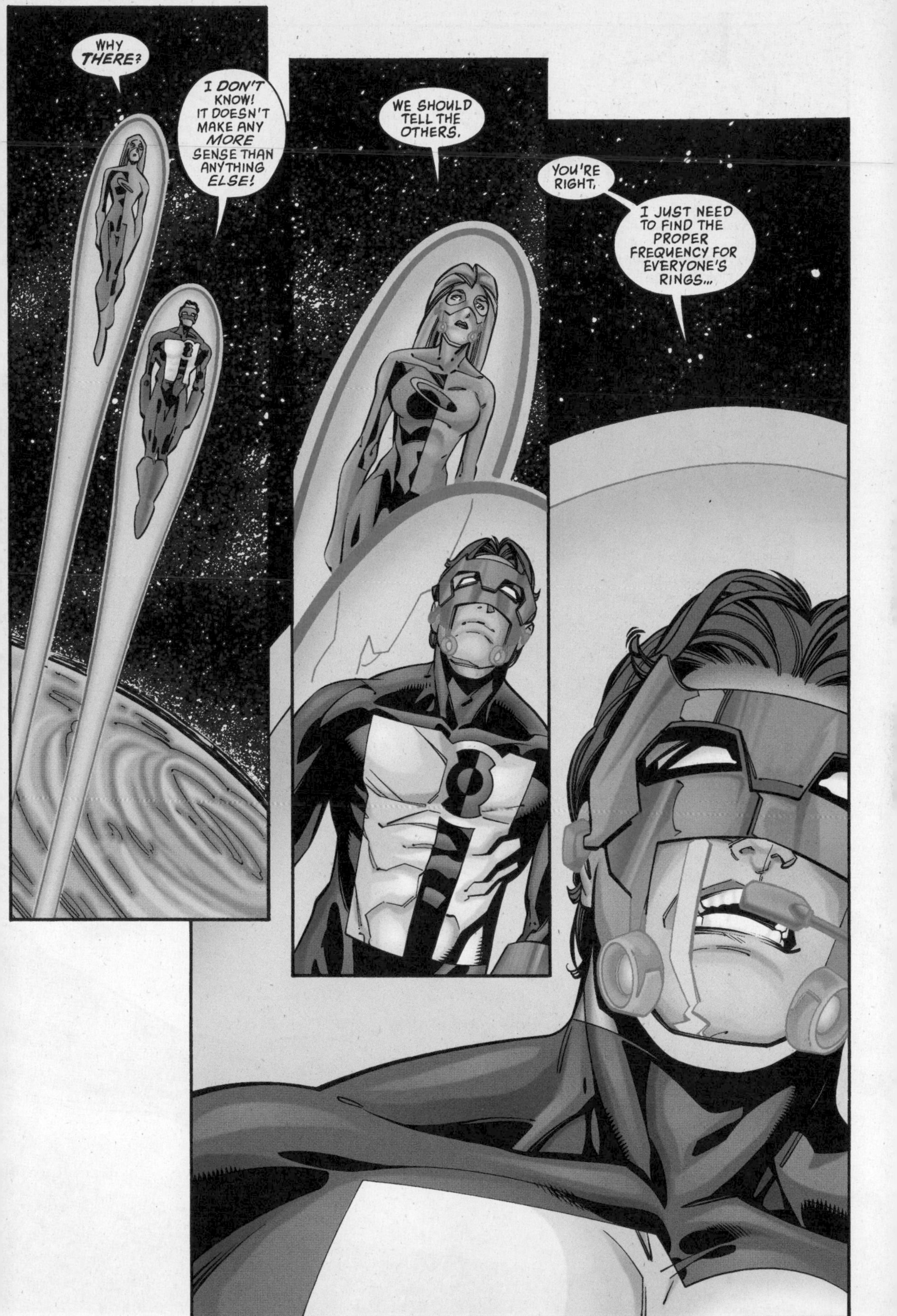
WHY THERE?
I DON'T KNOW! IT DOESN'T MAKE ANY MORE SENSE THAN ANYTHING ELSE!
WE SHOULD TELL THE OTHERS.
YOU'RE RIGHT.
I JUST NEED TO FIND THE PROPER FREQUENCY FOR EVERYONE'S RINGS...

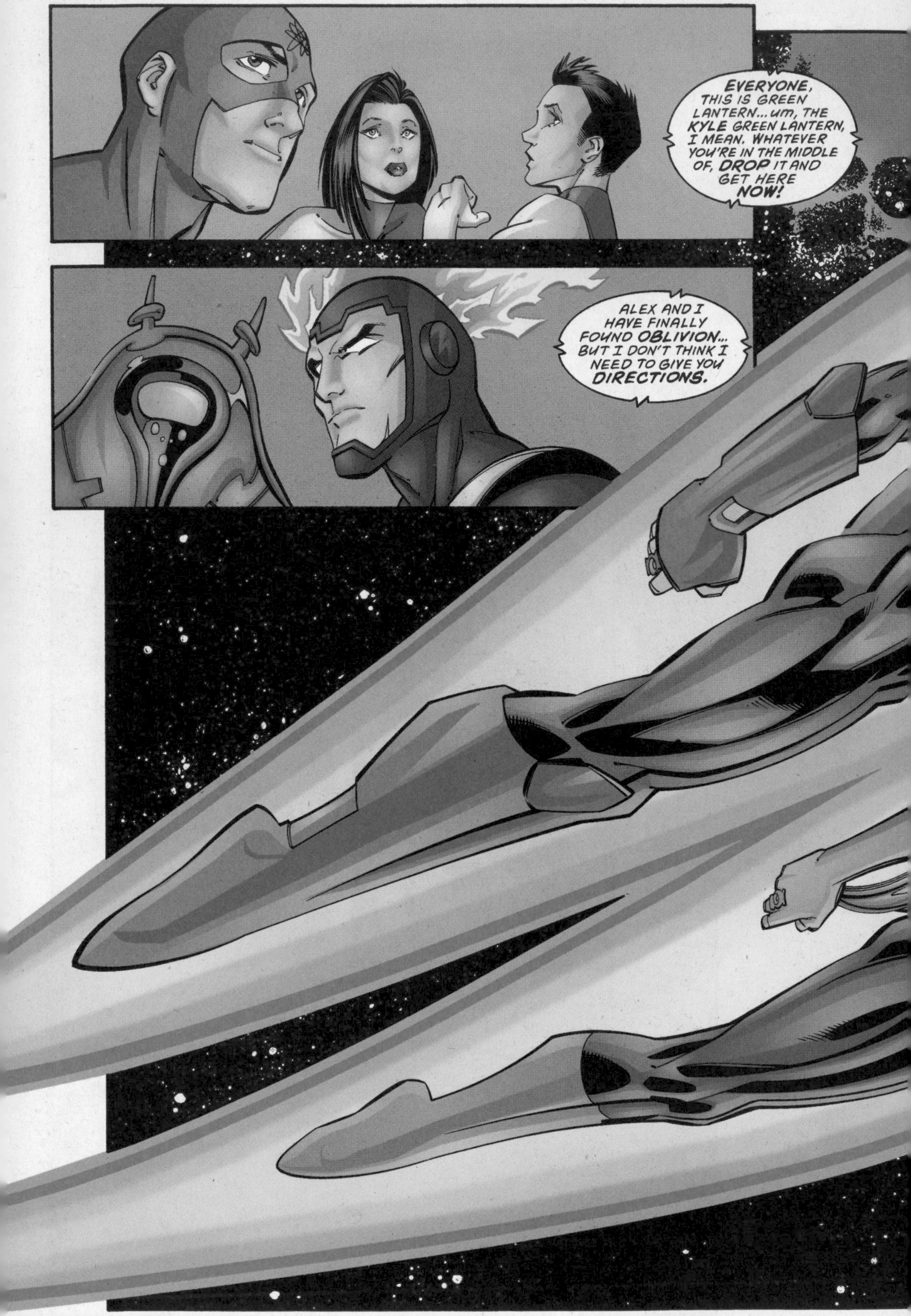
EVERYONE, THIS IS GREEN LANTERN... um, THE KYLE GREEN LANTERN, I MEAN. WHATEVER YOU'RE IN THE MIDDLE OF, DROP IT AND GET HERE NOW!
ALEX AND I HAVE FINALLY FOUND OBLIVION... BUT I DON'T THINK I NEED TO GIVE YOU DIRECTIONS.

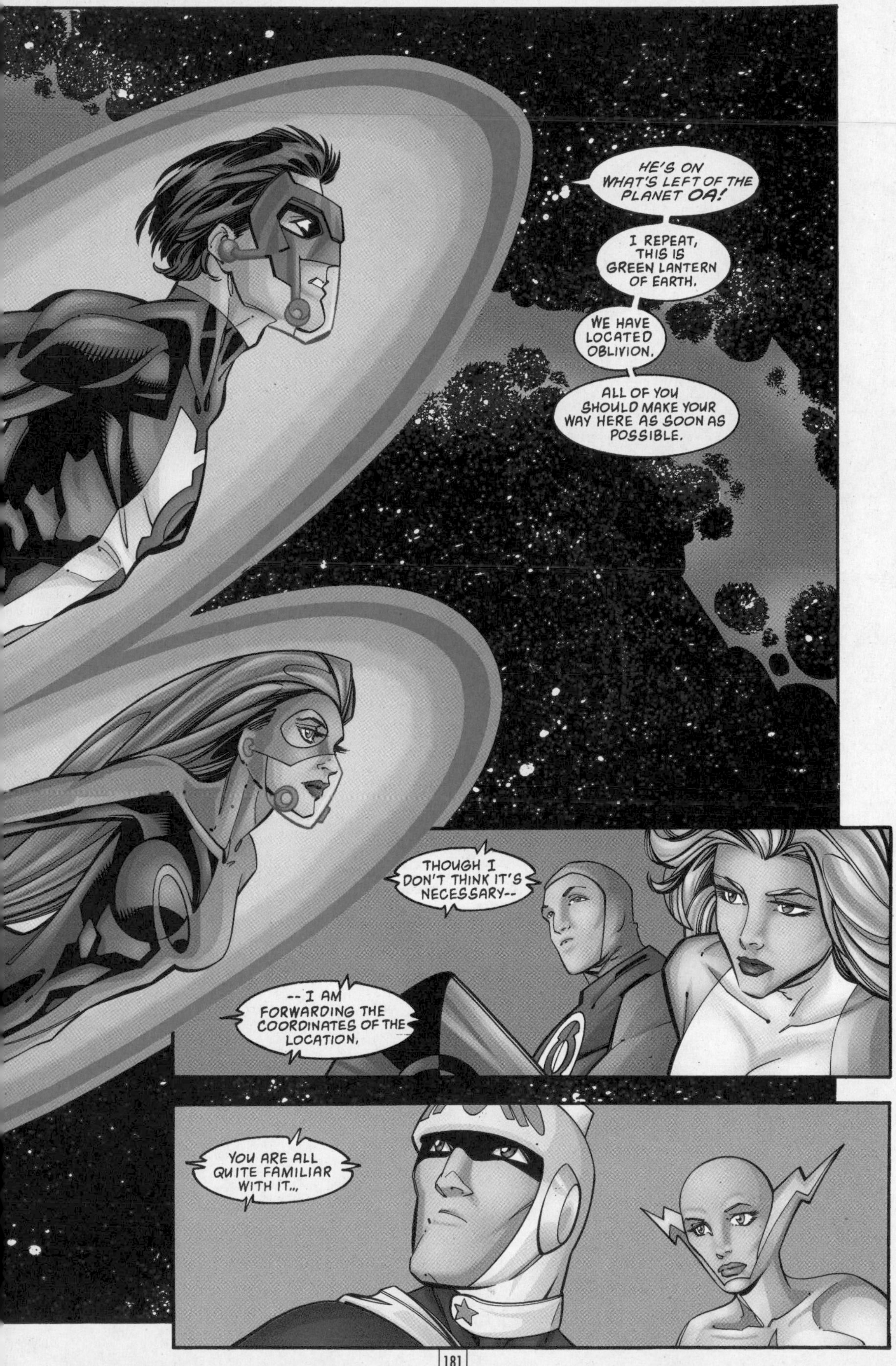
HE'S ON WHAT'S LEFT OF THE PLANET OA!
I REPEAT, THIS IS GREEN LANTERN OF EARTH.
WE HAVE LOCATED OBLIVION.
ALL OF YOU SHOULD MAKE YOUR WAY HERE AS SOON AS POSSIBLE.
THOUGH I DON'T THINK IT'S NECESSARY--
--I AM FORWARDING THE COORDINATES OF THE LOCATION.
YOU ARE ALL QUITE FAMILIAR WITH IT...

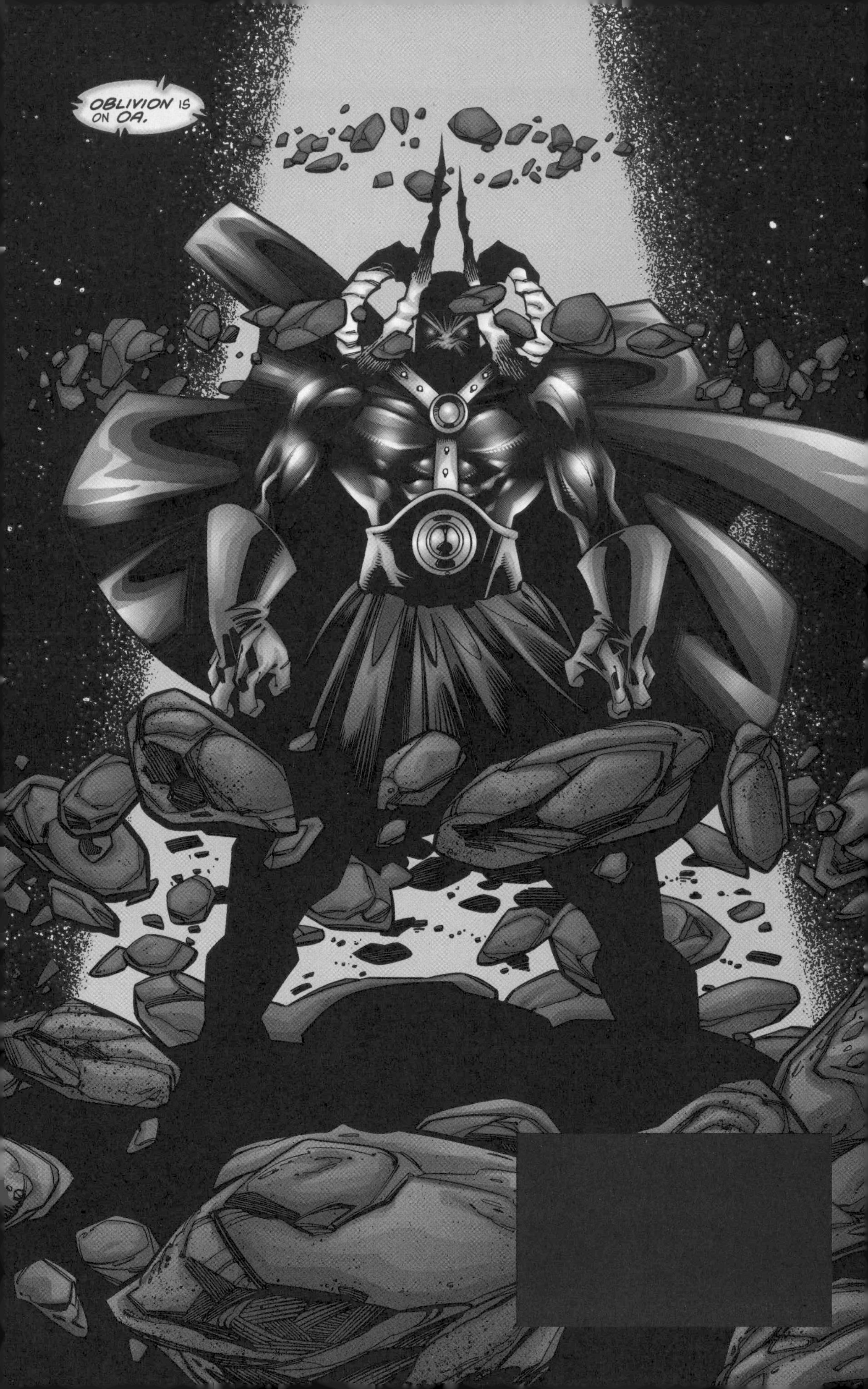
OBLIVION IS ON OA.
[redacted]

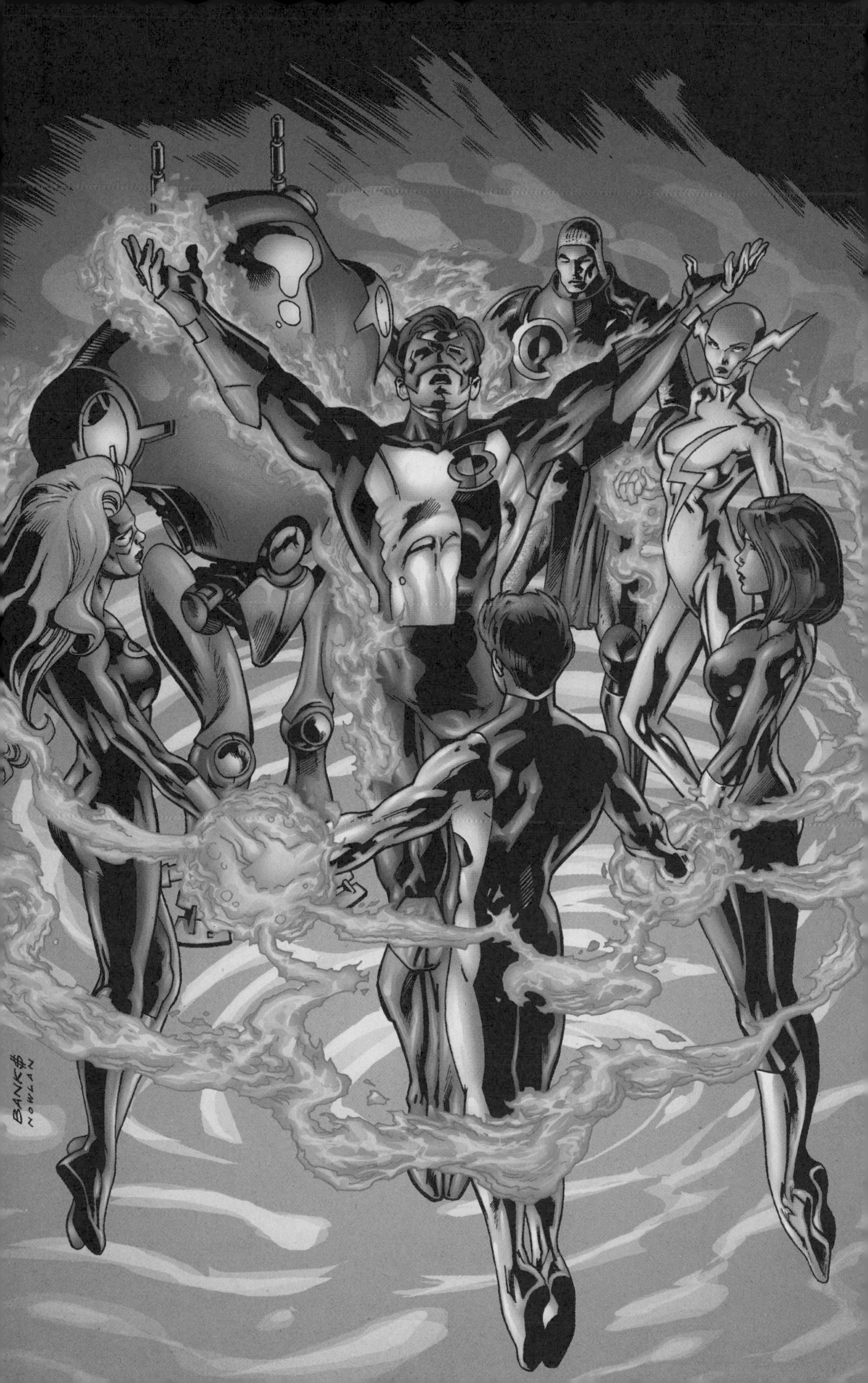
BANKS
NOWLAN

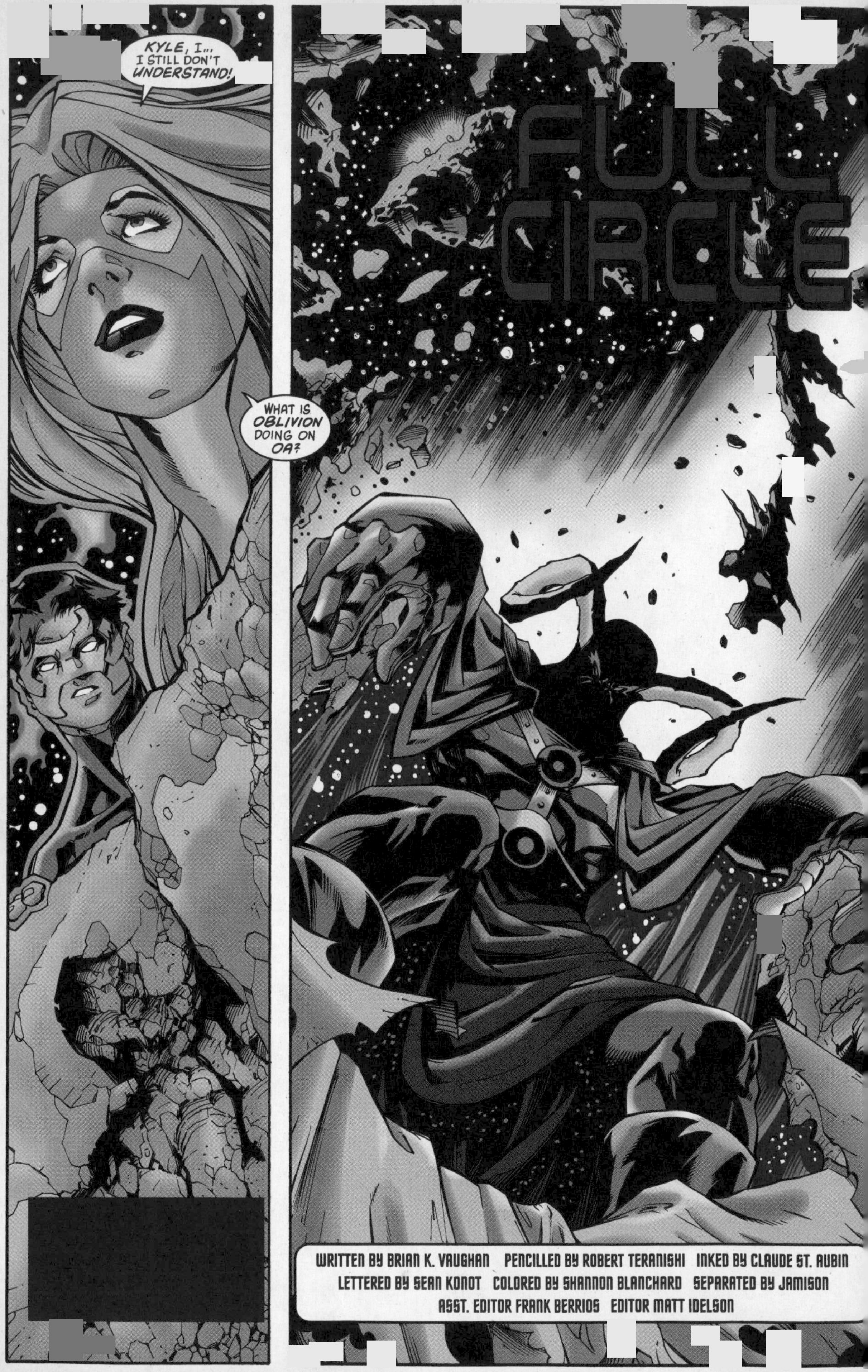
KYLE, I... I STILL DON'T UNDERSTAND!
WHAT IS OBLIVION DOING ON OA?
[redacted]
FULL CIRCLE
WRITTEN BY BRIAN K. VAUGHAN PENCILLED BY ROBERT TERANISHI INKED BY CLAUDE ST. AUBIN
LETTERED BY SEAN KONOT COLORED BY SHANNON BLANCHARD SEPARATED BY JAMISON
ASST. EDITOR FRANK BERRIOS EDITOR MATT IDELSON

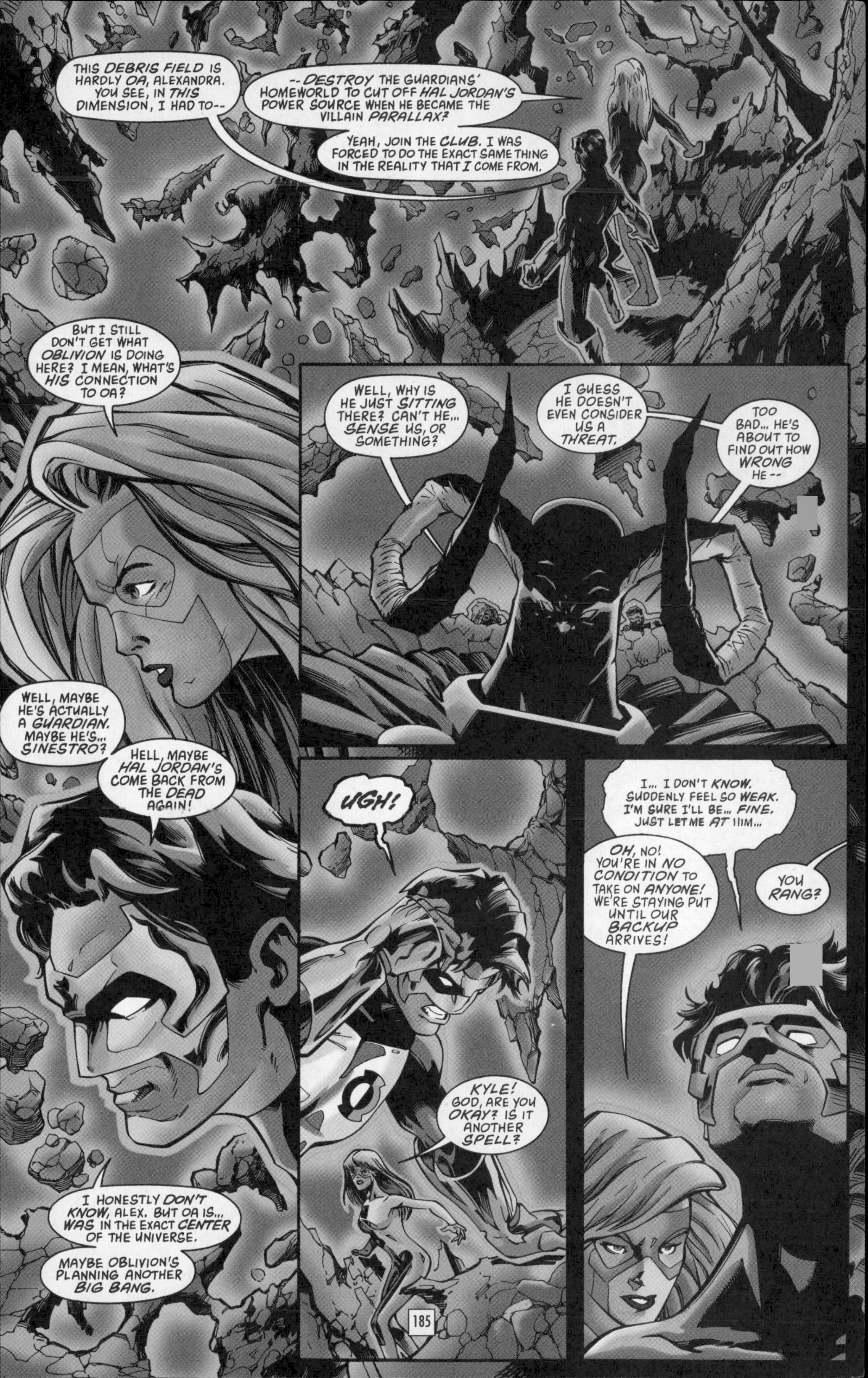
THIS DEBRIS FIELD IS HARDLY OA, ALEXANDRA. YOU SEE, IN THIS DIMENSION, I HAD TO--
--DESTROY THE GUARDIANS' HOMEWORLD TO CUT OFF HAL JORDAN'S POWER SOURCE WHEN HE BECAME THE VILLAIN PARALLAX?
YEAH, JOIN THE CLUB. I WAS FORCED TO DO THE EXACT SAME THING IN THE REALITY THAT I COME FROM.
BUT I STILL DON'T GET WHAT OBLIVION IS DOING HERE? I MEAN, WHAT'S HIS CONNECTION TO OA?
WELL, MAYBE HE'S ACTUALLY A GUARDIAN. MAYBE HE'S... SINESTRO?
HELL, MAYBE HAL JORDAN'S COME BACK FROM THE DEAD AGAIN!
I HONESTLY DON'T KNOW, ALEX. BUT OA IS... WAS IN THE EXACT CENTER OF THE UNIVERSE.
MAYBE OBLIVION'S PLANNING ANOTHER BIG BANG.
WELL, WHY IS HE JUST SITTING THERE? CAN'T HE... SENSE US, OR SOMETHING?
I GUESS HE DOESN'T EVEN CONSIDER US A THREAT.
TOO BAD... HE'S ABOUT TO FIND OUT HOW WRONG HE--
UGH!
KYLE! GOD, ARE YOU OKAY? IS IT ANOTHER SPELL?
I... I DON'T KNOW. SUDDENLY FEEL SO WEAK. I'M SURE I'LL BE... FINE. JUST LET ME AT HIM...
OH, NO! YOU'RE IN NO CONDITION TO TAKE ON ANYONE! WE'RE STAYING PUT UNTIL OUR BACKUP ARRIVES!
YOU RANG?

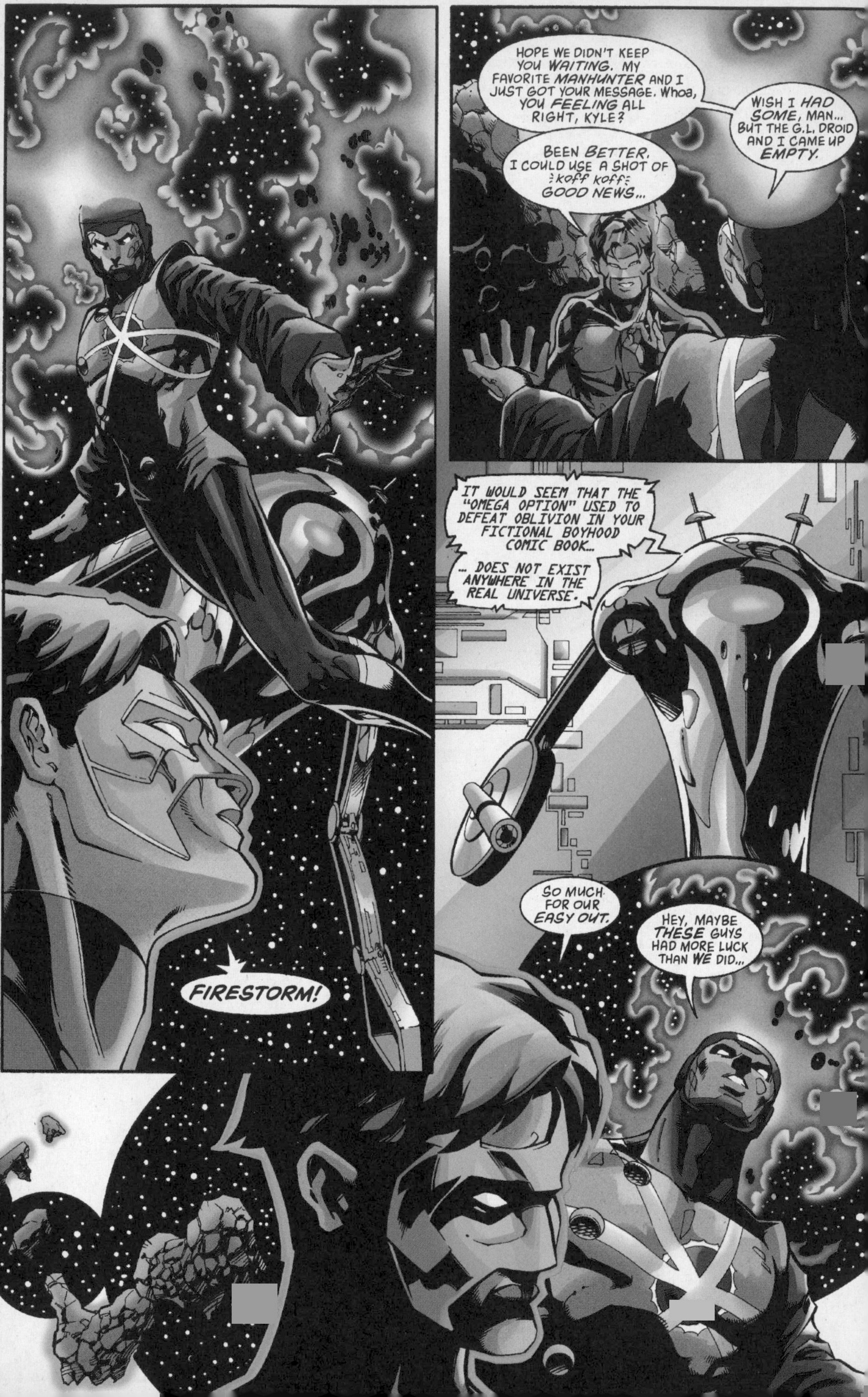
FIRESTORM!
HOPE WE DIDN'T KEEP YOU WAITING. MY FAVORITE MANHUNTER AND I JUST GOT YOUR MESSAGE. Whoa, YOU FEELING ALL RIGHT, KYLE?
BEEN BETTER. I COULD USE A SHOT OF koff koff GOOD NEWS...
WISH I HAD SOME, MAN... BUT THE G.L. DROID AND I CAME UP EMPTY.
IT WOULD SEEM THAT THE "OMEGA OPTION" USED TO DEFEAT OBLIVION IN YOUR FICTIONAL BOYHOOD COMIC BOOK...
... DOES NOT EXIST ANYWHERE IN THE REAL UNIVERSE.
SO MUCH FOR OUR EASY OUT.
HEY, MAYBE THESE GUYS HAD MORE LUCK THAN WE DID...

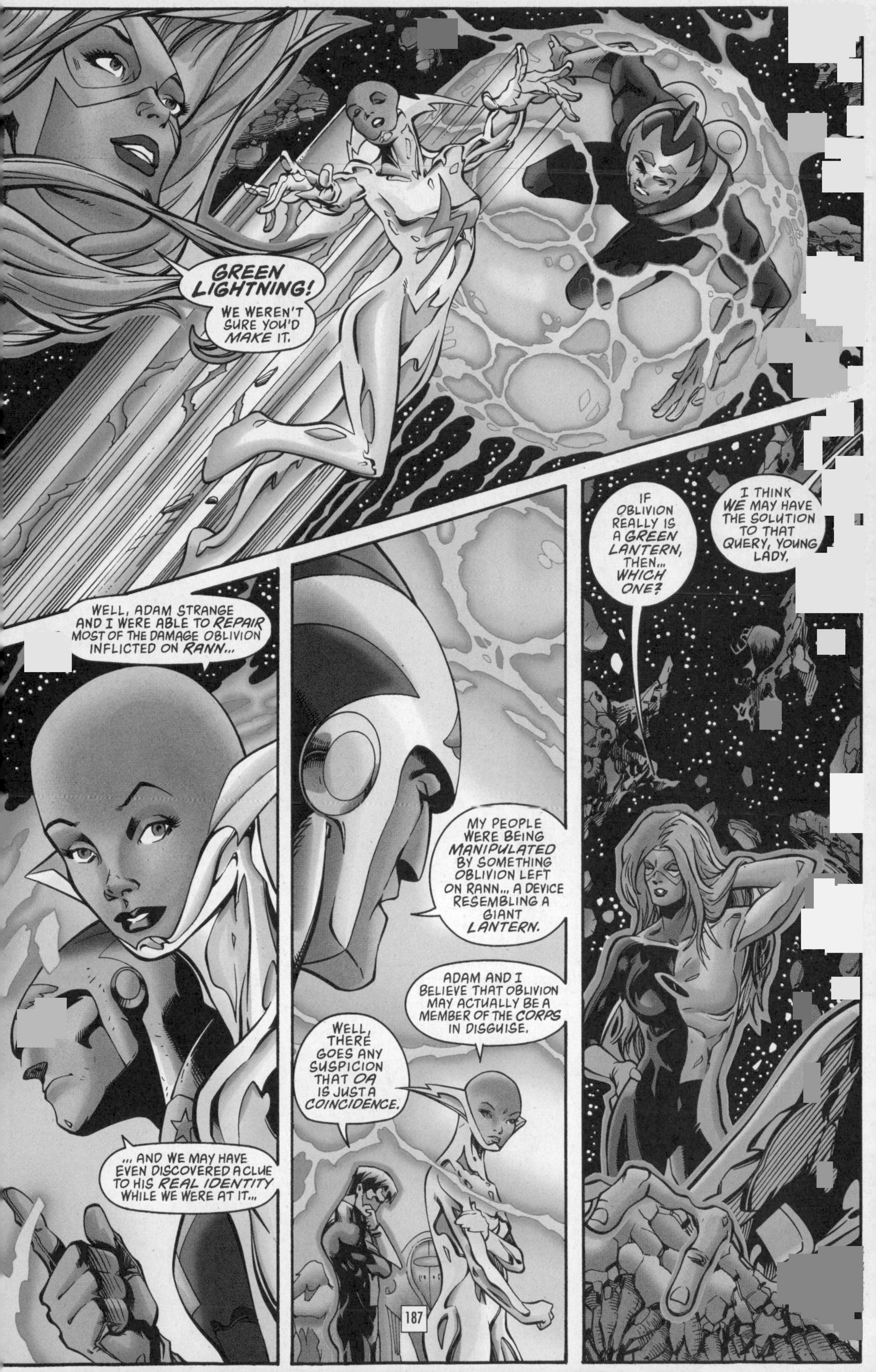
GREEN LIGHTNING! WE WEREN'T SURE YOU'D MAKE IT.
WELL, ADAM STRANGE AND I WERE ABLE TO REPAIR MOST OF THE DAMAGE OBLIVION INFLICTED ON RANN...
...AND WE MAY HAVE EVEN DISCOVERED A CLUE TO HIS REAL IDENTITY WHILE WE WERE AT IT...
MY PEOPLE WERE BEING MANIPULATED BY SOMETHING OBLIVION LEFT ON RANN... A DEVICE RESEMBLING A GIANT LANTERN.
ADAM AND I BELIEVE THAT OBLIVION MAY ACTUALLY BE A MEMBER OF THE CORPS IN DISGUISE.
WELL, THERE GOES ANY SUSPICION THAT OA IS JUST A COINCIDENCE.
IF OBLIVION REALLY IS A GREEN LANTERN, THEN... WHICH ONE?
I THINK WE MAY HAVE THE SOLUTION TO THAT QUERY, YOUNG LADY.

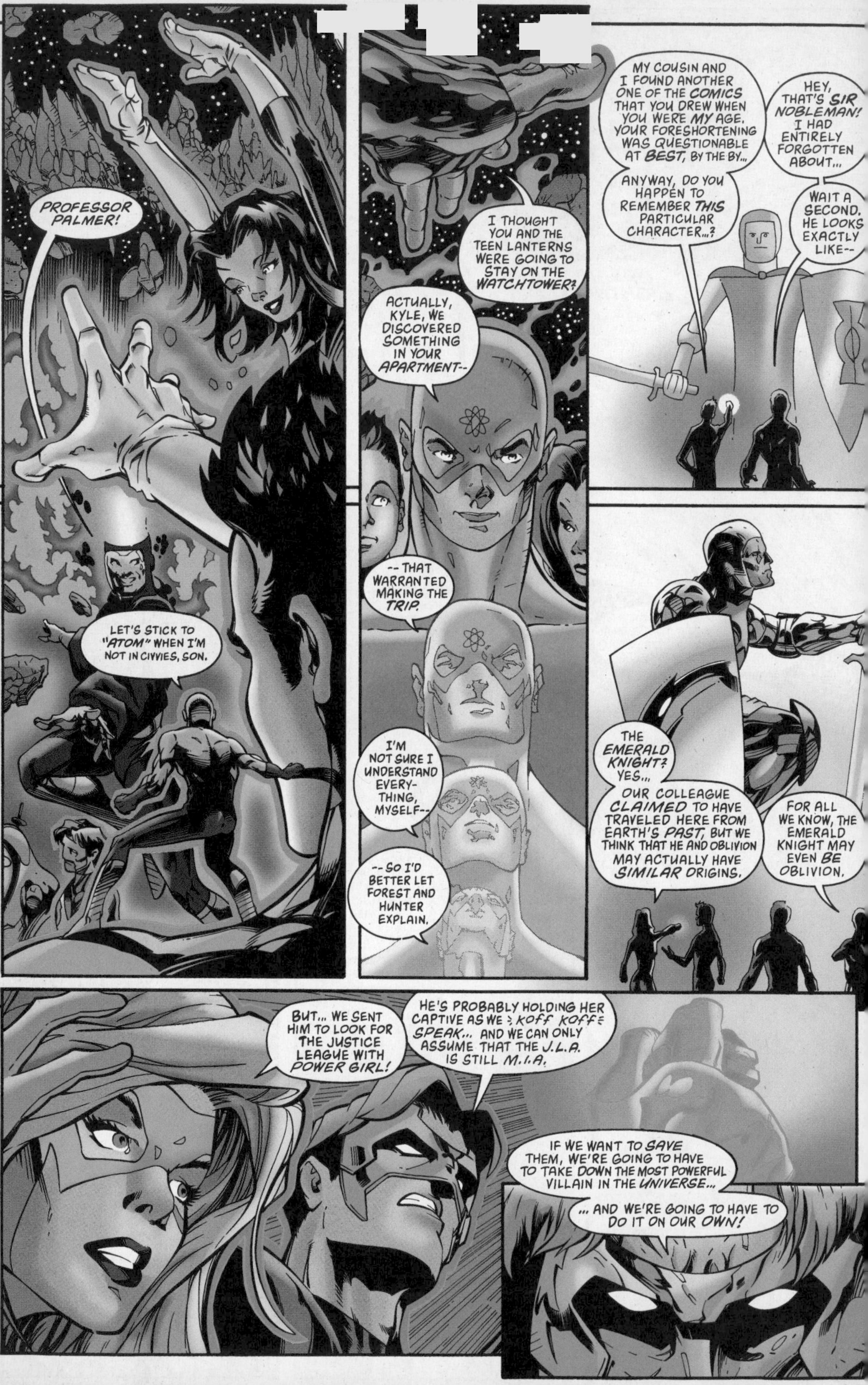
PROFESSOR PALMER!
LET'S STICK TO "ATOM" WHEN I'M NOT IN CIVVIES, SON.
I THOUGHT YOU AND THE TEEN LANTERNS WERE GOING TO STAY ON THE WATCHTOWER?
ACTUALLY, KYLE, WE DISCOVERED SOMETHING IN YOUR APARTMENT--
--THAT WARRANTED MAKING THE TRIP.
I'M NOT SURE I UNDERSTAND EVERY-THING, MYSELF--
--SO I'D BETTER LET FOREST AND HUNTER EXPLAIN.
MY COUSIN AND I FOUND ANOTHER ONE OF THE COMICS THAT YOU DREW WHEN YOU WERE MY AGE. YOUR FORESHORTENING WAS QUESTIONABLE AT BEST, BY THE BY...
ANYWAY, DO YOU HAPPEN TO REMEMBER THIS PARTICULAR CHARACTER...?
HEY, THAT'S SIR NOBLEMAN! I HAD ENTIRELY FORGOTTEN ABOUT...
WAIT A SECOND. HE LOOKS EXACTLY LIKE--
THE EMERALD KNIGHT? YES...
OUR COLLEAGUE CLAIMED TO HAVE TRAVELED HERE FROM EARTH'S PAST, BUT WE THINK THAT HE AND OBLIVION MAY ACTUALLY HAVE SIMILAR ORIGINS.
FOR ALL WE KNOW, THE EMERALD KNIGHT MAY EVEN BE OBLIVION.
BUT... WE SENT HIM TO LOOK FOR THE JUSTICE LEAGUE WITH POWER GIRL!
HE'S PROBABLY HOLDING HER CAPTIVE AS WE ≈KOFF KOFF≈ SPEAK... AND WE CAN ONLY ASSUME THAT THE J.L.A. IS STILL M.I.A.
IF WE WANT TO SAVE THEM, WE'RE GOING TO HAVE TO TAKE DOWN THE MOST POWERFUL VILLAIN IN THE UNIVERSE...
...AND WE'RE GOING TO HAVE TO DO IT ON OUR OWN!

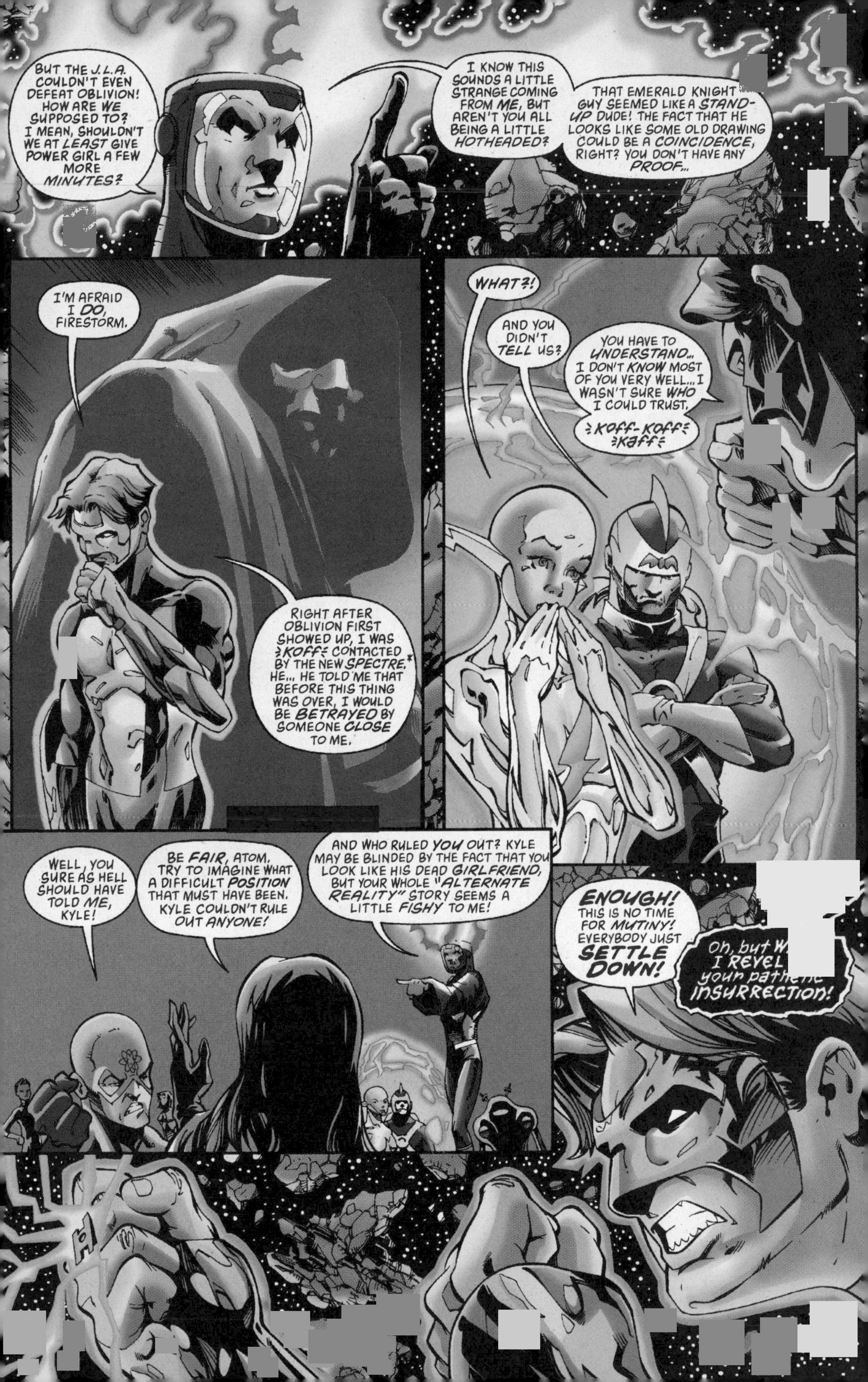

BUT THE J.L.A. COULDN'T EVEN DEFEAT OBLIVION! HOW ARE WE SUPPOSED TO? I MEAN, SHOULDN'T WE AT LEAST GIVE POWER GIRL A FEW MORE MINUTES?
I KNOW THIS SOUNDS A LITTLE STRANGE COMING FROM ME, BUT AREN'T YOU ALL BEING A LITTLE HOTHEADED?
THAT EMERALD KNIGHT GUY SEEMED LIKE A STAND-UP DUDE! THE FACT THAT HE LOOKS LIKE SOME OLD DRAWING COULD BE A COINCIDENCE, RIGHT? YOU DON'T HAVE ANY PROOF...
I'M AFRAID I DO, FIRESTORM.
RIGHT AFTER OBLIVION FIRST SHOWED UP, I WAS ≷KOFF≶ CONTACTED BY THE NEW SPECTRE.* HE... HE TOLD ME THAT BEFORE THIS THING WAS OVER, I WOULD BE BETRAYED BY SOMEONE CLOSE TO ME.
WHAT?!
AND YOU DIDN'T TELL US?
YOU HAVE TO UNDERSTAND... I DON'T KNOW MOST OF YOU VERY WELL... I WASN'T SURE WHO I COULD TRUST.
≷KOFF-KOFF≶ ≷KAFF≶
WELL, YOU SURE AS HELL SHOULD HAVE TOLD ME, KYLE!
BE FAIR, ATOM. TRY TO IMAGINE WHAT A DIFFICULT POSITION THAT MUST HAVE BEEN. KYLE COULDN'T RULE OUT ANYONE!
AND WHO RULED YOU OUT? KYLE MAY BE BLINDED BY THE FACT THAT YOU LOOK LIKE HIS DEAD GIRLFRIEND, BUT YOUR WHOLE "ALTERNATE REALITY" STORY SEEMS A LITTLE FISHY TO ME!
ENOUGH! THIS IS NO TIME FOR MUTINY! EVERYBODY JUST SETTLE DOWN!
Oh, but W I REVEL your pathetic INSURRECTION!

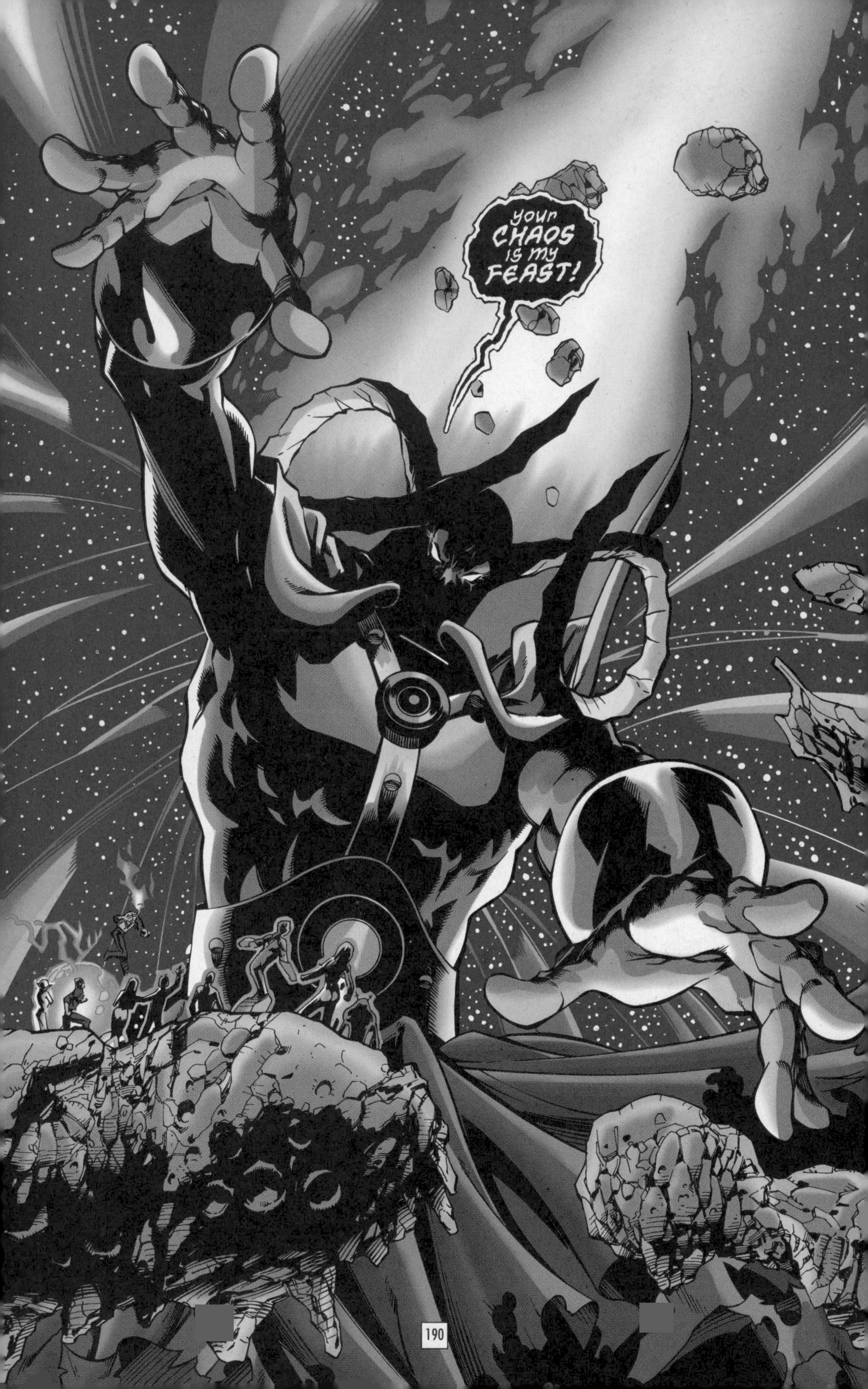
your CHAOS is my FEAST!

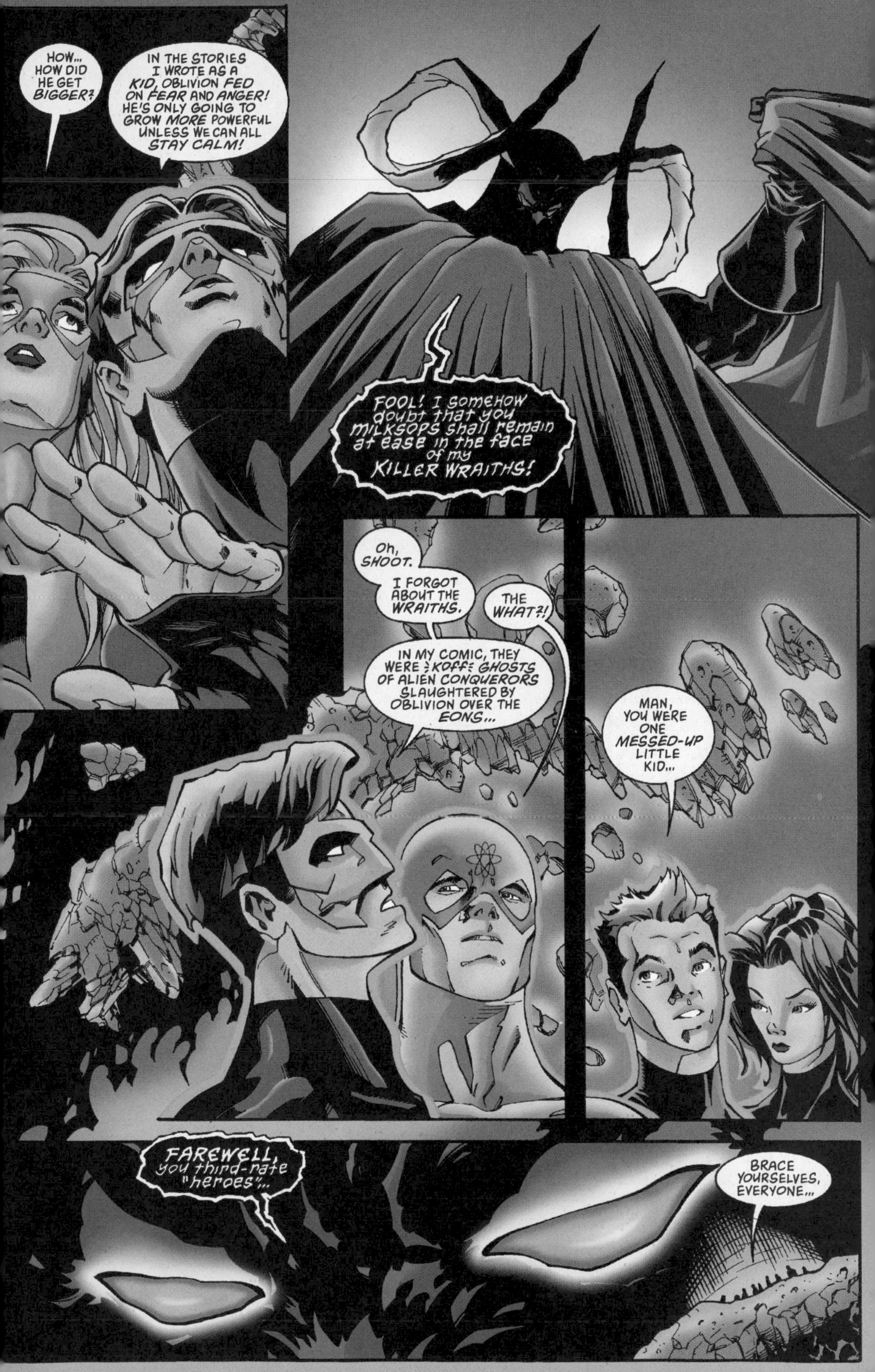
HOW... HOW DID HE GET BIGGER?
IN THE STORIES I WROTE AS A KID, OBLIVION FED ON FEAR AND ANGER! HE'S ONLY GOING TO GROW MORE POWERFUL UNLESS WE CAN ALL STAY CALM!
FOOL! I SOMEHOW doubt that you milksops shall remain at ease in the face of my KILLER WRAITHS!
Oh, SHOOT.
I FORGOT ABOUT THE WRAITHS.
THE WHAT?!
IN MY COMIC, THEY WERE =KOFF= GHOSTS OF ALIEN CONQUERORS SLAUGHTERED BY OBLIVION OVER THE EONS...
MAN, YOU WERE ONE MESSED-UP LITTLE KID...
FAREWELL, you third-rate "heroes"...
BRACE YOURSELVES, EVERYONE...

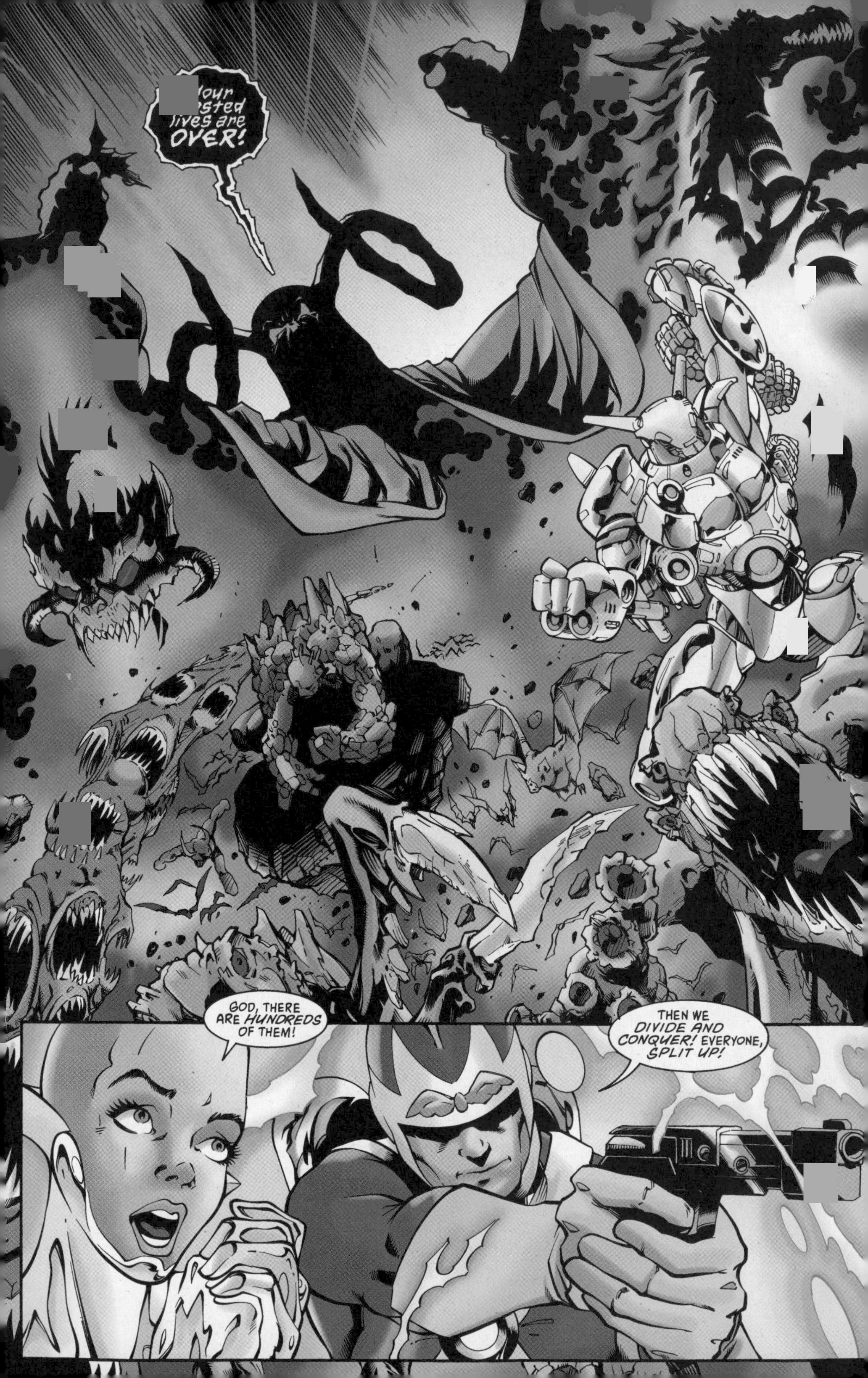
our sted lives are OVER!
GOD, THERE ARE HUNDREDS OF THEM!
THEN WE DIVIDE AND CONQUER! EVERYONE, SPLIT UP!

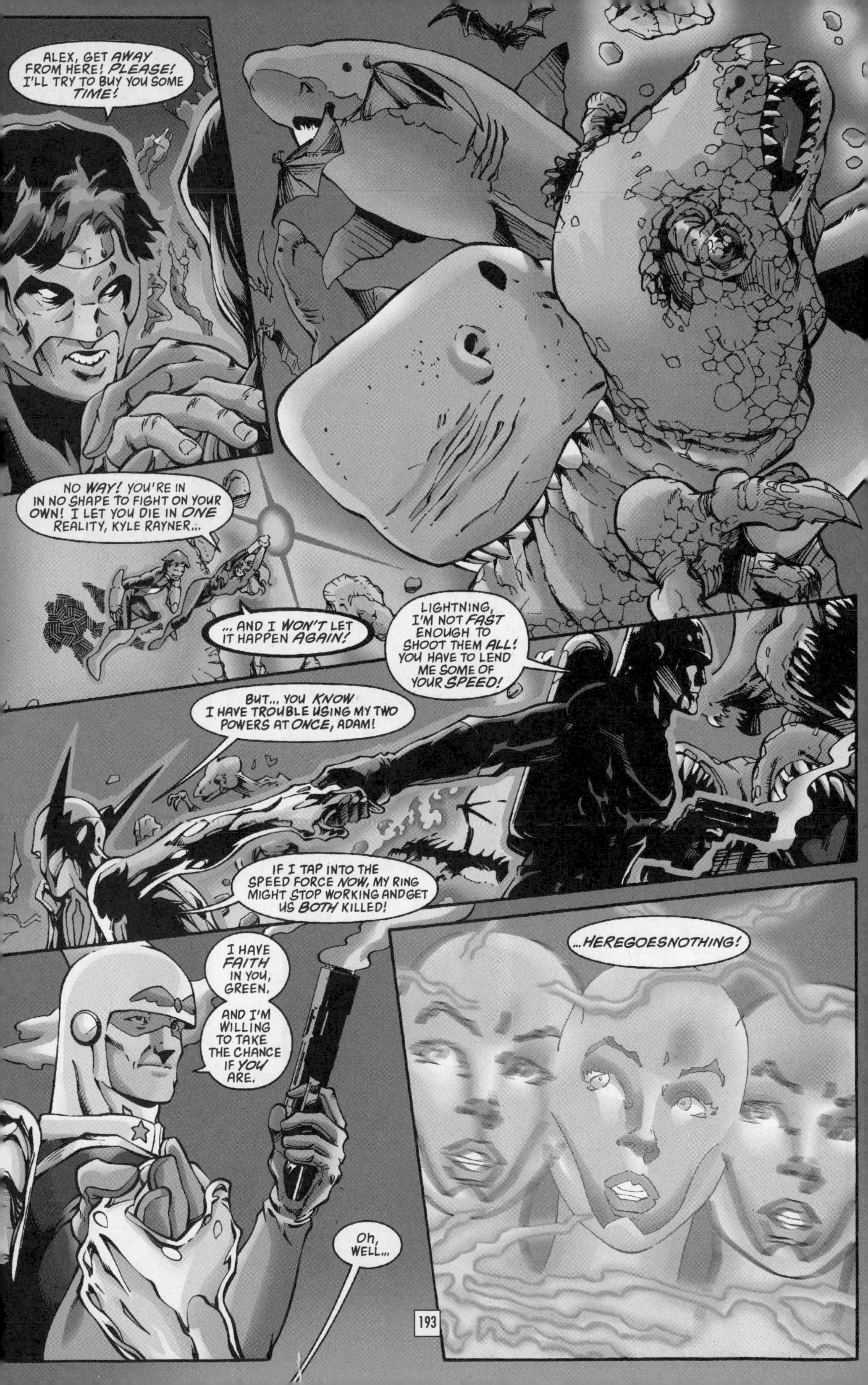

ALEX, GET AWAY FROM HERE! PLEASE! I'LL TRY TO BUY YOU SOME TIME!
NO WAY! YOU'RE IN IN NO SHAPE TO FIGHT ON YOUR OWN! I LET YOU DIE IN ONE REALITY, KYLE RAYNER...
...AND I WON'T LET IT HAPPEN AGAIN!
LIGHTNING, I'M NOT FAST ENOUGH TO SHOOT THEM ALL! YOU HAVE TO LEND ME SOME OF YOUR SPEED!
BUT... YOU KNOW I HAVE TROUBLE USING MY TWO POWERS AT ONCE, ADAM!
IF I TAP INTO THE SPEED FORCE NOW, MY RING MIGHT STOP WORKING AND GET US BOTH KILLED!
I HAVE FAITH IN YOU, GREEN.
AND I'M WILLING TO TAKE THE CHANCE IF YOU ARE.
Oh, WELL...
...HEREGOESNOTHING!

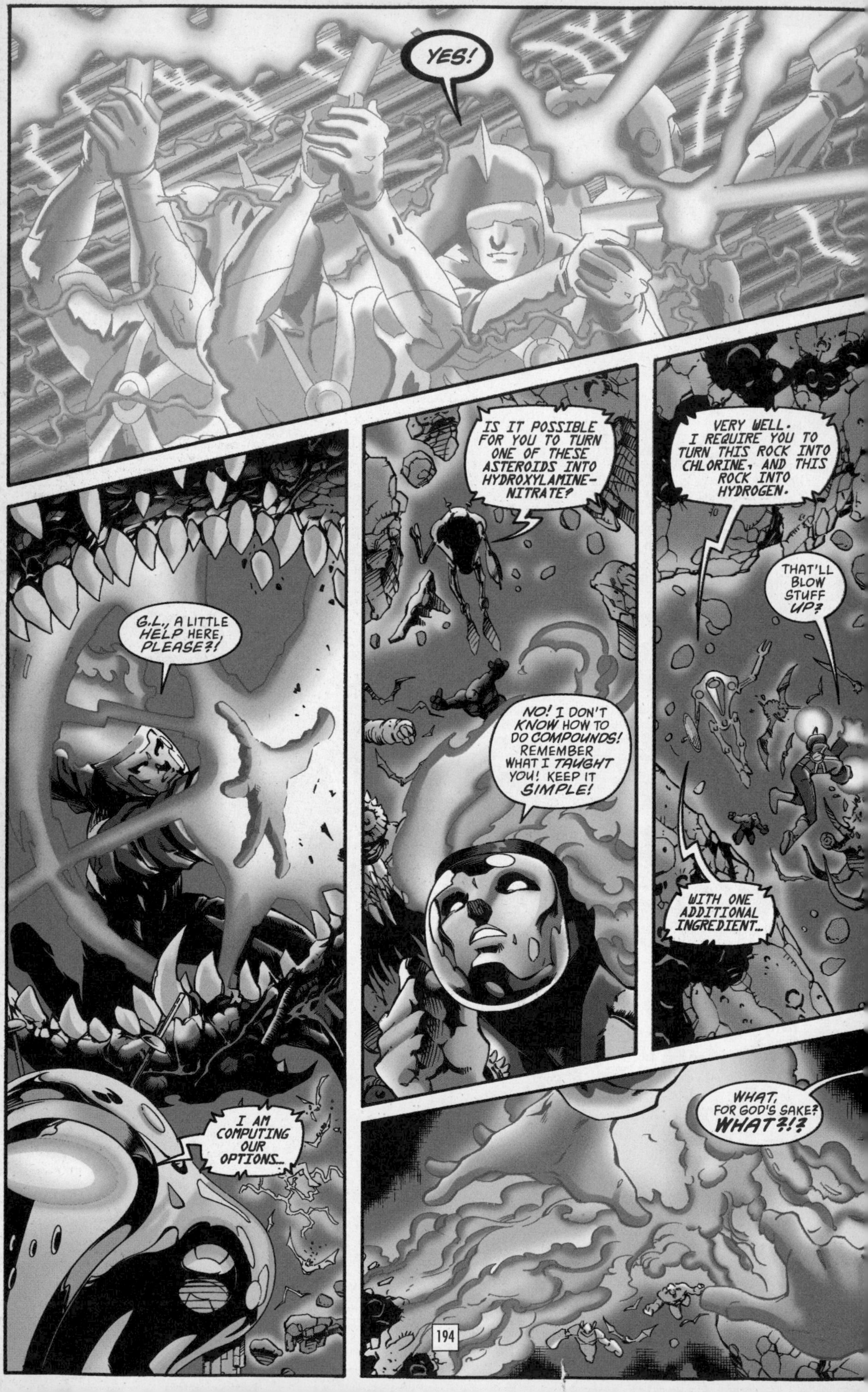
YES!
IS IT POSSIBLE FOR YOU TO TURN ONE OF THESE ASTEROIDS INTO HYDROXYLAMINE-NITRATE?
VERY WELL. I REQUIRE YOU TO TURN THIS ROCK INTO CHLORINE, AND THIS ROCK INTO HYDROGEN.
G.L., A LITTLE HELP HERE, PLEASE?!
NO! I DON'T KNOW HOW TO DO COMPOUNDS! REMEMBER WHAT I TAUGHT YOU! KEEP IT SIMPLE!
THAT'LL BLOW STUFF UP?
WITH ONE ADDITIONAL INGREDIENT...
I AM COMPUTING OUR OPTIONS...
WHAT, FOR GOD'S SAKE? WHAT?!?

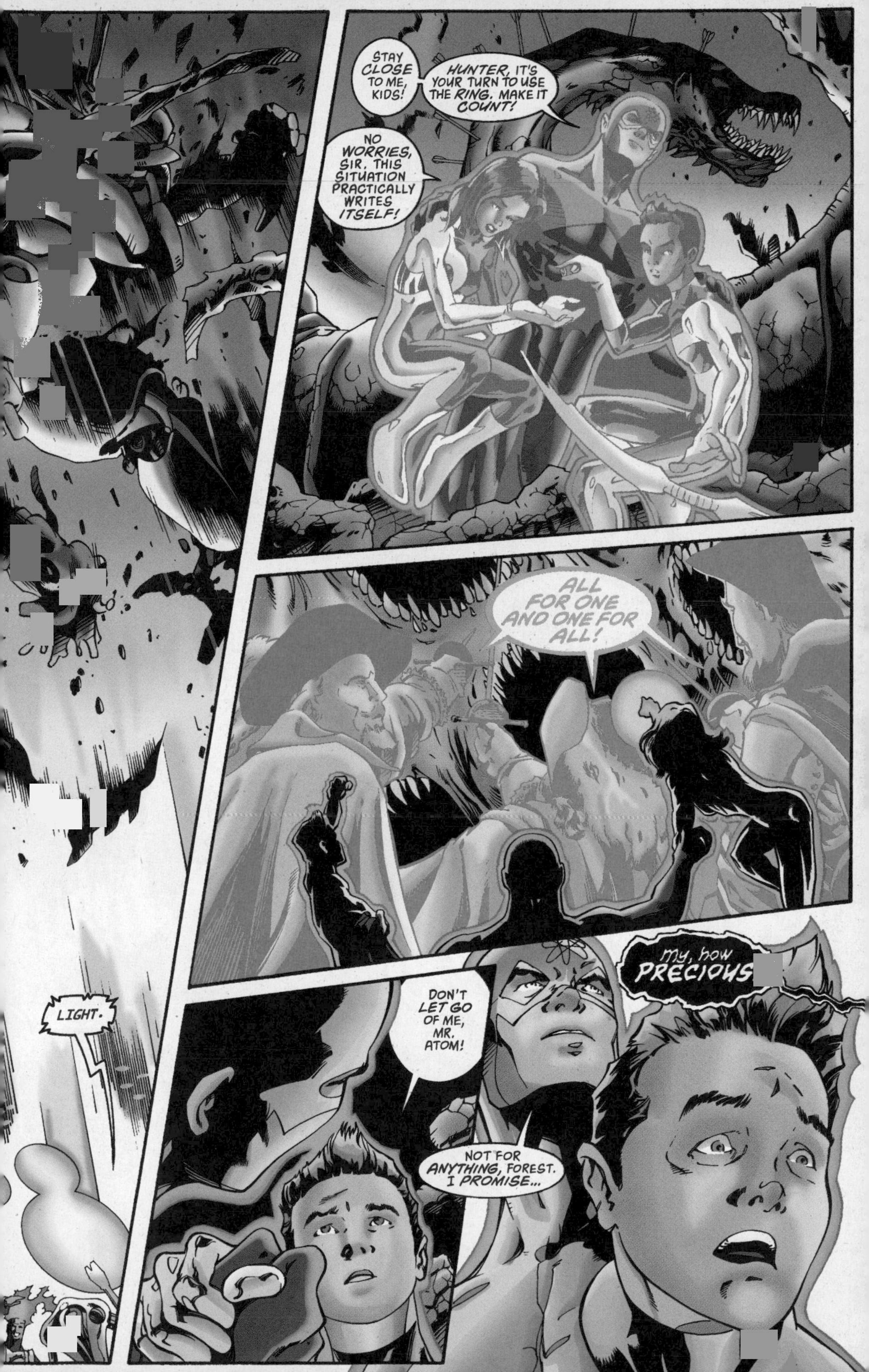

LIGHT.
STAY CLOSE TO ME, KIDS!
HUNTER, IT'S YOUR TURN TO USE THE RING. MAKE IT COUNT!
NO WORRIES, SIR. THIS SITUATION PRACTICALLY WRITES ITSELF!
ALL FOR ONE AND ONE FOR ALL!
my, how PRECIOUS
DON'T LET GO OF ME, MR. ATOM!
NOT FOR ANYTHING, FOREST. I PROMISE...

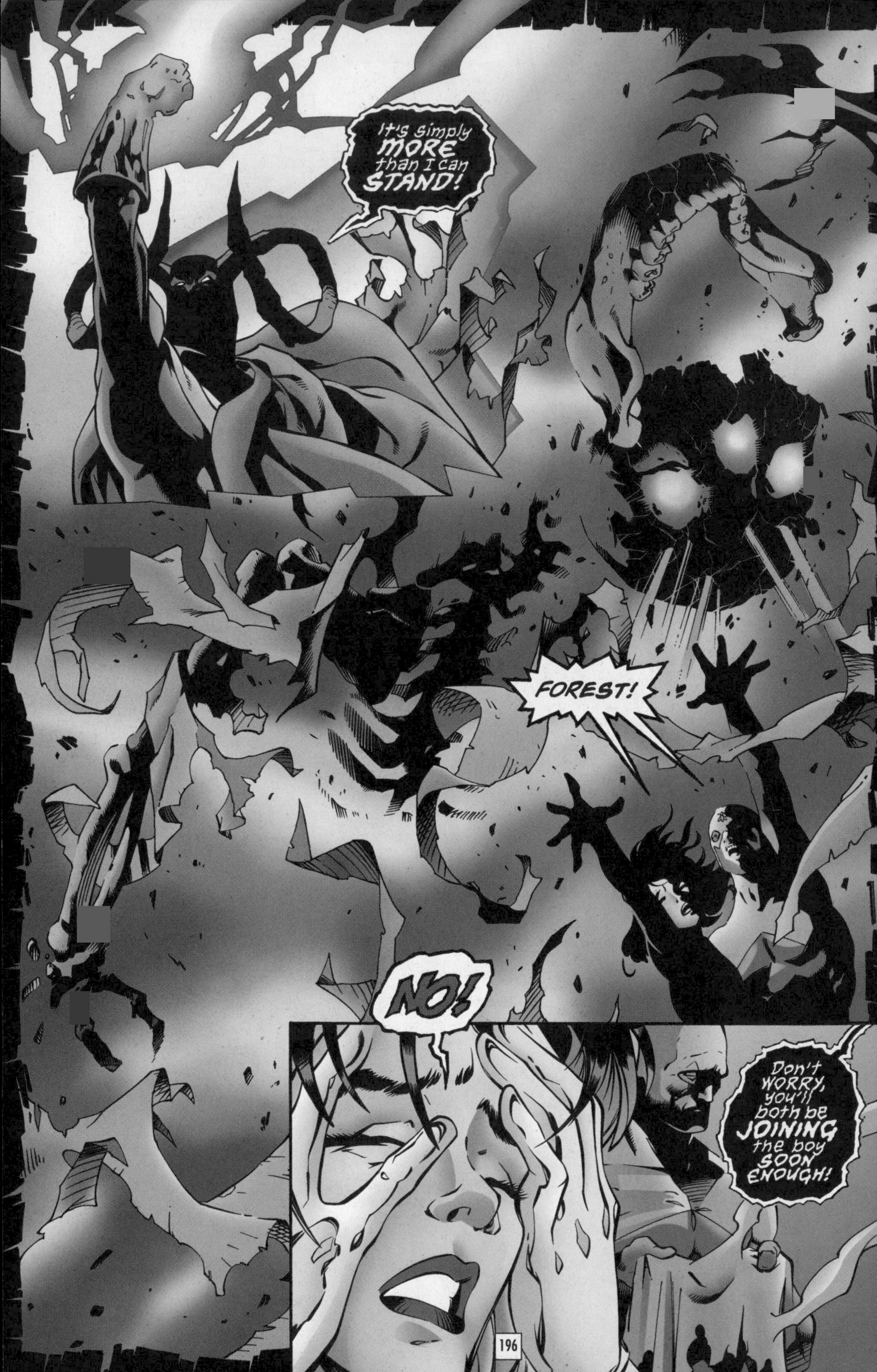
It's simply MORE than I can STAND!
FOREST!
NO!
Don't WORRY, you'll both be JOINING the boy SOON ENOUGH!

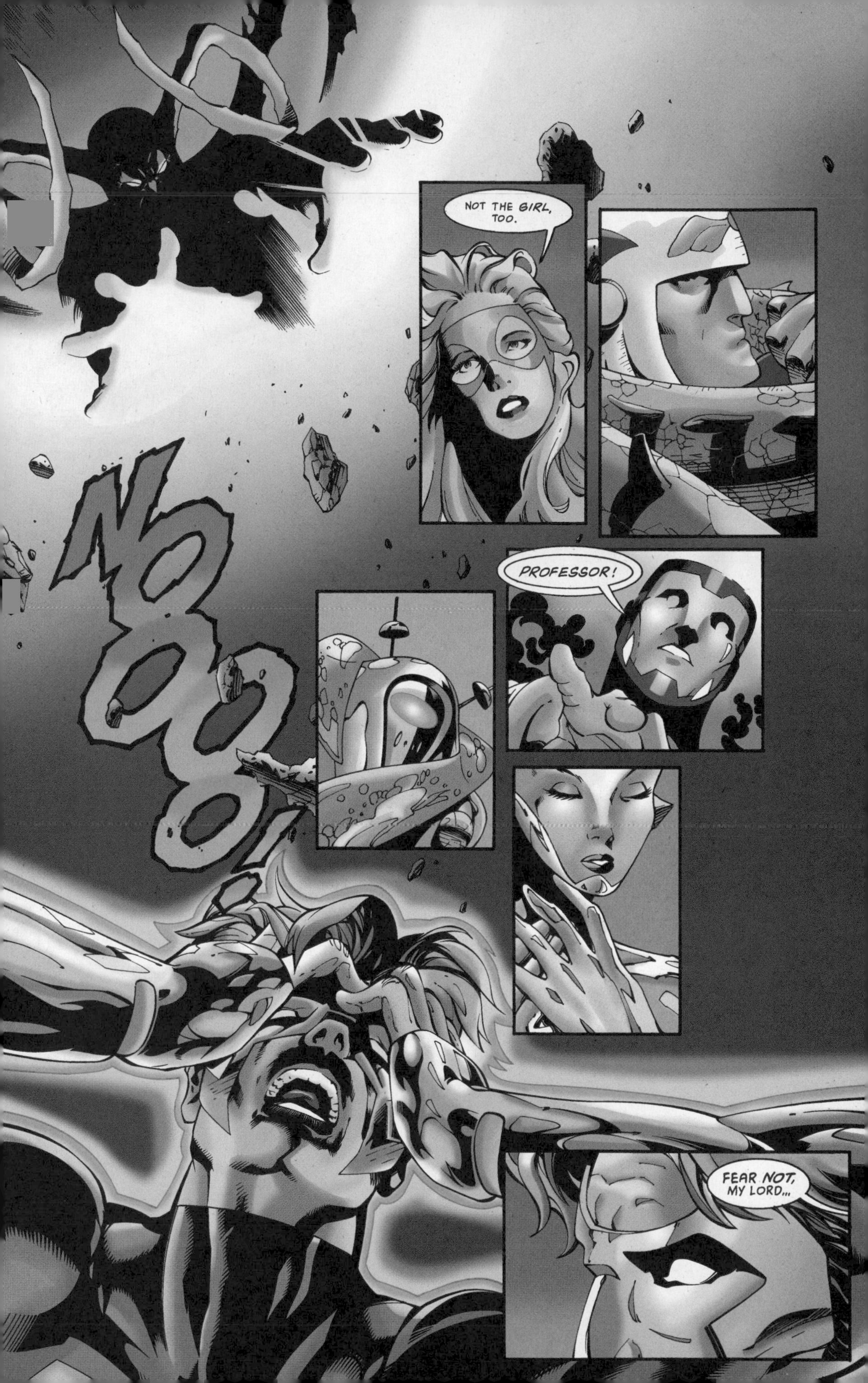
NOT THE GIRL, TOO.
NOOOOO!
PROFESSOR!
FEAR NOT, MY LORD...

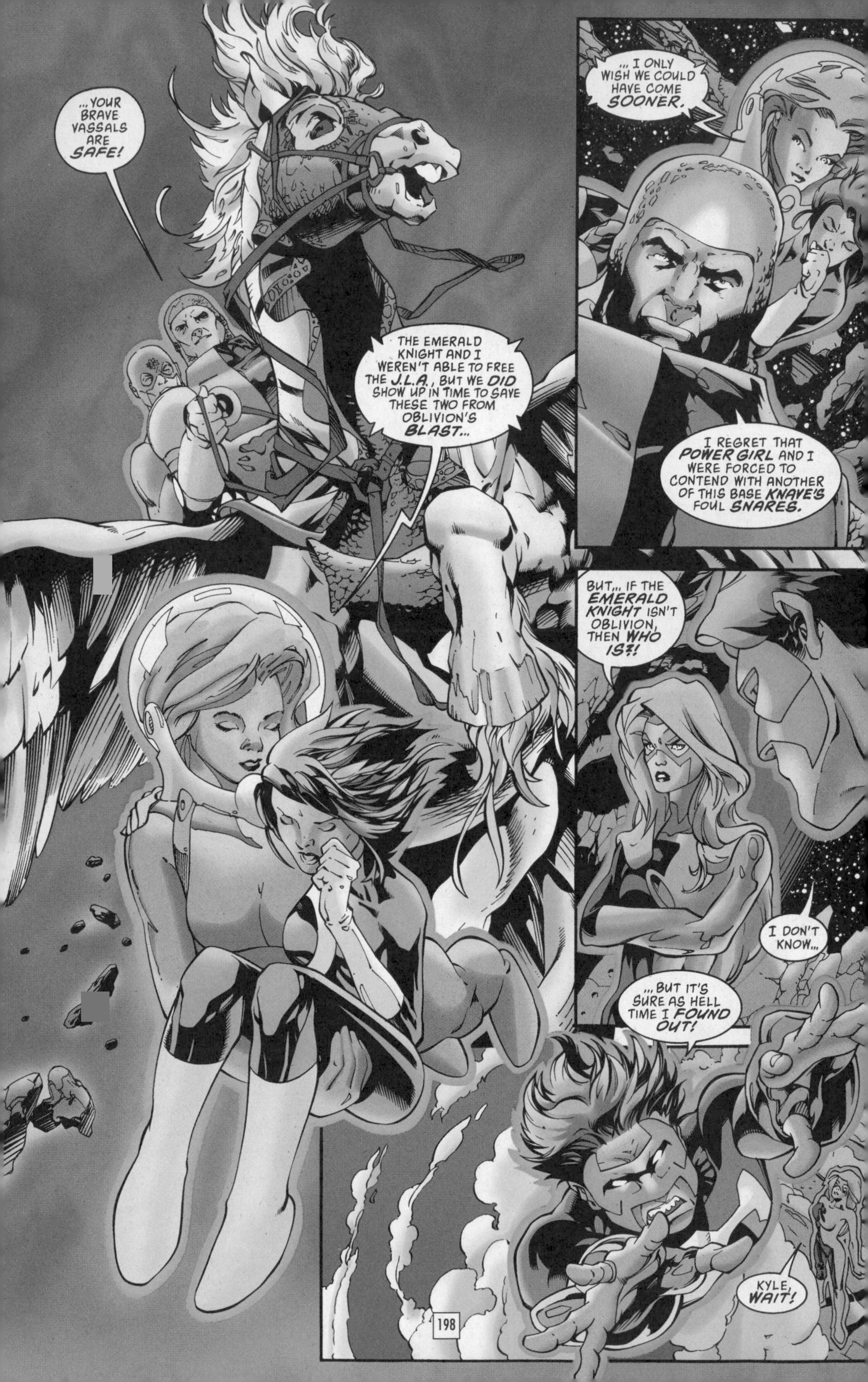
...YOUR BRAVE VASSALS ARE SAFE!
THE EMERALD KNIGHT AND I WEREN'T ABLE TO FREE THE J.L.A., BUT WE DID SHOW UP IN TIME TO SAVE THESE TWO FROM OBLIVION'S BLAST...
...I ONLY WISH WE COULD HAVE COME SOONER.
I REGRET THAT POWER GIRL AND I WERE FORCED TO CONTEND WITH ANOTHER OF THIS BASE KNAVE'S FOUL SNARES.
BUT... IF THE EMERALD KNIGHT ISN'T OBLIVION, THEN WHO IS?!
I DON'T KNOW...
...BUT IT'S SURE AS HELL TIME I FOUND OUT!
KYLE, WAIT!

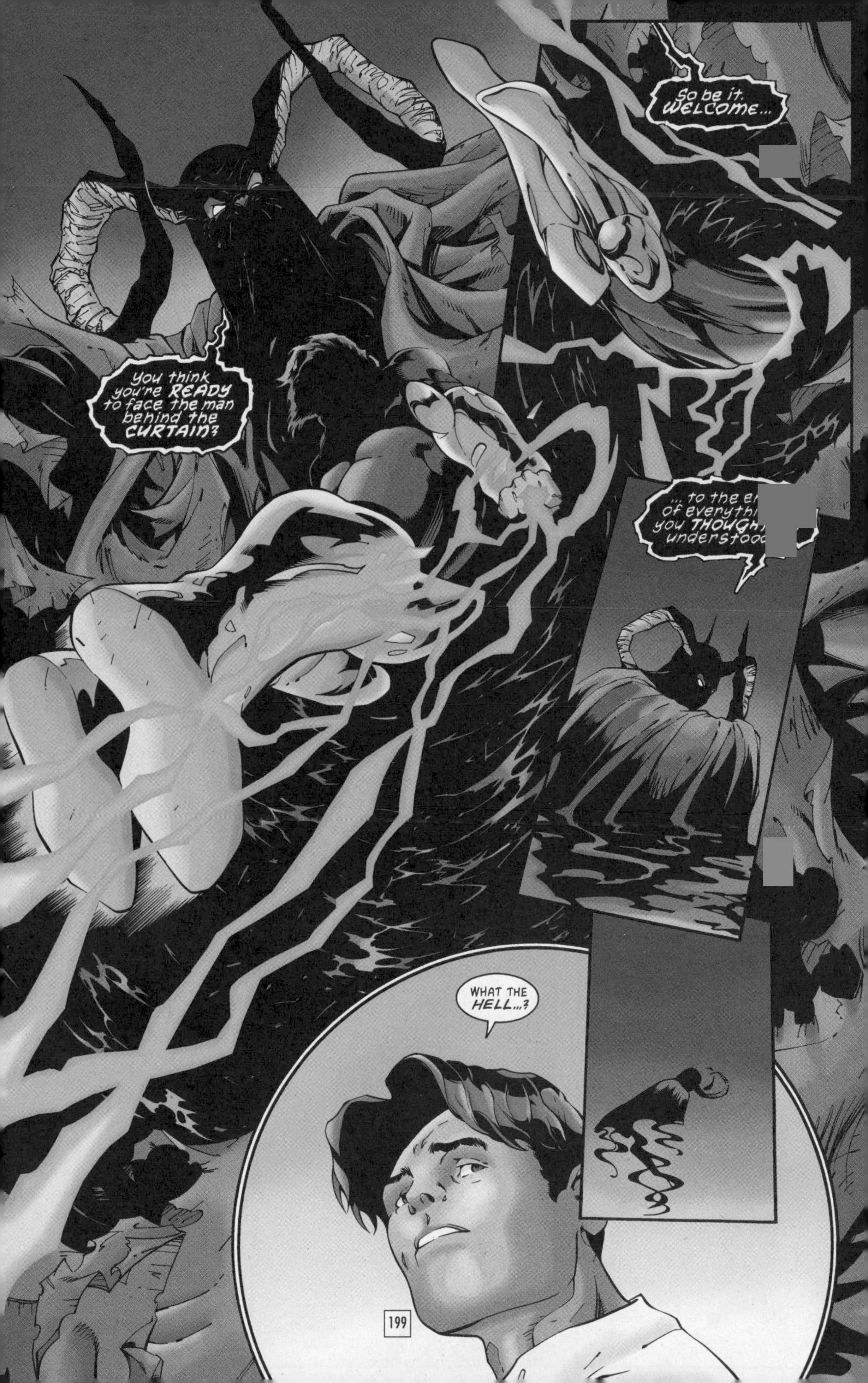
So be it. WELCOME...
You think you're READY to face the man behind the CURTAIN?
... to the en
of everythi
you THOUGH
understood
WHAT THE HELL...?

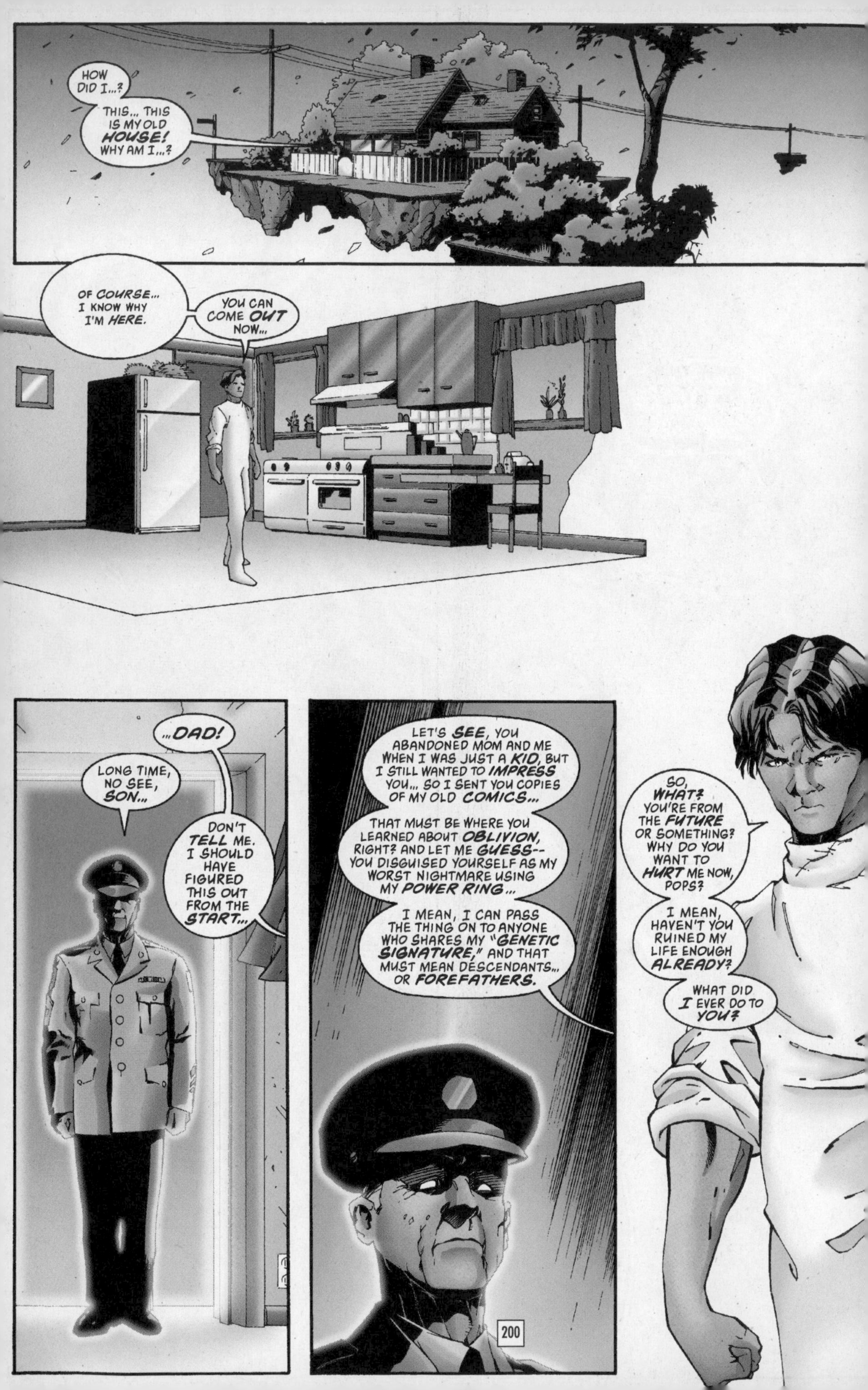
HOW DID I...?
THIS... THIS IS MY OLD HOUSE! WHY AM I...?
OF COURSE... I KNOW WHY I'M HERE.
YOU CAN COME OUT NOW...
LONG TIME, NO SEE, SON...
...DAD!
DON'T TELL ME. I SHOULD HAVE FIGURED THIS OUT FROM THE START...
LET'S SEE, YOU ABANDONED MOM AND ME WHEN I WAS JUST A KID, BUT I STILL WANTED TO IMPRESS YOU... SO I SENT YOU COPIES OF MY OLD COMICS...
THAT MUST BE WHERE YOU LEARNED ABOUT OBLIVION, RIGHT? AND LET ME GUESS-- YOU DISGUISED YOURSELF AS MY WORST NIGHTMARE USING MY POWER RING...
I MEAN, I CAN PASS THE THING ON TO ANYONE WHO SHARES MY "GENETIC SIGNATURE," AND THAT MUST MEAN DESCENDANTS... OR FOREFATHERS.
SO, WHAT? YOU'RE FROM THE FUTURE OR SOMETHING? WHY DO YOU WANT TO HURT ME NOW, POPS?
I MEAN, HAVEN'T YOU RUINED MY LIFE ENOUGH ALREADY?
WHAT DID I EVER DO TO YOU?

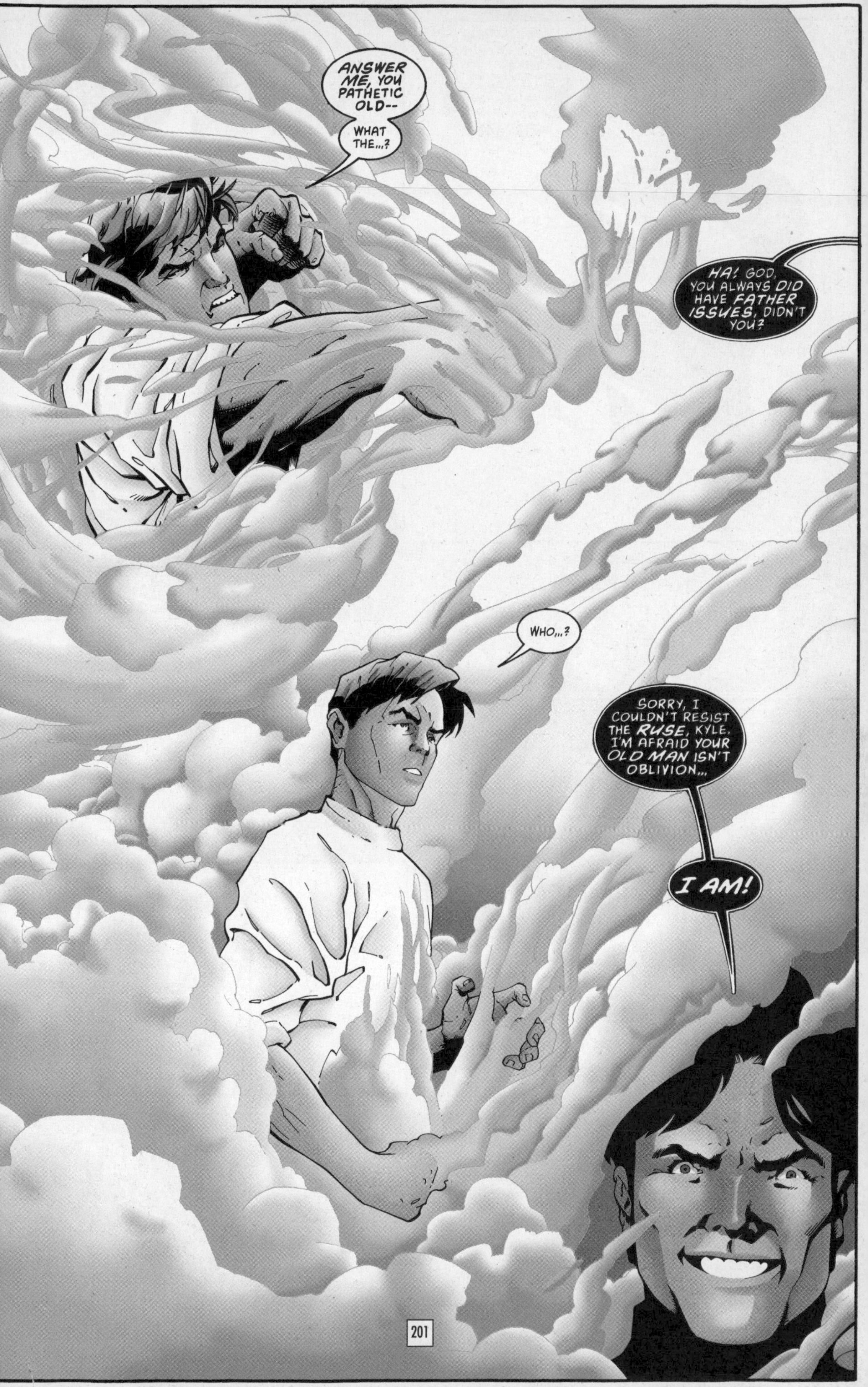
ANSWER ME, YOU PATHETIC OLD--
WHAT THE...?
HA! GOD, YOU ALWAYS DID HAVE FATHER ISSUES, DIDN'T YOU?
WHO...?
SORRY, I COULDN'T RESIST THE RUSE, KYLE. I'M AFRAID YOUR OLD MAN ISN'T OBLIVION...
I AM!

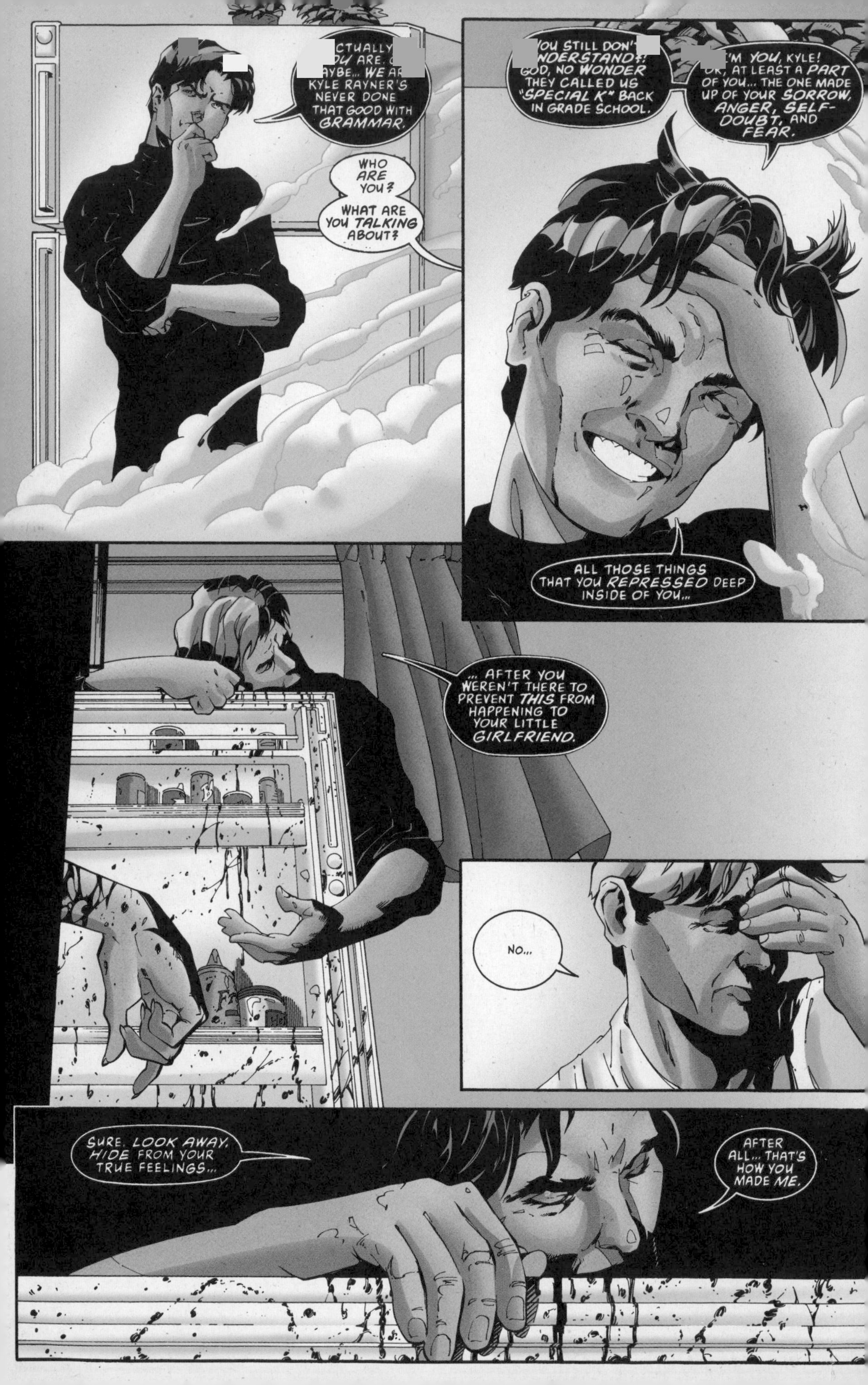

…CTUALLY …OU ARE. … …AYBE… WE AR… KYLE RAYNER'S NEVER DONE THAT GOOD WITH GRAMMAR.
WHO ARE YOU?
WHAT ARE YOU TALKING ABOUT?
…OU STILL DON'… …NDERSTAND?! GOD, NO WONDER THEY CALLED US "SPECIAL K" BACK IN GRADE SCHOOL.
…'M YOU, KYLE! …R, AT LEAST A PART OF YOU... THE ONE MADE UP OF YOUR SORROW, ANGER, SELF-DOUBT, AND FEAR.
ALL THOSE THINGS THAT YOU REPRESSED DEEP INSIDE OF YOU...
... AFTER YOU WEREN'T THERE TO PREVENT THIS FROM HAPPENING TO YOUR LITTLE GIRLFRIEND.
NO...
SURE. LOOK AWAY. HIDE FROM YOUR TRUE FEELINGS...
AFTER ALL... THAT'S HOW YOU MADE ME.

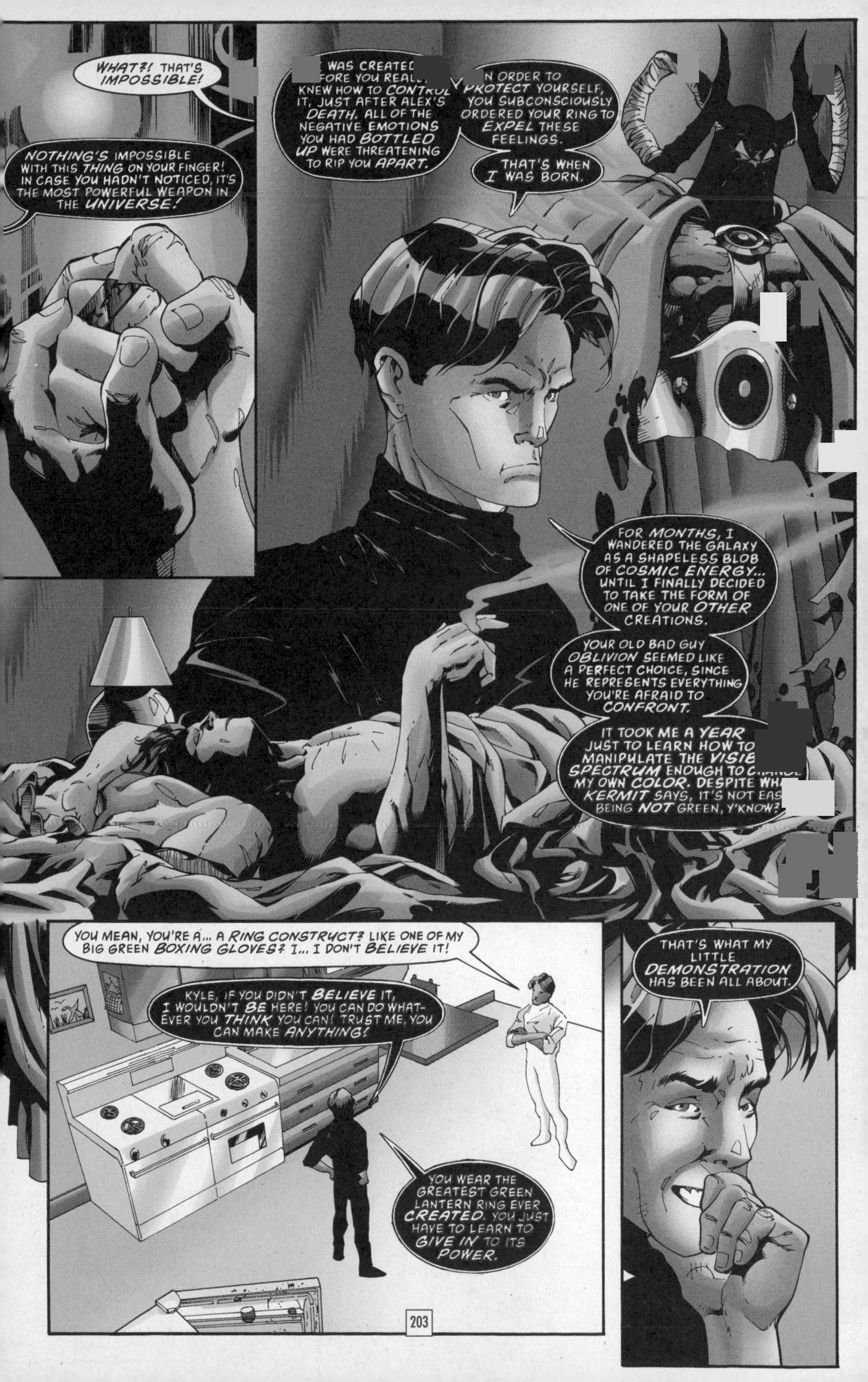
WHAT?! THAT'S IMPOSSIBLE!
NOTHING'S IMPOSSIBLE WITH THIS THING ON YOUR FINGER! IN CASE YOU HADN'T NOTICED, IT'S THE MOST POWERFUL WEAPON IN THE UNIVERSE!
WAS CREATED FORE YOU REAL KNEW HOW TO CONTROL IT, JUST AFTER ALEX'S DEATH. ALL OF THE NEGATIVE EMOTIONS YOU HAD BOTTLED UP WERE THREATENING TO RIP YOU APART.
N ORDER TO PROTECT YOURSELF, YOU SUBCONSCIOUSLY ORDERED YOUR RING TO EXPEL THESE FEELINGS.
THAT'S WHEN I WAS BORN.
FOR MONTHS, I WANDERED THE GALAXY AS A SHAPELESS BLOB OF COSMIC ENERGY... UNTIL I FINALLY DECIDED TO TAKE THE FORM OF ONE OF YOUR OTHER CREATIONS.
YOUR OLD BAD GUY OBLIVION SEEMED LIKE A PERFECT CHOICE, SINCE HE REPRESENTS EVERYTHING YOU'RE AFRAID TO CONFRONT.
IT TOOK ME A YEAR JUST TO LEARN HOW TO MANIPULATE THE VISIB SPECTRUM ENOUGH TO C MY OWN COLOR. DESPITE WH KERMIT SAYS, IT'S NOT EAS BEING NOT GREEN, Y'KNOW?
YOU MEAN, YOU'RE A... A RING CONSTRUCT? LIKE ONE OF MY BIG GREEN BOXING GLOVES? I... I DON'T BELIEVE IT!
KYLE, IF YOU DIDN'T BELIEVE IT, I WOULDN'T BE HERE! YOU CAN DO WHATEVER YOU THINK YOU CAN! TRUST ME, YOU CAN MAKE ANYTHING!
YOU WEAR THE GREATEST GREEN LANTERN RING EVER CREATED. YOU JUST HAVE TO LEARN TO GIVE IN TO ITS POWER.
THAT'S WHAT MY LITTLE DEMONSTRATION HAS BEEN ALL ABOUT.

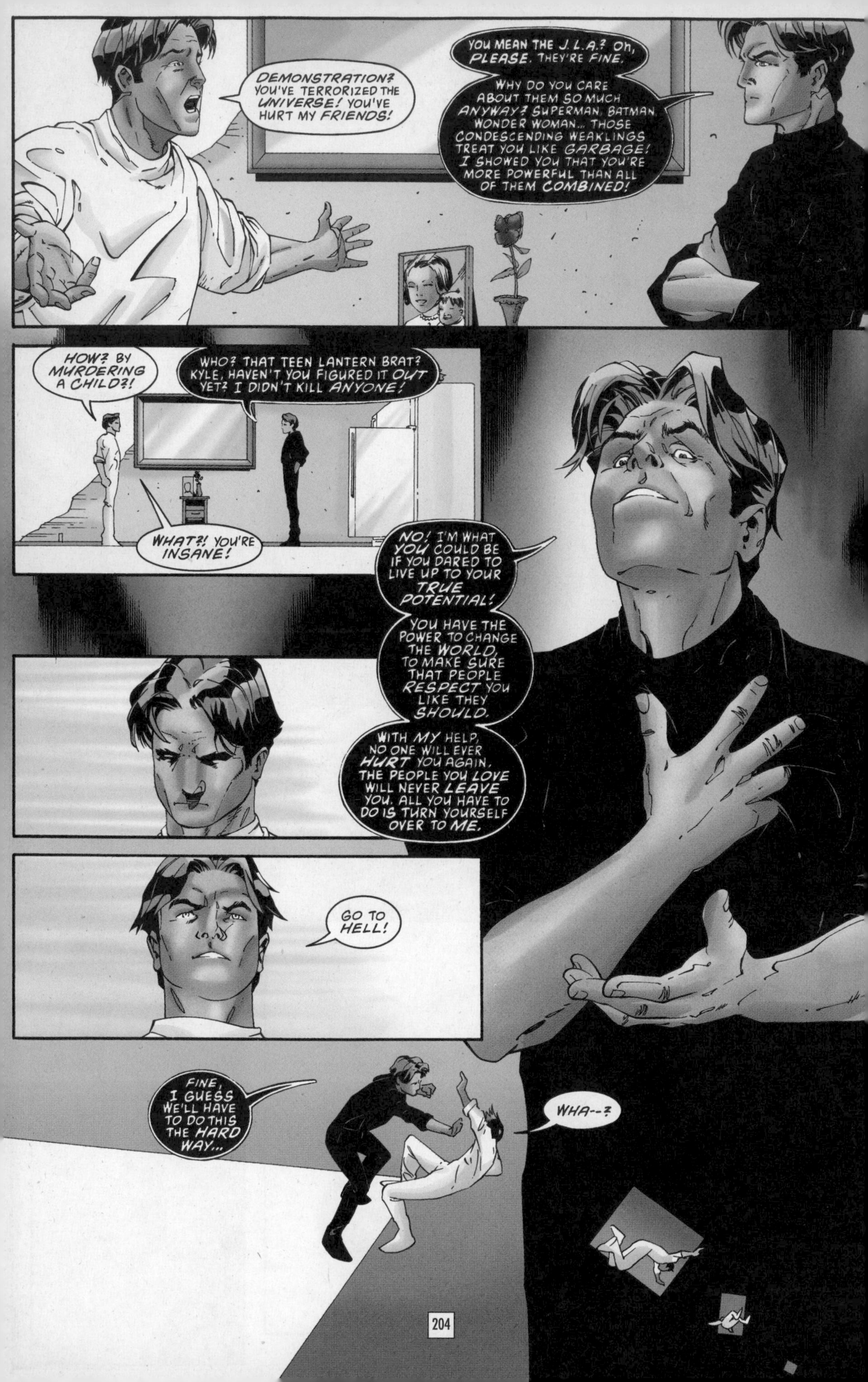

DEMONSTRATION? YOU'VE TERRORIZED THE UNIVERSE! YOU'VE HURT MY FRIENDS!
YOU MEAN THE J.L.A.? OH, PLEASE. THEY'RE FINE.
WHY DO YOU CARE ABOUT THEM SO MUCH ANYWAY? SUPERMAN, BATMAN WONDER WOMAN... THOSE CONDESCENDING WEAKLINGS TREAT YOU LIKE GARBAGE! I SHOWED YOU THAT YOU'RE MORE POWERFUL THAN ALL OF THEM COMBINED!
HOW? BY MURDERING A CHILD?!
WHO? THAT TEEN LANTERN BRAT? KYLE, HAVEN'T YOU FIGURED IT OUT YET? I DIDN'T KILL ANYONE!
WHAT?! YOU'RE INSANE!
NO! I'M WHAT YOU COULD BE IF YOU DARED TO LIVE UP TO YOUR TRUE POTENTIAL!
YOU HAVE THE POWER TO CHANGE THE WORLD, TO MAKE SURE THAT PEOPLE RESPECT YOU LIKE THEY SHOULD.
WITH MY HELP, NO ONE WILL EVER HURT YOU AGAIN. THE PEOPLE YOU LOVE WILL NEVER LEAVE YOU. ALL YOU HAVE TO DO IS TURN YOURSELF OVER TO ME.
GO TO HELL!
FINE, I GUESS WE'LL HAVE TO DO THIS THE HARD WAY...
WHA--?

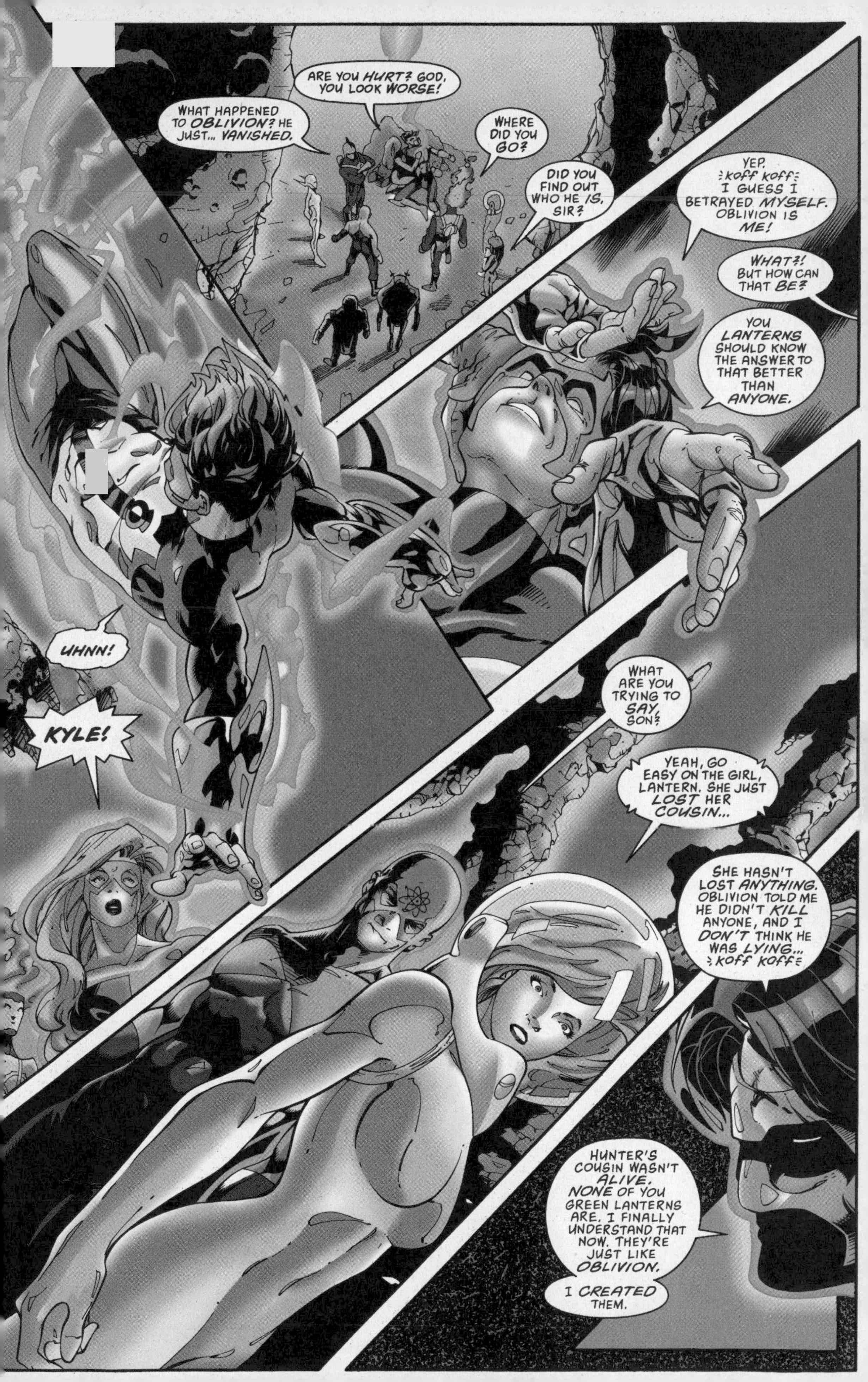
WHAT HAPPENED TO OBLIVION? HE JUST... VANISHED.
ARE YOU HURT? GOD, YOU LOOK WORSE!
WHERE DID YOU GO?
DID YOU FIND OUT WHO HE IS, SIR?
YEP. koff koff I GUESS I BETRAYED MYSELF. OBLIVION IS ME!
WHAT?! BUT HOW CAN THAT BE?
YOU LANTERNS SHOULD KNOW THE ANSWER TO THAT BETTER THAN ANYONE.
UHNN!
KYLE!
WHAT ARE YOU TRYING TO SAY, SON?
YEAH, GO EASY ON THE GIRL, LANTERN. SHE JUST LOST HER COUSIN...
SHE HASN'T LOST ANYTHING. OBLIVION TOLD ME HE DIDN'T KILL ANYONE, AND I DON'T THINK HE WAS LYING... koff koff
HUNTER'S COUSIN WASN'T ALIVE. NONE OF YOU GREEN LANTERNS ARE. I FINALLY UNDERSTAND THAT NOW. THEY'RE JUST LIKE OBLIVION.
I CREATED THEM.

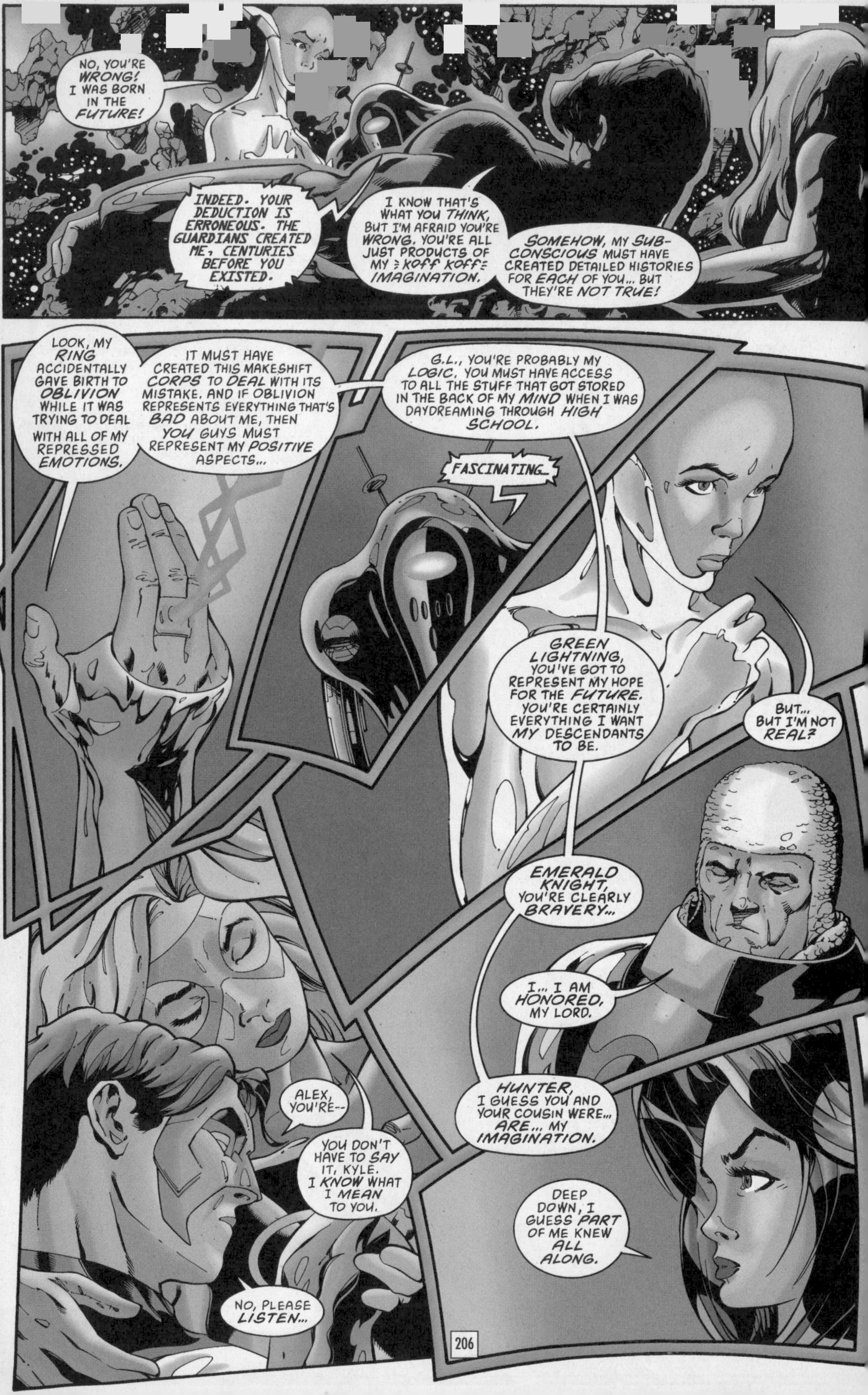
NO, YOU'RE WRONG! I WAS BORN IN THE FUTURE!
INDEED. YOUR DEDUCTION IS ERRONEOUS. THE GUARDIANS CREATED ME, CENTURIES BEFORE YOU EXISTED.
I KNOW THAT'S WHAT YOU THINK, BUT I'M AFRAID YOU'RE WRONG. YOU'RE ALL JUST PRODUCTS OF MY ≷KOFF KOFF≶ IMAGINATION.
SOMEHOW, MY SUB-CONSCIOUS MUST HAVE CREATED DETAILED HISTORIES FOR EACH OF YOU... BUT THEY'RE NOT TRUE!
LOOK, MY RING ACCIDENTALLY GAVE BIRTH TO OBLIVION WHILE IT WAS TRYING TO DEAL WITH ALL OF MY REPRESSED EMOTIONS.
IT MUST HAVE CREATED THIS MAKESHIFT CORPS TO DEAL WITH ITS MISTAKE. AND IF OBLIVION REPRESENTS EVERYTHING THAT'S BAD ABOUT ME, THEN YOU GUYS MUST REPRESENT MY POSITIVE ASPECTS...
G.L., YOU'RE PROBABLY MY LOGIC. YOU MUST HAVE ACCESS TO ALL THE STUFF THAT GOT STORED IN THE BACK OF MY MIND WHEN I WAS DAYDREAMING THROUGH HIGH SCHOOL.
FASCINATING...
GREEN LIGHTNING, YOU'VE GOT TO REPRESENT MY HOPE FOR THE FUTURE. YOU'RE CERTAINLY EVERYTHING I WANT MY DESCENDANTS TO BE.
BUT... BUT I'M NOT REAL?
EMERALD KNIGHT, YOU'RE CLEARLY BRAVERY...
I... I AM HONORED, MY LORD.
HUNTER, I GUESS YOU AND YOUR COUSIN WERE... ARE... MY IMAGINATION.
DEEP DOWN, I GUESS PART OF ME KNEW ALL ALONG.
ALEX, YOU'RE--
YOU DON'T HAVE TO SAY IT, KYLE. I KNOW WHAT I MEAN TO YOU.
NO, PLEASE LISTEN...

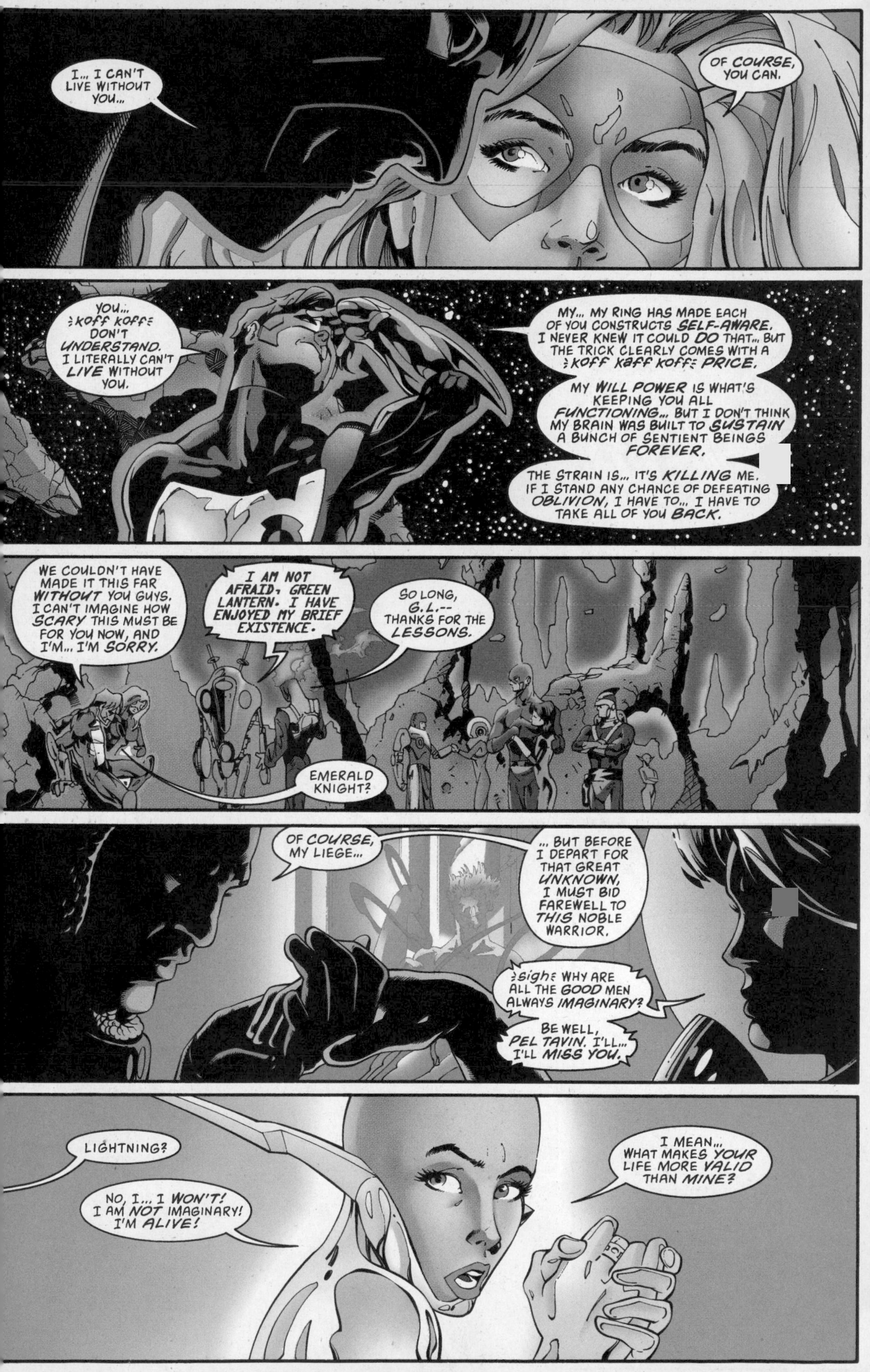

I... I CAN'T LIVE WITHOUT YOU...
OF COURSE, YOU CAN.
YOU... ≷koff koff≷ DON'T UNDERSTAND. I LITERALLY CAN'T LIVE WITHOUT YOU.
MY... MY RING HAS MADE EACH OF YOU CONSTRUCTS SELF-AWARE. I NEVER KNEW IT COULD DO THAT... BUT THE TRICK CLEARLY COMES WITH A ≷koff kaff koff≷ PRICE.
MY WILL POWER IS WHAT'S KEEPING YOU ALL FUNCTIONING... BUT I DON'T THINK MY BRAIN WAS BUILT TO SUSTAIN A BUNCH OF SENTIENT BEINGS FOREVER.
THE STRAIN IS... IT'S KILLING ME. IF I STAND ANY CHANCE OF DEFEATING OBLIVION, I HAVE TO... I HAVE TO TAKE ALL OF YOU BACK.
WE COULDN'T HAVE MADE IT THIS FAR WITHOUT YOU GUYS. I CAN'T IMAGINE HOW SCARY THIS MUST BE FOR YOU NOW, AND I'M... I'M SORRY.
I AM NOT AFRAID, GREEN LANTERN. I HAVE ENJOYED MY BRIEF EXISTENCE.
SO LONG, G.L.-- THANKS FOR THE LESSONS.
EMERALD KNIGHT?
OF COURSE, MY LIEGE...
... BUT BEFORE I DEPART FOR THAT GREAT UNKNOWN, I MUST BID FAREWELL TO THIS NOBLE WARRIOR.
≷sigh≷ WHY ARE ALL THE GOOD MEN ALWAYS IMAGINARY?
BE WELL, PEL TAVIN. I'LL... I'LL MISS YOU.
LIGHTNING?
NO, I... I WON'T! I AM NOT IMAGINARY! I'M ALIVE!
I MEAN... WHAT MAKES YOUR LIFE MORE VALID THAN MINE?

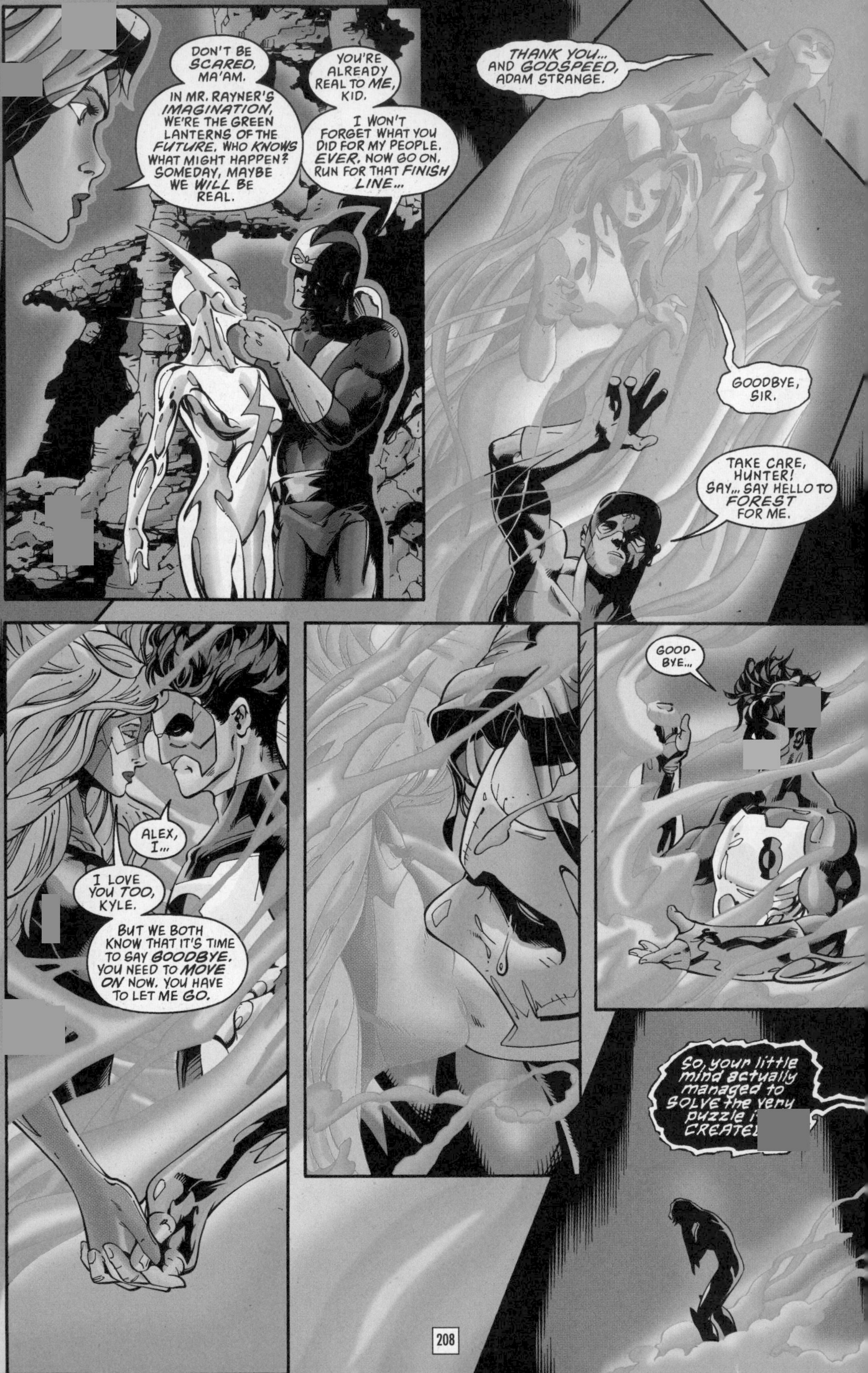
DON'T BE SCARED, MA'AM.
IN MR. RAYNER'S IMAGINATION, WE'RE THE GREEN LANTERNS OF THE FUTURE. WHO KNOWS WHAT MIGHT HAPPEN? SOMEDAY, MAYBE WE WILL BE REAL.
YOU'RE ALREADY REAL TO ME, KID.
I WON'T FORGET WHAT YOU DID FOR MY PEOPLE. EVER. NOW GO ON, RUN FOR THAT FINISH LINE...
THANK YOU... AND GODSPEED, ADAM STRANGE.
GOODBYE, SIR.
TAKE CARE, HUNTER! SAY... SAY HELLO TO FOREST FOR ME.
ALEX, I...
I LOVE YOU TOO, KYLE.
BUT WE BOTH KNOW THAT IT'S TIME TO SAY GOODBYE. YOU NEED TO MOVE ON NOW. YOU HAVE TO LET ME GO.
GOOD-BYE...
So, your little mind actually managed to SOLVE the very puzzle i CREATED

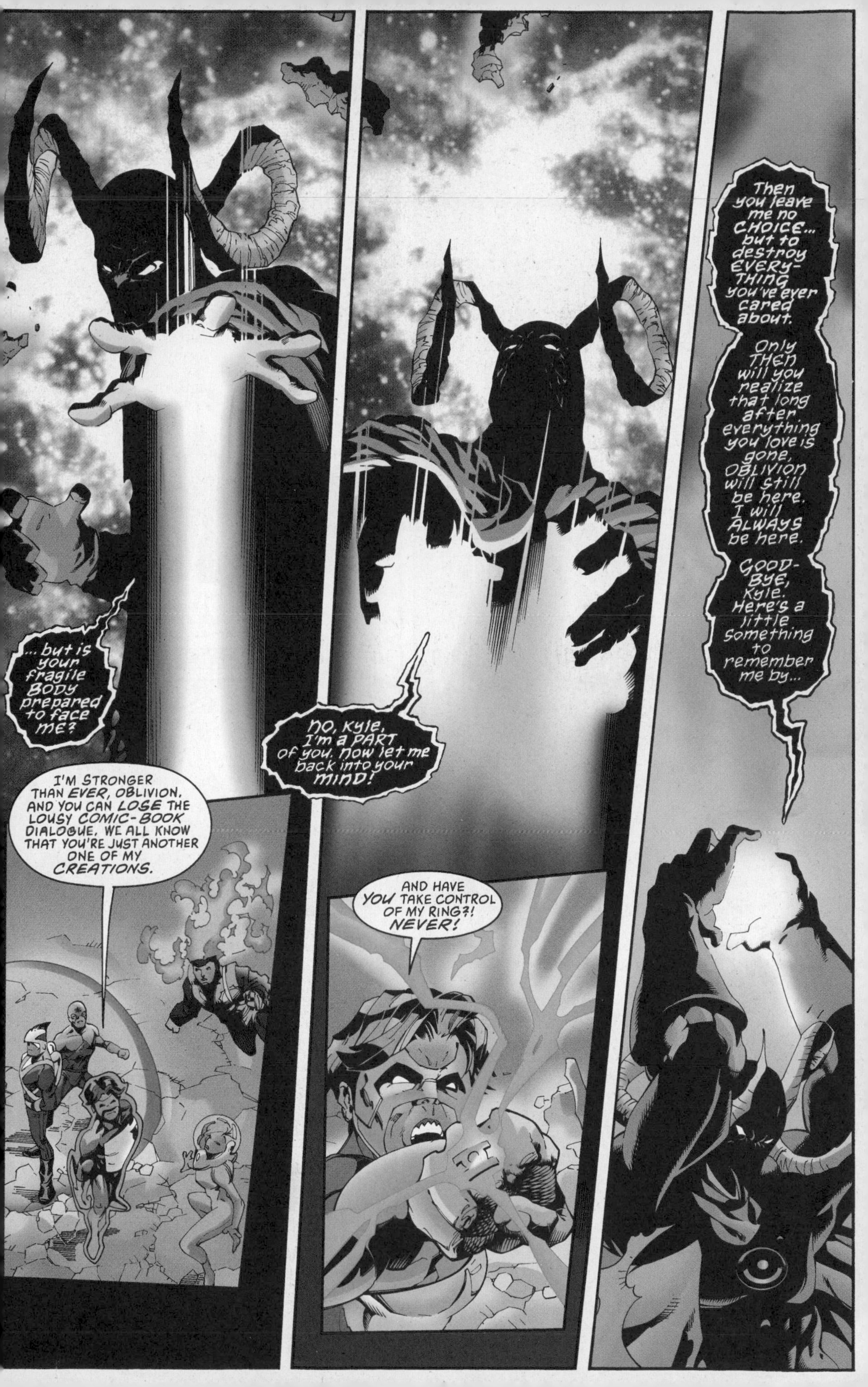
...but is your fragile BODY prepared to face me?
I'M STRONGER THAN EVER, OBLIVION. AND YOU CAN LOSE THE LOUSY COMIC-BOOK DIALOGUE. WE ALL KNOW THAT YOU'RE JUST ANOTHER ONE OF MY CREATIONS.
No, Kyle. I'm a PART of you. Now let me back into your MIND!
AND HAVE YOU TAKE CONTROL OF MY RING?! NEVER!
Then you leave me no CHOICE... but to destroy EVERYTHING you've ever cared about.
Only THEN will you realize that long after everything you love is gone, OBLIVION will still be here. I will ALWAYS be here.
GOOD-BYE, Kyle. Here's a little something to remember me by...

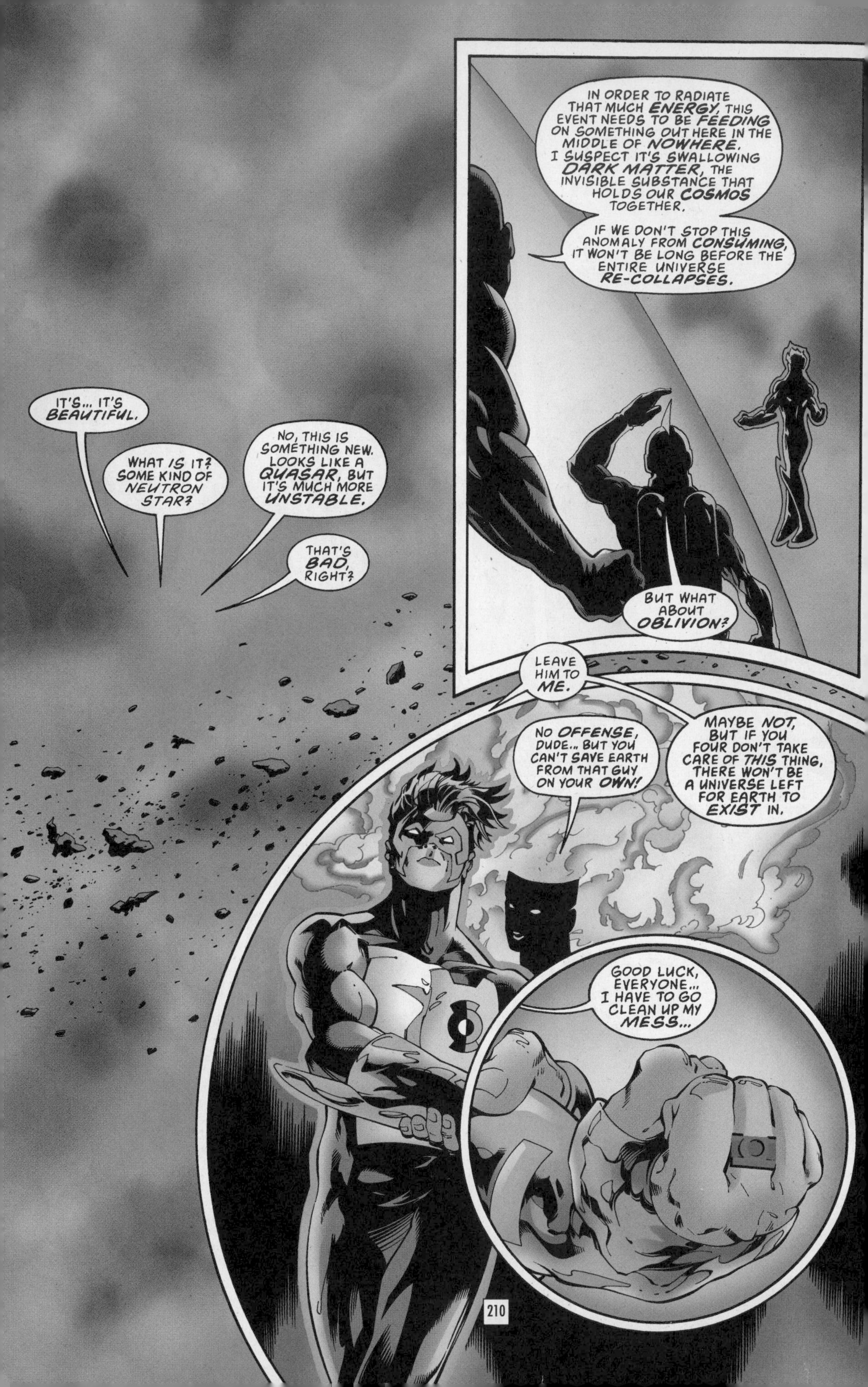
IT'S... IT'S BEAUTIFUL.
WHAT IS IT? SOME KIND OF NEUTRON STAR?
NO, THIS IS SOMETHING NEW. LOOKS LIKE A QUASAR, BUT IT'S MUCH MORE UNSTABLE.
THAT'S BAD, RIGHT?
IN ORDER TO RADIATE THAT MUCH ENERGY, THIS EVENT NEEDS TO BE FEEDING ON SOMETHING OUT HERE IN THE MIDDLE OF NOWHERE. I SUSPECT IT'S SWALLOWING DARK MATTER, THE INVISIBLE SUBSTANCE THAT HOLDS OUR COSMOS TOGETHER.
IF WE DON'T STOP THIS ANOMALY FROM CONSUMING, IT WON'T BE LONG BEFORE THE ENTIRE UNIVERSE RE-COLLAPSES.
BUT WHAT ABOUT OBLIVION?
LEAVE HIM TO ME.
NO OFFENSE, DUDE... BUT YOU CAN'T SAVE EARTH FROM THAT GUY ON YOUR OWN!
MAYBE NOT, BUT IF YOU FOUR DON'T TAKE CARE OF THIS THING, THERE WON'T BE A UNIVERSE LEFT FOR EARTH TO EXIST IN.
GOOD LUCK, EVERYONE... I HAVE TO GO CLEAN UP MY MESS...

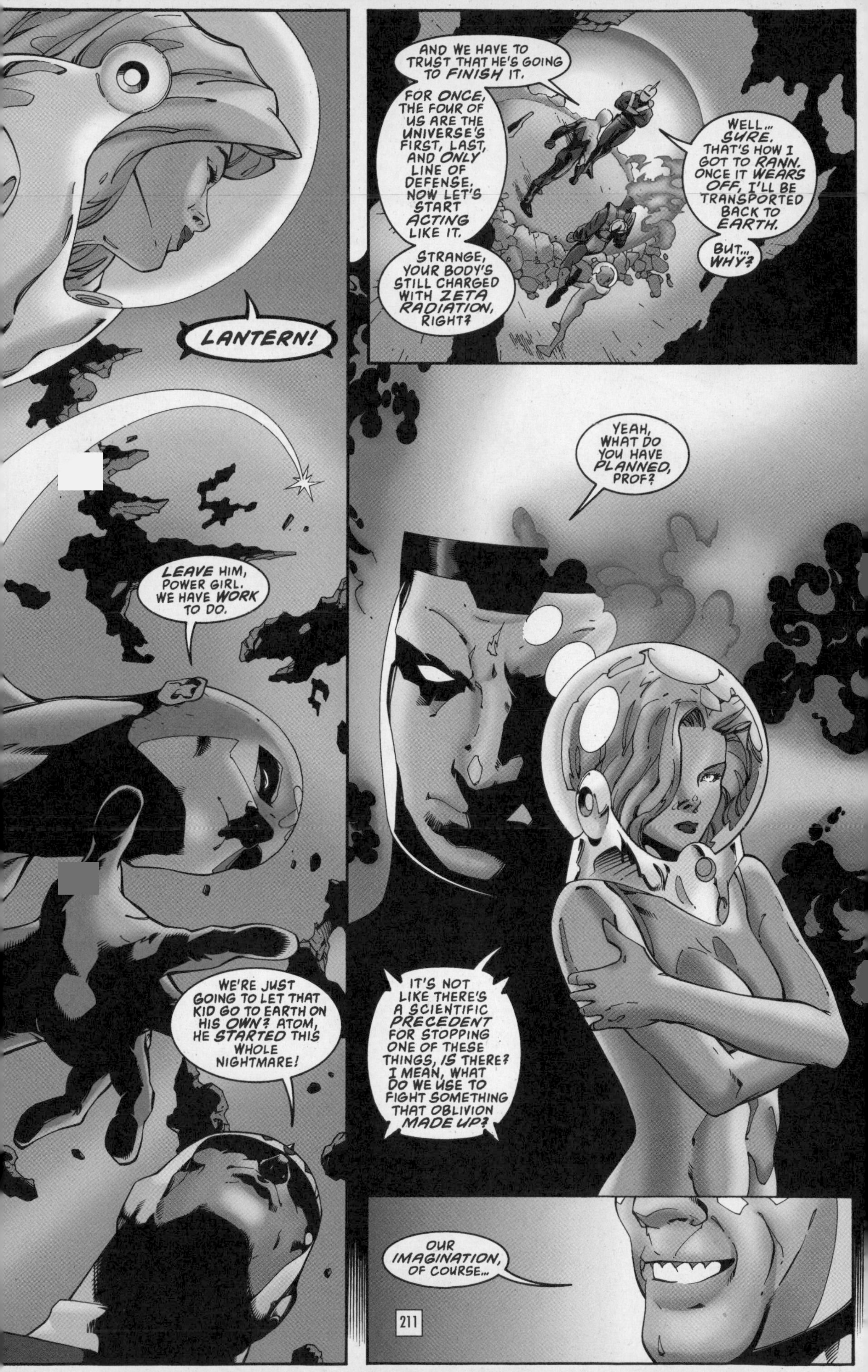
LANTERN!
AND WE HAVE TO TRUST THAT HE'S GOING TO FINISH IT.
FOR ONCE, THE FOUR OF US ARE THE UNIVERSE'S FIRST, LAST, AND ONLY LINE OF DEFENSE. NOW LET'S START ACTING LIKE IT.
STRANGE, YOUR BODY'S STILL CHARGED WITH ZETA RADIATION, RIGHT?
WELL... SURE. THAT'S HOW I GOT TO RANN. ONCE IT WEARS OFF, I'LL BE TRANSPORTED BACK TO EARTH.
BUT... WHY?
LEAVE HIM, POWER GIRL. WE HAVE WORK TO DO.
WE'RE JUST GOING TO LET THAT KID GO TO EARTH ON HIS OWN? ATOM, HE STARTED THIS WHOLE NIGHTMARE!
YEAH, WHAT DO YOU HAVE PLANNED, PROF?
IT'S NOT LIKE THERE'S A SCIENTIFIC PRECEDENT FOR STOPPING ONE OF THESE THINGS, IS THERE? I MEAN, WHAT DO WE USE TO FIGHT SOMETHING THAT OBLIVION MADE UP?
OUR IMAGINATION, OF COURSE...

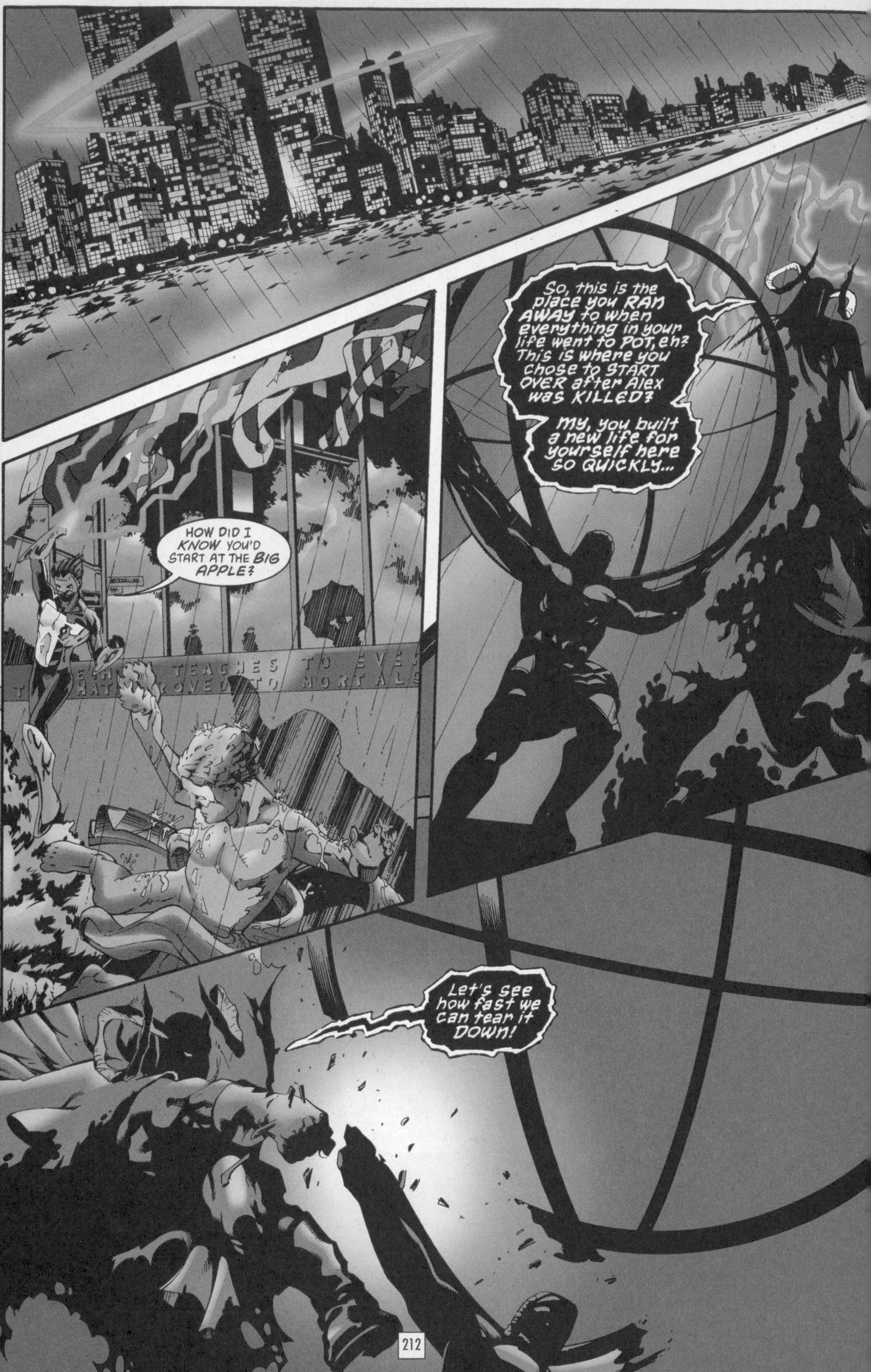
So, this is the place you RAN AWAY to when everything in your life went to POT, eh? This is where you chose to START OVER after Alex was KILLED?
My, you built a new life for yourself here so QUICKLY...
HOW DID I KNOW YOU'D START AT THE BIG APPLE?
Let's see how fast we can tear it DOWN!

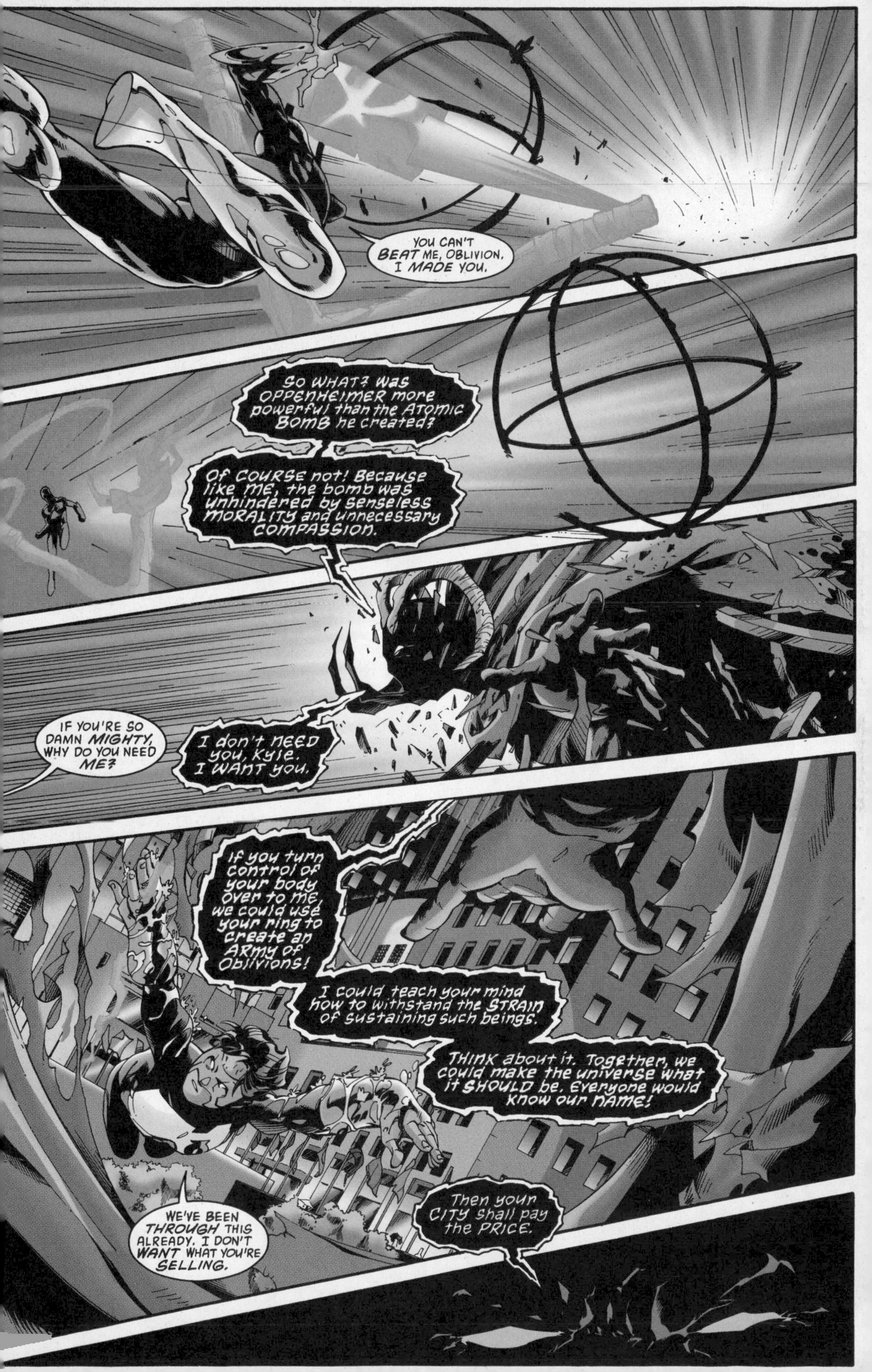
YOU CAN'T BEAT ME, OBLIVION. I MADE YOU.
So WHAT? Was OPPENHEIMER more powerful than the ATOMIC BOMB he created?
Of COURSE not! Because like ME, the bomb was unhindered by senseless MORALITY and unnecessary COMPASSION.
IF YOU'RE SO DAMN MIGHTY, WHY DO YOU NEED ME?
I don't NEED you, Kyle. I WANT you.
If you turn control of your body over to me, we could use your ring to create an ARMY of Oblivions!
I could teach your mind how to withstand the STRAIN of sustaining such beings.
THINK about it. Together, we could make the universe what it SHOULD be. Everyone would know our NAME!
WE'VE BEEN THROUGH THIS ALREADY. I DON'T WANT WHAT YOU'RE SELLING.
Then your CITY shall pay the PRICE.

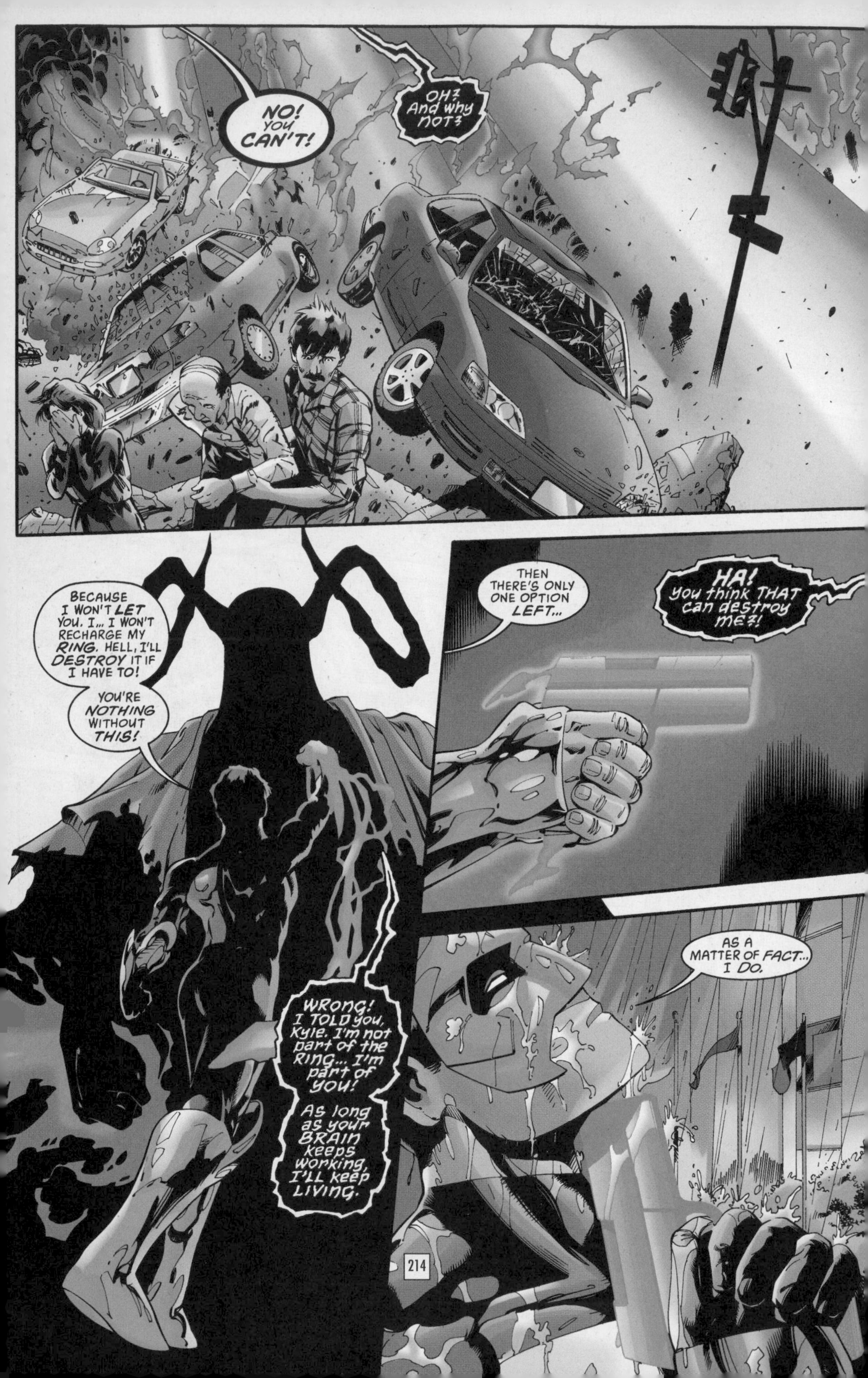
NO! YOU CAN'T!
OH? And why NOT?
BECAUSE I WON'T LET YOU. I... I WON'T RECHARGE MY RING. HELL, I'LL DESTROY IT IF I HAVE TO!
YOU'RE NOTHING WITHOUT THIS!
WRONG! I TOLD you, Kyle. I'm not part of the RING... I'm part of YOU!
As long as your BRAIN keeps working, I'LL keep LIVING.
THEN THERE'S ONLY ONE OPTION LEFT...
HA! You think THAT can destroy ME?!
AS A MATTER OF FACT... I DO.

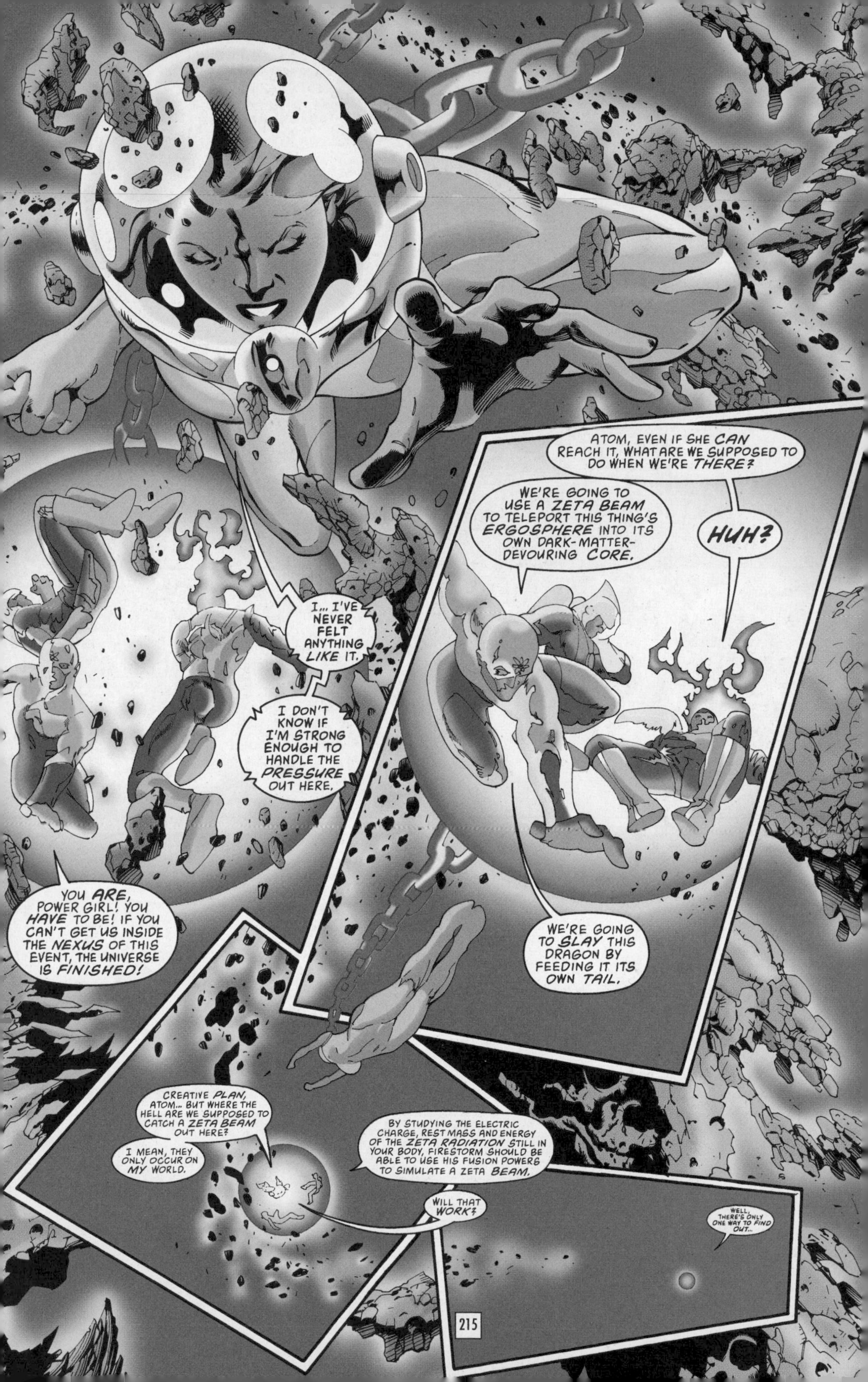

I... I'VE NEVER FELT ANYTHING LIKE IT.
I DON'T KNOW IF I'M STRONG ENOUGH TO HANDLE THE PRESSURE OUT HERE.
YOU ARE, POWER GIRL! YOU HAVE TO BE! IF YOU CAN'T GET US INSIDE THE NEXUS OF THIS EVENT, THE UNIVERSE IS FINISHED!
ATOM, EVEN IF SHE CAN REACH IT, WHAT ARE WE SUPPOSED TO DO WHEN WE'RE THERE?
WE'RE GOING TO USE A ZETA BEAM TO TELEPORT THIS THING'S ERGOSPHERE INTO ITS OWN DARK-MATTER-DEVOURING CORE.
HUH?
WE'RE GOING TO SLAY THIS DRAGON BY FEEDING IT ITS OWN TAIL.
CREATIVE PLAN, ATOM... BUT WHERE THE HELL ARE WE SUPPOSED TO CATCH A ZETA BEAM OUT HERE?
I MEAN, THEY ONLY OCCUR ON MY WORLD.
BY STUDYING THE ELECTRIC CHARGE, REST MASS AND ENERGY OF THE ZETA RADIATION STILL IN YOUR BODY, FIRESTORM SHOULD BE ABLE TO USE HIS FUSION POWERS TO SIMULATE A ZETA BEAM.
WILL THAT WORK?
WELL, THERE'S ONLY ONE WAY TO FIND OUT...

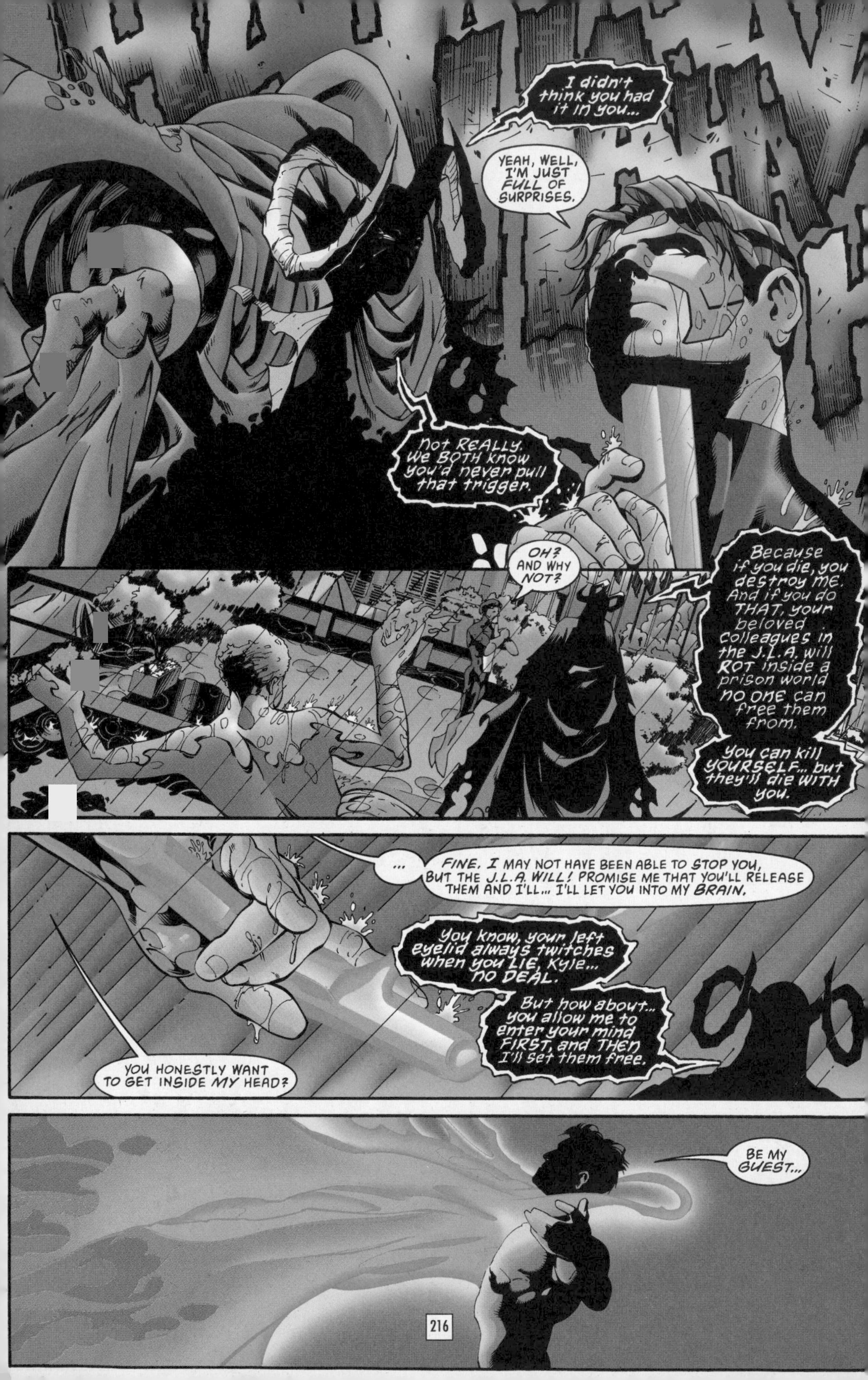
I didn't think you had it in you...
YEAH, WELL, I'M JUST FULL OF SURPRISES.
Not REALLY. We BOTH know you'd never pull that trigger.
OH? AND WHY NOT?
Because if you die, you destroy me. And if you do THAT, your beloved colleagues in the J.L.A. will ROT inside a prison world no one can free them from.
You can kill YOURSELF... but they'll die WITH you.
...
FINE. I MAY NOT HAVE BEEN ABLE TO STOP YOU, BUT THE J.L.A. WILL! PROMISE ME THAT YOU'LL RELEASE THEM AND I'LL... I'LL LET YOU INTO MY BRAIN.
You know, your left eyelid always twitches when you LIE, Kyle... no DEAL.
But how about... you allow me to enter your mind FIRST, and THEN I'll set them free.
YOU HONESTLY WANT TO GET INSIDE MY HEAD?
BE MY GUEST...

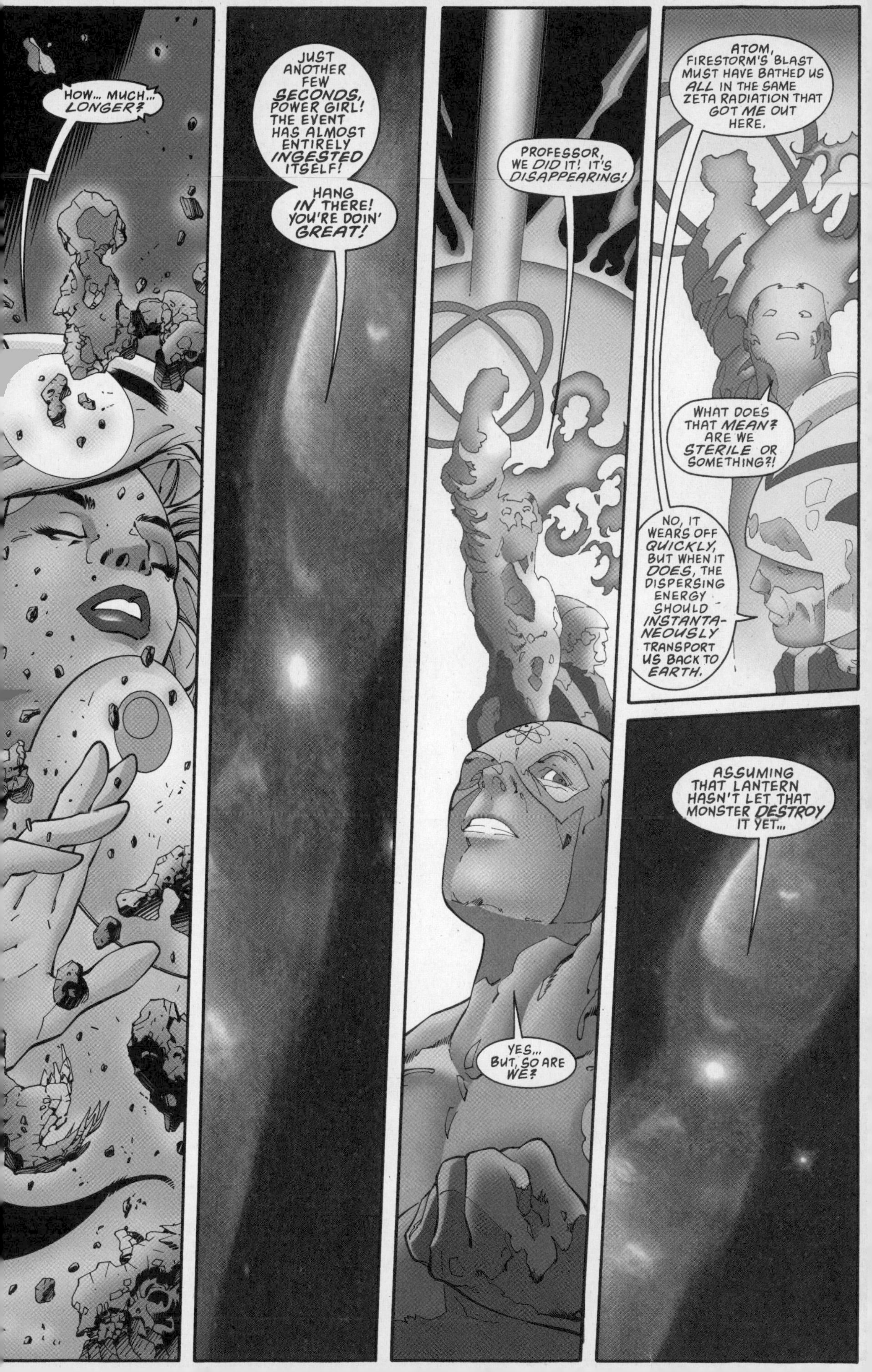
HOW... MUCH... LONGER?
JUST ANOTHER FEW SECONDS, POWER GIRL! THE EVENT HAS ALMOST ENTIRELY INGESTED ITSELF!
HANG IN THERE! YOU'RE DOIN' GREAT!
PROFESSOR, WE DID IT! IT'S DISAPPEARING!
YES... BUT, SO ARE WE?
ATOM, FIRESTORM'S BLAST MUST HAVE BATHED US ALL IN THE SAME ZETA RADIATION THAT GOT ME OUT HERE.
WHAT DOES THAT MEAN? ARE WE STERILE OR SOMETHING?!
NO, IT WEARS OFF QUICKLY, BUT WHEN IT DOES, THE DISPERSING ENERGY SHOULD INSTANTANEOUSLY TRANSPORT US BACK TO EARTH.
ASSUMING THAT LANTERN HASN'T LET THAT MONSTER DESTROY IT YET...

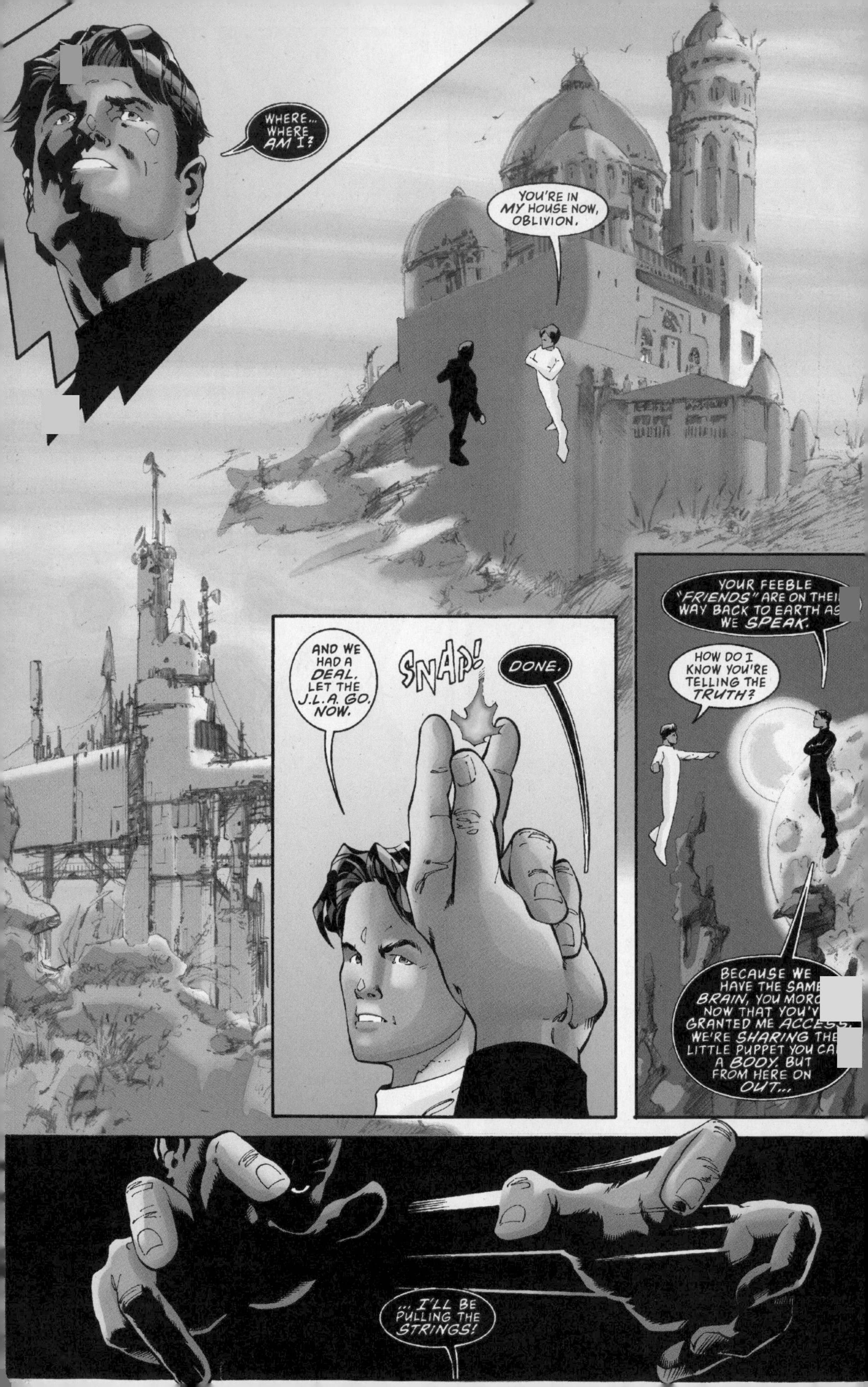
WHERE... WHERE AM I?
YOU'RE IN MY HOUSE NOW, OBLIVION.
AND WE HAD A DEAL. LET THE J.L.A. GO. NOW.
SNAP!
DONE.
YOUR FEEBLE "FRIENDS" ARE ON THEI WAY BACK TO EARTH AS WE SPEAK.
HOW DO I KNOW YOU'RE TELLING THE TRUTH?
BECAUSE WE HAVE THE SAME BRAIN, YOU MORO NOW THAT YOU'V GRANTED ME ACCES WE'RE SHARING THE LITTLE PUPPET YOU CA A BODY. BUT FROM HERE ON OUT...
... I'LL BE PULLING THE STRINGS!

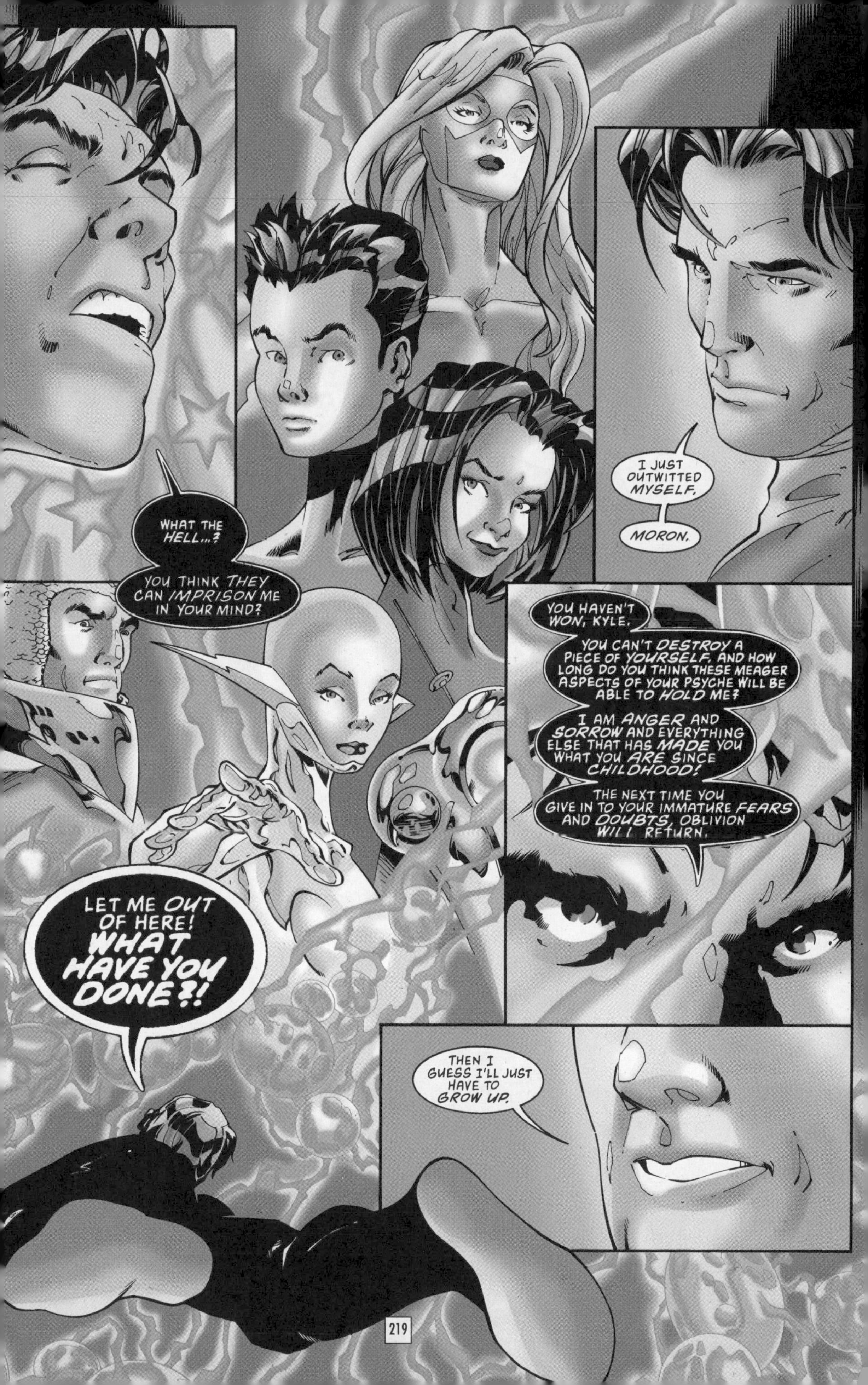
WHAT THE HELL...?
YOU THINK THEY CAN IMPRISON ME IN YOUR MIND?
I JUST OUTWITTED MYSELF.
MORON.
YOU HAVEN'T WON, KYLE.
YOU CAN'T DESTROY A PIECE OF YOURSELF, AND HOW LONG DO YOU THINK THESE MEAGER ASPECTS OF YOUR PSYCHE WILL BE ABLE TO HOLD ME?
I AM ANGER AND SORROW AND EVERYTHING ELSE THAT HAS MADE YOU WHAT YOU ARE SINCE CHILDHOOD!
THE NEXT TIME YOU GIVE IN TO YOUR IMMATURE FEARS AND DOUBTS, OBLIVION WILL RETURN.
LET ME OUT OF HERE! WHAT HAVE YOU DONE?!
THEN I GUESS I'LL JUST HAVE TO GROW UP.

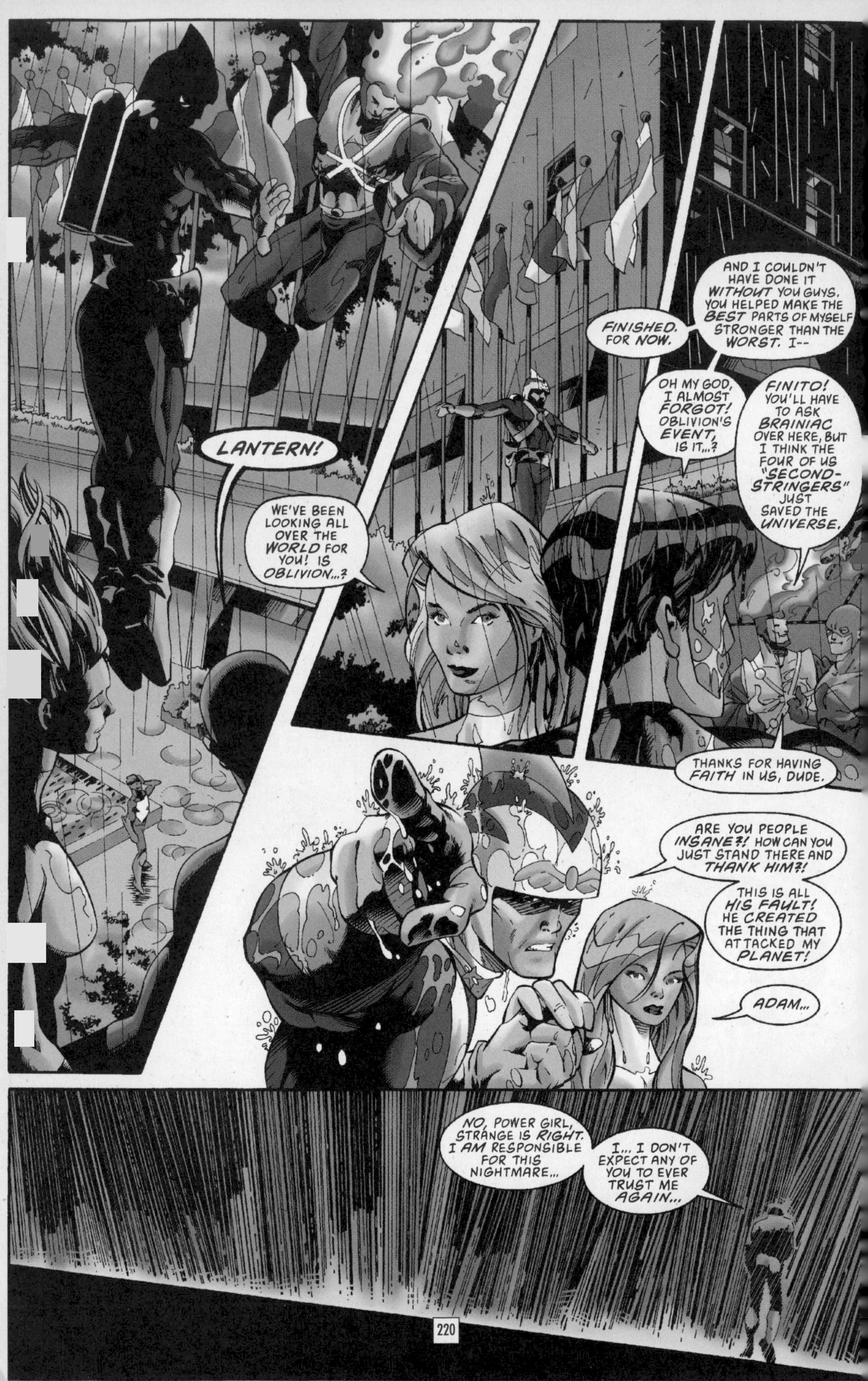
LANTERN!
WE'VE BEEN LOOKING ALL OVER THE WORLD FOR YOU! IS OBLIVION...?
FINISHED. FOR NOW.
AND I COULDN'T HAVE DONE IT WITHOUT YOU GUYS. YOU HELPED MAKE THE BEST PARTS OF MYSELF STRONGER THAN THE WORST. I--
OH MY GOD, I ALMOST FORGOT! OBLIVION'S EVENT, IS IT...?
FINITO! YOU'LL HAVE TO ASK BRAINIAC OVER HERE, BUT I THINK THE FOUR OF US "SECOND-STRINGERS" JUST SAVED THE UNIVERSE.
THANKS FOR HAVING FAITH IN US, DUDE.
ARE YOU PEOPLE INSANE?! HOW CAN YOU JUST STAND THERE AND THANK HIM?!
THIS IS ALL HIS FAULT! HE CREATED THE THING THAT ATTACKED MY PLANET!
ADAM...
NO, POWER GIRL, STRANGE IS RIGHT. I AM RESPONSIBLE FOR THIS NIGHTMARE...
I... I DON'T EXPECT ANY OF YOU TO EVER TRUST ME AGAIN...

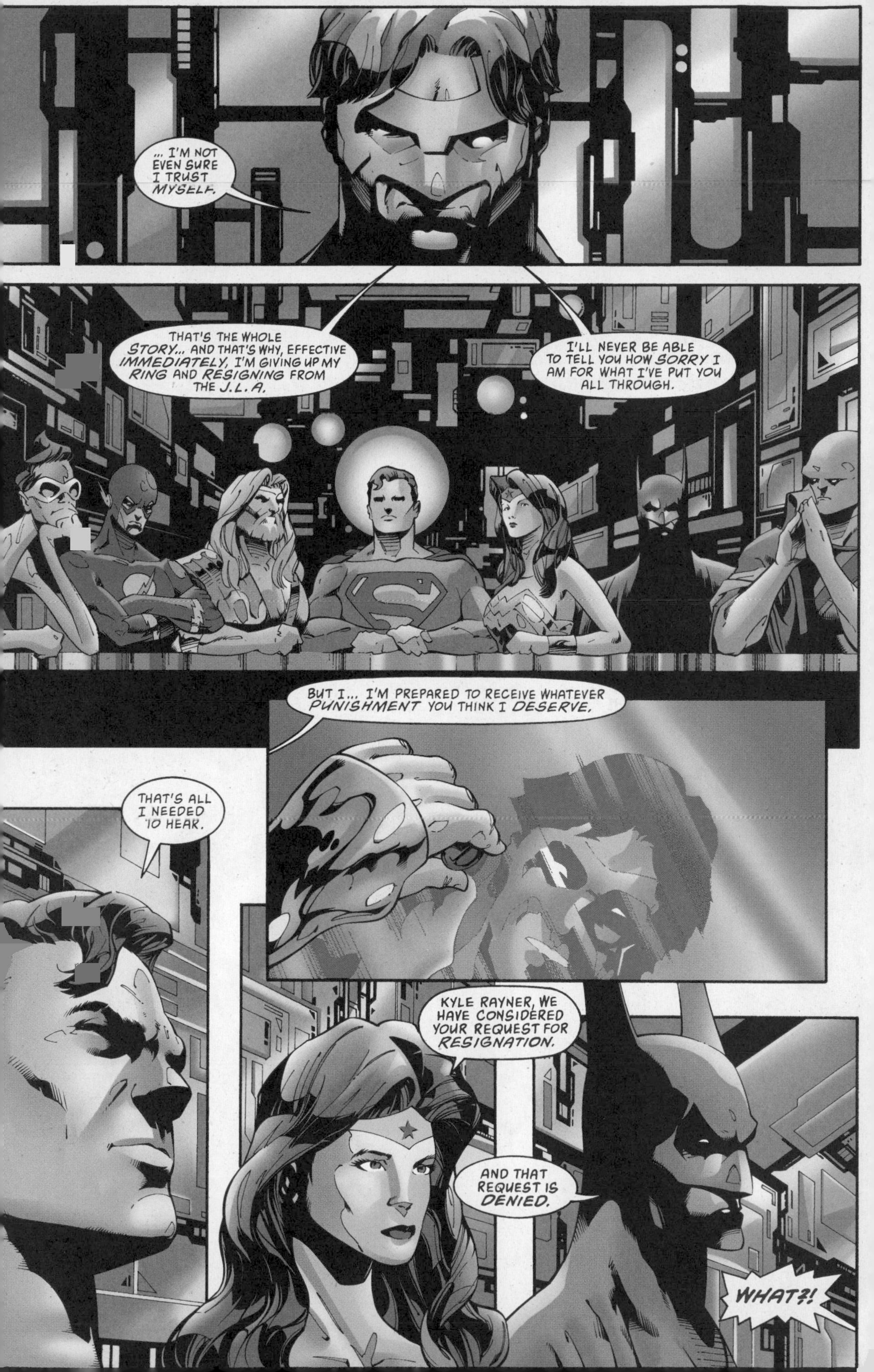
... I'M NOT EVEN SURE I TRUST MYSELF.
THAT'S THE WHOLE STORY... AND THAT'S WHY, EFFECTIVE IMMEDIATELY, I'M GIVING UP MY RING AND RESIGNING FROM THE J.L.A.
I'LL NEVER BE ABLE TO TELL YOU HOW SORRY I AM FOR WHAT I'VE PUT YOU ALL THROUGH.
BUT I... I'M PREPARED TO RECEIVE WHATEVER PUNISHMENT YOU THINK I DESERVE.
THAT'S ALL I NEEDED TO HEAR.
KYLE RAYNER, WE HAVE CONSIDERED YOUR REQUEST FOR RESIGNATION.
AND THAT REQUEST IS DENIED.
WHAT?!

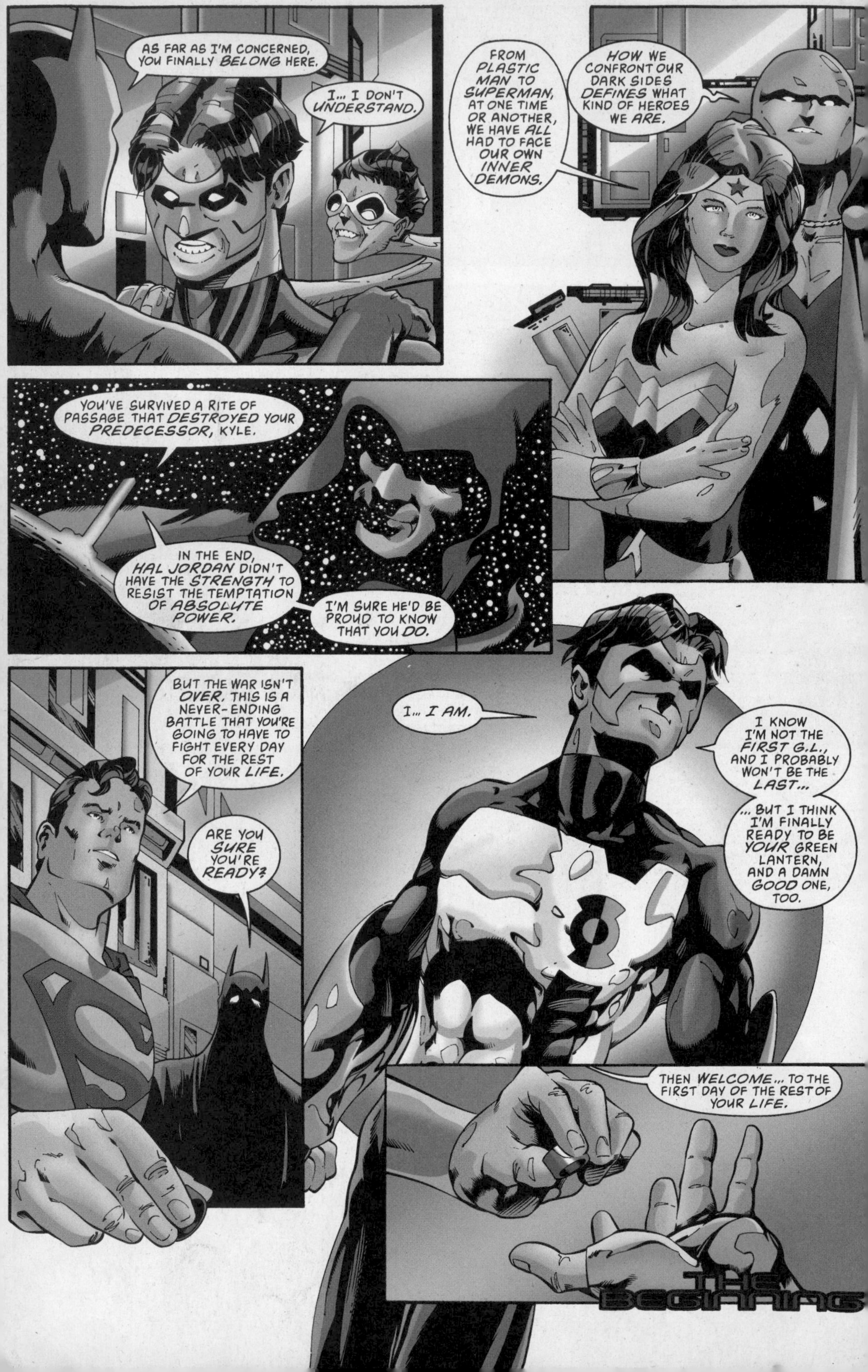
AS FAR AS I'M CONCERNED, YOU FINALLY BELONG HERE.
I... I DON'T UNDERSTAND.
FROM PLASTIC MAN TO SUPERMAN, AT ONE TIME OR ANOTHER, WE HAVE ALL HAD TO FACE OUR OWN INNER DEMONS.
HOW WE CONFRONT OUR DARK SIDES DEFINES WHAT KIND OF HEROES WE ARE.
YOU'VE SURVIVED A RITE OF PASSAGE THAT DESTROYED YOUR PREDECESSOR, KYLE.
IN THE END, HAL JORDAN DIDN'T HAVE THE STRENGTH TO RESIST THE TEMPTATION OF ABSOLUTE POWER.
I'M SURE HE'D BE PROUD TO KNOW THAT YOU DO.
BUT THE WAR ISN'T OVER. THIS IS A NEVER-ENDING BATTLE THAT YOU'RE GOING TO HAVE TO FIGHT EVERY DAY FOR THE REST OF YOUR LIFE.
ARE YOU SURE YOU'RE READY?
I... I AM.
I KNOW I'M NOT THE FIRST G.L., AND I PROBABLY WON'T BE THE LAST...
... BUT I THINK I'M FINALLY READY TO BE YOUR GREEN LANTERN, AND A DAMN GOOD ONE, TOO.
THEN WELCOME... TO THE FIRST DAY OF THE REST OF YOUR LIFE.
THE BEGINNING